The New French Baker

The New

French Baker

Perfect Pastries and Beautiful

Breads from Your Kitchen

Sheila Linderman

William Morrow and Company, Inc. / New York

Library of Congress Cataloging-in-Publication Data

Linderman, Sheila.
    The new French baker : perfect pastries and beautiful breads from your kitchen / Sheila Linderman. — 1st ed.
        p.   cm.
    Includes index.
    ISBN 0-688-14325-3
    1. Pastry.   2. Cookery, French.   3. Bread.   I. Title.
    TX773.L493   1998
    641.8'65—dc21   98-26185
                                                                           CIP

Printed in the United States of America

First Edition

1   2   3   4   5   6   7   8   9   10

BOOK DESIGN BY RICHARD ORIOLO

www.williammorrow.com

To Alan, Hannah, Jeremy, and Sarah.

You inspire me daily.

Acknowledgments

No one is alone in writing a cookbook. It is a huge endeavor: the culmination of years of research, recipe collecting and testing, and just plain experience. Many people have helped me along the way, some of whom are not even aware of their contributions. I want all of them to know that not a day goes by, not a cookie gets baked, without my thinking of them with infinite gratitude. Without any one of these people, this book would have suffered in a most radical way. I would like to thank them in the order in which they appeared in my life.

Logically, then, I must first thank my parents, Max and Dee Linderman, who may not always have agreed with the various paths I followed in my life, but who always trusted my instincts and supported my choices. I hope that I have made them proud.

The first cakes and pastries I ever made, so many years ago, were from Maida Heatter's wonderful books. I daresay that it was Maida who inspired me to switch from reading biology texts to cookbooks. I am also extremely grateful to Alice Medrich, the former owner of Cocolat and a fabulous cookbook author. She encouraged me to go to France and become the best professional I could be. She also taught me that one could make thirty-six génoises at a time and that they could all be perfect.

Once in France, Madame Couzelin, then the director of the Société de Saint-Michel, an organization of pastry chefs, took me under her wing. She placed me in some of the best pastry shops in the Paris area. That is where I learned most of the tricks I know today. Of course, I was working with eighteen-year-olds who could bake circles around me, but no matter, I was on a mission. The chefs with whom I worked, most notably Serge LeCourbe and Gérard Rever, taught me more than I could have ever learned from books or in baking courses. Most important, they taught me *how* to work.

Back in Los Angeles, I was given the opportunity to show off what I had learned in France. I am particularly grateful to Claude Alrivy, the former chef and owner of Le Chardonnay Restaurant, and Leonard Schwartz, of Maple Drive Restaurant, for letting me spread my wings. Leonard also gave me my first writing opportunity as coauthor of his book *Salads*. I would say that he opened a whole new chapter in my career.

Leonard also introduced me to my agents, Maureen and Eric Lasher, without whom this book simply would not exist. They suggested that I write the book, and their vast knowledge, unflagging support, and seemingly infinite patience helped me see it through to the end.

My very dear friend Judy Hing has been there through it all. Not only were we roommates for several years, but Judy, who shares my passion for France and its food, accompanied me to France. I could not have asked for a better traveling companion—or friend.

Millane Spector played a large part in keeping me focused and on track by calling me daily to ask about the status of the manuscript. Millane and David Darwish, both of Van Rex Gourmet Foods, also made the best possible ingredients available to me in bulk quantities.

While researching this book, I had a great deal of help from pastry chefs of the old school and the new. Jean Néret and Mary Crochet not only took me into their home, Jean let me shadow him at the highly acclaimed pastry shop that he runs with Solange Néret in Loches. Jean shared dozens of recipes for chocolates, pastries, and cakes with me. He also shared the all-important tricks of the trade, and he did so with total openness. His good friend, Jean-Pierre Gonfroy, is the director of the École Nationale Supérieure de la Pâtisserie in Yssingeaux. Messieurs Néret and Gonfroy are among the founders of modern French pastry. Recipes are great, but the history and anecdotes that they provided cannot be found in books; they are what makes this book different from others.

My closest friends in France, Pascaline Simar and Susan Inahara, acted as my on-site agents, constantly sending me recipes or telling me whose pastries and breads I simply had to try.

There were many friends who contributed their efforts on this side of the Atlantic as well. Lisa Gardner, my good friend and former assistant at Maple Drive Restaurant (where she is currently the pastry chef), has truly come into her own. I was thrilled to include her recipe for Caramel-Berry Sauce with Chocolate. And my pastry chef friend Scooter Kanfer's Brown Butter Fruit Tart is the stuff legends are made of. They, along with Dorte Lambert of Michael's (Michael McCarty's restaurant in Santa Monica), also shared their knowledge as they very patiently let me bounce ideas off them.

Of course, writing a book is one thing; publishing it is quite another. Without all the great staff at William Morrow and Company, as well as their associates, this would not be a book at all. I am, therefore, eternally grateful to the following people: Justin Schwartz, senior editor, for pulling the whole thing together; Jennifer Kaye, associate editor, who took a pile of papers and organized them into a book; Susan Derecskey, the copy editor, who has a phenomenal eye for detail and a vast knowledge of French pastry; Lisa Koenig, Karen Pickus, and Janet Bowblis, the photographer, food stylist, and prop stylist, respectively, who made this book gorgeous; Stacy Heller, illustrator and close friend, who made the recipes accessible; Carrie Weinberg, head of cookbook publicity at Morrow, for helping put this on the bookshelf.

I really am not sure where to put my husband, Alan Schiff, in this chronology. Should he be at the beginning? After all, we did meet in high school. Or, should he be toward the end, since we became reacquainted at our twentieth high school reunion? He actually fits everywhere: I am convinced that he has always been with me in spirit. Thank you, Alan, for believing in me and for being the only partner I will ever need. Thank you especially for bringing Hannah, Jeremy, and Sarah into my life. You all inspire me to give everything in life my best effort.

Contents

Introduction

France's culinary traditions may not go back as far as its history, but they may well be more glorious. It is difficult to think of French food and wine without admiration, if not salivation, especially French baking. Even if you do not fancy yourself a lover of sweets, French bread is hard to pass up.

Whereas the ability to cook is a birthright in France, and eating out is much more the exception than the rule, the opposite is true of baking. A typical block in Paris has two to three bread bakeries *(boulangeries)*, at least one of which will also produce its own pastries *(pâtisseries)*. Some, of course, are better and more refined than others. Some may display the sign *pur beurre*, indicating that all their products are made with pure butter, never margarine.

Every shop has its loyal clientele. Walk down the street at 6 P.M. on any day and you will see thirty percent of the pedestrians carrying their daily baguette home. On Saturday and Sunday, typically days for family get-togethers, you'll see artfully wrapped packages of pastries swinging from shoppers' hands. When these shops close for their annual monthlong holiday, which usually occurs in July or August in Paris but may vary in Province (everything outside Paris, at least according to the Parisians), the local customers either diet or take their own vacations.

In the large cities, and to some extent in Province, the French rarely bake. For one thing, it is their long-standing tradition to leave baking to the boulangeries and pâtisseries and the masters who run them. After all, the baguette and the croissant, for example, are such important parts of the French economy that their prices are regulated by the government. On a more practical level, many Parisian apartments do not have kitchens, let alone ovens (I shared a 300-square-foot apartment that had only two hot plates in its kitchen, and I use the term "kitchen" loosely). Slowly, the French are opening up to the idea of making desserts and some pastries at home, but it is a rare city dweller who bakes bread.

In Province, bread is still purchased more often than it is baked at home. There are, of course, some farmwives who bake huge, crusty loaves to be enjoyed by their large families. Desserts, however, are another matter. This is where you'll find the big earthenware bowl of *Teurgoule* (Normandy Rice Pudding) that has been baking all night in a cooling oven. It is in Province that all the seasonal traditions live on.

Here, in America, our traditions are quite different. Up until the early 1990s, most Americans bought their bread in a supermarket. Now, more artisan breads are popping up but their cost is high. Bread is not a part of our culinary history as it is in France, but we do love experimenting with it at home. Desserts and pastries, on the other hand, have always been associated more with home than with bakeries. Bakeries try to produce things that look "homemade." There are as many people who think of themselves as good bakers as there are those who think of themselves as good cooks (oddly, few think of themselves as both).

Therein lies my reason for writing this book. Having worked in Parisian pastry shops for three years, I wanted to bring all those recipes and tricks back home so that we can play with them in the comfort of our own kitchens and not have to seek out bakery-produced creations, however homey *or* refined. One thing that we definitely have going for us is our openness to trying new things; another is the ever-increasing availability of quality ingredients and once-obscure equipment. Since our own traditions don't go back quite as far as those in France, we can think of these traditions as a work in progress and not be bogged down by them (not to imply that the French are, of course).

The New French Baker is organized into chapters that closely resemble the different sections of a French bakery. The breads, of course, are found in their own chapter, as in a French bakery they are often produced in a separate room using a special steam-injected oven. The cookies, or *petits fours secs*, usually require the help of several bakers, as large quantities must be shaped quickly before they cool. Rolled pastries, called *viennoiserie* because the first croissants came from Vienna, are made in the section of the bakery called *le tour* (not to be confused with *la tour*, meaning "the tower"). This is where croissant dough and puff pastry are turned (from the French word *tourner*, to turn). Large cakes that are displayed like jewels are assembled and finished in their own section of *entremets*. Ice creams and chocolates cannot be made near the ovens, of course, nor near flour dust. Instead, they are made in temperature-controlled areas known as the *glacerie* and the *chocolaterie*, respectively.

Not to imply that the pastry shop is a metaphor for life (although some pastry chefs might disagree), I must say that, as with so many things in life, a good knowledge of the basics will open the door to infinite possibilities. With that in mind I have included an extensive chapter on the basics—*Les Recettes de base*. It is my hope that once you master these, even the most difficult recipe in any book will become simple, and even better, you will find the confidence and inspiration to create your own recipes.

The Baker's Elements

Ingredients

ALL OF THE INGREDIENTS in this book are available at your neighborhood supermarket, a specialty store, or through mail-order suppliers. You may want to stock up on nonperishable specialty items.

Whatever the ingredient, buy the freshest and best quality available. This is particularly important for such basics as eggs, dairy products, and fruit. If you start with quality ingredients and follow the recipes, you will end up with a quality product. If you start with inferior ingredients, you can follow the recipes to the last letter, but the results will be mediocre.

Butter

Unless otherwise noted, all the butter in these recipes is unsalted. Unsalted butter is more neutral in flavor than salted butter and preferable for pastries. It also contains less water than salted butter. In terms of the quality of the butter you choose, personal taste is certainly a factor. Store brands are usually not of the highest quality, but more expensive does not necessarily mean better quality. Shop around, and if you come across an unsalted block of butter from a small dairy, give it a try.

In France, there are two types of unsalted butter available to the baking industry: wet butter and dry butter. Both are available in twenty-kilo blocks called *mottes*.

Wet butter is a general-use butter. It is good for cakes, cookies, butter creams, and so on. Dry butter is specifically used in rolled doughs; it is especially useful in puff pastry and croissant dough, where a high moisture content in the butter could cause water blisters to form during baking and might eventually lead to soggy, heavy pastry with an uneven rise. Wet butter does not spread evenly between the dough layers; it breaks up and gives the appearance of large curd cottage cheese under the dough.

Dry butter is produced, frozen, and set aside for professional pastry bakers in January and February. During this period, dairy cows are not grazing in the pastures, and the cream they produce is much richer than that of the rest of the year. The dry butter produced from this cream is remarkable in its smooth consistency. It is much more expensive than its wet counterpart and therefore reserved only for *le tour*, or rolled and turned doughs.

Alas, dry butter is not available to the general public, neither in France nor in America. But there are ways of achieving the same consistency:

- First and foremost, always choose a high-quality unsalted butter. Lightly salted butter is used in some traditional baked goods from Brittany, and recipes for those products will specify salted butter.

- When you can get butter in one-pound blocks, do so. Butter that has been divided into quarter-pound sticks has some water added. Furthermore, four sticks have a great deal more surface area than a one-pound block, leaving more area to absorb moisture from the atmosphere, impurities, and so on.

- Always work with chilled butter, as warm butter may begin to ooze and you will not see the water in the butter.

How to Dry Butter Determine how wet the butter is. Even within a given brand of butter, the moisture content may vary according to the season. Test the butter by pounding it with the side of your rolling pin. This mechanical action will force any droplets of water to the surface. Pat the water away with a lint-free absorbent cloth.

Continue to pound the butter and pat it dry until no more droplets appear, then form the butter into the block you will be using for your puff pastry or croissant dough.

If you have determined that your butter is wet but if for some reason the pounding and wiping method does not appeal to you or if you have a very large quantity of butter to dry out, cut up the butter and blend it with all-purpose flour, using one to two tablespoons of flour per pound of butter. The flour will absorb the moisture in the butter; while some flour will be added to the recipe, the percentage is quite small. Mix the butter and flour in an electric mixer, not in a food processor, as the motor of a processor may heat the butter and cause it to separate. Blend the butter and flour until all the flour is absorbed and the mixture is of an even, spreadable consistency. Form the butter into the block needed for the dough you're making.

If you expect to be making a lot of puff pastry or croissants, prepare several blocks of butter, in whatever weights are appropriate, ahead of time. Wrap the butter tightly in plastic and freeze for up to one month.

Clarified butter, which is the pure, fat portion of butter, is prepared by slowly melting unsalted butter over a low flame. The pan must not be disturbed during the melting process, so as to allow the whey solids to rise to the top and any water contained in the butter to sink to the bottom of the pan. After the butter has melted, skim the foamy whey from the butter's surface, then decant the fat into a bowl, leaving the water in the bottom of the pan.

Because whey solids burn at a lower temperature than does butterfat, their removal makes clarified butter a better choice for sautéing. Removal of the water makes clarified butter less likely to spatter when heated. This butter is also less likely to turn rancid at room temperature.

Chocolate

The types of chocolate available today, even in supermarkets, cover a range that far surpasses what was available ten years ago. With all the new chocolates on the market, it's important to realize that expensive chocolate is not necessarily better chocolate. Always taste the chocolate.

For bonbon centers, ganaches, mousses, and fillings, choose a chocolate that tastes great to you. I like extra bittersweet, because of its strong taste, which stands up to various other ingredients, such as cream, caramel, and alcohols. For dipping, be sure to use a chocolate with a higher cocoa butter content. When this information is available on the wrapper, choose a dipping chocolate with a maximum of 60 percent cocoa paste or liqueur. Taste the chocolate. It should not coat the roof of your mouth or feel greasy. Read the ingredients, but the most important thing is to taste the chocolate.

You are probably familiar with the following types of chocolate, which are listed according to ascending proportion of sugar and cocoa butter:

Cocoa powder Be sure to choose European- or Dutch-process cocoa powder, which is neutralized with an alkali. It has a milder taste and darker color than the others. Good quality cocoa is ideal for dusting truffles or sprinkling on cakes, leaving a velvety finish without a bitter aftertaste.

Unsweetened chocolate This chocolate is rather coarse in its flavor and can only be used to flavor things. Unsweetened chocolate available in one-ounce cubes is acceptable in any recipe that calls for unsweetened chocolate. Do not use pre-melted unsweetened chocolate, which contains chemicals that keep it fluid.

Bittersweet chocolate This chocolate is ideal for ganaches, mousses, bonbon centers, or anything that calls for a strong chocolate flavor. It is not ideal for dipping, since there is not enough cocoa butter to keep it fluid when melted.

Couverture Also known as coating chocolate, it can be tempered and used for dipping bonbons or wrapping cakes. Proper tempering ensures the couverture's shine, pliability, and smooth texture. Couverture may be dark (semisweet) or milk chocolate, but must contain no more than 60 percent cocoa paste or liqueur. As the cocoa paste content is inversely proportional to that of cocoa butter and sugar, a couverture that is lower in cocoa paste will be higher in cocoa butter and much easier to temper.

Semisweet chocolate This can be used in the same ways as bittersweet chocolate as well as for dipping.

Chocolate chips Chips can be used in ganaches and creams, but not for dipping. Paraffin is often added to chocolate chips so that they hold their shape when baked. This makes chocolate chips difficult to temper for dipping. Avoid them for glazing as well.

White chocolate This consists only of cocoa butter, sugar, milk, lecithin, and flavorings, with no chocolate liqueur whatsoever. It is suitable for decorations, especially if the cake you are decorating will be refrigerated. White chocolate is difficult to temper because it burns easily, but it can be used for dipping if melted at a low temperature.

Eggs

All the recipes in this book call for large eggs. Using extra large eggs may not affect the recipe drastically.

How to Freeze Eggs Many recipes call for either egg yolks or egg whites. Obviously, if you do not have any in the freezer, you will have to separate whole eggs. If you do, freeze whatever is left, yolk or white, in an airtight container. Zipper bags are ideal for this, because you can remove all the air and later peel away the bag from its frozen contents quite easily. Be sure to mark the date and the number or volume of egg whites or yolks on the outside of the bag. If you forget to do so, here are some guidelines (you can weigh the bags while the contents are still frozen):

Weights and Volumes of Frozen Eggs

5 whole large eggs weigh	8½ ounces
5 large whites weigh	5¾ ounces
5 large yolks weigh	2¾ ounces
4 large eggs measure	¾ cup
8 large whites measure	1 cup
5 large yolks measure	⅓ cup

In other words, 1 cup holds 6 whole eggs, 8 whites, or 15 yolks

Frozen egg yolks and egg whites thaw quickly at room temperature. It is better, however, to thaw yolks more slowly, in the refrigerator. Peel away the plastic bag and place the yolks in a bowl, then cover the bowl and refrigerate. Thawed yolks are difficult to remove from plastic bags.

Recipes that call for separated eggs, or egg whites that will be whipped to a meringue, require that the eggs be separated very cleanly. There should be no whites in the yolks (whites cook faster, so if they are clinging to the yolks, they could curdle your mixture), nor should there be yolks in the whites. Because they are fat, egg yolks inhibit whites from taking on volume. By the same token, the bowl and the whisk used for whipping whites must be very clean. If there is water in the bowl, do not dry it if there is a chance that your towel is greasy. A little water won't hurt, but grease will.

It is crucial that the eggs be extremely fresh. Follow the directions in each recipe for proper cooking and cooling techniques, especially for egg-based custards. Egg whites are considerably less risky than yolks. Whites whip better at room temperature, so leave them out before whipping.

Flour

Most of the recipes in this book can be made with all-purpose flour. Some bread recipes do call for bread flour, for its higher gluten content, but if you do not have any on hand, use all-purpose flour. On the other hand, if you only have bread flour, do not make anything but bread with it. A pastry dough made from bread flour will be tough. However, none of the recipes in this book calls for pastry flour.

Choose the right flour for the baked product you are making. The commonly available types of white flour are in descending order of gluten content:

High-gluten flour Great for bagels and bialys and other dense, extremely chewy yeasted products.

Bread flour This is a generally good flour for all types of white breads and to add to whole wheat and rye flours as well as other milled grains, which are low in gluten.

All-purpose flour All-purpose flour may be bleached or unbleached. Bleaching changes the appearance of the flour drastically, without changing its properties. Unbleached flour does not contain chemical additives and is therefore preferable. You can use this flour for anything, *but be aware that the amount of mixing, kneading, or rolling will dictate the texture of your baked product.*

Cake flour Rarely used in France, this finely milled flour yields cakes with a good deal of body, yet a fine crumb.

Pastry flour This grade of flour contains the least gluten of all. It is suitable only for rolled doughs and some cookies.

Measuring Flour

Precise measurement is the key to success in baking, and the key to precise measurement is a good kitchen scale. Weigh your flour and other ingredients; don't measure them out in cups and spoons. A pound of flour always weighs a pound, but may fill a different volume every time you measure it, depending on its texture and density. I have given both weight and volume measurements wherever necessary. They are correct but may look a little odd. You may notice that 1 cup of flour doesn't equal 8 ounces, despite what your measuring cup says. This is because a cup is meant to measure fluid ounces. Only water weighs (in dry ounces) and measures (in fluid ounces) the same. The fluid ounces of a measuring cup were originally based on the weight of water. If ever in doubt, remember that a pint's a pound and both are 16 ounces.

Sift your flour after weighing it. You may shake flour and other dry ingredients through a medium-mesh strainer to combine them and remove lumps.

Fruit

In keeping with the spirit of this book, I recommend using fresh fruit whenever possible. That said, high-quality frozen and canned fruit also have a place in the pastry kitchen; better choices, in fact, than out-of-season or poor-quality fresh fruit. It all depends on how the fruit is to be used. For example, an apricot mousse made with puréed canned apricots is likely to taste better than one made with the tasteless, mealy fruit that is often all that is available at the supermarket. Frozen fruit, or even frozen fruit purées, tends to be very consistent in quality within a given brand. Their processors have huge quantities available to them at the peak of the season so that the quality tends to average out, in general toward the high end. Of course, nothing beats the quality at a local farmers' market, so if you happen upon a bushel of great peaches or plums, take advantage by preserving or canning them yourself.

Fruit Facts Fruit has certain characteristics: fleshy, acidic, watery, and so on. It is the acidity that makes a slice of pineapple seem to cut the grease after a heavy meal. Some restaurants that specialize in steak soak the meat in enzymatic fruit juices, such as papaya juice, to tenderize it. Old recipes for jams and jellies sometimes call for an apple core or seeds wrapped in cheesecloth to add natural pectin to the mix.

Gelatin is composed of amino acids. These molecules link together in very long chains that bind with either other gelatin chains or with whatever is surrounding them, such as cream or fruit puree.

Certain naturally occurring compounds break apart the long gelatin protein molecules. Acids, for example, will break down proteins into their component amino acids. Enzymes, which are themselves proteins, act on specific molecules. In the case of the papaya, the enzymes in its juice break down muscle fiber, also made of protein. That is why papaya-soaked steak is so tender. What happens when these compounds are mixed with gelatin?

- In the case of lemon juice, whose acidity goes a long way to keep the eggs in Lemon Cream (page 315) from curdling, gelatin will be completely broken down and useless. If you want to make a lemon mousse, make lemon cream first. The mousse will have a strong lemon flavor, but the acidity of the juice will be tempered.

- Other citrus juices may not react as strongly with gelatin, since their acidity is considerably less than that of lemon juice. I still recommend making a citrus cream first. The final mousse will be much smoother.

- Pineapple does not puree smoothly, because of the high fiber content, and absolutely cannot be mixed with gelatin. Even the sweetest-tasting pineapple is loaded with citric acid, which will cut right through gelatin. And because pineapple puree does not cook smoothly, a pineapple cream is not the answer. Even chunks of pineapple in an otherwise well-composed mousse, such as a mango mousse with tropical fruit, will eat away at the surrounding gelatin and simply fall out. If you are really craving a pineapple dessert, try a roasted whole pineapple (see page 126) or Caramelized Pineapple Tart (page 114).

- If it's papaya mousse you want, you're in for some frustration. The powerful enzymes in the papaya make it impossible to combine with gelatin.

Here are a couple of rules of thumb that will help you determine if a certain fruit will make a good mousse, puree, sauce, or custard:

1. When pureed, the result should be completely smooth, never chunky. It should not separate when left to stand for a while. Examples of smooth purees: mango, raspberry, strawberry, lemon cream. Not-so-smooth purees: melon, pineapple, kiwi, papaya.

2. When eaten raw, the fruit should not taste acidic.

Pectin is another naturally occurring binder. It is also a protein, but it consists of a much shorter chain of amino acids than gelatin. Commercial pectin is added to fruit preserves to gel them. It can be found in the baking section of the supermarket. With commercial pectin, you can cook preserves less, and thereby reduce the volume less, and fruit cooked with pectin tends to have a brighter color. So, pectin is a money-saver. That being said, I do not recommend its use. I believe that the best way to make jam is the old-fashioned way: long, slow cooking. The apple-core-in-the-cheesecloth trick is a good one. This adds a very small amount of natural pectin, which changes the preserves' consistency only slightly.

Gelatin

Gelatin is a protein that is extracted either from the collagen in the hooves of certain animals or, in the case of kosher gelatin, from plant materials (often certain types of seaweed, which also give us agar-agar). American gelatin comes in granular form in jars or one-tablespoon packets; European gelatin comes in transparent sheets. Their uses are the same.

Whichever gelatin you use, it must be softened before it can be blended into a liquid. This does not mean melted. Softened gelatin, be it sheet or granulated, will still retain its integrity, making it possible to transfer it to the warm liquid in which it will be melted.

How to Soften Gelatin Sprinkle 1 tablespoon gelatin over the surface of ¼ cup *cold* water. Once the gelatin has swollen and has become translucent, drain the water and add the softened gelatin to warm liquid (110°F) to melt it. The liquid need not be hotter than that. To soften sheet gelatin, slide the sheets, one by one, into a bowl of cold water. Be sure to separate the sheets; sandwiched sheets will remain hard. Once the gelatin has completely softened, drain the water or pour the gelatin and water through a mesh strainer. Place the gelatin in warmed liquid.

Three sheets of gelatin are the equivalent of one tablespoon of granulated gelatin. As a general rule, it takes sixteen sheets or five tablespoons plus one teaspoon of granulated gelatin to bind one quart of fruit puree for a mousse. This will yield a mousse that stands up well in a refrigerated case, without tasting like gelatin. For the recipes calling for gelatin in this book, I have cut back slightly on the gelatin. If you are preparing a mousse that needs extra staying power, increase the gelatin slightly.

Grease for Pans

Many recipes call for greased or buttered baking pans. This butter is not included in the ingredients, because it is rarely of a fixed quantity. It is best to use soft but not melted butter to grease a pan; this will not burn. I usually keep a small amount of butter out of the refrigerator for just such a purpose. In most cases, unless specifically mentioned, you can substitute spray-on grease for butter on pans. Do not, however, use spray-on olive oil, except for savory recipes.

Milk and Cream

The milk called for in this book is always whole and cream is always whipping. If you can only find heavy whipping cream, that is fine. Do not, however, replace cream with half-and-half or whole milk with low-fat or nonfat milk. With few exceptions, the butterfat content of the dairy product is important to the success of the recipe.

Crème Fraîche

How to Make Crème Fraîche Stir 1 tablespoon well-mixed cultured buttermilk into 1 cup of heavy whipping cream (not ultra-high-temperature [UHT] pasteurized cream). Cover this mixture with plastic wrap and leave it at room temperature for 12 hours to thicken. Refrigerate the cream for up to one week.

Nuts

Nuts—almonds, hazelnuts, walnuts, pistachios, pine nuts—can change the flavor, texture, and crunch of a cake, pastry, chocolate, or even bread. Use only the freshest nuts, bearing in mind that what is available in supermarkets has been packaged for a while. Get vacuum-packed nuts if possible. If you know of a bulk nut supplier, get your nuts there. Properly wrapped, they will keep for six months in the freezer. If you do a lot of baking, it's a good idea to store nuts in different forms, blanched, ground, and chopped.

Nuts are very different in France, however. France grows a great deal of very flavorful bitter almonds, from which almond extract is derived, along with the sweet variety like the almonds grown in California. Sweet almonds need to be toasted to bring out their flavor but are relatively tasteless in their raw form. Since it is in this form that most almonds are used in baking, a small amount of almond extract may be needed to make the almonds identifiable. Use this extract cautiously, as it is pungent and overuse may give the final product an artificial taste. When almonds are added to an unbaked product, or after baking for texture, toast them first (see page 10). You may also purchase roasted almonds, but be sure that they are not salted.

France and Italy are famous for their hazelnuts (filberts). Fortunately, the hazelnuts of the Pacific Northwest really hold their own. Toast them to bring out their flavor, even in recipes that call for baking with hazelnuts, such as Chocolate-Spread Hazelnut Wafers (page 162). Toasted hazelnuts are considerably richer in flavor than raw, and since they take a while to fully toast, merely baking them in a cake may not do the trick.

Pastries made with walnuts also benefit from toasting. This is especially true of savory pastries, such as Roquefort Pinwheels (page 232), since toasted walnuts have an almost meaty taste.

We Americans do not revere the walnut as do the French. October is walnut season, especially in the region around Grenoble. Town festivals are centered on the walnut. Local restaurants present their walnut specialties. Markets are overflowing with fresh nuts. And fresh is what they are. (Walnuts sold in the United States are dried to increase their shelf life.) October walnuts in France are consumed just after harvest. Their meat is soft, juicy, and sweet. Walnut aficionados use special tools to dig the nutmeat out of its shell without damaging it. Some fanatics I have known actually grow their fingernails for the season!

Pecans are not grown in France. If you prefer the sweet taste of pecans to the flavor of walnuts, simply replace the walnuts in any of the recipes in this book with an equal amount of pecans. The flavor will definitely change, perhaps for the better.

Pistachios have long been adding color, flavor, and texture to French desserts and confections, particularly those with Provençal roots. While some pistachios are grown in France, the bulk of the nuts come from Turkey and Iran. You may not find California pistachios as flavorful as those from Asia Minor, but they are readily available in various forms: shelled or in the shells, roasted or raw. Whichever you choose, be sure they are unsalted.

Pine nuts, or pignoli, are quite common in Italian-influenced Provençal recipes, such as the spinach tart on page 92. These are available shelled in many specialty markets, and while they are somewhat costly, just a few add a soft crunch to any recipe. Toast them for 5 minutes at 375°F to bring out their flavor.

Only recently have macadamias, native to Hawaii and Polynesia, made their way into French pastries. The process required to shell macadamias makes them costly, but they add a wonderful richness and crunch, as well as a tropical touch, to cookies. Purchase raw or roasted unsalted macadamias, but avoid toasting them at home, as their oil makes them susceptible to burning.

How to Toast Nuts Spread the nuts on a foil-lined baking sheet. Bake at 375°F until light to medium brown, 7 to 10 minutes for walnuts and pistachios; 10 to 15 minutes for almonds and hazelnuts; 5 minutes for pine nuts. Stir the nuts halfway through the toasting time. Lift the nuts off the pan by picking up the corners of the foil. If you are grinding the nuts, cool them completely first. If you are making Caramelized Hazelnut Paste (page 320), keep the nuts warm while caramelizing the sugar.

How to Blanch Nuts For hazelnuts, toast the nuts as directed. When the skins split, remove the nuts from the oven and rub them between 2 towels to remove the skins. Do this while the nuts are still warm. Or rub toasted hazelnuts over a sieve or strainer. The friction will remove the skins. The advantage to the towel system is that the skins cling to the towel; with the sieve system, they just move around with the nuts. The disadvantage to the towel system is that the skins cling to the towel seemingly forever.

For almonds and pistachios, boil the nuts in water for 5 minutes. Drain thoroughly. While they are still warm, squeeze each nut between your thumb and forefinger to pop them out of their skin, or rub them between 2 towels, and the skins will cling to the towels. Do not use a sieve, or the points of the almonds will get nicked. Let the nuts dry before toasting or grinding.

How to Grind Nuts Start with blanched nuts. Blanched almonds must be completely dry. Toasted nuts must be completely cool. Put the nuts in a nut grinder or a food processor fitted with a steel knife. Process in small batches for even grinding. Grind as finely as possible, without turning the nuts into a paste. Press the ground nuts through a medium mesh sieve and discard any large pieces that remain. Freeze in airtight containers or zipper bags.

Walnuts can never be ground as finely as almonds or hazelnuts. For ground walnuts, process with some of the sugar or flour from the recipe.

How to Store Nuts Nuts of all kinds and in all forms can be frozen for up to three months in airtight containers. Zipper bags and plastic containers are ideal for this. I keep a large plastic container filled will bags of nuts in the freezer. They are all labeled and dated.

Phyllo Dough

Phyllo, from the Greek word for leaf, is made of flour, water, and salt. Frozen phyllo dough is available in the frozen pastry section of most supermarkets. It is sold in one-pound packages of 16 to 22 rolled sheets, depending upon the brand and the size of the sheets. Thaw frozen dough in the refrigerator overnight, but work with it at room temperature. (*Thawed phyllo dough may be refrigerated for up to 1 week.*) Always keep the pile of dough sheets covered, first with a piece of wax paper, then a slightly damp tea towel, folding back the covers, only when you need to take out more sheets.

Phyllo is a great replacement in many, but not all, recipes requiring puff pastry. As a rule of thumb, it works well in recipes that require sheets or flat pieces of dough, such as Napoleons (page 41) and strudels (see pages 94-96), but does not work in recipes that call for rolled-up or folded puff pastry. A recipe made with phyllo will be lighter than if made with puff pastry since there will be many fewer layers of dough and butter. Baked phyllo layers are considerably more fragile than puff pastry as well. Bear this in mind when you come up with your own creations.

Phyllo's biggest advantage is the convenience. You can decide to make a dessert with phyllo just hours before serving time. Versatility is another advantage. You can use this pastry for sweet or savory recipes, always brushing butter between the layers. The layers can be sprinkled with slivered almonds, toasted sesame seeds, or grated Parmesan. You can even drizzle honey between the layers.

Sugar

Unless otherwise specified, all sugar is granulated sugar. Do not substitute powdered, and especially not brown, sugar for granulated. They are not the same. You may substitute superfine sugar, using the weight measurement; superfine sugar is much more compact than granulated. Try to use cane rather than beet sugar. If it does not say cane on the box, it is probably beet. Beet sugar is processed differently, producing a granulated sugar with a lot of impurities. This is particularly noticeable when cooking sugar by itself: a gray film rises to the top.

Vanilla

Many recipes in this book call for vanilla beans, and a few call for vanilla extract. Vanilla extract, which is made from vanilla beans, barely exists in France, and what does exist is more of an essence; it is not alcohol-based like American extract.

I strongly urge you to use vanilla beans rather than vanilla extract wherever possible. Extract is best when baked into something; the heat forces the alcohol to evaporate and leaves the vanilla flavor behind.

If you live in an area where you have had trouble finding vanilla beans, buy a quarter pound (about twenty-five pieces) at a time from one of the mail-order companies listed in the back of the book. You can store them for up to a year. Vanillin is the main flavor component in Bourbon vanilla. Vanillin may also be produced synthetically and added to boost the flavor of a vanilla extract, in which case the extract must be called "natural and artificial," or to make artificial vanilla extract.

How to Store Vanilla Beans Store vanilla beans in a glass jar with a tight-fitting lid, or wrapped in wax paper, then placed in an airtight metal box. Do not store vanilla beans in plastic, at least not for long; plastic reacts with the organic elements in vanilla. Keep the beans in a cool dry place. It is not necessary to refrigerate them, unless you live in an extremely hot, humid area, where the beans might get moldy. Vanilla beans will keep at room temperature in a jar or tin for up to 1 year. They may dry a bit but will remain flavorful.

How to Make Vanilla Sugar You can make vanilla sugar by burying 1 split vanilla bean in 1 pound of sugar in a jar.

The bean will still be usable afterward, though somewhat less flavorful, and the sugar will taste great. Vanilla sugar lasts as long as unflavored sugar. It takes about 1 week for the flavor to infuse. Stir every 2 days to distribute the seeds.

Many French chefs reuse vanilla beans after making a recipe. They wash them off and let them air-dry. I do not recommend this. If, for example, you have just made *Crème Anglaise* or something else with egg yolks, the risk of bacteria remaining in the vanilla beans may not be great, but it hardly seems worth taking.

Yeast

I prefer fresh cake yeast to active dry yeast, although all the recipes requiring yeast have measurements for both. Fresh yeast can be crumbled directly into a mixing bowl with the other ingredients (except in the case of croissant dough). Active dry yeast must be proofed in tepid water, to verify that it is still alive. Note that cake yeast is no longer widely available. Since it's perishable, check the sell-by date.

Active dry yeast is available in ¼-ounce (2¼-teaspoon) packets or small jars. One of these packets has the rising power equivalent to one package of fresh yeast, weighing .6 ounce. This is enough to rise a dough made with one pound of flour. Should you decide to make a double batch of bread, do not double the yeast. Since yeast cells multiply exponentially, starting out with too many cells will cause them to multiply too quickly, with explosive results.

Fresh compressed yeast is available commercially in 1-pound blocks, and active dry yeast can be purchased in jars. These quantities are convenient if you are planning to make a lot of bread on a regular basis. They must be properly stored, however, as some of the yeast cells may die once exposed to air.

Be Prepared

This is not just the Scouts' motto; it should become yours as well. A good *mise en place*, or preparation, can be the difference between taking hours to make a single tart and making it within an hour because many of the elements have been prepared ahead and frozen. Once you've decided which pastries or desserts you like to make most often, follow these tips:

Freeze cookie dough: For those times when you need a batch of cookies but do not have the time to start from scratch, freeze a half recipe of Almond Shortbread Cookies (page 174), Palm Leaf Cookies (page 150), Straws (page 152), or Rolled Butter Cookies (page 172), unbaked. Thaw the shortbread in the refrigerator (it thaws quickly) and cut and bake the cookies. Cut the puff pastry–based cookies while still partially frozen (after about fifteen minutes at room temperature or about two hours in the refrigerator). Freeze the butter cookies after cutting rounds from the rolled dough. Once frozen, transfer the rounds of dough to an airtight container and keep in the freezer until ready to bake. These can go directly from the freezer into the oven.

Freeze tart shells: If tarts are your forte, make a batch of Sweet Short Dough (page 294), form disks, and chill them for one hour. Roll the dough and line several tart pans, of various sizes if you wish, then wrap and freeze the tart shells, unbaked. If you like, chill the shell and spread a thin layer (up to ¼ inch thick) of Almond Cream (page 314) on the bottoms of the shells before freezing. If you do this, prepare the tart dough, then the cream. The latter will be at the perfect consistency for spreading. Refrigerate or freeze any unused dough or cream.

Freeze toppings for tarts: Keep bags of Streusel (page 326) in the freezer. The topping can be broken up and used while still frozen. Also keep 1/2-cup containers of Glaze for Fruit Tarts and Desserts (page 325) in the freezer, especially during the summer, when you'll be making a lot of fresh fruit desserts.

Freeze creams and fillings: Keep small amounts of Chocolate Ganache (page 318), Raspberry Preserves (page 338), Apricot Preserves (page 336), and any other spreads or fillings you find yourself using often, in the refrigerator or freezer. Ganache makes a great chocolate sauce, and it thaws quickly. Heat it in a double boiler; it will burn easily if warmed over direct heat. You can make Almond Cream (page 314) ahead and freeze it in small batches for up to one month. Thaw only what you need. Do not make egg yolk–based custards and creams, such as Pastry Cream or *Crème Anglaise*, too far in advance; these do not keep as long as other fillings.

Freeze nuts: Keep nuts of all kinds on hand in the freezer (see page 11). When you toast almonds for one recipe, toast more than you need and keep the unused almonds in the freezer for next time. Date the containers, since nuts should not stay in the freezer longer than three months.

Store nut brittles at room temperature: Keep some Caramelized Hazelnut Paste (page 320) or Almond Brittle (page 319) on hand for those recipes that call for either. These will keep for a month, ground or in chunks, in an airtight container, at room temperature, not refrigerated or frozen. If the chunks stick together, roll over them with a rolling pin or break them apart in a food processor.

Store rum-soaked raisins in the refrigerator: Keep a covered jar of raisins completely covered with dark rum in the refrigerator. These can be used after soaking for twenty-four hours. When you drain the raisins, pour the rum back into the jar and replace the raisins. If you do not have rum-soaked raisins on hand and need some for a recipe, cover the needed amount of raisins with dark rum, then heat the mixture in a small saucepan, just until it simmers. Cool before using. This method is less desirable, since much of the alcohol is driven off when heated.

The Classics

Les Recettes classiques

FROM CUSTARDS TO SOUFFLÉS, from tarts to Napoleons, these dishes have been prepared in French restaurants and pastry shops for generations. Many of them have intimidated the home baker, particularly in Paris, where many apartments are not equipped with ovens. The recipes in this chapter have been modified to make them doable for today's home cook.

These recipes will put your growing knowledge of basic techniques to good use, as many classics combine two or more basic recipes. As you become more comfortable with some standard equipment, such as your mixer and candy thermometer, they will, in turn, become your best friends. Your "feel" for what is going on in the mixing bowl or that pot of boiling sugar will help to make these recipes become part of your regular repertoire and, hopefully, will inspire you to create your own classics.

In baking, much more so than in cooking, consistency and precision are key. Hence the use of precision instruments, such as a good candy thermometer. The most important instrument, in my opinion, is a good kitchen scale. Try to get into the habit of weighing your dry ingredients instead of measuring their volume. Remember that a pound of flour may fill a different volume every time you measure it, depending upon how you do so and under what conditions, but it will always weigh a pound. Remember, too, that if a dessert or pastry is to become a classic, it should be the same every time you prepare it.

Pears Poached in White Wine / *Poires pochées au vin blanc*
    Pears Poached in Red Wine / *Poires pochées au vin rouge*

Vanilla-poached Pears / *Poires pochées à la vanille*

Lemon Tart / *Tarte au citron*

Fresh Fruit Tart / *Tarte aux fruits frais*

Brown Butter Fruit Tart I and II / *Tarte aux fruits et au beurre noisette I et II*

Italian Prune Plum Tart / *Tarte aux quetsches*

Rustic Apple Tartlets / *Tartelettes aux pommes "Bonne-Mère"*

Tarte Tatin

Gâteau de Pithiviers

Paris-Brest
    Chestnut Paris-Brest / *Paris-Brest aux marrons*

Éclairs
    Mini-Éclairs / *Carolines*

Cream Puffs / *Choux à la crème*

Napoleons / *Millefeuilles*

Crêpes

Caramel Custard / *Crème caramel renversée*
    Large Caramel Custard / *Crème caramel*
    Coconut Caramel Custard / *Crème caramel à la noix de coco*
    Coffee Caramel Custard / *Crème caramel au café*

Crème Brûlée
    Black and White Crème Brûlée / *Crème brûlée noire et blanche*

Floating Classics
    Snow Eggs / *Oeufs à la neige*
    Floating Islands / *Îles Flottantes*
    Islands Floating on the Red Sea / *Îles Flottantes sur la Mer Rouge*
    Mysterious Islands / *Îles du mystère*

Individual Chocolate Soufflés / *Petits soufflés au chocolat*

Chocolate Mousse / *Mousse au chocolat*

Pears Poached in White Wine

Poires pochées au vin blanc

Pears are in season in the fall. I suggest that you take advantage of this versatile fruit by always keeping some poached pears in your refrigerator. Note that the weight of the poaching liquid is twice that of the sugar. This is a good rule of thumb for the syrup used to poach any fruit.   **Makes 8 pear halves**

2 lemons

4 Bartlett pears, all about the same size, slightly green

2 cups water

2 cups dry white wine, such as Chardonnay or Sancerre

2¼ cups (1 pound) sugar

1. Squeeze the juice of 1 lemon into a bowl of cold water. Peel the pears, taking care to not gouge or bruise them. Halve the pears, starting from the stem and cutting down. Using a melon baller or the tip of a paring knife, cut out the core. Using the paring knife, cut out the woody strip that extends from the stem to the core. Cut away the bottom dimple of the pear. As you finish peeling each half, place it in the bowl of lemon water.

2. Prepare the poaching liquid. Cut a circle of parchment paper or wax paper to fit just inside the pan you will be using. Combine the water and wine in a wide, shallow braising pan. Cut the remaining lemon in half and squeeze the juice into the pan, then add the lemon halves as well. Stir in the sugar. Bring to a boil, then lower the heat and simmer for 5 minutes.

3. Drain the pear halves, and using a large spoon, slide them into the poaching liquid, cut side up. Cover the surface of the poaching liquid with the paper circle. Bring the contents back up to a boil, then lower the heat again so that the liquid is just simmering under the paper.

4. Poach the pears for 15 to 20 minutes, or until they begin to look translucent around the edges. They will continue to cook in the hot liquid, so do not overpoach. Leave the pears covered with the paper to cool completely in the pan.

5. Once the pears have cooled, remove them with a slotted spoon and place them in a storage container. Discard the lemon halves. Ladle some of the poaching liquid over the pears, being sure there is enough liquid to completely surround the pears, or they will discolor. Place another piece of parchment or wax paper on the surface of the liquid, then cover the container and refrigerate. The pears will keep, refrigerated, for 3 weeks.

Pears Poached in Red Wine *Poires pochées au vin rouge*

Replace the lemon in the poaching liquid with 2 cinnamon sticks and the white wine with a young red wine, such as a Gamay (Beaujolais). Proceed as for Pears Poached in White Wine, leaving the cinnamon sticks with the poached pears instead of discarding them for storage.

Vanilla-poached Pears

Poires pochées à la vanille

Makes 8 pear halves

Juice of 1 lemon

4 Bartlett pears, all about the same size, slightly green

4 cups water

2 vanilla beans, split lengthwise in half

2¼ cups (1 pound) sugar

1. Pour the lemon juice into a bowl of cold water. Prepare the pears for poaching as in Step 1 of Pears Poached in White Wine.

2. Prepare the poaching liquid. Cut a circle of parchment paper or wax paper to fit just inside the pan you will be using. Combine the water and the vanilla beans in a wide, shallow braising pan. Stir in the sugar. Bring to a boil, then lower the heat and simmer for 5 minutes. Drain and add the pears, cut side up. Cover with paper and bring the contents back up to a boil, then lower the heat again so that the liquid is just simmering under the paper.

3. Poach and store as in Steps 3, 4, and 5 of Pears Poached in White Wine, leaving the vanilla beans with the poached pears for storage.

Lemon Tart

Tarte au citron

This perennial American favorite is rarely seen topped with meringue in France. In fact, when a pastry shop does display a *tarte au citron méringuée* with perfectly piped and browned meringue on top, the tart underneath is usually at least one day old and not presentable unadorned. This recipe does include a meringue option, however. The choice is yours.

Tarte au citron has its roots in Menton, near Nice, which is often referred to as the Lemon Capital of France. There the fruit is so revered, it is celebrated for the entire week before Mardi Gras.

If you are making a tray of *petits fours frais*, or petit fours that need refrigeration, tiny lemon tartlets are a perfect addition. Fully bake the tartlet shells with a dab of almond cream, then pipe on a few teaspoons of Lemon Cream. Top with fresh berries or sliced fruit—kiwi works well here—or meringue.   Makes one 10-inch tart, for 8 servings

¼ recipe (8 ounces) Sweet Short Dough (page 294), chilled but not frozen, or frozen and thawed overnight in the refrigerator, or 1 frozen tart shell, preferably frozen with a layer of Almond Cream (see page 314)

½ cup Almond Cream (page 314), softened (if shell was not frozen with Almond Cream)

Italian Meringue made from 3 egg whites and 1 cup minus 2 tablespoons (6 ounces) sugar (page 288) (optional)

½ recipe (1½ cups) Lemon Cream (page 315)

1.   Place the dough on a lightly floured surface and tap it a few times with a rolling pin. Roll it out to a 13-inch circle ⅛ inch thick and fill a 10-inch tart pan. Refrigerate for 1 hour. Or remove the frozen tart shell from the freezer.

2.   Preheat the oven to 375°F.

3.   Spread the Almond Cream, if using, evenly over the bottom of the tart shell and bake for 10 minutes. Check that the bottom of the tart shell is not puffing up. If it is, prick it with a sharp knife or a skewer. Bake for about 20 minutes more, or until the shell and the Almond Cream are golden brown. Remove the tart from the oven, leaving the oven on.

4.   If topping with meringue, prepare the meringue and let it cool on the mixer while the tart is baking. (If you do not have a free-standing mixer, prepare the meringue after the Lemon Cream filling). During the last 10 minutes of baking, prepare the Lemon Cream. When you remove the tart shell from the oven, strain the Lemon Cream directly into the shell, moving the strainer around so that the cream fills the shell evenly. If not covering the tart with meringue, return the tart to the oven for 5 minutes, or until no cream sticks to your finger when you touch the top of the tart very lightly. Do not overbake: The filling should not bubble or brown. This tart is self-glazing.

5.   If topping the tart with meringue, increase the oven temperature to 400°F. Fill the tart with lemon cream. Using a ½-inch open star tip, pipe the meringue on top. Use a regular pattern, such as ropes, braids, or stars, or free-form swirls. Bake the topped tart for 10 minutes, or until the meringue is lightly browned.

6.   Cool the tart completely at room temperature before serving. If the tart pan has two parts, remove the ring by holding the bottom with one hand while guiding the ring down with the other. Place the cooled tart on the table and set ring aside. Either remove the bottom by loosening it with a small paring knife and sliding it onto a serving platter or place the tart with the bottom on the serving platter. There is no need to refrigerate. If the tart is topped with meringue, refrigeration would cause the topping to weep. If using meringue, do not prepare the tart more than 4 hours ahead of serving time. An unadorned tart may be prepared up to 8 hours ahead.

Fresh Fruit Tart *Tarte aux fruits frais*

When you think of classic French pastries, this has to be one of the first that comes to mind. Every pastry shop in France displays its tarts proudly; every French pastry shop in America makes them as well. Those that go on display require a protective layer of apricot glaze to help them get through the day in the refrigerator. Fortunately, you will not need this at home.

I prefer to make fresh fruit tarts in the summer when berries are at their peak. In the fall and winter I switch to baked tarts, such as Italian Prune Plum Tart (page 26) or apple tarts.

If you're feeling exotic, use Mango Cream to fill the tart, then cover it with sliced kiwi, banana, and fresh mango, or other tropical fruits. In this case, you will need a glaze to prevent the fruit from drying or turning brown.   Makes one 10-inch tart, for 8 servings

¼ recipe (8 ounces) Sweet Short Dough (page 294), chilled but not frozen, or frozen and thawed overnight in the refrigerator, or 1 frozen tart shell, preferably frozen with a layer of Almond Cream (see page 314)

½ cup Almond Cream (page 314), softened (if shell was not frozen with Almond Cream)

1 cup Pastry Cream (page 308) or Mango Cream (page 310), chilled

2 teaspoons Kirschwasser, Grand Marnier, or dark rum (optional)

2 to 3 cups sliced fruit or berries or whole berries

½ cup strained Apricot Preserves, homemade or store-bought (page 336) (optional)

Powdered sugar, for dusting (optional)

½ cup Glaze for Fruit Tarts and Desserts (page 325) (optional)

1.   Place the dough on a lightly floured surface and tap it a few times with a rolling pin. Roll it out to a 13-inch circle ⅛ inch thick and fill a 10-inch tart pan. Refrigerate for 1 hour. Or remove the frozen tart shell from the freezer.

2.   Preheat the oven to 375°F.

3.   Spread the Almond Cream, if using, evenly over the bottom of the tart shell and bake for 10 minutes. Check that the bottom of the tart is not puffing up. If it is, prick it with a sharp knife or a skewer. Bake for about 20 minutes more, or until the shell and the Almond Cream are golden brown. Cool on a wire rack.

4.   If the tart pan has two parts, remove the ring by holding the bottom with one hand while guiding the ring downward with the other. Place the cooled tart shell on the table and set the ring aside. Either leave the tart on the pan bottom or loosen it with a small paring knife and slide it onto a platter.

5.   Whisk the Pastry Cream filling to loosen it, and add the liqueur, if desired. Spread the cream evenly over the bottom of the tart and cover it completely with sliced fruit or berries. If using sliced fruit, be sure to overlap it. If using a mixture of fruits, lay them in overlapping concentric circles.

6.   If you are glazing with apricot preserves, heat the preserves in a small pot with enough water to make a glaze with the consistency of maple syrup. Brush the hot glaze evenly over the tart. If you have used fruit such as whole raspberries that will not dry or turn brown, dust the tart with a thin veil of powdered sugar just before serving. (*The tart may be refrigerated for up to 8 hours.*) Or melt the Glaze for Fruit Tarts and Desserts in a double boiler and brush it over sliced fruit.

> **Most tart pans with removable bottoms are made of tin or metal other than stainless steel and will rust if washed and not dried immediately. I usually wash a new tart ring once, then just wipe it clean after each use. Since it usually comes in contact only with dough, and the butter in the dough makes the pan release easily, this wipe-down is an easy task. If, however, you feel more comfortable washing the tart pan after each use, be sure to dry it thoroughly and immediately. Place the dried pan in a turned-off oven, just in case any water remains. Do not wash these pans in the dishwasher.**

Brown Butter Fruit Tart I

Tarte aux fruits et au beurre noisette I

The French call brown butter *beurre noisette*, or hazelnut butter, because it has such a lovely nutty flavor. This recipe is incredibly easy, and like the Italian Prune Plum Tart (page 26), it is a great way to take advantage of summer stone fruit. In addition to the fruits named in that recipe, you can make this tart with sliced fresh peaches or nectarines. Make a rolled-out crust or a simple press-in crust.

This recipe comes from my friend Scooter Kanfer, who is an amazing chef.   Makes one 10-inch tart, for 8 servings

CRUST
¼ recipe (8 ounces) Sweet Short Dough (page 294), chilled but not frozen, or frozen and thawed overnight in the refrigerator, or 1 frozen tart shell, preferably frozen with a layer of Almond Cream (see page 314)

½ cup Almond Cream (page 314), softened (if shell was not frozen with Almond Cream)

FRUIT AND FILLING
2½ pounds stone fruit

5 ounces (1¼ sticks) unsalted butter, cut into small pieces

1 vanilla bean, split lengthwise

1 cup (7 ounces) sugar

3 tablespoons unsifted unbleached all-purpose flour

2 large eggs

1 large egg yolk

Whipped Cream (page 307) or vanilla ice cream, for serving

1. Place the dough on a lightly floured surface and tap it a few times with a rolling pin. Roll it out to a 13-inch circle ⅛ inch thick and fill a 10-inch tart pan. Refrigerate for 1 hour. Or remove the frozen tart shell from the freezer.

2. Preheat the oven to 375°F.

3. Spread the bottom of the tart shell evenly with Almond Cream and bake for 10 minutes. Check that the bottom of the tart shell is not puffing up. If it is, prick it with a small knife or a skewer. Remove from the oven, turning the temperature down to 350°F. Cool completely on a wire rack.

4.　Wash, dry, and halve the fruit, discarding the pits. If using plums, cut halfway down each piece of fruit, starting from the blossom end of each half. The pieces will open up as the tart bakes. If using peaches or nectarines, cut them in half and remove the pits, then cut the fruit into ½-inch wedges. Set aside.

5.　To prepare the filling, place the butter and the vanilla bean, split lengthwise, seeds scraped out, in a small, heavy saucepan and cook over medium heat until the butter foams and is light brown. It should have a nutty aroma. Remove the vanilla bean with a pair of tongs and scrape any remaining seeds into the butter. Allow the butter to cool slightly while preparing the other ingredients. Place the sugar and flour in the bowl of an electric mixer and stir to blend. Add the eggs and the egg yolk, one at a time, mixing on low speed until smooth. With the mixer still on low speed, add the butter in a thin stream until well incorporated. Scrape any remaining butter solids or vanilla seeds from the pot into the mixing bowl.

6.　Pour the filling into the shell. Lay plums on top, as you would for a plum tart. Lay peach or nectarine wedges in the filling in concentric circles.

7.　Bake for 45 to 60 minutes, or until the filling is puffed, browned, and set. Cool on a wire rack. If the tart pan has two parts, remove the ring by holding the bottom with one hand while guiding the ring down with the other. Place the cooled tart on the table and set the ring aside. Either remove the bottom by loosening it with a small paring knife and sliding it onto a serving platter or place the tart with the bottom on the serving platter. Serve at room temperature or slightly warmed with whipped cream or vanilla ice cream.

Brown Butter Fruit Tart II

Tarte aux fruits et au beurre noisette II

**Here is a variation on the previous recipe, using the same filling baked in a press-in crust. The prepa-
ration is somewhat simpler, as the crust requires no rolling. The resulting tart will be slightly richer
and more fragile, and absolutely delectable.**   Makes one 10-inch tart, for 8 servings

PRESS-IN CRUST
4 ounces (1 stick) frozen unsalted butter, cut into small pieces

1 cup (about 5½ ounces) unbleached all-purpose flour, unsifted

⅓ cup (about 2½ ounces) sugar

One-third of the seeds from 1 vanilla bean (use the rest for filling)

1.   Place all the crust ingredients in the workbowl of a food processor and pulse until there are
no butter pieces remaining and the mixture resembles coarse cornmeal.

2.   Preheat the oven to 375°F.

3.   Pour the mixture into a 10-inch tart pan and press it firmly and evenly into the bottom and
sides of the pan. Bake for 10 minutes, or until the crust just begins to color. Remove from the
oven and lower the oven temperature to 350°F. Cool on a wire rack.

4.   Prepare the fruit as in Step 4 of the recipe for Brown Butter Fruit Tart I.

5.   Prepare the filling as in Step 5, using the remaining two-thirds of the vanilla bean, and fill
the tart as in Step 6. Bake, cool, and serve the tart as in Step 7.

Italian Prune Plum Tart *Tarte aux quetsches*

**The Germans call it *Zwetschgendatschi*, and the classic French version definitely has its roots in
Alsace, where prune plums are plentiful. This is one of the simplest and most satisfying tarts you can
make. The tips of the quartered plums brown as they bake, and the juices run down into the almond
cream base, leaving the crust crisp. Serve this with a dollop of lightly sweetened whipped cream.**

**This type of tart lends itself well to summer stone fruits, such as apricots, peaches, cherries,
and other kinds of plums (see color insert). No topping is required, although you may want to add a
layer of Streusel for extra crunch.**   Makes one 10-inch tart, for 8 servings

½ recipe (8 ounces) Sweet Short Dough (page 294), chilled but not frozen, or frozen and thawed overnight in the refrigerator, or 1 frozen tart shell, preferably frozen with a layer of Almond Cream (see page 314)

2½ pounds Italian prune plums, or other oval plums

⅓ recipe (1 cup) Almond Cream (page 314), softened (use only ½ cup if shell was frozen with Almond Cream)

Granulated sugar, for sprinkling (optional)

1 recipe (1½ cups) Streusel (page 326) (optional)

1. Place the dough on a lightly floured surface and tap it a few times with a rolling pin. Roll it out to a 13-inch circle ⅛ inch thick and fill a 10-inch tart pan. Refrigerate for 1 hour. Or remove the frozen tart shell from the freezer.

2. Preheat the oven to 375°F.

3. Prick the bottom of the tart shell all over with a fork. Bake for 10 minutes, or until the shell is just beginning to brown. Remove from the oven, leaving the oven on. Cool completely on a wire rack.

4. Wash, dry, and halve the plums, discarding the pits. Starting from the blossom end of each half, cut halfway down the piece of fruit. The pieces will open up as the tart bakes.

5. Spread the Almond Cream evenly over the bottom of the tart shell. Place the plum halves, cut ends pointing up and skins down, against the rim of the tart. The halves should overlap a bit. Cover the tart with overlapping concentric circles of fruit.

6. If not using Streusel, sprinkle lightly with granulated sugar and bake for 15 minutes. Sprinkle with more sugar and bake for 20 to 30 minutes more, or until the crust is well browned, the Almond Cream is puffed and set, and the tips of the plums are browned.

If topping with Streusel, crumble the topping all over the tart and bake for 30 to 45 minutes, or until the Streusel is golden brown.

7. Serve warm or at room temperature. If the tart pan has two parts, remove the ring by holding the bottom with one hand while guiding the ring down with the other. Place the cooled tart on the table and set the ring aside. Either remove the bottom by loosening it with a small paring knife and sliding it onto a serving platter or place the tart with the bottom on the serving platter. *The tart, covered lightly with plastic, can be stored at room temperature for up to 24 hours.*

Rustic Apple Tartlets

Tartelettes aux pommes "Bonne-Mère"

These tartlets will serve equally well as a snack for the kids when they get home from school or as dessert, served warmed with whipped cream or vanilla ice cream, after a winter meal. The apple-sauce should not be watery, which would make the pastry soggy. The tartlets may also be made with sliced apples. Use Golden Delicious apples here; they give off the least amount of water during baking, hence holding their shape, and they are readily available.   Makes 8 tartlets

½ recipe (1 pound) fully turned Puff Pastry (page 296) or 1 package store-bought pastry, cold

2 cups stiff applesauce, homemade (see page 333) or store-bought, chilled, or 2 large ripe Golden Delicious apples, peeled, cored, quartered lengthwise, and thinly sliced perpendicular to the core

2 tablespoons granulated sugar mixed with a pinch of ground cinnamon (optional)

1 large egg yolk

Powdered sugar, for dusting

1. If using homemade pastry, line a baking sheet with parchment paper. Roll out the pastry on a lightly floured surface to a 20 × 10-inch rectangle ⅛ inch thick. Cut the sheet in half to form 2 squares. Place the dough in a single layer on the baking sheet and cover lightly with plastic wrap. Refrigerate for at least 1 hour to allow the gluten to relax, and thus minimize shrinkage. If using store-bought pastry, let it rest at room temperature for 5 minutes to prevent cracking, then unfold both sheets. Store-bought pastry does not need to be rolled out. Trim the dough around all the edges to square it off and to eliminate any folds in the dough. Cut eight 5-inch squares of dough. Freeze any scraps, without rolling them into a ball. Use a fork to prick a 3-inch round in the center of each square.

2. Place ¼ cup of applesauce or one quarter of an apple in the middle of each square. For sliced apples, keep the slices together and press them down at a slight angle to fan them; they will bake more evenly and the pastry will be easier to close. Sprinkle sliced apples with cinnamon sugar, if desired.

3. Use your fingers or a pastry brush to dampen the corners of the pastry square with water. Draw the corners in and pinch them over the applesauce or apple, leaving the sides gapped. Transfer to ungreased or parchment-lined baking sheets, leaving 3 inches between for even browning, and refrigerate for at least 1 hour. (*The tartlets, covered with plastic wrap, can be refrigerated for up to 24 hours.*)

4.   Adjust the oven racks to divide the oven into thirds and preheat to 400°F.

5.   Mix the egg yolk with 1 teaspoon water. Remove the pastries from the refrigerator and brush the tops evenly with the egg wash. Bake until puffed and golden, 35 to 45 minutes. The tarts may open up during baking. Cool on wire racks.

6.   Serve at room temperature or warm for 10 minutes at 350°F. Dust with powdered sugar.

Cinnamon was virtually unknown in French pastries, except for a few Alsatian or German-influenced specialties, until recently. But now some contemporary pastry chefs are discovering this spice and using it in new ways.

Tarte Tatin

Accidents happen, often with positive results. At the end of the nineteenth century, the Tatin sisters owned a small hotel across from the train station in Lamotte-Beuvron (in Sologne, a region just south of Paris known for game hunting). One day, Fanny Tatin was about to place an apple tart in the oven when she dropped it. Without missing a beat, she slid a tray under the upside-down tart and baked it, still upside down. Much to her surprise and her customers' pleasure, the creation was a huge success and became a classic.

Like every French classic, *Tarte Tatin* has its own set of tools, molds, and utensils and, in this case, few are available here. I replaced my Tatin mold with a 9-inch enameled cast-iron skillet about 3 inches deep, which conducts the heat wonderfully. Any heavy-bottomed nonreactive pan will do. Do not use a pan larger than 9 to 10 inches in diameter, though, or your tart will be difficult to unmold.

Over the years I have been disappointed in Tartes Tatin that look great, are perfectly caramelized, yet have a soggy crust. Traditional recipes call for partially baking the apples, then topping them with a thin layer of puff pastry (usually from scraps) or Flaky Pastry Dough, so the pastry cooks on top. It never seems to bake through. In this recipe, the crust is baked separately and excess juice from the apples is drained before they are turned onto the crust. The result is a tart that can sit for hours without getting soggy.

Use apples that hold their shape during baking but are not too hard. Golden Delicious apples are ideal for Tarte Tatin.   Makes one 9-inch tart, for 8 servings

> 8 ounces puff pastry scraps (see page 349) or Flaky Pastry Dough (page 293), chilled
>
> 1 cup (about 7 ounces) sugar
>
> 4 ounces (1 stick) unsalted butter
>
> About 4½ pounds Golden Delicious apples, peeled, halved lengthwise, and cored
>
> Whipped Cream (page 307), crème fraîche (see page 9), or vanilla ice cream, for serving

1.   Line a baking sheet with parchment paper. Roll out the dough on a lightly floured surface ⅛ to ¼ inch thick. Lift the dough off the table and put it back down to relax it. Using the bottom of a pan or a tart ring as a guide, cut a 10-inch circle of dough. Discard the scraps; they will be too tough to use for anything else. Transfer the dough to the baking sheet and cover lightly with plastic wrap. Refrigerate for 30 to 60 minutes.

2.   Arrange the oven racks to divide your oven into thirds and preheat the oven to 400°F. Place a piece of aluminum foil on the floor of the oven to catch any caramel or juices that drip.

3. Place the sugar and butter in a 9-inch cast-iron skillet or the mold of your choice and melt over medium heat. Place the apple halves in the pan, so that the cut side of one half is against the round side of the next. Pack the apples in tight concentric circles, with the cut sides perpendicular to the side of the pan (the apples will be higher than the top of the pan). The sugar will begin to caramelize. Cook the apples on the top of the stove for 20 minutes, or until the lightly caramelized sugar is bubbling around the fruit.

Arrange halved apples vertically in concentric circles.

4. Place the pan in the oven on the upper rack and bake for 20 to 30 minutes, or until the apples have sunk somewhat into the pan, are deep brown in color, and a thin knife can be inserted with only slight resistance.

5. As soon as you put the apples in the oven, remove the dough round from the refrigerator and prick it all over with a fork. Bake the round for 10 to 15 minutes on the lower rack, or until golden brown. Remove the crust from the oven and cool on a wire rack.

6. When the apples are cooked, remove the pan from the oven and let it cool for 15 minutes on a wire rack. Place a closely woven rack on top of the apples and carefully invert the apples onto the rack. Set the rack with the apples over a pan to collect the juices as they drain. Leave the skillet on top of the apples.

7. After 10 minutes, invert the apples again and place the crust over the apples. Cover this with a flat serving platter and invert the tart with the crust onto the platter. Lift the skillet off the apples.

Drain baked apples on a wire rack before placing them on the baked crust.

8. Pour the juices back into the skillet and reduce over high heat until very thick. Pour this sauce over the tart.

9. Serve the tart warm or at room temperature. It will not retain its crispness for more than 8 hours. Cut with a heavy knife or a finely serrated one, and serve with a dollop of Whipped Cream or crème fraîche, or a scoop of vanilla ice cream on the side.

Gâteau de Pithiviers

Pithiviers is a town in the Orléanais region of France, about sixty miles southeast of Paris. I was born in that region, and while I was not raised there, I like to believe that this fact accounts for my affinity for this dessert.

In Paris and elsewhere, this cake has also become known as *galette des rois,* literally, kings' cake, or Twelfth Night Cake, although in some parts of France this designation is used for a filled yeasted ring cake. Huge numbers of these cakes are prepared by pastry shops (I recall making 1,500 myself one season) for Epiphany, January 6. The cake is sold with a gold crown. A *fève,* literally "bean," is baked into the cake. Whoever gets the piece with the fève wears the crown. The French take this so seriously that in recent years, after many decades of plastic fèves, a whole new industry of fancy porcelain fèves of various shapes has grown. There is even a *Châteaux de France* series!   **Makes one 9-inch round cake, for 8 servings**

½ recipe (1 pound) fully turned Puff Pastry (page 296) or 1 package store-bought pastry, cold

⅓ recipe (1 cup) Almond Cream (page 314), softened

1 egg yolk, mixed with 1 teaspoon water, for egg wash

1.   Line 2 baking sheets with parchment paper. If using homemade pastry, roll it out on a lightly floured surface to a 20 × 10-inch rectangle ⅛ inch thick. Cut the sheet in half to form 2 squares. Place 1 square of dough on each baking sheet and cover lightly with plastic wrap. Refrigerate for at least 1 hour to allow the gluten to relax and thus minimize shrinkage. If using store-bought pastry, let it rest at room temperature for 5 minutes to prevent cracking, then unfold both sheets. Store-bought pastry does not need to be rolled out any further.

2.   Use an inverted 9-inch cake pan to trace a circle, without cutting, on 1 square of dough. Trace another circle inside that one, 7 inches in diameter. Prick the dough all over the inner circle with a fork. Using a small offset spatula or icing spatula, spread the Almond Cream over the inner circle in a flat, even layer.

After pricking the dough, spread the Almond Cream in the middle of the traced circle.

3.   Dip a pastry brush in cold water and shake off the excess. Dampen the dough between the Almond Cream layer and the outer traced circle.

Press the air out of the covered filling, sealing the dough.

4.   Roll the other square of Puff Pastry around the rolling pin and hold 1 edge of the dough over the edge of the cream-topped square nearest you. Lay the dough over the square without stretching it. Take care not to trap any air underneath. The back edges of dough may not quite meet up. Using the sides of your hands and gently curving your fingers to follow the circle of filling, press down on the top layer of dough just at the inner circle's edge. This will seal the 2 pieces together, while forcing any air from the inside to the edge of the dough. Invert the same 9-inch cake pan and trace the perimeter of the cake, again without cutting into the dough. Make sure that the filling is centered within this circle.

5. Stir the egg wash and glaze the top of the circle, stopping just beyond the outer circle's perimeter. Slide the pastry onto a baking sheet and refrigerate for at least 1 hour. (*The pastry may be covered with plastic wrap after the glaze has dried and refrigerated for up to 24 hours.*)

6. Place a rack in the middle of the oven and preheat the oven to 425°F.

7. Remove the baking sheet from the refrigerator. Invert the same 9-inch cake pan over the pastry, making sure that the filling is centered, and cut through both layers of dough with the tip of a sharp paring knife. Remove the excess dough and save as scraps (see page 349). Cut a ¼-inch hole through the very top of the pastry to allow steam to escape during baking. Use the tip of the knife to cut arched spokes from the center hole to the edge of the filling, leaving a 1-inch unmarked border. Do this by simply resting the knife on the dough, without pressing.

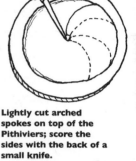

Lightly cut arched spokes on top of the Pithiviers; score the sides with the back of a small knife.

8. Use the dull side of the knife, with the tip resting on the pan, to trace vertical or slightly angled marks ¼ inch apart along the perimeter of the pastry. If you wish, slide a piece of parchment paper under the pastry. Refrigerate for 10 minutes. (*At this point, the pastry can be wrapped with plastic resting directly on the dough to avoid air pockets and frozen for up to 1 month, provided the Almond Cream was not previously frozen. The frozen pastry, unwrapped, can go directly from the freezer to a baking sheet and into the oven.*)

A baked Pithiviers

9. Bake the pastry for 10 minutes at 425°F, then lower the temperature to 400°F and bake for 25 to 30 minutes more, or until deep brown on top and golden on the sides. Be sure the sides are done; if not, the pastry will collapse when removed from the oven.

10. Using 2 wide metal spatulas, transfer the pastry to a wire rack to cool. Serve warm or at room temperature. (*This pastry, wrapped in plastic, can be kept at room temperature for up to 24 hours, then reheated in a 425°F oven for 5 minutes to bring back its crispness.*)

> **By cutting both pieces of dough at once, rather than trying to match up two circles of dough, you have two pieces of exactly the same size that rise together in the oven. Also, by glazing with egg before marking the top of the dough and letting the glaze dry, you can be sure that the egg wash won't seal the decorative marks. The dough will split at those marks during baking, revealing a less shiny finish to contrast with the glazed dough. Even more important, since the pastry is trimmed only after glazing, the egg wash cannot run down the sides and seal the dough, which would prevent it from rising evenly.**

continued

It is very important to let all pastries composed of Puff Pastry cut into a specific shape rest for at least one hour, refrigerated, to allow the gluten to relax. Gluten builds up with the mechanical action of rolling, and if it does not relax, the dough will shrink, often unevenly. Since this particular pastry has two layers of dough that fit together, it is especially important to rest the dough, to prevent the two pieces from shrinking away from each other or in different directions.

Paris-Brest

Brest is a city in Brittany and we all know where Paris is, but this dessert is popular all over France. Traditionally, it consists of a ring of baked Choux Paste filled with a mixture of Butter Cream, Caramelized Hazelnut Paste, and Pastry Cream. I have always found this to be delicious for about two bites, after which the filling becomes cloyingly sweet. Here is a lighter version plus a variation that's perfect for Thanksgiving or Christmas.

This recipe is easily doubled, or you can make individual cakes.   Makes one cake, for 6 servings, or 10 individual cakes

¼ recipe (6 ounces) Choux Paste (page 295), freshly made or frozen and thawed

¼ cup (1 ounce) chopped, sliced, or slivered blanched almonds

¼ recipe (1½ cups) Pastry Cream (page 308), chilled

½ recipe (½ cup) Caramelized Hazelnut Paste (page 320)

1 cup whipping cream, cold

¼ cup very finely chopped Caramelized Hazelnut Paste (page 320) (optional)

Powdered sugar, for dusting

I. Preheat the oven to 400°F. If making a large cake, use the bottom of an 8-inch cake pan to trace a circle on a piece of parchment paper. For individual pastries, use an inverted bowl with a 4-inch diameter to trace smaller circles. Place the paper, ink or pencil facing down, on a baking sheet.

2. Fill a large pastry bag fitted with a ⅜-inch open star tip with Choux Paste. Place the tip against the paper and holding the pastry bag at a 30-degree angle to the pan, pipe around the circle or circles once. For the larger circle, pipe another ring of dough inside the first, then a third circle on top of the first two. Sprinkle evenly with almonds.

3. Bake for 15 minutes, or until the dough begins to puff. Avoid opening the oven door earlier, as the rush of cooler air may cause the pastry to collapse. Prop the door open with a wooden spoon and continue to bake until the pastry is even, golden, and firm. This will take 15 to 20 minutes for the large ring, 5 to 10 minutes for individual rings. Remove the pan from the oven and immediately transfer the ring or rings to a wire rack to cool completely.

4.   Meanwhile, prepare the filling. Whisk the Pastry Cream slightly just to loosen, then add the hazelnut paste and whisk until smooth and even. Whip the cream until stiff but still very smooth. Gently fold the 2 creams together, taking care to not overmix. Fold in the chopped hazelnut paste, if desired.

5.   Using a serrated knife, cut the cream puff circle or circles horizontally. Set the top or tops aside. Fill a pastry bag fitted with a ½-inch open star tip with the hazelnut cream filling. Have a toothpick handy to clean the tip if the hazelnut paste plugs it. Using a swirling motion that goes from the inside to the outside edge of the ring, fill it. Place the top of the ring on the cream and press down gently.

6.   Transfer the dessert to a serving platter, wrap loosely in plastic, and refrigerate for 1 to 4 hours to set the cream (after four hours, the pastry will lose some of its crunch). Just before serving, dust lightly with powdered sugar. Cut the large ring with a serrated knife or pie-server.

Chestnut *Paris-Brest* *Paris-Brest aux marrons*

Prepare the above recipe, replacing the hazelnut paste with Chestnut Cream with Vanilla (page 339) or canned sweetened chestnut puree. Replace the chopped hazelnut paste with an equal amount of drained and chopped chestnuts in syrup, available in many gourmet shops and supermarkets around the holidays.

Éclairs

Here is a pastry that is a classic on both sides of the Atlantic. As ubiquitous as éclairs are in bakeries, however, even in the most avant-garde ones at that, they are rarely prepared at home. They do require several steps: preparation of Choux Paste, preparation and chilling of the Pastry Cream, and preparation of some sort of glaze. There are, of course, tricks and shortcuts that will enable you to make as many or as few pastries as you want, whenever you want.

Typically, Parisian pastry shop éclairs are filled with Grand Marnier-, chocolate-, or coffee-flavored pastry cream, then glazed with white, chocolate, or coffee fondant, respectively. The pastry cream is simple to prepare, and you can even combine flavors or prepare your pastry cream with Caramelized Hazelnut Paste for *éclairs pralinés*. The fondant is a bit trickier; even professionals must master this glaze, composed of sugar, water, and glucose, in order to maintain its shine and suppleness. I prefer to dispense with fondant entirely (it is virtually unavailable in the retail market and a mess to make at home) and glaze my éclairs with either a chocolate glaze or caramelized sugar.

Makes 10 éclairs

½ recipe (¾ pound) Choux Paste (page 295), freshly made or frozen and thawed

⅓ recipe (2 cups) Pastry Cream (page 308), flavored with Grand Marnier, chocolate, coffee, or Caramelized Hazelnut Paste (page 320)

½ recipe (1¼ cups) Chocolate Glaze II (page 324), or 2 cups granulated sugar (14 ounces) and 2 teaspoons freshly squeezed lemon juice

1. Adjust the oven racks to divide your oven into thirds and preheat the oven to 400°F. Line 2 baking sheets with parchment paper, placing a bit of Choux Paste under each corner of the paper to attach it to the pan.

2. Spoon about 1½ cups of dough into a large pastry bag fitted with a ¾-inch plain tip. Rest the tip on the baking sheet and angle the bag up about 30 degrees. Moving the bag in a straight line and squeezing evenly, pipe out a 5-inch log. As you reach the end, stop squeezing and lift the tip up sharply to cut the flow of dough (lift the bag with the hand that is not squeezing). Repeat this until you have used all the dough, leaving 2 inches between logs, refilling the pastry bag as needed.

3. Use a damp pastry brush to press down any dough peaks, then brush over each log to smooth it. Lightly score each log with an inverted fork. At this point, if the dough has not been previously frozen, you may wrap the pans in plastic and freeze them for up to 1 month. Thaw in the refrigerator, then allow the dough to come to room temperature before baking.

4. Place the pans in the oven and close immediately. Check the éclairs after about 10 minutes, through the oven window if possible. Avoid opening the door unnecessarily, which may cause the

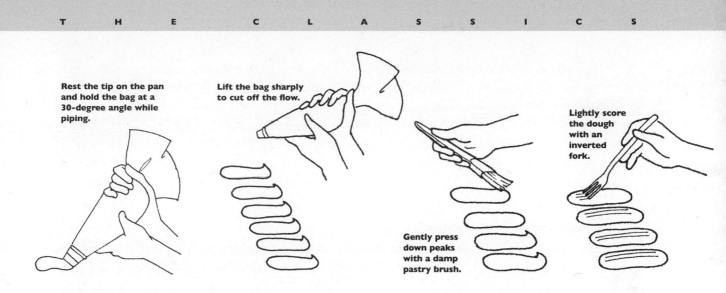

Rest the tip on the pan and hold the bag at a 30-degree angle while piping.

Lift the bag sharply to cut off the flow.

Gently press down peaks with a damp pastry brush.

Lightly score the dough with an inverted fork.

éclairs to collapse. They should be expanding with smooth tops and just starting to brown. At this point, prop the oven door open with a wooden spoon to let steam escape, which will give the éclairs a smooth, thin, crisp crust and a dry interior.

5.   After a total of 20 to 25 minutes, the éclairs should be an even, deep brown and should feel quite firm when squeezed. Remove the pans from the oven and cool the éclairs completely on wire racks. Once cooled, the éclairs may be wrapped in plastic zipper bags and frozen for up to 1 month, refrigerated for up to 1 week, or left at room temperature for 24 hours. To re-crisp, place the éclairs on a baking sheet and bake for 5 minutes at 400°F. Do not overbake, as they will become brittle.

6.   Take a pastry tip with the smallest opening possible and wedge it under a cooling rack, so that the tip points through the rack and remains in place. Spoon half the Pastry Cream into a pastry bag fitted with a ¼-inch plain tip. Using the wedged pastry tip as a spike, pierce three holes in the bottom (flat side) of an éclair, then immediately insert the pastry bag's tip and squeeze Pastry Cream into each hole. Squeeze until you feel that the section of the éclair is filled; you will feel resistance once this has happened. Scrape any oozing Pastry Cream back into the cream's bowl, then replace the filled éclair, pierced side up, on the rack and repeat with the remaining pastries. Place the rack in the refrigerator while preparing the glaze.   *continued*

Wedge a fine pastry tip under the cooling rack.

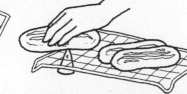

Pierce the bottom of each éclair three times with the tip, then . . .

. . . immediately fill each pastry, squeezing pastry cream into each hole.

Invert each éclair into glaze or caramel.

7.   **For chocolate-glazed éclairs,** melt the Chocolate Glaze in a double boiler until it is fluid, stirring often. It should be no warmer than 95°F (slightly cool to the touch) to maintain its sheen. Pour the glaze into a shallow bowl large enough to insert an éclair horizontally. Remove the éclairs from the refrigerator and invert each into the glaze, dipping to about one-third the thickness of each pastry. Shake off the excess glaze, then invert the éclairs onto the rack. The glaze will set quickly. Place the éclairs directly onto a serving platter or into elongated paper pastry or muffin cups. Serve immediately, or refrigerate loosely covered with plastic, for up to 8 hours. Note that the éclairs will lose some of their crispness with refrigeration.

8.   **For caramel-glazed éclairs,** combine 2 cups of sugar with the lemon juice and ½ cup of water in a small, heavy saucepan. If you have an unlined copper caramelizing pot, clean it (with salt and vinegar) and use it here. Brush down any sugar crystals clinging to the inside of the pot with a damp pastry brush. Cook the sugar over a medium flame until it begins to boil clear. Do not move the pot until this point; it could cause the sugar to crystallize. Meanwhile, fill a bowl that is larger than the pot halfway with ice cubes and cover with cold water. On a very flat, work surface (wood or metal), lay a sheet of aluminum foil. Grease the foil very lightly with a few drops of tasteless vegetable oil. Place the rack of filled éclairs and a wadded kitchen towel next to the foil.

9.   Swirl the pot from time to time, to even the cooking. Once the sugar begins to color, watch it carefully. When it has reached a deep amber color (365°F on a candy thermometer), remove it from the heat and immediately dip the bottom of the pot into the ice water to stop the cooking. Lift it out, swirl it a few times, then dip it again for just a few seconds. Carefully dry off the bottom of the pot, then place it on the table with one side propped up on the wadded towel, so that the pot is at an angle.

10.   Dip the unpierced side of each éclair in the caramel, taking care not to touch the caramel or the pot with your fingers, as they are still extremely hot. Dip to about one-fourth the thickness of each pastry. Place each caramelized éclair on the oiled foil and press down gently, so that the caramel flattens. This caramel will harden quickly and the éclairs should release easily from the foil. Place the éclairs on a serving platter, in paper cups if desired, and serve immediately, or refrigerate for up to 4 hours. Since the caramel tends to soften under refrigeration, you may want to leave the éclairs unglazed until just before serving.

Mini-Éclairs *Carolines*

In a pastry shop these would fall into the category of *petits fours frais*, or chilled petit fours. They are wonderful mouthfuls that look impressive on a platter with other small pastries. All the components can be made ahead, then assembled several hours before serving.   **Makes 50 pieces**

½ recipe (¾ pound) Choux Paste (page 295)

About ⅓ recipe (2 cups) Pastry Cream (page 308), flavored with Grand Marnier, chocolate, coffee, or Caramelized Hazelnut Paste (page 320)

About 2 cups Chocolate Glaze II (page 324), or 2½ cups granulated sugar (about 17½ ounces) and 1 tablespoon freshly squeezed lemon juice

Follow the recipe for Éclairs, with the following modifications:

- Use a ⅜-inch plain tip to pipe the dough, making sticks that are 3 inches in length and about 1 inch apart on the pans. Run a dampened pastry brush over the piped dough, but do not score with a fork.

- Bake for about 15 minutes total, propping the door open after 5 to 7 minutes (when the mini-éclairs begin to puff).

- Pierce each mini-éclair only twice, then fill. Each pastry will require less than a tablespoon of Pastry Cream.

- Use a skewer to invert each mini-éclair into its glaze to avoid dropping them or burning your fingers with hot caramel.

- Do not refrigerate chocolate-glazed or unglazed mini-éclairs for more than 4 hours. Caramelized mini-éclairs should not remain refrigerated for more than 2 hours.

Cream Puffs *Choux à la crème*

Traditionally, cream puffs are filled with whipped cream, and while they are extremely simple to prepare, they are not particularly fascinating. I prefer to place a dollop of pastry cream in the bottom of each puff before filling it with whipped cream. If you're feeling really adventurous, fill your cream puffs with the hazelnut cream used in the Paris-Brest on page 34. **Makes 10 to 12 pastries**

½ recipe (¾ pound) Choux Paste (page 295), freshly made or frozen and thawed

¼ cup (1 ounce) chopped blanched almonds

¼ recipe (1½ cups) Pastry Cream (page 308), flavored with Grand Marnier, chocolate, coffee, or Caramelized Hazelnut Paste (page 320)

1½ recipes (3 cups) Whipped Cream (page 307)

Powdered sugar for dusting puffs

1.   Adjust the oven racks to divide your oven in half and preheat the oven to 400°F. Line a baking sheet with parchment paper, placing a bit of Choux Paste under each corner of the paper to attach it to the pan.

2.   Spoon about 1½ cups of dough into a large pastry bag fitted with a ¾-inch plain tip. Holding the tip about ½ inch above the pan, pipe out round mounds of dough about 2 inches in diameter and ¾ inch thick. Leave 3 inches between mounds. If you do not want to use a pastry bag, you may drop dollops of dough from a tablespoon. This will yield cream puffs that look somewhat more rustic.

3.   Use a damp pastry brush to press down any dough peaks, then brush over each puff to smooth it. This will help you reshape puffs that have been spoon-formed. Sprinkle with chopped almonds. At this point, if the dough has not been previously frozen, you may wrap the pan in plastic and freeze for up to 1 month. Thaw in the refrigerator, then allow the dough to come to room temperature before baking.

4.   Place the pans in the oven and close immediately. Check the puffs after about 10 minutes, through the oven window if possible. Avoid opening the door unnecessarily, which may cause the puffs to collapse. They should be expanding with smooth tops and just starting to brown. At this point, prop the oven door open with a wooden spoon to let steam escape, which will give the puffs a smooth, thin, crisp crust and a dry interior.

5.   After a total of about 25 to 30 minutes, the puffs should be an even, deep brown and should feel quite firm when squeezed. Remove the pans from the oven and cool the puffs completely on wire racks. Once cooled, the puffs may be wrapped in plastic zipper bags and frozen for up to 1 month, refrigerated for up to 1 week, or left at room temperature for 24 hours. To re-crisp, place the puffs on a baking sheet and bake for 5 minutes at 400°F. Do not overbake, as they will become brittle.

6.   Cut the puffs with a serrated knife. Your cut should make a 30-degree angle with the horizontal and be about three-quarters of the way through the puffs, so that they will open like clamshells. Place half the Whipped Cream in a pastry bag fitted with a ¾-inch star tip. Open each puff slightly and spread the bottom with about 2 tablespoons of Pastry Cream. Then, pipe a large rosette of Whipped Cream on top of the Pastry Cream so that the swirls of the whipped cream just pass the edge of the puffs. Close the puffs and press down lightly. Dust with powdered sugar and place the cream puffs on a serving platter, in paper muffin cups if desired. They may be covered loosely with plastic wrap and refrigerated for up to 8 hours. Dust with more powdered sugar before serving.

Napoleons *Millefeuilles*

In France, what we call a Napoleon is available in the best *pâtisseries* and the most humble neighborhood *boulangeries*, but it is called a *Millefeuilles*. Classically, it is made from three layers of very flat, crisp puff pastry filled with a Crème Mousseline, which is Pastry Cream beaten with butter. Proper presentation requires a steady hand and a great deal of patience. This recipe is for a simplified version.

One big difference between the classic method for preparing *Millefeuilles* and this one is in the baking of the puff pastry. In most shops, the pastry chef bakes large sheets of dough, then cuts them into strips, fills and stacks the strips, then ices the top and cuts the pastries. The big advantage to this method is that shrinkage of the pastry sheet is minimized. At the risk of some shrinkage, I prefer cutting the dough into even pieces before baking, then filling and stacking them. This method results in pastries that are somewhat less uniform in appearance and somewhat more homey looking.

I'll give away a trade secret: Some of those fabulous pastry shops fold puff pastry scraps into fresh dough to keep it from rising too much and to make it less delicate and less perishable. Some also add gelatin to the filling to keep the sides perfectly straight.   Makes 8 pastries

continued

½ recipe (1 pound) fully turned Puff Pastry (page 296), 1 package store-bought pastry, cold, or ½ pound Puff Pastry scraps and ½ pound fully turned Puff Pastry

2 ounces (½ stick) unsalted butter, at room temperature

2 tablespoons Grand Marnier, Kirschwasser, or dark rum (optional)

½ recipe (3 cups) Pastry Cream (page 308), chilled

1 cup raspberries, picked over (optional)

Powdered sugar, for dusting

24 raspberries, for garnish

8 mint leaves, for garnish

Fresh Berry Sauce (page 331) (optional)

1.　Preheat the oven to 400°F. Set out at least 2 to 4 very flat baking sheets that can be stacked evenly.

2.　If using homemade Puff Pastry, line 2 baking sheets with parchment paper. Roll out the pastry on a lightly floured surface to a 10 × 20-inch rectangle ¼ to ⅛ inch thick. Cut the dough in half to form 2 squares. Place 1 square of dough on each baking sheet and cover lightly with plastic wrap. Refrigerate for at least 1 hour to allow the gluten to relax and thus minimize shrinkage. Store-bought dough does not need to be rolled out. Cut pastry while it is cold and work quickly so that all pieces are the same size. Place uncut dough in the freezer for a few minutes if it seems to be stretching. Using a sharp heavy knife, cut off about ¼ inch around the edges of the dough and discard these scraps. Using 2 forks, prick the dough all over. Using a ruler as a guide, cut each square into three 3-inch strips, then cut each strip into 4 even pieces. Line a baking sheet with parchment paper and place 12 rectangles on the pan ½ inch apart. Cover with another sheet of parchment and another pan, to keep the pastry pieces evenly thin and flat. (If you have 4 baking sheets, use them all at once. Otherwise, bake 12 rectangles, then wait for the first pans to cool before baking the rest.) Bake for 15 minutes. Remove the upper pan and the parchment. If the pastry pieces no longer look raw and translucent and have begun to crust on top, remove the pan and paper and return the pastry to the oven for browning. If the dough appears uncooked on top, replace the paper and upper pan and bake for 5 minutes more. When the rectangles are evenly browned and crisp, remove them from the oven and cool on a rack. Bake the remaining 12 rectangles, if you have not already done so. Cool completely before filling.

3.　To prepare the filling, beat the butter with an electric mixer until extremely light. Add in the liqueur, if using, and mix thoroughly. On medium speed, add the Pastry Cream in thirds, mixing until well incorporated. The mixture should remain very light.

4.　When preparing the individual pastries, you may either fold the optional berries into the cream filling before assembling, or place a few on each layer of cream. In the former case, some of the berries may crush and leave streaks of pink. This is also the faster method. Either method will yield lovely results.

5.   Set aside 8 of the flattest pastry rectangles as toppers. Place 8 others on a work surface. Using an icing spatula, spread about 3 tablespoons of filling on each. The filling need not go all the way to the edge. If desired, place a few berries on each layer of filling, if not already mixed into the filling. Top with another layer of pastry. Press down gently but evenly and repeat the filling process. Top with a flat piece of pastry, and press down lightly but evenly. Dust with powdered sugar, decorate each pastry with 3 raspberries and a mint leaf, and serve on individual plates with berry sauce or on a pastry platter with other individual pastries. (*This pastry may be refrigerated for up to 4 hours. Remove it from the refrigerator about 30 minutes before serving.*)

> To use Puff Pastry scraps, unfold the fully turned fresh Puff Pastry and cover the top evenly with scraps. The scraps may be either individual pieces or horizontal slices from a stack of scraps. Do not overlap the scraps or cut vertically from a mound, or the scraps will rise in all directions. Refold the dough, completely enclosing the scraps. If the dough has warmed, chill it, then roll it as you would fresh homemade dough. Do not let the weight of the scraps used exceed that of the fresh dough, or the mixed dough will shrink considerably during baking and might be tough.
>
> If you have a blowtorch, you can caramelize the pastries. Place the top layers close together on a baking sheet so as not to waste sugar and not to burn the work surface. Sprinkle a thin layer of powdered sugar over each one. Light the torch and move the flame across all the pastries, without staying in any one spot, as this pastry will burn quickly. The nozzle should be 4 to 6 inches from the pastry. Stop torching when the sugar beads up and begins to caramelize. The caramel may remain in beads, but it will still add a lovely flavor and crunch. Place the toppers on the pastries and top with 3 raspberries and a mint leaf, if desired.

Crêpes

There is no question that crêpes are enjoyed all over France, if not the world. But their origin is definitely Breton, and in Brittany, the concentration of *crêperies* is up there with that of cafés in Paris. Galettes, savory crêpes, also originated in Brittany, where the Bretons were desperate to find as many uses as possible for buckwheat, which was almost all they had to eat during leaner times, though it still provided good nutrition.

Using the proper pan is extremely important. An uncoated steel or cast-iron crêpe pan is preferable. My crêpe pan is 8 inches in diameter with a slightly sloped rim about 1 inch wide. This provides a 6-inch frying space, but the gradual slope of the rim allows for a slightly wider crêpe as well. It should be well seasoned, so that additional grease is not necessary. Too much grease—or even nonstick coating—may cause the batter to roll around on the pan instead of sticking in a thin film.

Makes twelve 8-inch crêpes

¾ cup (4 ounces) unbleached all-purpose flour

1 tablespoon sugar

Pinch of salt

2 large eggs

1 cup minus 2 tablespoons whole milk

2 tablespoons unsalted butter, melted

1. Sift the flour into a medium mixing bowl. Add the sugar and salt and stir to mix. Add the eggs and mix with a whisk until smooth. The mixture may be quite thick. Add the milk in thirds, whisking thoroughly after each addition. Pour the batter through a medium mesh strainer into another bowl or a pitcher. Let the batter sit at room temperature for 1 hour, to allow the flour to absorb the liquids.

2. When ready to cook, whisk in the melted butter. Heat an 8-inch crêpe pan over medium heat. Test the pan with a drop of batter, which should bead and sizzle immediately but not burn. Using a 1-ounce ladle, pour batter along one edge of the pan and turn the pan as you are pouring to distribute the batter evenly. (If you don't have such a ladle, fill a 2-ounce ladle halfway and pour.) If the pan is the right temperature, you can do this evenly with one rotation. Too hot, and the batter will seize and bubble before it has a chance to spread; not hot enough, the batter will spread, then stick to the pan. At the right temperature, a crêpe will cook to golden brown within 45 seconds.

3. When the crêpe is golden, loosen it with a metal spatula and turn it onto a wire rack to cool. The pan will retain its heat, so you can cook another crêpe immediately. Do not let the crêpes overlap when cooling, as they will stick. It is not necessary to turn the crêpe and cook both sides; once one side is brown, the entire crêpe is set and cooked.

4. Fill the crêpes immediately or stack them, wrapped airtight in plastic, and refrigerate or freeze them. (*Crêpes may be refrigerated for up to 24 hours or frozen for 2 weeks. If frozen, thaw in the refrigerator overnight. Let the crêpes come to room temperature—this will take about 1 hour—before unwrapping and peeling apart.*)

Caramel Custard *Crème caramel renversée*

If you are a custard-lover, as am I, this recipe for baked custard is a must-do. It satisfies the following criteria, set forth by the authority on perfect custards, namely, us, the diners:

- It must be creamy throughout, and a wedge from a large custard must not crack at any point.
- It must have absolutely no holes on the sides, which are a result of overbaking.

The creaminess comes from using a combination of milk and cream as well as both egg yolks and whole eggs. The absence of holes comes from baking the custard in a hot-water bath.

I prefer to make this dessert in individual ramekins rather than a large dish, although I have given instructions for that option as well. Ramekins bake faster and more evenly, and unmolding each one separately makes for a nicer presentation than cutting the custard into wedges.

As always when working with caramel, be sure to use a heavy pot holder and not to splash the caramel on your skin. Sugar begins to caramelize at 340°F; sugar that is deep amber in color, almost burnt, may be as hot as 410°F. And, caramelized sugar will cling to your skin.   Makes 12 individual custards

2 cups (14 ounces) sugar

2½ cups whole milk

1½ cups whipping cream

1 vanilla bean, split lengthwise

6 large eggs

4 large eggs yolks

1.   Place 1 cup of the sugar in a small heavy-bottomed saucepan. If you have an unlined copper caramelizing pot with a pour spout, clean it first with salt and white vinegar, then use it here; this is the ideal pot for caramelizing, as it conducts heat so quickly and evenly. Add ¼ cup water to wet all the sugar without dissolving it, or even making it pourable. Prepare an ice bath in a mixing bowl with a diameter about twice that of the saucepan. Fill the bowl halfway with ice cubes and cold water.

2.   Begin heating the sugar over low to medium heat. The heat should remain on the bottom of the saucepan; flames should not come up the side of the pan at any time. Wash any crystals clinging to the inside of the pot into the rest of the sugar, using a pastry brush dipped in water. Do this before the pan gets too hot, so that the water from the brush does not simply evaporate against the pan and the brush does not burn. If you notice sugar crystals still clinging to the pan once it heats, try to wash them down with a more generous dose of water on the brush.

3.   Heat the sugar without disturbing the pot or stirring until the sugar begins to boil clear. Once the sugar boils clear, swirl it from time to time to distribute the heat within the syrup. When the sugar just begins to take on a light amber color, watch it carefully and swirl the pan often. It will go to deep caramel within just a few minutes. Once the caramel has reached 370°F, turn off the heat and carefully plunge the bottom of the pan into the ice bath, to stop further cooking of the sugar. Hold the pan in the ice bath, submerged only to the depth of the caramel, for 3 seconds. Lift the pan out of the water, swirl it, then dip it into the ice bath for 3 seconds more. Lift the pan out of the water and dry the bottom.

4.   Pour a thin layer of caramel in the bottom of each of twelve 5-ounce ramekins. Tilt and turn the molds to spread the caramel, making sure that the entire bottom is covered. Work quickly, so that the caramel does not harden in the pot. If it does, heat it briefly over very low heat. If you have any caramel left after all the molds have been lined, heat it, then pour it into a metal container. Save this caramel for Coffee Flavoring (page 342). Clean the remaining caramel out of the pot by boiling water in the pot.

5.   Place the oven rack in the middle of the oven and preheat the oven to 325°F.

6.   Combine the milk, cream, vanilla bean, and ½ cup sugar together in a large saucepan. Bring to a boil and whisk immediately to prevent a skin from forming.

7.   Meanwhile, whisk the eggs and egg yolks in a large mixing bowl. Add the remaining ½ cup sugar and whisk well. Pour the hot milk into the egg mixture and whisk immediately. Place a medium mesh strainer over a pitcher or large measuring cup and pour the custard mixture through. The strainer will catch the egg membranes and the vanilla bean. Using a small knife, scrape the seeds out of the vanilla bean into the custard and whisk again.

8.   Place the caramelized ramekins in a large roasting pan or baking dish. Leave out 1 ramekin but leave space for it in the pan. Fill the ramekins with custard to ¼ inch from the top. Pour very hot tap water or boiling water into the pan, taking care not to splash any into the ramekins, nearly halfway up the ramekins. Place the last ramekin in the pan. Carefully slide the pan into the oven, taking care not to get any water into the custard.

9.   Bake for 30 minutes, or until the custards feel set when lightly touched and a small sharp knife inserted in the middle of 1 or 2 custards comes out clean. Carefully remove the pan from the oven and cool on a wire rack until the ramekins can be lifted out. Dry the bottoms of the ramekins, place them on a baking sheet, and cool completely. Refrigerate for at least 4 hours. (*The custards may be refrigerated for up to 3 days, covered lightly with plastic wrap.*)

10.   To unmold, run a small sharp knife around each custard. Turn it over onto a dessert plate and shake to release the custard. If it refuses to come out, slide the knife down 1 side of the ramekin and gently push the custard inward, allowing air into the bottom of the mold. Turn the custard over again; air will rush in as the custard slides out.

Large Caramel Custard *Crème Caramel*

For a large custard, follow the recipe for individual ramekins. Caramelize 1 cup of the sugar and pour the caramel into a 2-quart soufflé dish or baking dish with an angled (not rounded) bottom. Prepare the custard and pour it into the dish. Bake for 1 to 1¼ hours in a hot-water bath, testing with a small knife. Refrigerate for at least 6 hours before serving. Unmold onto a rimmed platter. Serves 12.

Coconut Caramel Custard *Crème caramel à la noix de coco*

The richness of coconut makes this custard very creamy. You must use unsweetened coconut for this, or the entire balance of the dessert will be disturbed. Use shredded coconut for maximum flavor. Serve this with Coconut-Macadamia Tile Cookies (page 165).   **Makes 12 individual custards**

2 cups (14 ounces) sugar

2¾ cups whole milk

1¾ cups whipping cream

1½ cups (4½ ounces) unsweetened shredded coconut

2 to 4 tablespoons hot milk, if needed

6 large eggs

4 egg yolks

1 teaspoon pure vanilla extract

1. Follow the recipe for Caramel Custard through Step 4, omitting the vanilla bean but adding the coconut to the milk, cream, and sugar. Bring to a boil, turn off the heat, cover the pot, and let the liquid steep for 20 minutes.

2. Pour the liquid through a fine mesh strainer into a large measuring cup. Press the liquid out of the coconut. If you do not have 4 cups of liquid in the cup, make up the difference with hot milk. Discard the coconut.

3. Proceed with Step 5. Add the vanilla extract to the eggs and sugar in Step 6. Continue with Steps 7, 8, and 9.

Coffee Caramel Custard *Crème caramel au café*

Top this with whipped cream and call it Cappuccino Custard. The custard may contain some very fine coffee grinds that sneak through the strainer. That way, everyone will know that you used real coffee. Make sure to choose coffee of good quality.   Makes 12 individual custards

2 cups (14 ounces) sugar

2¾ cups whole milk

1¾ cups whipping cream

¾ cup (3 ounces) freshly drip-ground coffee, packed

2 to 4 tablespoons hot milk, if needed

6 large eggs

4 large egg yolks

1 teaspoon pure vanilla extract

1.   Follow the recipe for Caramel Custard through Step 4, omitting the vanilla bean but adding the coffee to the milk, cream, and sugar. Bring to a boil, turn off the heat, cover the pot, and let the liquid steep for 20 minutes.

2.   Pour the liquid through a fine mesh strainer into a large measuring cup. Press the liquid out of the coffee. If you do not have 4 cups of liquid in the cup, make up the difference with hot milk. Discard the coffee.

3.   Proceed with Step 5. Add the vanilla extract to the eggs and sugar in Step 6. Continue with Steps 7, 8, and 9.

> **While the custard itself will set up enough to unmold within 4 hours, the caramel will not have liquefied and will remain in the cup. It takes at least 24 hours for the caramel to liquefy. At that point, when you unmold you will have liquid caramel spilling over the sides of a creamy custard—which is what Caramel Custard is all about.**

Crème Brûlée

Crème brûlée, **literally burned cream, is a cream and egg yolk custard topped with a hard caramel crust. It is only recently, however, that this so-called classic dessert started making an appearance on French restaurant menus and in French homes. It is actually a New Orleans creation, but the French, in their inimitable way, have taken it to new heights.**

I always prepare these as desserts in small soufflé dishes or ramekins, rather than shallow gratin dishes, which produce too much top crust and not enough baked cream.   Makes 8 individual custards

 4 cups whipping cream

 1 vanilla bean, split in half lengthwise

 9 large egg yolks

 9 tablespoons (4 ounces) sugar

 1 teaspoon pure vanilla extract

 Extra sugar for topping

1.   Place the oven rack in the middle of the oven and preheat the oven to 325°F.

2.   Put the cream and the vanilla bean in a heavy saucepan and bring to a boil. Keep a whisk in the pot, and if the cream starts to boil over, turn off the heat and stir it down.

3.   Meanwhile, whisk together the egg yolks and the sugar in a large mixing bowl. Pour the hot cream over the egg yolks and whisk immediately. Remove the vanilla bean with a pair of tongs and let it cool. Whisk in the vanilla extract. Using a small knife, scrape the seeds out of the vanilla bean and whisk them into the custard mixture, without creating foam on top. Discard the pod. Place a medium mesh strainer over a pitcher or large measuring cup and pour the custard through. Place eight 5-ounce ramekins in a shallow baking pan about the same depth as the ramekins themselves. Fill the ramekins with custard to about ⅛ inch from the top.

4.   Remove one of the ramekins from the pan and pour hot tap or boiling water into the pan halfway up the ramekins. Avoid splashing any water into the custard. Replace the last ramekin in the pan. Carefully slide the pan into the oven, taking care not to get any water in the custard.

5.   Bake for about 30 minutes, or until the tops feel set but still quite loose when lightly touched. Carefully remove the pan from the oven and cool on a wire rack until the ramekins can be lifted out. As soon as you are able, remove the dishes from the water bath and allow them to cool to room temperature on a wire rack. Once cooled, wipe the outside of the dishes. (They will be dry, but may have a film on them if any custard got into the water bath.) Refrigerate for at least

4 hours. The custards will thicken and their consistency will be ideal after 1 day. (*The custards may be refrigerated for up to 3 days.*)

6.   Up to 1 hour before serving, remove the ramekins from the refrigerator. Spread about 2 teaspoons sugar in a thin layer on top of each custard. If you have a blowtorch, light it and, holding the nozzle about 8 inches above the surface, move the flame in a circle on the surface of each ramekin. Tilt and swirl the browning sugar slightly for even coverage. Repeat the sugaring and caramelizing for a double coating of caramel.

To caramelize under a broiler, place the rack so that the tops of the ramekins will be about 4 inches from the source of heat. Preheat the broiler. Sugar the tops of the custards and place the ramekins on a baking sheet so that the heat will be evenly exposed over all the dishes and all the ramekins can be moved at one time. Watch carefully so that the tops do not burn. Remove from the broiler, sugar again, and repeat the caramelizing process. Serve immediately or return to the refrigerator for up to 1 hour. After that time, the caramel begins to weep.

Black and White *Crème Brûlée* Crème brûlée noire et blanche

What could be better than plain vanilla Crème Brûlée? Vanilla Crème Brûlée with a thick layer of chocolate on the bottom. This recipe is sinfully rich and incredibly simple.   Makes 8 individual custards

About ½ recipe (2 cups) Chocolate Ganache (page 318), at room temperature

2 egg yolks

½ recipe Crème Brûlée (page 50), using a whole vanilla bean

9 tablespoons (4 ounces) sugar, for caramelizing

1.   Place the ganache in a heatproof bowl and warm it in a simmering water bath until it just begins to liquefy. It should be only tepid, not hot. Stir to even the consistency. Remove from the water bath and stir in the egg yolks. Fill each of eight 5-ounce ramekins halfway with the chocolate mixture.

2.   Prepare the Crème Brûlée through Step 3. Pour the cream custard over the chocolate in each ramekin. Continue with Steps 4 and 5. Caramelize as directed in Step 6.

Floating Classics

If you are looking for desserts that can be prepared ahead of time and/or in very little time, that call for readily available ingredients, and that lend themselves to adaptation, creating signature desserts out of classics, Snow Eggs and Floating Islands are for you.

All the components can be made up to twenty-four hours ahead of time and are simple to put together. You will find all the ingredients on a trip to the local supermarket: eggs, milk, sugar, maybe a vanilla bean, and some nuts. And both can be transformed from classic to modern with a few very simple changes as in Islands Floating on the Red Sea, with a berry coulis, or Mysterious Islands, with a dollop of ganache buried inside.

The classic desserts are similar in that meringues are set afloat on a pool of Crème Anglaise. For the Snow Eggs, the meringues are poached; for the Floating Islands, the meringues, which include caramelized nuts, are baked.

Snow Eggs *Oeufs à la neige*

You can make these as elegant or as homey as you like, depending on the shape of the meringues. Either pipe out mounds using a pastry bag fitted with a ½-inch open star tip or spoon mounds of meringue directly into the simmering liquid. You will need a large wide shallow pan to poach the meringues. When you make the Crème Anglaise, reserve the egg whites for the meringues in this recipe.   Makes 6 servings

> 2 cups milk
>
> 4 cups water
>
> 5 large egg whites, at room temperature
>
> ¾ cup (about 5½ ounces) sugar
>
> 1 recipe (3 cups) Crème Anglaise (page 328), chilled

1.   Combine the milk and water in a large shallow pan and heat to a bare simmer (about 200 °F).

2.   Put the egg whites in a clean mixing bowl or the bowl of an electric mixer. Using the whisk attachment, mix on low speed until the whites begin to froth, then increase to medium speed and whip until the whites hold soft peaks. Gradually add the sugar in a thin stream. Once all has been added, increase to high speed and whip until the whites are stiff but not dry.

3.   To form meringues with a pastry bag, fill the bag, avoiding any air bubbles. Pipe either 6 large, 12 small, or 18 very small rosettes onto a sheet of aluminum foil or parchment paper. Using a wet metal spatula, gently transfer 1 rosette at a time to the simmering liquid, without allowing them to touch. These swell during poaching. Poach in batches if necessary.

To form meringues with spoons, take scoops of meringue with 1 spoon and push the meringue into the simmering liquid with another. This method will give the meringues a cloud-like look. Or, form dumplings by using a large wet spoon and forming egg shapes. Carefully drop the meringues into the poaching liquid without touching.

4. Poach the meringues for 3 to 7 minutes on 1 side. The meringues should puff slightly and not stick to your fingers when lightly touched. The time depends on the size. Carefully turn with a spatula and poach for 3 minutes on the other side. The meringues should be firm and spring back when lightly squeezed. Using a slotted spoon, carefully remove the meringues and drain on a clean kitchen towel or on paper towels. (*The meringues, on the towel, can be refrigerated for up to 24 hours, lightly covered with plastic.*)

5. To serve, ladle about ½ cup of the Crème Anglaise into each of 6 soup plates. Top with 1 or more eggs.

Floating Islands *Îles Flottantes*

Traditionally, this dessert is prepared as one large island and served in wedges, with Crème Anglaise ladled around the wedge. It is not particularly easy to serve that way, and it is difficult to decorate the large island with poured or spun caramel. I prefer to make individual islands in 10-ounce soufflé cups or ramekins.

When you make the Crème Anglaise, reserve the egg whites for the meringues in this recipe.

Makes 6 servings

Butter, for greasing ramekins

5 large egg whites, at room temperature

1¼ cups (about 9 ounces) sugar

½ cup coarsely chopped Caramelized Hazelnut Paste (see page 320; do not grind caramelized nuts into a paste)

1 recipe (3 cups) Crème Anglaise (page 328), chilled

1. Adjust the oven racks to divide the oven into thirds and preheat the oven to 350°F. Cut 12 parchment circles that will fit inside a 10-ounce soufflé cup or ramekin. Butter all the paper rounds, then line each ramekin with 1 round, buttered side up. Generously butter the sides of the ramekins.

continued

2. Put the egg whites into a clean mixing bowl or the bowl of an electric mixer. Using the whisk attachment, mix on low speed until the whites begin to froth, then increase to medium speed and whip until the whites hold soft peaks. Gradually add ¾ cup sugar in a thin stream. Once all has been added, increase to high speed and whip until the whites are stiff but not dry. Gently fold the chopped hazelnut paste into the meringue.

3. Spoon some meringue into each of the ramekins, evenly covering the bottom and sides of each. Use the back of the spoon to spread a layer of meringue all over, then fill to the top. Level the top with a metal spatula and cover with a paper round, buttered side down. Place the ramekins in a shallow roasting pan or baking dish. Remove one of the ramekins to fill the pan. Using a pitcher, pour hot tap water into the pan, halfway up the ramekins, without getting water in any of the meringues. Replace the last ramekin,

4. Bake for 20 to 25 minutes, or until the meringues are firm and spring back when lightly touched (remove one of the papers to test). Remove from the oven and cool slightly in the pan, then remove the ramekins carefully and cool to lukewarm on a wire rack.

5. Serve immediately or refrigerate for no longer than 8 hours (any longer and the hazelnut paste will melt). If serving immediately, remove the paper covers and run a thin, small knife around each meringue, then turn each island over onto a soup plate. If serving later, turn the islands onto a platter or baking sheet. These must be unmolded while still slightly warm. If chilled, the congealed butter will make it difficult to unmold them.

6. Just before serving, caramelize the remaining ½ cup of sugar in a small heavy saucepan. Place the sugar in a small heavy-bottomed saucepan. If you have an unlined copper caramelizing pot with a pour spout, clean it first with salt and white vinegar, then use it here; this is the ideal pot for caramelizing, as it conducts heat so quickly and evenly. Add about 2 tablespoons water to wet all the sugar without dissolving it, or even making it pourable. Prepare an ice bath in a mixing bowl with a diameter about twice that of the saucepan. Fill the bowl halfway with ice cubes and cold water.

7. Begin heating the sugar over a low to medium heat. The heat should remain on the bottom of the saucepan; flames should not come up the side of the pan at any time. Wash any crystals clinging to the inside of the pot into the rest of the sugar, using a pastry brush dipped in water. Do this before the pan gets too hot, so that the water from the brush does not simply evaporate against the pan and the brush does not burn. If you notice sugar crystals still clinging to the pan once it heats, try to wash them down with a more generous dose of water on the brush.

8. Heat the sugar without disturbing the pot or stirring until the sugar begins to boil clear. Once the sugar boils clear, swirl it from time to time to distribute the heat within the syrup. When the sugar just begins to take on a light amber color, watch it carefully and swirl the pan often. It will go to deep caramel within just a few minutes. Once the caramel has reached 370°F, turn off the heat and carefully plunge the bottom of the pan into the ice bath to stop further cooking of the sugar. Hold the pan in the ice bath, submerged only to the depth of the caramel, for 3 seconds. Lift the pan out of the water, swirl it, then dip it into the ice bath for 3 seconds more. Lift the pan out of the water and dry the bottom.

9.   Ladle ½ cup of Crème Anglaise around each island. Drizzle caramel over each island. Or use 2 forks back-to-back to form fine strands of caramel by dipping the tines in the caramel and flicking it over each island to form a nest.

Islands Floating on the Red Sea *Îles Flottantes sur la Mer Rouge*

Replace the Crème Anglaise with 3 cups of Fresh Berry Sauce (page 331). Use leftover or frozen and thawed egg whites for the meringues. To make the dessert fat free, omit the chopped hazelnut paste and poach the meringues, as you would Snow Eggs (page 52), instead of baking them.

Mysterious Islands *Îles du mystère*

Many cafés and restaurants in France that do not employ a pastry chef buy desserts and ice creams either from local bakeries or from manufacturers. One very common ice cream dessert is the *Mystère*, or mystery. It is a large ball or cone of ice cream with a surprise inside: a little piece of meringue. *Mystère* was the inspiration for this dessert. Instead of meringue, the mysterious center is ganache, and the meringue is on the outside. You can create your own version with a different filling, as long as that filling can withstand its surroundings and will not sink. A piece of poached pear or another poached fruit would be fine, but not berries, which will explode during baking. You can also change the sauce, replacing the Crème Anglaise with Fresh Berry Sauce (page 331) or Caramel Sauce (page 330).   Makes 6 servings

   1 recipe Floating Islands (page 53)

   6 tablespoons Chocolate Ganache (page 318), at room temperature

1.   Follow Steps 1 and 2 of the Floating Islands recipe.

2.   Spoon some meringue into each of the ramekins, evenly covering the bottom and sides of each. Drop in 1 tablespoonful of ganache and cover it with meringue. Fill to the top and level the top with a metal spatula. Cover with a paper round, buttered side down.

3.   Continue with Step 4 of the master recipe.

4.   Serve at room temperature, so that the ganache remains creamy.

Individual Chocolate Soufflés

Petits soufflés au chocolat

Claude Alrivy, former chef and owner of Le Chardonnay Restaurant in Los Angeles, was kind enough to share this wonderful recipe with me. He would prepare individual soufflés at the beginning of the dinner service and leave them at room temperature until they were ordered. Whether prepared ahead of time or baked immediately, the soufflés rise straight up and stay there. Serve them with very lightly whipped cream on the side.   Makes 10 individual soufflés

Butter and granulated sugar, for lining the ramekins

14 ounces semisweet or bittersweet chocolate, coarsely chopped

6 large egg yolks, at room temperature

3 tablespoons dark rum (optional)

8 egg whites, at room temperature

1 cup (about 7 ounces) granulated sugar

Powdered sugar, for sifting over the tops

1 cup whipping cream lightly whipped with 2 tablespoons powdered sugar

1.   Brush the inside of ten 5-ounce soufflé dishes with butter and coat evenly with sugar. Tap out the excess sugar. Place the dishes on a baking sheet and set aside. If baking immediately, preheat the oven to 375°F. Otherwise, do so 30 minutes before serving.

2.   Put the chocolate in a medium mixing bowl and melt it in a simmering water bath. When it begins to melt, remove the bowl from the heat and whisk until smooth. Let cool to room temperature. Whisk in the egg yolks and the rum, if using.

3.   Put the egg whites in a medium mixing bowl or the bowl of an electric mixer. Using the whisk attachment, mix on low speed until the whites begin to froth, then increase to medium speed and whip until the whites hold soft peaks. Gradually add the sugar in a thin stream. Once all has been added, increase to high speed and whip until the whites are stiff but not dry.

4.   Using a rubber spatula, gently fold one-third of the whites into the chocolate mixture, without overmixing. Fold in another third, again without overmixing. Fold the chocolate mixture back into the remaining whites, this time folding until no streaks of white are visible.

5.   Divide the batter evenly among the soufflé dishes, filling to within ¼ inch of the top. Sift a thin layer of powdered sugar evenly over each soufflé. Set the soufflés aside until ready to bake.

6. Bake for about 15 minutes, or until the soufflés have risen to 1 inch above the rim of the dishes and have stopped rising. They should be firm on the outside but still loose inside. Carefully remove them from the oven, sift more powdered sugar over the tops, and serve on individual dessert plates. Serve the whipped cream for guests to pour into the middle of their soufflés.

- **When separating eggs, make sure that there are no flecks of yolk in the whites. Put them in a very clean bowl. Any grease will keep the whites from whipping to maximum volume. In fact, it is better to leave a few drops of water in the mixing bowl than to dry it with a towel that may be greasy.**

- **If you are planning to bake something that will require an egg wash, save the extra yolks for that. Refrigerate them in a small bowl, covered with plastic directly on the yolks, for up to 24 hours. You can also freeze the yolks for up to 1 month. Mark the container with the number of yolks and the date.**

Chocolate Mousse *Mousse au chocolat*

From the French word meaning "foam," *mousse* should be both creamy and fluffy. Pipe or spoon this mousse into dessert cups, or use it to fill Crêpes (page 44) or to make a charlotte. Combine it with other mousses, top it with fresh fruit or with whipped cream and a chocolate curl. Don't forget a cookie on the side—Almond Shortbread Cookies (page 174) or Rolled Cigarette Cookies (page 166)— it's the classic way!

Most French chocolate mousse recipes call for raw egg yolks, and while this may seem scary to Americans, the French insist that scientific studies have proven that chocolate actually inhibits salmonella. You can choose to believe this or not. In any event, egg yolks are necessary to emulsify the chocolate, so that it can be mixed in with the beaten egg whites. If the yolks are left out, the chocolate and whites may not combine evenly. In this recipe, the whipped egg whites are mixed with a ganache, not just with melted chocolate and butter. The yolks, then, add richness but are not necessary to the blending of all the ingredients.   Makes 6 servings

8 ounces semisweet or bittersweet chocolate, chopped

¼ cup whipping cream

2 ounces (½ stick) unsalted butter, at room temperature

2 large egg yolks

5 large egg whites

1 tablespoon granulated sugar

¾ recipe (1½ cups) lightly Whipped Cream (page 307) (optional)

Chocolate curls (see page 182) (optional)

continued

1. Put the chocolate in a medium mixing bowl. Boil the cream in a small saucepan and pour it over. Let the mixture stand for 5 minutes, then whisk until smooth. Add the butter, 1 tablespoon at a time. Whisk in the egg yolks.

2. Put the egg whites in a clean mixing bowl or the bowl of an electric mixer. Using the whisk attachment, mix on low speed until the whites begin to froth, then increase to medium speed and whip until the whites hold soft peaks. Gradually add the sugar in a thin stream. Once all has been added, increase to high speed and whip until the whites are stiff but not dry.

3. With a rubber spatula, gently fold one-third of the whites into the chocolate mixture to lighten it. Fold in another third of the whites, then fold the chocolate mixture into the remaining whites. Fold gently until no streaks of egg white remain.

4. Refrigerate the mousse in a large decorative bowl or in individual bowls. Or pipe the mousse into glass dessert cups using a pastry bag fitted with a ¾- or 1-inch open star tip. Refrigerate for at least 2 hours but no more than 24 hours, covered loosely with plastic wrap (avoid contact with the mousse).

5. Serve the mousse as is or topped with a dollop of whipped cream and a chocolate curl.

Pastry Shop Cakes and Pastries

Pâtisserie de boutique

THE FRENCH TERM FOR window-shopping is *lèche-vitrines*, literally lick the windows. This expression was undoubtedly coined by someone looking longingly inside a pastry shop! The French are very proud of their window-dressing skills; this is considered a true art. Of course, in a pastry shop, the job is much easier, since the cakes and pastries themselves are pieces of art.

The recipes for these cakes will give you some insight into how organized a pastry kitchen has to be. Each of these cakes represents the assembly of several elements: sponge or pastry layers, syrups, mousse, butter cream, poached or puréed fruit, preserves, glazes. None of these can be whipped together in an hour, but if you're organized, and if you have a good *mise en place*, or preparation, you should be undaunted by all the steps and richly rewarded by the results, not to mention the kudos you will receive.

Many of these recipes call for stainless steel frames or rings. The French like to build their cakes in these, often leaving the sides exposed so that all the layers are visible. Frames and rings can be found at some better shops or ordered by mail (see page 360). In most cases and with just a few extra steps, pans can be substituted. Most of the straight-sided cake pans available in the States, however, are made of aluminum, which will react when it comes in contact with, say, a fruit mousse, discoloring it. For this reason, I recommend investing in a few sheets of thin acetate, available in art supply stores. Cut the sheets to line the insides of the pan. The acetate will not react with the ingredients nor will it wrinkle as would plastic wrap, and it can be wiped clean and reused.

In French pastry lingo, these cakes are not referred to as *gâteaux*, but rather as *entremets*, a contraction for *entre les mets*, or between courses. Smaller versions of these entremets are called either *entremets réduits*, reduced entremets, or *petits gâteaux*, little cakes. The latter category also includes certain pastries such as Napoleons (page 41), Éclairs (page 36), and various tartlets.

Gâteau Saint-Honoré
   Individual Gâteaux Saint-Honoré

Opera Cake / *L'Opéra*

Chocolate and Hazelnut Truffle Torte/ *L'Alhambra*

Coffee-Walnut Cake/ *Le Noyer*

Hazelnut Praline Torte / *Succès*
   Individual Succès

Strawberry Cream Torte / *Fraisier*

Raspberry Mousse Cake / *Miroir de framboises*
   Apricot Mousse Cake / *Miroir d'abricots*

Blackberry and Mascarpone Charlotte / *Charlotte au fromage blanc et aux mûres*
   Tiramisù

Pear Charlotte/ *Charlotte aux poires*
   Chocolate-Pear Charlotte / *Charlotte Belle-Hélène*

Gâteau Saint-Honoré

Considering that Saint Honoré is the patron saint of pastry chefs, it would be unthinkable not to include a recipe for the dessert created in his honor. Not surprisingly, it is a recipe that calls for several complicated elements, namely, Puff Pastry, Choux Paste, *crème chiboust*, and caramelized sugar.

This particular recipe strays from the classic a bit. It still requires a lot of work and an organized mind, but the results are spectacular and worth all the effort. Plan ahead: In fact, many of the elements can be prepared ahead and frozen. Note, however, that the *Saint-Honoré* should not be completed more than one hour before serving it, as it deteriorates when refrigerated.

As always when working with caramel, be sure to use a heavy pot holder and not to splash the caramel on your skin. Sugar begins to caramelize at 340°F; sugar that is deep amber in color, almost burnt, may be as hot as 410°F. And, caramelized sugar will cling to your skin.   Makes one 9-inch cake, for 8 servings

> 7 ounces Puff Pastry scraps (see page 349), chilled
>
> ⅓ recipe (8 ounces) Choux Paste (page 295), freshly made or frozen and thawed
>
> ¼ recipe (1½ cups) Pastry Cream (page 308), flavored with Grand Marnier, chilled
>
> Vegetable oil, do not use olive oil
>
> 1 cup (about 7 ounces) sugar
>
> 1 teaspoon freshly squeezed lemon juice
>
> 1 recipe (2 cups) lightly Whipped Cream (page 307)

I. Line a baking sheet with parchment paper. Use a disk of Puff Pastry scraps that is already fairly flat. This can even be a slice from a larger piece of scraps. Roll the dough into a round, no more than ⅛ inch thick (the thinner the better, but scraps are hard to roll). Place the dough on the baking sheet and refrigerate for at least 1 hour.

2. Preheat the oven to 425°F.

3. Fill a large pastry bag fitted with a ⅜-inch plain tip with Choux Paste. Remove the pastry piece from the refrigerator, and using a 9-inch cake pan as a template, cut the piece into a 9-inch disk. Prick the dough all over with a fork. Pipe a circle of Choux Paste on top of the pastry disk, right at the edge but not falling over the edge. Pipe another circle just inside the first one; they should be touching but not overlapping. Pipe a small disk of Choux Paste in the very middle of the disk, then a ring of paste between the center and outer rings. About 1 inch from the disk and 1 inch from each other, pipe 16 little puffs, using about 1 tablespoon of dough for each. Use a dampened pastry brush to press down any points that the little puffs may have on top.

4. Bake for about 15 minutes, or until the little puffs begin to crust and are very lightly browned on top. Lower the temperature to 400°F, and continue to bake until the little puffs are golden brown. Remove them from the oven and cool on a wire rack. Continue to bake the disk until it, too, is golden brown all over, about 15 to 20 minutes. Remove the pan from the oven and, using 2 metal spatulas, transfer the disk to a wire rack to cool. (*The cake can be prepared to this point up to 8 hours in advance. If you are in a humid area and the disk and little puffs lose their crispness, crisp them in a 400°F oven for 5 minutes, then cool again, before proceeding.*)

5. When you are ready to assemble the cake, place a large wire rack on the work table. Take your smallest, pointiest pastry tip and wedge it under one corner of the rack, so that the open part of the tip is flat against the table and the rack is slightly raised at the corner. (This may ruin this tip for later piping.) Lay a sheet of aluminum foil as smoothly as possible on a flat heatproof surface. Grease the foil lightly with a few drops of oil. Wad a kitchen towel next to it.

6. Whisk the Pastry Cream just to make it smooth. Place the Pastry Cream in a pastry bag fitted with a ¼-inch tip. Hold the bag tautly in your stronger hand. With the other hand, pierce the side of each baked puff using the point of the stationary tip, now anchored by the rack. Immediately pipe Pastry Cream into the puffs, just until the filling begins to ooze from the opening. Place the filled puffs on the rack as you work.

7. Place the sugar in a small heavy-bottomed saucepan. If you have an unlined copper caramelizing pot with a pour spout, clean it first with salt and white vinegar, then use it here; this is the ideal pot for caramelizing, as it conducts heat so quickly and evenly. Add the lemon juice and just enough water to wet all the sugar without dissolving it, or even making it pourable. Prepare an ice bath in a mixing bowl with a diameter about twice that of the saucepan. Fill the bowl halfway with ice cubes and cold water.

8. Begin heating the sugar over low to medium heat. The heat should remain on the bottom of the saucepan; flames should not come up the side of the pan at any time. Wash any crystals clinging to the inside of the pot into the rest of the sugar, using a pastry brush dipped in water. Do this before the pan gets too hot, so that the water from the brush does not simply evaporate against the pan and the brush does not burn. If you notice sugar crystals still clinging to the pan once it heats, try to wash them down with a more generous dose of water on the brush.

9. Heat the sugar without disturbing the pot or stirring until the sugar begins to boil clear. Once the sugar boils clear, swirl it from time to time to distribute the heat within the syrup. When the sugar just begins to take on a light amber color, watch it carefully and swirl the pan often. It will go to deep caramel within just a few minutes. Once the caramel has reached 370°F, turn off the heat and carefully plunge the bottom of the pan into the ice bath to stop further cooking of the sugar. Hold the pan in the ice bath, submerged only to the depth of the caramel, for 3 seconds. Lift the pan out of the water, swirl it, then dip it into the ice bath for 3 seconds more. Lift the pan out of the water and carefully dry off the bottom of the pan, then place it on the table with one side propped up on the wadded towel, so that the pot is at an angle.

10. Dip the flat side of each puff in the caramel, taking care not to touch the caramel or the pot with your fingers, as they are still extremely hot. Place each dipped puff on the oiled foil and press down gently, so that the caramel flattens. This caramel will harden quickly and the puffs should release easily from the foil.

11. When you have caramelized all the puffs, attach them to the outer ring of the disk by dipping the rounded end of each puff in a very small amount of the caramel. Make sure that the punctures where you filled the puffs are facing into the ring, and that the puffs are evenly spaced. Place the caramel, which will have thickened considerably, over very low heat.

12. Fill a large pastry bag fitted with a 1-inch open star tip with the whipped cream and pipe rosettes and swirls of cream into the middle of the ring of puffs. If there is any space between puffs, pipe a little cream there.

13. Remove the caramel from the heat and swirl the pan to even out the color. If it is very hot and the caramel continues to darken, stop the cooking by dipping the pan in the ice water bath. Prop the pan on the wadded towel again and, holding 2 forks back-to-back, dip the forks into the caramel, then flick it over the cream to create a caramel nest. Strands of caramel will fall from the forks. Serve immediately, if possible. (There is no way to preserve the spun sugar nest once you cut the cake.)

Individual *Gâteaux Saint-Honoré*

It will seem that these take ten times the work of a large Saint-Honoré, but at least your spun caramel nest will not be destroyed! Follow the recipe for the large cake, making the changes indicated below.   **Makes 10 individual pastries**

1½ pounds Puff Pastry scraps (see page 349), chilled

½ recipe (12 ounces) Choux Paste (page 295), freshly made or frozen and thawed

½ recipe (3 cups) Pastry Cream (page 308), flavored with Grand Marnier, chilled

2 cups whipping cream

2¼ cups (1 pound) sugar

2 teaspoons freshly squeezed lemon juice

Vegetable oil

1.   Roll out the Puff Pastry scraps into a ⅛-inch-thick sheet. Refrigerate for 1 hour. Cut ten 3½-inch disks with a plain cookie cutter.

2.   When piping the Choux Paste onto the disks, pipe 1 ring around each rim, and 1 very small dab in the middle of each disk.

3.   Use three little puffs for each individual pastry.

4.   When filling each ring with whipped cream, pipe rosettes of cream between the puffs, then a large rosette in the middle.

Opera Cake *L'Opéra*

A classic for the past twenty years, the *Opéra* was created for those who unabashedly choose chocolate and butter cream over fruit desserts. What makes this low, flat cake more modern than any of its predecessors is its shape (usually square or rectangular), and its undecorated sides that show all the layers.

L'Opéra is traditionally composed of layers of *Biscuit Joconde,* an almond sponge, that have been thoroughly soaked with coffee syrup. The sponge layers are spread with alternating layers of coffee and chocolate butter cream. I have also made Opera Cakes where the chocolate butter cream was replaced by chocolate ganache. This way, the cake has contrasting consistencies, but it is no less wonderful. The glaze for this cake is shiny and smooth. It takes a fair amount of practice. Do not panic if you do not achieve a perfectly smooth glaze. That is why they invented decorations. Some pastry shops decorate the top with the word *Opéra,* written in ganache with all the swirls that the French love so much. I prefer a very simple decoration: tiny pieces of edible gold leaf laid randomly on top of the glaze with a small paint brush.

In a pastry shop, Opera Cake is usually prepared in a large frame that covers a commercial-size sheet pan. After glazing, the large sheet is cut into squares and rectangles of various sizes, depending upon the orders for the day or what is needed to fill the display case. Since you may not need to make more than one cake at a time, this recipe has been reduced to the size of an 8-inch square pan. The cake can also be cut into 1-inch squares, each with its own dot of gold leaf, then placed in pastry cups for a platter of petit fours.   **Makes one 8-inch square cake, for 8 servings**

½ recipe (1 sheet) Almond Sponge Sheets (page 284), freshly made or frozen and thawed

2 ounces bittersweet or semisweet chocolate, melted and cooled

1½ cups Simple Syrup (page 334), cold or at room temperature

1 cup very strong brewed coffee, cold or at room temperature

¼ cup Coffee Flavoring, homemade (page 342) or store-bought

1 recipe (3 cups) Butter Cream (page 316), half flavored with coffee and half flavored with unsweetened chocolate, or ½ recipe (1½ cups) Coffee Butter Cream (page 317) and 1½ cups Chocolate Ganache (page 318), at room temperature

⅓ recipe (1 cup) Chocolate Glaze I (page 323)

Edible gold leaf, for decoration (optional)

⅓ recipe (1 cup) Crème Anglaise (page 328), for serving (optional)

8 chocolate coffee beans, for decoration (optional)

1. If you have an 8-inch square stainless steel frame that is 2 inches deep, place it on a foil-lined baking sheet. Otherwise, use a metal baking pan. The corners of the pan should be squared off, not rounded. Line the bottom and two of the sides of the pan with a 16-inch-long sheet of foil folded in half lengthwise for strength, leaving flaps of foil over the 2 sides. Smooth the lining. Or if you have sheets of acetate (see page 351), cut rectangles to line all the sides of the pan and a square for the bottom. Stick these in place with a dab of oil.

2. Using a ruler as a guide, cut the Almond Sponge Sheet in half to make 2 pieces 12 × 8 inches in size. Cut each piece to make one 8-inch square and one 8 × 4-inch rectangle. The 2 small pieces will make a third 8-inch square.

3. Using a small offset metal spatula, spread 1 side of one of the squares with a thin, even layer of melted chocolate. Place it on a baking sheet, chocolate side up, and refrigerate until the chocolate is firm, 3 to 5 minutes.

4. Stir together the syrup, coffee, and Coffee Flavoring. Remove the chocolate-covered sponge layer from the refrigerator and place it, chocolate side down, in the prepared pan or frame. Using a wide pastry brush, generously soak the sponge layer with the coffee syrup. Check various spots on the sponge with the tip of a paring knife to see that the syrup has gone all the way through. If you see any white spots, keep soaking.

5. Spread evenly with 1 cup of the coffee butter cream, reserving about ½ cup for the top layer, using a small offset spatula. Check randomly with the small knife to make sure that the butter cream is of even thickness all over. Cover the coffee butter cream with the 2 small layers of sponge, joining them in the middle without overlapping. Soak with coffee syrup and check for saturation with the knife. Spread all the chocolate butter cream or ganache over the soaked split sponge. Even the layer with the small offset spatula. Cover with the last piece of sponge and soak it with syrup. If you have syrup left over, strain it to remove any sponge crumbs and freeze it for your next coffee dessert.

6. Spread the remaining coffee butter cream over the top of the cake. This will be a thin layer, but it must be extremely flat, since it will be glazed. It is all right if the butter cream layer is higher than the top rim of the pan. Simply take a large spatula, one with a blade longer than 8 inches, wipe it with a damp cloth, and smooth the top in one motion.

7. Refrigerate the cake for 15 minutes, or until the top begins to harden. Cover with a piece of plastic wrap, not foil, taking care not to have air bubbles underneath. A sheet of acetate works well here too. If you have lined the pan with foil, fold the flaps over the top. Refrigerate the cake for at least 4 hours or up to 8 hours. (*The cake may be wrapped well and frozen for up to 3 weeks. To wrap the cake for freezing, chill it for 30 minutes, or until the Butter Cream sets, then wrap around the entire pan with several layers of plastic, making sure that it lies flat on the cream with no air bubbles underneath. The cake can be glazed while still frozen.*)

continued

8.   At least 1 hour before serving, melt the Chocolate Glaze in a double boiler as described on page 373, stirring with a wooden spoon, not a whisk. Take care not to overheat the glaze, or it will not be shiny.

9.   Remove the Opera Cake from the refrigerator or freezer. Leave the plastic wrap or acetate on top of the cake. If the pan is lined with acetate, simply invert the cake onto a baking sheet, remove the pan and the bottom square of acetate, then reinvert the cake onto another baking sheet. If the pan is lined with foil, run a hot knife along the sides that were not lined, and lift the cake out with the foil flaps. Leave these up against the sides of the cake, once it's removed from the pan. Place the cake on a baking sheet.

10.   Place 2 small ramekins under a short side of the baking sheet, to tilt it. Remove the plastic from the top of the cake. Take the melted glaze out of the double boiler and dry the bottom. Starting at the raised edge of the cake, pour the glaze along the edge and down the top. Remove the ramekins and level the pan. Gently tap the pan a few times to level the still-liquid glaze. Then, with one sweeping motion, level the top of the glaze with a long metal spatula, preferably offset. Refrigerate the cake, on the baking sheet, until just before cutting.

11.   When you are ready to cut the cake or present it whole, or up to 1 hour before, take it out of the refrigerator. Carefully pull away the pieces of acetate from the sides or pull down the flaps of foil. If you used acetate, the sides and exposed layers should be perfectly clean. This cake is now ready to cut into portions. If you used foil, at least two of the sides will have accumulated some glaze, and the other two may not be all that clean. Dip a long, sharp, heavy knife in hot water, dry it, and cut away ¼ inch from 1 side. Cut away ¼ inch from the other 3 sides, dipping and drying the knife between cuts. Decorate the top of the cake with a few small pieces of gold leaf.

12.   If you are presenting the cake whole, transfer it to a serving platter using 2 wide metal spatulas. If you are cutting it into portions, use the long heavy knife, heating it between slices. Serve with Crème Anglaise decorated with a chocolate coffee bean, if desired, on the side.

> **To keep a syrup from soaking all the way through the sponge layer on which it has been brushed—which would make moving the pastry from pan to plate nearly impossible—coat the bottom of the lowest layer of sponge with a thin layer of melted chocolate. As it hardens, the chocolate forms a barrier between the drenched sponge and the plate.**

Chocolate and Hazelnut Truffle Torte *L'Alhambra*

This extremely decadent chocolate cake is a specialty of one of the pastry shops where I worked in Paris, Pâtisserie Hardel, in the Sixteenth Arrondissement. The cake is extremely easy to prepare and assemble, and because it is made up of layers of hazelnut-chocolate cake spread with dark chocolate ganache, a little bit goes a long way.

At Hardel, a dozen of these cakes were made at once and frozen. These were made in 1½-inch-deep rings. Extreme care was taken to ensure that the outsides of the cakes, where the ganache hit the rings, were completely smooth. The rings were removed while the cakes were still frozen and then—and this was one of the most thrilling things I ever experienced in a pastry kitchen—the cakes were sprayed with chocolate. Each cake was set on a small pedestal with a cardboard shield around three sides. A paint sprayer was filled with melted bittersweet chocolate that had been thinned with melted cocoa butter to the consistency of paint, and each cake got a thin sprayed-on coating. The result was like velvet. As the chocolate spray hit the frozen cake, it froze in fine droplets. The cake was refrigerated to thaw slowly, then put on display with no decoration, save for the pastry shop's simple gold label. Now that's dramatic! You can achieve a similar effect by dusting the top of the cake with a thin layer of cocoa.   **Makes one 10-inch cake, for 16 servings**

½ recipe (one 9-inch cake) Hazelnut-Chocolate Sponge (page 282), freshly made or frozen and thawed

1 recipe (4 cups) Chocolate Ganache (page 318), prepared the day before and left at room temperature

Unsweetened cocoa powder, for dusting

16 whole blanched hazelnuts, for decoration (optional)

1. Using a long serrated knife, cut the sponge horizontally into two ½-inch-thick layers. (If you have a third layer left over, wrap it well in plastic and freeze it for up to 2 weeks even if it was previously frozen.) Place 1 layer in the bottom of a 10-inch springform pan. Or if you have a 10-inch stainless steel ring 1½ or 2 inches deep, place it on a foil-lined baking sheet and put a layer of sponge in the middle.

2. Fill a pastry bag fitted with a ½-inch plain tip with ganache. Pipe a ring of ganache around the bottom of the pan, filling the space between it and the sponge layer. Pipe a spiral of ganache onto the entire layer of sponge, then spread it evenly with a small offset spatula. Using a metal icing spatula, spread the ganache up the inside of the pan, stopping about ½ inch from the top, to prevent air bubbles from showing on the outside of the cake.

continued

3.   Place the other layer of Hazelnut-Chocolate Sponge on the ganache. Fill the ring with the remaining ganache, spreading it very evenly. If the level of the ganache is lower than where you stopped spreading the ganache up the sides, scrape the excess ganache down with a small rubber spatula, with a wet towel, or with your finger.

4.   Refrigerate the cake for 30 minutes to set the ganache. Cover the ganache with plastic wrap or a 10-inch round of acetate set directly on the chocolate. Make sure that there are no air bubbles underneath. Place in the freezer overnight. (*The cake may be frozen for up to 3 weeks.*)

5.   At least 4 but not more than 8 hours before serving, remove the cake from the freezer. If you have a blowtorch, light it and run the flame quickly but evenly around the side of the springform pan. If not, turn the pan on its side and roll it quickly over a low open flame or the hot burner of an electric range. (The heat will loosen the ganache from the pan without melting it. If you were to release the outside of the pan without heating it first, the ganache might crack away.) Once you've heated the ring, release it and immediately smooth the ganache with a metal spatula. If you made the cake in a ring, heat it in the same manner, then place the still-frozen cake on an inverted cake pan smaller in diameter and deeper than the ring. Place your hands on opposite sides of the ring and slide it down.

6.   Run a wide metal spatula under the cake to loosen it, then transfer the cake to a large piece of wax paper on a flat surface. Sift a thin layer of cocoa over the top, then transfer the cake to a serving platter. Thaw in the refrigerator until ready to serve.

7.   Space the hazelnuts evenly around the top edge of the cake, if desired. Cut with a sharp, heavy knife, dipping the knife in hot water and wiping it clean between cuts.

> **You can also use a straight-sided 10 x 2-inch round cake pan for this. Line the bottom with parchment or with a round of acetate (see page 351). Cut strips of acetate, 2 inches wide, to line the inside of the pan (you will need a total length of about 32 inches). Prepare the cake as in Steps 1 through 4. When it is time to unmold the cake, invert it, still covered, onto a baking sheet, remove the pan and the acetate round, then reinvert the cake onto a piece of wax paper. Remove the acetate strips after sifting the cocoa over the top of the cake. The acetate will lift cleanly off the ganache.**

Coffee-Walnut Cake *Le Noyer*

This classic cake, the name of which means walnut tree, contains no walnuts, save for a few on top as decoration. How could this be? Traditionally, the cake is made with thin layers of egg white–based Almond Sponge (page 286)—and you may certainly use this—but if you really want it to be a walnut cake, use Walnut Sponge. Whichever you choose, it does not need to be brushed with syrup, which makes this cake very simple to assemble.

Another traditional component of *Le Noyer* is a thin layer of coffee-flavored almond paste as the topping. The coffee flavor is good, but the almond paste, which is fifty percent sugar, is terribly sweet. I prefer to top each piece of cake with a rosette of whipped cream, topped with a chocolate coffee bean or a toasted walnut half. **Makes one 8-inch square cake, for 8 servings**

1 recipe Walnut Sponge (page 281), baked in an 8-inch square pan, freshly made or frozen and thawed.

1 recipe (3 cups) Coffee Butter Cream (page 317)

½ recipe (1 cup) lightly Whipped Cream (page 307)

8 chocolate coffee beans or 8 perfect walnut halves, toasted

⅓ recipe (1 cup) Chocolate Caramel Sauce (page 331), warmed (optional)

1. If you have an 8-inch square stainless steel frame that is 2 inches deep, place it on a foil-lined baking sheet. Otherwise, use a metal baking pan. The corners of the pan should be squared off, not rounded. Line the bottom and two of the sides of the pan with a 24-inch-long sheet of foil folded in half lengthwise for strength, leaving flaps of foil over the 2 sides. Smooth the lining. Or if you have sheets of acetate (see page 351), cut rectangles to line all the sides of the pan and a square for the bottom. Stick these in place with a dab of oil.

2. Using a serrated knife, cut the Walnut Sponge horizontally into 3 even layers. Set aside.

3. Measure out 1 cup of the butter cream. Put it in the frame or pan and spread it evenly using a small offset spatula. Place one of the walnut layers on top of the cream and press gently to make sure that it is completely flat. Repeat the layering process, making sure that each layer of butter cream is spread very evenly. By the time you top the cake with the third layer of sponge, it may be higher than the top of the pan. Cover the cake loosely with plastic wrap, and refrigerate for at least 2 hours. (*The cake may be frozen, tightly wrapped with plastic once the butter cream has set, for up to 3 weeks. Thaw for 3 hours in the refrigerator before unmolding.*)

4. Up to 8 hours before serving, unwrap the cake. Invert it onto a serving platter, lift off the frame or pan, and peel away the foil or acetate. The acetate can be wiped clean and reused. If the sides are not completely even and/or do not expose the layers of sponge and butter cream, trim

71

¼ inch from each side, using a sharp, heavy knife that has been dipped in hot water and wiped dry between cuts. Refrigerate until ready to serve.

5.   Just before serving, prepare the whipped cream. Cut the cake into eight 2 × 4-inch portions. Fill a large pastry bag fitted with a ½-inch star tip with the whipped cream and pipe a rosette on top of each portion. Place a chocolate coffee bean or walnut half on top of the cream. Serve with warmed Chocolate-Caramel Sauce, if desired.

Hazelnut Praline Torte *Succès*

This cake is usually constructed inside a ring and is packed with butter cream. Once the ring is removed, the outside of the cake is masked with ground nuts or cake crumbs, then powdered sugar is sifted on top. In this somewhat lighter and much easier version, the butter cream is piped in rosettes between the meringue layers, requiring about a third less cream and no side decoration. The resulting cake is even prettier than the classic one.

Just to show how subtle French pastry nomenclature can be, if you were to vary this recipe by replacing the ground almonds in the meringue layers with ground hazelnuts, the cake would be referred to as *Progrès*, or progress, instead of *Succès*, or success. Make whichever you prefer, depending on your state of mind!   Makes one 8-inch cake, for 8 servings

½ recipe (two 8-inch layers) Almond Meringue Layers (page 290)

½ recipe (1½ cups) Hazelnut Praline Butter Cream (page 317)

Powdered sugar, for dusting

I.   Place 1 meringue layer on a serving platter or in a pan, flat side down.

2.   If the butter cream is not at piping consistency or looks curdled, warm it very slightly, without melting it, in a double boiler, then beat it at high speed with an electric mixer. Fill a large pastry bag fitted with a ½-inch open star tip and pipe rosettes or swirls inside the edge of the meringue layer, then fill the center of the ring with butter cream. Top with the other meringue layer, flat side up. Refrigerate for at least 1 hour. (*The cake may be refrigerated, wrapped in plastic once the butter cream has set, for up to 3 days. It can be frozen, for up to 1 month, or up to the life of the butter cream. Thaw for 3 hours in the refrigerator.*)

3.   Before serving, sift powdered sugar evenly on top of the cake. Serve cold. Cut wedges with a serrated knife or pie server.

Individual *Succès*

These individual cakes are much easier to serve than one large one. And they are outstanding on a platter of mixed desserts.   **Makes 10 individual servings**

½ recipe (twenty 3-inch layers) Almond Meringue Layers (page 290)

1 recipe (3 cups) Hazelnut Praline Butter Cream (page 317)

Powdered sugar, for dusting

½ recipe (1½ cups) Crème Anglaise (page 328) or warmed Caramel Sauce (page 330), or 1½ cups Fresh Berry Sauce (page 331) or Chocolate Ganache (page 318), melted and kept warm

1.   Place 10 small meringue layers on a clean work surface, flat side down.

2.   Proceed with Steps 2 and 3 of the Hazelnut Praline Torte, using a pastry bag fitted with a ⅜-inch open star tip to fill the layers. It is not necessary to fill each pastry completely with butter cream, since these will not be cut into wedges.

3.   To serve, ladle about 2½ tablespoons of sauce onto each of 10 individual dessert plates. Tilt and turn the plates to spread the sauce evenly. Place a *Succès* in the middle of each. Serve immediately. The Succès may also be served on a large platter. Pass the sauce separately.

Strawberry Cream Torte *Fraisier*

Fraisier means strawberry plant in French, but that doesn't mean that this dramatic, yet light cake has to be limited to strawberries. Any fruit that is particularly attractive when cut in half or in slices, such as kiwis or figs, or a combination of several different fruits, can be substituted.

This cake can be made up to two days ahead, but it cannot be frozen—the fresh fruit will not survive. Classically, a Fraisier is topped with a thin layer of rolled almond paste, but I prefer to top it with a layer of the same fruit in thin slices.   Makes one 10-inch cake, for 12 servings

1 recipe Basic Sponge Cake (page 278), baked in a 10-inch pan, freshly made or frozen and thawed

¼ cup Simple Syrup (page 334)

2 tablespoons Kirschwasser, dark rum, or other alcohol (optional)

½ recipe (2¼ cups) Crème Mousseline (page 311)

2 to 3 pints (4 to 5 cups) strawberries, preferably small, washed and patted dry, stem side trimmed flat

½ cup Glaze for Fruit Tarts and Desserts (page 325)

1.   Cut the sponge horizontally into one 1-inch-thick layer and one ½-inch slice. (If you have a third layer left over, wrap it well in plastic and freeze it for up to 2 weeks, even if it was previously frozen.) Line the inside of a 10-inch springform pan with a 3-inch-wide strip of acetate (see page 351). If you don't have acetate, use neatly folded strips of aluminum foil. Set the 1-inch thick layer in the pan or inside a 3-inch deep stainless steel ring, set on a serving platter.

2.   Combine the syrup with the alcohol, if using, and generously brush the sponge. Trim the ½-inch-thick layer to 9 inches in diameter and set aside.

3.   Spread a thin layer of Crème Mousseline on the layer in the pan. Cut half of the strawberries, preferably those of equal height, in half from tip to stem. Place against the ring, cut side out and broad side down. The berries should be touching. Spoon about 1 cup of the mousseline onto the cake, against the uncut sides of the berries. Using a metal spatula, spread the cream across the backs of the berries and against the ring, plugging all the spaces between the strawberries, especially as they taper upward.

4.   Fill the inside of the cake with strawberries, standing them on the flat end, reserving the rest of the berries for the topping. Drop ½ to 1 cup mousseline from a spatula onto the strawberries, then spread to fill in all the spaces. Lay the reserved layer on top of the strawberries, avoiding the edges, and brush it with syrup. Finally, mask the sponge with ½ cup of mousseline and level the top by running a very long spatula over the top of the ring. Cover with plastic wrap and refrigerate for at least 2 hours. (*The torte may be refrigerated for up to 2 days.*)

5. If you made the torte in a ring, warm the ring, either by running a lit blowtorch quickly over the top half of the ring or by wrapping a hot towel around it. Lift the ring up. The torte will already be on a serving platter. If you assembled the torte in a springform pan, release the ring, then remove the acetate or foil strip.

6. Slice the remaining strawberries lengthwise ⅛ inch thick and lay these slices across the top in overlapping concentric circles, points facing outward. Warm the glaze until it is fluid, then brush it evenly over the sliced fruit. Refrigerate to set the glaze for at least 30 minutes or up to 4 hours.

7. Slice the cake with a serrated knife or pie server.

Raspberry Mousse Cake *Miroir de framboises*

One of the ubiquitous naked-sided mousse cakes in France is the *Miroir de cassis*, or black currant mirror. Black currants are plentiful in France, but not in the United States. If you can find fresh or frozen black currants in America, or even cassis puree, make this dessert with currants. Otherwise, use flavorful raspberries. Since you won't need any whole berries for the cake, frozen fruit is an option.

This cake is assembled upside down and then inverted in order to give the top a smooth mirror-like finish. If you are not satisfied with the smoothness of your glaze, pipe a rosette of whipped cream in the middle of each serving and top it with a raspberry.   Makes one 8-inch square cake, for 8 servings

½ recipe (1 sheet) Almond Sponge Sheets (page 284), freshly made or frozen and thawed

2 ounces bittersweet or semisweet chocolate, melted and cooled

1 cup plus 3 tablespoons strained raspberry puree

¼ cup (1¾ ounces) granulated sugar

1 packet (1 tablespoon) powdered gelatin, softened in ¼ cup cold water and drained

2 cups whipping cream, very cold

¼ cup (about ¾ ounce) powdered sugar

1½ cups Simple Syrup (page 334), cold or at room temperature

1 cup Chambord black raspberry liqueur, or Crème de Cassis, black currant liqueur, or good-quality raspberry syrup

¼ cup Glaze for Fruit Tarts and Desserts (page 325)

1 cup Fresh Berry Sauce (page 331) (optional)

1.   If you have an 8-inch square stainless steel frame that is 2 inches deep, place it on a foil-lined baking sheet. Otherwise, use a metal baking pan. The corners of the pan should be squared off, not rounded. Line the bottom and two of the sides of the pan with a 24-inch-long sheet of foil folded in half lengthwise for strength, leaving flaps of foil over the 2 sides. Smooth the lining. Or if you have sheets of acetate (see page 351), cut rectangles to line all the sides of the pan and a square for the bottom. Stick these in place with a dab of oil.

2.   Using a ruler as a guide, cut the Almond Sponge Sheet in half to make 2 pieces 12 × 8 inches in size. Cut each piece to make one 8-inch square and one 8 × 4-inch rectangle. The 2 small pieces will make an 8-inch square.

3.   Using a small offset metal spatula, spread 1 side of one of the squares with a thin, even layer of chocolate. Place it on a baking sheet, chocolate side up, and refrigerate until the chocolate is firm, 3 to 5 minutes.

4. Combine 1 cup of berry puree and the granulated sugar in a small stainless steel saucepan over low heat and heat to 150°F, or until the sugar is dissolved and the puree is very warm but not uncomfortable to the touch. Drain the gelatin completely and whisk it into the puree. Pour the puree into a small mixing bowl and allow it to cool to tepid.

5. Place the bowl and beaters or whisk attachment from an electric mixer in the freezer for at least 30 minutes. Remove and pour in the cold whipping cream and add the powdered sugar. Whip on low speed at first, until the cream begins to hold the trails of the beaters or whisk. Gradually increase the speed and whip the cream until stiff, but still very white and smooth. Gently fold the puree into the cream with a rubber spatula.

6. Measure out one-third of the mousse. Put it in the frame or pan and spread it evenly using a small offset spatula. Place the uncoated sponge square on top of the mousse and press gently to make sure that it is completely flat.

7. Stir together the syrup and liqueur, and using a large pastry brush, generously soak the sponge layer. Check various spots on the sponge with a paring knife to see that the syrup has gone all the way through. If you see any white spots, keep soaking.

8. Top the soaked sponge with half of the remaining mousse, spreading it evenly. Cover this layer with the sponge halves and soak them. Top with the remaining mousse, which may reach the top of your pan or frame. Remove the chocolate-coated sponge from the refrigerator. Invert it and soak it. If you have any syrup left over, strain and refrigerate it for later use.

9. Invert the chocolate-coated sponge onto the top layer of mousse so that the chocolate faces up. It may be higher than the edge of the pan. Refrigerate the cake for 1 hour, or until the mousse sets. Wrap in plastic and refrigerate for at least 4 hours or up to 2 days. (*The cake may also be wrapped well with plastic all around the pan and frozen for up to 3 weeks. The cake can be glazed while still frozen. Thaw in the refrigerator for 2 hours before cutting and serving.*)

10. Up to 8 hours before serving, remove the cake from the refrigerator or freezer. Invert it onto another baking sheet, cut along the unlined sides with a small hot knife, lift off the pan, and peel away the foil or acetate. Warm the glaze just until it melts and stir in the fruit puree. You can either pour the raspberry glaze over the top of the cake and quickly spread it with a metal spatula, or brush it on. Pouring will give you a smoother finish.

11. Using a long heavy knife dipped in hot water and dried, cut ¼ inch from each edge to expose the even layers of mousse and sponge. Dip the knife, then dry it between cuts. Transfer to a platter and refrigerate until it is time to serve.

12. Cut the cake into 8 pieces, each 2 × 4 inches, or into smaller, petit-four sizes. Dip the knife into hot water and dry it for each cut. Serve with berry sauce, if desired.

Apricot Mousse Cake *Miroir d'abricots*

I love deep-colored, sweet apricots, and very ripe, even mushy, ones are perfect for this mousse cake. Do not strain the puree—the little flecks of skin will enhance the look of the mousse. Serve it with a berry sauce. The contrast of colors on the plate will be striking. Makes one 10-inch cake, for 12 servings

¾ pound fresh apricots, pitted

½ recipe (1 sheet) Almond Sponge Sheets (page 284), freshly made or frozen and thawed

2 ounces bittersweet or semisweet chocolate, melted and cooled

¼ cup (1¾ ounces) granulated sugar

1 tablespoon freshly squeezed lemon juice

1 packet (1 tablespoon) powdered gelatin, softened in ¼ cup of cold water and drained

2 cups whipping cream, very cold

¼ cup (¾ ounce) powdered sugar

1½ cups Simple Syrup (page 334), cold or at room temperature

1 cup apricot brandy or liqueur or good-quality apricot syrup

¼ cup Glaze for Fruit Tarts and Desserts (page 325)

1 cup Fresh Berry Sauce (page 331) (optional)

1.   Puree the apricots in a blender or food processor. You should have 1¼ cups. Set aside.

2.   Follow the recipe for Raspberry Mousse Cake, Steps 1 through 3.

3.   Combine the apricot purée, the granulated sugar, and lemon juice in a small stainless steel saucepan over low heat, stirring often with a wooden spoon. Once the purée deepens in color, remove it from the heat and cool it to 150 degrees. Set aside ¼ cup of this puree for the glaze. Add the softened gelatin to the rest.

4.   Continue with Steps 5 and 6.

5.   If you use clear apricot brandy to flavor the syrup, in Steps 7 and 8, it will be difficult to know when the sponge layers are saturated. Just keep soaking.

6.   Continue with Steps 9 through 12.

Blackberry and Mascarpone Charlotte

Charlotte au fromage blanc et aux mûres

Surround a mousse with ladyfingers and it becomes a charlotte. Charlottes made of whatever the *mousse du jour* happens to be have become a fixture in most of France's pastry shops. This one is a slight departure, however. The mousse is based on *fromage blanc*, a creamy fresh cheese that has been common on French breakfast tables for years. Years ago, the great pastry chef Lenôtre started making a *gâteau au fromage blanc*, which was basically a simple sponge covered with a mousse made from this cheese, then covered with fresh fruit. Now the French have discovered Italian mascarpone and started making their gâteau au fromage blanc with that. (Imported and domestic mascarpone is available in gourmet food markets.)

Also appearing in many French restaurants and pastry shops: *Tiramisù!* Of course, the French have reinvented this classic Italian dessert. I have included a French *Tiramisù* recipe using the same techniques as in the berry charlotte but with coffee instead of berry flavoring.   **Makes one 9-inch cake, for 10 to 12 servings**

I recipe Basic Sponge Cake (page 278), baked in an 8-inch pan, freshly made or frozen and thawed, or two 8-inch Ladyfinger Rounds (page 281), freshly made or frozen and thawed

I cup Simple Syrup (page 334)

¼ cup Chambord, black raspberry liqueur, or good-quality blackberry syrup

I recipe (30) Ladyfingers (page 280)

½ cup plus I tablespoon (about 4 ounces) granulated sugar

2 large egg whites

I cup whipping cream

I teaspoon powdered gelatin, softened in I tablespoon cold water and drained

I small (250 grams/8½ ounces) tub mascarpone, very cold

2 tablespoons whole milk

3 cups blackberries

½ cup Glaze for Fruit Tarts and Desserts (page 325) or powdered sugar, for decoration

I½ cups Fresh Berry Sauce (page 331), made with blackberries

I. If you have a 9-inch stainless steel ring that is 3 inches deep, place it on a serving platter. Or assemble a 9-inch springform pan.

continued

2.   If you are using a sponge cake, cut 2 horizontal layers, ½ inch thick, using a serrated knife. If you have any cake left, wrap it in plastic and freeze for later use. Place either a sponge cake layer or a Ladyfinger Round in the bottom of the pan or ring, leaving a ½-inch border all around.

3.   Stir the syrup with the Chambord. Brush the cake layer generously with this syrup. Lightly brush the flat side of each biscuit with syrup, then stand the biscuits inside the pan with the lower ends between the cake and the pan and the flat sides facing in. Place the biscuits so they are touching but not crowded or overlapping. Crumple a large piece of wax paper or aluminum foil and place it inside the pan, to keep the biscuits in place.

4.   Put ½ cup sugar in a small heavy saucepan with 2 tablespoons water. Wash down any crystals clinging to the inside of the saucepan with a wet pastry brush. Place the saucepan over medium heat and heat, without stirring, until the sugar begins to boil. When the sugar boils clear, begin whisking the egg whites on low speed until they begin to froth. Increase the speed to medium and whip until the whites hold a soft peak. With the mixer on low speed gradually add the remaining tablespoon sugar and continue beating. When the sugar reaches 244°F, increase the speed to high. When the sugar reaches 248°F, remove it from the heat. With the mixer on low speed, add the sugar to the whites in a thin stream. Increase to high speed and whip for 5 minutes, then lower the speed and beat the meringue on low speed until it cools to room temperature.

5.   Heat ¼ cup of the cream to a simmer in a small pot, then pour it over the drained gelatin to melt it. Whisk until there are no gelatin strands.

6.   Stir the mascarpone to loosen it, then add the cold milk. Whisk in the cream with the melted gelatin, mixing thoroughly so that the gelatin is evenly dispersed.

7.   Whip the remaining cream until stiff. Fold together the meringue and the whipped cream. Some streaks may remain. Using a rubber spatula, gently fold in the mascarpone mixture.

8.   Remove the paper from the mold. Distribute one-quarter of the berries over the bottom layer of sponge. Cover with half the mousse, spreading it very evenly. Place the remaining sponge layer over the mousse and brush it with syrup. Distribute a third of the remaining berries over the sponge and cover with the remaining mousse. Set aside the remaining berries for decoration. The mousse may be slightly higher in the middle. Freeze for 1 hour, or refrigerate for 8 hours.

9.   To serve, remove the ring or springform sides from the charlotte. Top the mousse with blackberries, standing on their stem ends. Melt the glaze and glaze the top, or sift powdered sugar over the berries. Serve cold with berry sauce on the side.

Tiramisù

Traditional *tiramisù* is made in a deep rectangular pan and is quite rustic. Squares of this rich dessert expose ladyfingers laid on their sides and brushed with coffee syrup. This seems an awful waste of ladyfingers, but good-quality biscuits are available even in supermarkets in France and Italy. If you're going to take the time to make these biscuits, though, I think you should show them off on the outside of the cake.   Makes one 9-inch cake, for 10 to 12 servings

> 1 recipe Basic Sponge Cake (page 278), baked in an 8-inch pan, freshly made or frozen and thawed, or two 8-inch Ladyfinger Rounds (page 281), freshly made or frozen and thawed
>
> ¾ cup Simple Syrup (page 334), cold or at room temperature
>
> ½ cup very strong brewed coffee, cold or at room temperature
>
> 2 tablespoons Coffee Flavoring, homemade (page 342) or store-bought
>
> 1 recipe (30) Ladyfingers (page 280)
>
> ½ cup plus 1 tablespoon (4 ounces) sugar
>
> 2 large egg whites
>
> 1 cup whipping cream
>
> 1 teaspoon powdered gelatin, softened in 1 tablespoon cold water and drained
>
> 1 small tub (250 grams/8½ ounces) mascarpone, very cold
>
> 2 tablespoons whole milk
>
> Unsweetened cocoa powder or chocolate shavings or curls (see page 182), for decoration

1.   Follow Steps 1 and 2 for the Blackberry and Mascarpone Charlotte.

2.   In Step 3 of the master recipe, mix together the syrup, coffee, and Coffee Flavoring. Brush the bottom cake layer and the flat side of the ladyfingers.

3.   Continue with Steps 4 through 9, omitting the berries.

4.   Just before serving, sift cocoa powder over the top or top with chocolate decorations.

Pear Charlotte *Charlotte aux poires*

According to Jean-Pierre Gonfroy, director of the French National School of Pastry in Yssingeaux, this charlotte came to be when the president of the Brotherhood of Pastry Chefs had an overabundance of pears in his orchard and did not know what to do with them. The French were growing tired of cakes laden with butter cream and chocolate—they were ready for some lighter desserts.

Today, *Charlotte aux poires* can be found in every corner pastry shop in France. The better establishments poach their own pears, which you can do (see pages 18–19). Others buy good-quality canned pears, and you can do that too. You'll be in good company. You will need four whole pears or seven to eight halves.

The mousse contains a bit of gelatin, mostly to keep it upright in a pastry case. If you are going to eat your charlotte the day it is prepared, you can cut down on the gelatin. You should not eliminate it entirely, though, as it will help you cut the cake. I've reduced the quantity of gelatin from the standard pastry shop amount with this in mind, so try the recipe as written, then reduce the gelatin next time, if you like.   **Makes one 10-inch cake, for 12 servings**

    1 recipe Basic Sponge Cake (page 278), baked in an 8-inch pan, freshly made or frozen and thawed, or two 8-inch Ladyfinger Rounds (page 281), freshly made or frozen and thawed.

    1 cup Simple Syrup (page 334)

    ¼ cup Poire William, or other pear brandy, such as pear schnapps, or ¼ cup pear syrup or poaching liquid

    1 recipe (30) Ladyfingers (page 280)

    3 to 4 poached or canned pear halves, drained, juices reserved

    2 tablespoons poaching liquid or canned pear syrup

    4 large eggs, separated

    1 tablespoon (1 packet) gelatin, softened in cold water and drained

    1 cup plus 2 tablespoons (8½ ounces) sugar

    ⅔ cup whipping cream, very cold

    2 poached or canned pear halves, cut into ½-inch cubes

    2 perfect poached or canned pear halves, for decoration

    ½ cup Glaze for Fruit Tarts and Desserts (page 325)

    1½ to 2 cups Fresh Berry Sauce (page 331)

1.   If you have a 9-inch stainless ring that is 3 inches deep, place it on a serving platter. Or assemble a 9-inch springform pan.

2.   If you are using a sponge cake, cut 2 horizontal layers, ½ inch thick, using a serrated knife. If you have any cake left, wrap it in plastic and freeze for later use. Place either a sponge cake layer or a Ladyfinger Round inside the pan or ring, leaving a ½-inch border all around.

3.   Stir the syrup with the Poire William or poaching liquid. Brush the cake layer generously with this syrup. Lightly brush the flat side of each biscuit with syrup, then stand the biscuits inside the pan with the lower ends between the cake and the pan and the flat sides facing in. Place the biscuits so they are touching but not crowded or overlapping. Crumple a large piece of wax paper or aluminum foil and place it inside the pan, to keep the biscuits in place.

4.   Combine 3 to 4 pear halves with the poaching liquid or pear syrup in a blender or food processor and process to a fine puree. You should have 1 cup puree. Pour the puree into a medium stainless steel pot and heat over medium heat, stirring often with a wooden spoon. Whisk the egg yolks to an even consistency. When the puree comes to a boil, pour one-third of it over the yolks and whisk immediately. Pour the pear–egg yolk mixture back into the pot and cook over low heat, stirring constantly, until the mixture coats the back of a spoon (175°F on a candy thermometer). Remove from the heat and immediately whisk in the softened gelatin. Pour the pear mixture into a small bowl and let stand at room temperature.

5.   Put 1 cup sugar in a small heavy saucepan with 2 tablespoons water. Wash down any crystals clinging to the inside of the saucepan with a wet pastry brush. Place the saucepan over medium heat and heat, without stirring, until the sugar begins to boil. When the sugar boils clear, whisk the egg whites on low speed until they begin to froth. Increase the speed to medium and whip until the whites hold soft peaks. Gradually add the remaining 2 tablespoons sugar and continue beating. When the sugar reaches 244°F, increase the speed to high. When the sugar reaches 248°F, remove it from the heat, and with the mixer on low speed, add half the sugar to the whites in a thin stream. Increase the speed to medium and add the remaining sugar. Increase the speed to high and whip for 5 minutes. Reduce the speed to medium and beat the meringue until it cools to room temperature.

6.   Whip the cream until it just barely holds stiff peaks. Fold together the meringue and the whipped cream. Some streaks may remain. Using a rubber spatula, fold in the pear mixture in thirds, scraping the bottom of the bowl with the spatula.

7.   Remove the wax paper or foil from the mold and spread half the pear cubes over the bottom layer of sponge. Pour half the mousse on top, then cover with a round of sponge. Brush generously with pear syrup, spread with the remaining cubed pears, and fill the mold with the remaining mousse. The mousse may be slightly higher in the middle. Refrigerate for 15 minutes, then cover the top with plastic wrap and refrigerate for at least 4 hours. (*The charlotte may be refrigerated for up to 24 hours. It can also be frozen for up to 3 weeks. Wrap all around the pan with plastic for freezing. Thaw overnight in the refrigerator.*)

continued

8.   At least 15 minutes or up to several hours before serving, slice the perfect pear halves cross-wise into even, thin slices, perpendicular to the stem. Remove the charlotte from the refrigerator and lay the slices on the mousse inside the ladyfingers, in a flower pattern. Or spread the slices across the top, maintaining the pear shape. Brush evenly with a thin layer of glaze, and refrigerate for at least 15 minutes to set the glaze.

9.   To serve, remove the ring or springform sides and place the charlotte on a serving platter (if it is not already on one). Use a serrated knife or cake server to cut wedges. Dip the knife in warm water between slices, so that the wedges come out cleaner. Ladle berry sauce around each wedge and serve.

- **If you are poaching pears for this recipe, poach them in white wine (page 18) or with vanilla (page 19), not red wine. When pureed and mixed with the other ingredients, the flavor of the red wine will be lost and even more important, the color of the mousse will be a rather unappetizing pale pink.**

- **Whether you are using canned pears in syrup or pears that you have poached yourself, reserve some of the syrup or poaching liquid to brush onto the sponge layers. This gives the dessert a certain continuity. If you do not have cooled Simple Syrup on hand, use pear syrup only.**

Mango Napoleons *(Millefeuilles à la mangue)*, **page 118**

Madeleines, page 169

Palm Leaf Cookies (Palmiers), page 150

Rolled Cigarette Cookies (Cigarettes), page 166

Little Brioches *(Brioches individuelles),* **page 273**

Walnut Bread *(Pain aux noix)*, **page 266**

Nice-style Pizza *(Pissaladière niçoise)*, page 236

Four-tiered Chocolate Mousse (*Mousse aux quatre chocolats*), **page 57**

Chocolate-Pear Charlotte *Charlotte Belle-Hélène*

In the world of French pastry, *Belle-Hélène*, literally beautiful Helena, refers to a combination of chocolate and pears. Many desserts bear this name. In this one, a layer of chocolate mousse is topped with a layer of pear mousse. Makes 10 to 12 servings

I recipe Basic Sponge Cake (page 278), baked in an 8-inch pan, freshly made or frozen and thawed, or two 8-inch Ladyfinger Rounds (page 281), freshly made or frozen and thawed

I cup Simple Syrup (page 334)

¼ cup Poire William, or any other pear brandy (such as pear schnapps), or ¼ cup pear syrup or poaching liquid

I recipe (30) Ladyfingers (page 280)

1½ to 2 poached or canned pears halves, drained, the juices reserved

I tablespoon poaching liquid or pear syrup

2 large egg yolks

1½ teaspoons (½ packet) gelatin, softened in cold water and drained

4 large egg whites

I cup plus 2 tablespoons (8½ ounces) sugar

⅔ cup whipping cream, very cold

6 ounces extra bittersweet chocolate, melted and cooled to room temperature

2 perfect poached or canned pear halves

½ cup Glaze for Fruit Tarts and Desserts (page 325)

1½ to 2 cups Fresh Berry Sauce (page 331)

1. Follow Steps 1, 2, and 3 for the Pear Charlotte.

2. In Step 4 of the master recipe, prepare the pear–egg yolk mixture using the amounts of pears, poaching liquid, egg yolks, and gelatin listed above.

3. Continue with Steps 5 and 6. Divide the meringue-cream mixture in half. Fold the pear puree into one half and the melted chocolate into the other half.

4. Assemble the charlotte as in Step 7, using the chocolate mousse on the bottom and the pear mousse on top.

5. Continue with Steps 8 and 9.

Regional Specialties

Les Spécialités régionales

FRENCH PASTRIES AND DESSERTS are every bit as steeped in history as are the other foods and the wines of France. Every specialty tells a story—about the culture, religion, local products, traditions, and history of that particular region. Many specialties have a very prominent place in the region's history, such as the cake that Joan of Arc brought to King Charles VII. That cake is still being made today at local pastry shops, such as Pâtisserie Néret in Loches in the Loire Valley. Still others typify what is available in the region, such as honey nougat or apple strudel.

Many regional desserts and pastries were created at monasteries and convents, often to commemorate a local saint or a holy day. These are usually very simple and take advantage of locally available ingredients. Because of the isolation of each region before the advent of the railroad and the automobile or truck, each region was limited to what it produced. Even in France, people now take all these ingredients for granted, so that it is not unusual for someone in Brittany to make an Alsatian specialty. By the same token, it is perfectly reasonable for an American to make that same specialty.

Normandy Apple Tart / *Tarte normande*

Provençal Spinach Tart / *Tourte de blettes*

Alsatian Apple Strudel / *Strudel aux pommes à l'alsacienne*
    Plum or Cherry Strudel / *Strudel aux quetsches ou aux cerises*

Basque Cake / *Gâteau basque*

Almond Sponge Cookies from Lorraine / *Visitandines*

Baked Cherry Custard from Limousin / *Clafoutis limousin*

Caramelized Upside-down Bread Pudding from Burgundy / *Rigodon*

Normandy Rice Pudding / *Teurgoule*

Two Chestnut Specialties
    Chestnut Soufflés / *Soufflés de marrons d'Aurillac*
    Mont Blanc / *Mont-Blanc aux marrons*

Honey Nougat / *Nougat au miel*

Soft Nougat from Provence / *Nougat tendre de Provence*

Normandy Apple Tart *Tarte normande*

In the springtime, the rolling hills of Normandy, the northwestern coastal region of France, are covered with blooming apple trees, a striking contrast to the rain-filled skies and green fields. It is no wonder that apples find their way into so many specialties of Normandy.

Here is just one version of a classic that is both rustic and refined. The crisp caramel on top makes it somewhat of a challenge to serve gracefully, but individual tarts require tall individual ring molds that are difficult to find. A large tart, on the other hand, can be made with ease in a springform pan.

For this recipe, make a chunky applesauce using half Golden Delicious, half tart apples, such as Granny Smith, with butter. It will help the tart wedges keep their shape when cut.   Makes one 10-inch tart

¼ recipe (8 ounces) Sweet Short Dough (page 294), chilled but not frozen or frozen and thawed overnight in the refrigerator

½ cup Almond Cream (page 314), at room temperature

1 recipe (3 cups) Chunky Applesauce (page 333), made with 2 ounces (½ stick) unsalted butter, cold

½ recipe (3 cups) Meringue-lightened Pastry Cream (page 312), made with Calvados (Normandy apple brandy) if desired, warm

About ½ cup (3½ ounces) sugar, for caramelizing the top

1.   Place the dough on a lightly floured surface and tap it a few times with a rolling pin. Roll it out to a 13- or 14-inch circle ⅛ inch thick. Line an ungreased 9- or 10-inch springform pan. Without stretching it, press the dough evenly against the inside of the pan. With a small knife, trim the top of the dough in a straight line so that the band of dough goes halfway up the pan, about 1½ inches high. Refrigerate for 1 hour.

2.   Preheat the oven to 375°F.

3.   Line the bottom and sides of the dough with aluminum foil, making sure that the foil is flush against the dough at all points. Fill the foil with rice, beans, or pie weights and bake for 15 minutes, or until the dough begins to set. Remove from the oven and carefully lift out the weights with the foil. Allow the tart to cool.

4.   Spread the bottom of the tart evenly with Almond Cream and return it to the oven for 15 to 20 minutes, or until the crust is golden and the Almond Cream is set. Turn off the oven. Cool the tart shell in the pan on a wire rack. (*The shell may be left out at room temperature for up to 8 hours.*)

5.   Fill the shell with applesauce, spreading it evenly. Cover and refrigerate. (*The filled shell may be refrigerated for up to 4 hours.*)

6. No more than 4 hours before serving, prepare the Meringue-lightened Pastry Cream. Pour it over the chilled tart and spread the top to level it. If there is extra pastry cream, put it in a bowl and refrigerate it. Freeze the tart on a very level rack for 30 minutes or refrigerate it for at least 1 hour, so that the gelatin in the pastry cream sets up. If you have any pastry cream left over, fill a pastry bag fitted with a ½-inch open star tip or a ¼-inch plain tip. Pipe a border of rosettes of cream just inside the rim.

7. No more than 1 hour before serving, adjust the broiler rack to about 6 inches below the source of heat and preheat the broiler.

8. Spread half the sugar in a thin, even layer over the top of the pastry cream, avoiding the very edge where the cream comes in contact with the pan. Caramelize under the broiler for 30 to 45 seconds, or just until the sugar melts and turns brown. Remove the tart and sprinkle with another thin layer of sugar, then caramelize again. If you have a blowtorch, you can use it instead of the broiler. The torch will give you considerably more control. Refrigerate for no more than 15 minutes.

9. Run a hot thin knife just inside the pan to loosen it. Remove the ring and place the tart on a platter to serve.

> **For a more dramatic presentation and more crunch, prepare the tart and top it with pastry cream ahead of time, then caramelize just before serving.**

Provençal Spinach Tart *Tourte de blettes*

A chard tart for dessert? My curiosity was piqued the first time I saw this *tourta de bléa* (as it is called in Provence) listed on a menu in a restaurant near Nice. I was not curious enough to try a pie made of chard, however, until I started seeing the regional specialty everywhere, including on my plate at a friend's home. To my delight, this delicate dessert was rich, only slightly sweet, and quite satisfying. I prefer to make it with spinach, which is sweeter and more tender than chard, but you can use young chard leaves whose stems are no thicker than ½ inch.   Makes one 10-inch tart

Scant ½ cup (2 ounces) dried currants

¼ cup dark rum

¼ recipe (8 ounces) Flaky Pastry Dough (page 293), chilled but not frozen or frozen and thawed overnight in the refrigerator

1 pound tender spinach, stems removed

1 large egg

1 tablespoon pure olive oil

Finely grated zest of 1 lemon

⅓ cup (2 ounces) pine nuts, lightly toasted

About ½ pound tart-sweet apples, such as Granny Smith or Fuji, peeled, cored, and sliced into ⅛-inch pieces

1 large egg yolk mixed with 2 teaspoons cold water, for egg wash

Crème fraîche or whipped cream, for serving

1.   Soak the currants in the rum for at least 1 hour. Drain the rum and reserve it for another use.

2.   Roll out two-thirds of the dough on a lightly floured work surface into a circle about 14 inches in diameter and ⅛ inch thick. Carefully line a 10 × 1½-inch quiche pan, leaving about ½ inch of overhang. Refrigerate for 30 to 60 minutes. Refrigerate the remaining dough as well.

3.   Thoroughly wash the spinach and spin-dry. Place the leaves in a large saucepan, cover, and cook over medium heat just until the leaves wilt. They will cook in their own liquid. Drain and cool completely. Squeeze any remaining liquid out of the spinach, then coarsely chop it.

4.   Preheat the oven to 400°F.

5.   Lightly whisk the egg in a large mixing bowl. Add the olive oil and lemon zest. Add the spinach, currants, and pine nuts and mix thoroughly. Spread this mixture evenly across the tart shell. Cover the spinach mixture evenly with the sliced apples. Lightly brush the overhanging edge of the dough with water.

6. Roll out the remaining dough on a lightly floured surface into an 11-inch circle. Roll it up on the rolling pin, then lay the dough on the tart. Pinch the 2 layers of dough together to seal, then roll up this edge decoratively. Brush the top of the tart with the egg wash. Pierce the top of the tart several times with a fork or a paring knife. Bake for 35 to 40 minutes, or until golden brown. Serve chilled, at room temperature, or slightly warmed with crème fraîche or whipped cream.

Alsatian Apple Strudel

Strudel aux pommes à l'alsacienne

Germany's influence on French gastronomy is unmistakable, especially in regions like Alsace where the two countries share a border. This border has shifted back and forth over the years, making the region more or less French, more or less German, depending on the era. Alsatian cuisine is a delectable mix, the best of both worlds: savory specialties with smoked meats and fish, sauerkraut, and foie gras; pastries using the many fruits of the area—including phenomenal plums of countless varieties—cream, butter, and nuts, and spices not seen elsewhere in France.

This recipe is somewhat updated and even Americanized. I have replaced the traditional raisins with dried cranberries, which do not exist in France.

Use a fairly dry apple, like Golden Delicious, as a base; a juicier apple could leave you with a soggy pastry. Add a few chunks of a tart-sweet apple, such as Granny Smith, Pippin, or Braeburn, for contrast.

This strudel is best when eaten within twenty-four hours of baking. You can, however, prepare the strudel and freeze it unbaked. Serve warm or at room temperature with a dollop of *crème chantilly* on the side. Earl Grey tea, which is made with bergamot, also native to Alsace, is the ideal beverage accompaniment.   **Makes 10 servings**

5 ounces (1¼ sticks) unsalted butter

1¼ pounds apples, peeled, cored, and coarsely chopped

¾ cup (5½ ounces) granulated sugar

¼ cup fine, dry bread crumbs

½ teaspoon ground cinnamon

1 teaspoon grated fresh ginger (optional)

¾ cup (3 ounces) lightly toasted walnuts, chopped

½ cup (2 ounces) dried cranberries or cherries

8 to 10 sheets (½ pound) frozen phyllo dough, thawed overnight in the refrigerator

½ cup (2½ ounces) ground blanched or unblanched almonds (see pages 10–11)

Powdered sugar, for dusting

1.   Preheat the oven to 350°F. Line a baking sheet with parchment paper.

2.   Melt 1 stick of the butter over low heat. Let cool.

3. Combine the apples, sugar, bread crumbs, cinnamon, ginger, if using, walnuts, and cranberries in a large mixing bowl. Mix thoroughly with your hands or a large spoon. Set aside.

4. Remove the sheets of phyllo from the package, carefully reroll the remaining sheets, and tightly wrap them in plastic. Return to the refrigerator. (*Thawed phyllo may be refrigerated for up to 1 week.*) Stack the sheets on the work surface and cover with wax paper and a damp towel. Working with 1 sheet at a time while keeping the others covered, remove 1 sheet and lay it flat with a long edge closest to you. Brush it all over with melted butter and sprinkle evenly with 1 tablespoon of the ground almonds. Top with another sheet and repeat the process. Do this until you have used all the pastry sheets, ending with butter and almonds. Reserve some of the melted butter to brush the top of the strudel.

5. Place the apple mixture on the pastry, leaving a 4-inch-wide strip of dough along the edge closest to you and a 2-inch border at each end. Pack the mixture together, forming a 4-inch strip. Dot with the unmelted butter.

6. Fold the narrower ends of the dough over the filling, then fold the wide flap over the filling, then roll the strudel, shifting the apples if necessary. Turn so that the seam is on the middle of the bottom.

7. Using 2 long metal spatulas, transfer the strudel to the baking sheet. Brush with the remaining melted butter. (*If not baking immediately, refrigerate for 1 hour to let the butter set. Wrap strudel all around with plastic and freeze on the baking sheet. Bake the frozen strudel in a preheated oven. It will need an additional 10 minutes of baking time.*)

8. Bake for 45 to 60 minutes, or until the pastry is golden and crisp. Cool on the pan for at least 30 minutes, then transfer to a serving platter. Dust with powdered sugar. Slice with a serrated knife or pie server and serve warm or at room temperature. Store leftovers at room temperature, covered with plastic.

Plum or Cherry Strudel *Strudel aux quetsches ou aux cerises*

Either plums or cherries make a luscious, gooey filling. For that reason, you will need to increase the amount of bread crumbs, which will absorb some of the juices.   Makes 10 servings

5 ounces (1¼ sticks) unsalted butter

1¼ pounds Italian prune plums, pitted and quartered, or 1¼ pounds pitted dark cherries

¾ cup (5½ ounces) granulated sugar

¼ cup plus 2 tablespoons (1½ ounces) fine, dry bread crumbs

½ teaspoon ground cinnamon (optional)

Finely grated zest of 1 lemon

¾ cup (3 ounces) lightly toasted walnuts or almonds, chopped

½ cup (2 ounces) dried cranberries or cherries (optional)

8 to 10 sheets (½ pound) frozen phyllo dough, thawed overnight in the refrigerator

½ cup (2 ounces) ground blanched or unblanched almonds (see pages 10 –11)

Powdered sugar, for dusting

1.   Proceed as in Steps 1 and 2 of the recipe for Apple Strudel.

2.   In Step 3 of the master recipe, combine the plums or cherries, sugar, bread crumbs, cinnamon, if using, lemon zest, nuts, and dried cranberries, if using. Mix thoroughly and set aside.

3.   Prepare the phyllo as described in Step 4.

4.   Place the fruit mixture on the phyllo as described in Step 5. Roll the strudel as described in Step 6, transfer to a baking sheet as described in Step 7, and bake, cool, and serve as described in Step 8.

Basque Cake *Gâteau basque*

This rustic cake has its roots in Béarn, the region on the southwest coast of France. It is dense and rich, almost like a shortbread, with a baked-in pastry cream filling. When cherries are in season, the people in the region of Itxassou add the fruit to the filling. The juices run through the cream and into the surrounding dough. The cake is the centerpiece of that region's annual cherry festival. Makes one 9-inch cake, for 8 servings

4 large egg yolks

1 cup (7 ounces) sugar

6 ounces (1½ sticks) unsalted butter, cut into small pieces and softened

Finely grated zest of 1 lemon

½ teaspoon salt

2 cups minus 2 tablespoons (9 ounces) unbleached all-purpose flour

¼ cup (1 ounce) chopped almonds, toasted and cooled

¼ recipe (1 cup) Pastry Cream (page 308), at room temperature

1½ cups pitted fresh Bing cherries (optional)

1. Whisk together 3 of the egg yolks and the sugar in a medium mixing bowl until pale yellow and light in texture. Whisk in the butter, 1 or 2 tablespoons at a time, incorporating well with each addition. Whisk in the lemon zest and the salt. Sift or strain the flour and add it to the bowl in a stream, switching to a wooden spoon as the dough stiffens. Stir until the dough is very smooth. Scrape down the bowl with a rubber spatula, then cover and refrigerate for 30 minutes.

2. Preheat the oven to 350°F. Generously butter a 9-inch round cake pan.

3. Remove the dough from the refrigerator and turn it out onto a lightly floured work surface. Divide the dough into 2 pieces, two-thirds for the bottom of the cake and one-third for the top. Roll or pat the larger piece into a 12-inch circle. Lightly fold it in quarters, then place it in the pan and unfold it. Press the dough evenly into the bottom and sides of the pan without stretching it.

4. Whisk the almonds into the Pastry Cream, then spread the cream evenly over the dough, without getting any filling on the top edge of the dough. If you are using cherries, press them into the cream.

5. Roll out the remaining dough into a 10-inch circle. Using a pastry brush dipped in water, very lightly moisten the rim of the dough. Turn the disk over onto the filled cake, then pinch the edges to seal. You can crimp the edges as you would a pie or lay the edge back onto the top of the cake.

6. Mix the remaining egg yolk with 1 teaspoon water and brush this glaze over the top of the cake. Use the tines of a fork to crisscross the top, taking care not to pierce the dough. Prick the top a few times with the fork to allow steam to escape during baking.

7. Bake for 30 to 40 minutes, or until the top of the cake is well browned. Cool for 30 minutes on a wire rack. Invert the cake onto another rack, then invert it again onto a serving plate. Let the cake cool completely, right side up. Serve at room temperature. (*The cake, wrapped all around in plastic, will keep at room temperature for up to 5 days. It can be frozen in the pan, either baked or unbaked, for up to 1 month. If freezing a baked cake, thaw at room remperature, then heat for 5 minutes in a 350°F oven before unmolding.*)

Almond Sponge Cookies from Lorraine

Visitandines

Visitandines **come from Lorraine, a region adjacent to Alsace. Like many of France's regional specialties, they were created in a monastery, in this case, that of the Order of the Visitation. The monastery was founded in 1610 by Saint François de Sales and Sainte Jeanne de Chantal.**

These delicate little almond sponge cakes are light and buttery, perfect for dipping. You can top each with a whole blanched almond before baking, spread them with raspberry jam after baking, or eat them plain. These are traditionally baked in barquette molds, long oval- or lozenge-shaped tartlet tins, which are available in specialty cookware shops. Barquette molds are usually made of metal other than stainless steel and will rust if washed and not dried immediately. I recommend washing the tins once, when they are new, then simply wiping them out after each use. If you prefer to wash the tins each time you use them, dry them immediately with a towel, then put them in a turned-off oven to dry further. **Makes 3 dozen cookies**

> 4 ounces (1 stick) unsalted butter, melted and cooled
>
> 1 cup (5 ounces) packed ground blanched almonds
>
> 1 cup plus 2 tablespoons (8 ounces) sugar
>
> 3 tablespoons unbleached all-purpose flour, sifted or strained
>
> 5 egg whites, kept separate, at room temperature
>
> 1/4 teaspoon almond extract
>
> 18 whole blanched almonds, split in half (optional)

1.   Adjust the oven racks to divide the oven into thirds. Preheat the oven to 400°F. Use about 2 tablespoons of the melted butter to grease thirty-six 2-inch barquette molds.

2.   Place the ground almonds, sugar, and flour in a mixing bowl or the bowl of an electric mixer and stir to combine evenly. Add three of the egg whites and stir with a wooden spoon for 10 minutes or with an electric mixer on medium speed for 5 minutes. Add the almond extract and the remaining butter and stir until evenly combined.

3.   Place the remaining 2 egg whites in a clean bowl and whip by hand or with an electric mixer until stiff peaks form. Gently fold these into the almond mixture.

4.   Use a pastry bag fitted with a ½-inch plain tip to fill the molds three-quarters of the way with batter, without overfilling them; this batter will rise considerably. You may also drop heaping tablespoons of the batter into the molds. Top each with a halved almond, if desired, rounded side up. Place the barquettes on 1 or 2 baking sheets, leaving 1 inch between tins.

5.   Bake for 7 to 10 minutes, switching the pans between the racks and rotating to ensure even baking. The finished cookies should be puffed and golden, and spring back when lightly touched.

6.   Cool the cookies to room temperature before removing them from their molds. To do so, invert the tins and tap to loosen the cookies, or release with a small paring knife. (*The cookies may be stored at room temperature in airtight containers, with wax paper between the layers, for up to 1 week.*)

Baked Cherry Custard from Limousin

Clafoutis limousin

Clafoutis, a homey custardy cake, appears under various appellations in several regions of France. I prefer the version from Limousin, which includes the city of Limoges, famous for its porcelain; it is the simplest. The Alsatian version, for example, is baked in a crust.

Traditionally, clafoutis is baked with fresh *unpitted* cherries. The pits are believed to intensify the flavor of the cherries. True though this may be, I have never been tempted to risk teeth in the cause of tradition. Besides, pitted cherries tend to give off more juice during baking, lending an attractive pink ripple to the custard. You can replace the cherries with thick slices of fresh peaches or halved apricots. **Makes 6 to 8 servings**

⅔ cup (3½ ounces) unsifted unbleached all-purpose flour

½ cup (3½ ounces) sugar

Pinch of salt

3 large eggs

Seeds of 1 vanilla bean, split lengthwise and scraped out, or 1 teaspoon pure vanilla extract

1½ cups whole milk

2 tablespoons butter, melted

Butter, for greasing the baking dish

1 pound fresh Bing cherries, washed, dried, and pitted

Sugar, for sprinkling

Whipped Cream (page 307), for serving

1. Sift or strain the flour into a large mixing bowl. Add the sugar and salt, whisking to blend. Add the eggs, one at a time, mixing well after each addition. Whisk in the vanilla seeds or extract. Gradually whisk in the milk, mixing well to make a smooth batter. Pass the batter through a medium mesh strainer, then whisk in the melted butter. Let rest for 10 minutes.

2. Preheat the oven to 350°F. Generously butter a 13 × 9-inch glass baking dish or 2-quart gratin dish.

3. Spread the cherries over the bottom of the dish. Gently pour the batter over the cherries. The cherries should show through the batter.

4. Bake for 20 minutes. Sprinkle the top of the custard with a thin layer of sugar, then bake for 15 to 20 minutes more, or until the custard is slightly puffed and lightly browned. Cool slightly before serving.

5. Serve at room temperature with a dollop of Whipped Cream.

Caramelized Upside-down Bread Pudding from Burgundy *Rigodon*

This dessert is part of a long French tradition for using up leftovers. It is a wonderful way to finish off stale brioche or egg bread. Nontraditional though it may be, you can also use stale raisin bread for this recipe. Serve the bread pudding as is or with Crème Anglaise on the side.

As always when working with caramel, be sure to use a heavy pot holder and not to splash the caramel on your skin. Sugar begins to caramelize at 340°F; sugar that is deep amber in color, almost burnt, may be as hot as 410°F. And, caramelized sugar will cling to your skin. **Makes 6 servings**

1½ cups (10½ ounces) granulated sugar

1 teaspoon corn syrup

2 cups whole milk

1 vanilla bean, split lengthwise

3 large eggs

Butter, for greasing the baking dish

6 slices (about 4 ounces) of stale bread, cubed and lightly toasted

½ cup (2 ounces) walnut pieces, lightly toasted

½ cup (2 ounces) hazelnuts, toasted, skinned, and chopped (see page 10) (optional)

½ recipe (1½ cups) Crème Anglaise, made with 3 egg yolks (page 328) (optional)

1. Fill a bowl that is larger than the pan in which you will make the caramel with ice. If you have an unlined copper caramelizing pot with a pour spout, clean it first with salt and white vinegar, then use it here; this is the ideal pot for caramelizing, as it conducts heat so quickly and evenly. Place 1 cup of the sugar and the corn syrup in a small heavy-bottomed saucepan. Add ¼ cup water to wet all the sugar without dissolving it, or even making it pourable.

2. Begin heating the sugar over low to medium heat. The heat should remain on the bottom of the saucepan; flames should not come up the side of the pan at any time. Wash any crystals clinging to the inside of the pot into the rest of the sugar, using a pastry brush dipped in water. Do this before the pan gets too hot, so that the water from the brush does not simply evaporate against the pan and the brush does not burn. If you notice sugar crystals still clinging to the pan once it heats, try to wash them down with a more generous dose of water on the brush.

3. Heat the sugar without stirring or disturbing the pot until the sugar begins to boil clear. Once the sugar boils clear, swirl it from time to time to distribute the heat within the syrup. When the sugar just begins to take on a light amber color, watch it carefully and swirl the pan often. It will go to deep caramel within just a few minutes. Once the caramel has reached 370°F, turn off the heat and carefully plunge the bottom of the pan into the ice bath, to stop further cooking of the sugar. Hold the pan in the ice bath, submerged only to the depth of the caramel, for 3 seconds. Lift the pan out of the water, swirl it, then dip it into the ice bath for 3 seconds more. Lift the pan out of the water and dry the bottom.

4.   Pour the caramel into a 6-cup soufflé dish or glass baking dish with an angled, not rounded, bottom. Tilt the dish while the caramel is still hot to cover the bottom completely. Fill the pot halfway with water and boil to dissolve any remaining caramel, or reheat the caramel and pour it into a metal container for later use, as in Coffee Flavoring (page 342).

5.   Combine the milk, ¼ cup of the remaining sugar, and the vanilla bean in a heavy saucepan and bring to a boil. Whisk immediately to prevent a skin from forming.

6.   Meanwhile, whisk the eggs with the remaining ¼ cup sugar. Pour the hot milk over the eggs, whisking constantly. Place a medium mesh strainer over a pitcher or large measuring cup and pour the liquid through. Remove the vanilla bean and scrape the seeds into the custard, discarding the pod. Whisk again.

7.   Butter the inside of the baking dish above the caramel. Toss the bread cubes with the walnuts and hazelnuts, if using, and place them in the baking dish. Pour the custard over the bread and nuts, then cover with a plate or pot lid that fits just inside the baking dish. Let sit for 15 minutes to allow the bread to absorb the liquid.

8.   Preheat the oven to 325°F. Put a kettle of water on to boil.

9.   Place the baking dish in a larger dish or pan that is at least 2 inches deep. Remove the plate or lid. Fill the outer pan with boiling water to just below the depth of the pudding, not higher, or the inner dish will float. Take care not to splash water into the pudding.

10.   Bake for about 1 hour, or until a thin knife inserted into the middle of the pudding comes out clean. Carefully remove the larger pan from the oven, then remove the baking dish and let cool on a wire rack. When the pudding has reached room temperature, run a knife along the inside of the baking dish. Turn the pudding onto a lipped serving platter. Serve at room temperature, cut into wedges. Or refrigerate and serve chilled. (*Covered with plastic, this dessert will keep for 2 days refrigerated.*)

Note: If refrigerated in the baking dish, the caramel will liquefy beneath the pudding. When unmolded, this will create a caramel sauce.

Normandy Rice Pudding *Teurgoule*

In the mid-1980s, some friends of mine got married in his hometown of Rouen in Normandy. The couple had met while working at a three-star restaurant in Paris. Their wedding reception, held in an old mill house, complete with water wheel, was spectacular. The food was prepared by chefs from renowned restaurants.

The culinary high point for me, though, was an incredibly creamy rice pudding that the groom's grandmother had made. This traditional dish dates back to the time of coal- and wood-burning ovens. Late at night, as the embers were dying, the grandmother would place a mixture of milk, sugar, and rice in an earthenware terrine in the oven. In the morning, she would remove a thick custard that was completely smooth.

Today, Normandy grandmothers are still making *Teurgoule* in earthenware terrines, but in gas and electric ovens turned down low. It still makes a great breakfast, especially in the winter, but it is an equally wonderful dessert. If you have a glazed earthenware baking dish or terrine, use it here. A gratin dish or glass baking dish works equally well.   **Makes 6 to 8 servings**

2 quarts whole milk

1 vanilla bean, split

One 2-inch cinnamon stick or 2 teaspoons ground cinnamon

½ cup plus 1 tablespoon (4 ounces) sugar

1 cup short-grain Japanese rice or Italian Arborio rice, unrinsed

2 ounces (½ stick) unsalted butter

Pinch of salt

1. Preheat the oven to 200°F. Butter a 2½-quart shallow glazed earthenware or glass baking dish or a gratin dish.

2. Combine the milk, vanilla bean, cinnamon, and sugar in a large saucepan and bring to a boil. Stir in the rice and bring back to a boil, stirring constantly to prevent the rice from sticking to the bottom of the pan. Turn off the heat and whisk in the butter and salt. Pour the liquid into the buttered dish.

3. Bake for 5 hours, or until the custard has a thick crust and feels somewhat set.

4. Serve warm, at room temperature, or chilled, spooned into serving bowls.

Two Chestnut Specialties

Chestnuts, at their peak in fall and winter, are adored in France. Here are two regional French chestnut specialties. For either, you can peel your own chestnuts or take advantage of high-quality canned chestnut products, made in France and available in gourmet shops and larger supermarkets under the brand name Clément-Faugier. If you use canned chestnuts, you need not wait for the holidays to serve these desserts.

Chestnut Soufflés *Soufflés de marrons d'Aurillac*

Aurillac is a part of Auvergne, in the center of France. For centuries, the people of this region lived off reserves of chestnuts, which are extremely nutritious, when food was scarce. This dessert would qualify as a luxury by *auvergnat* standards.

Serve these soufflés with very lightly sweetened Whipped Cream (page 307) or Crème Anglaise (page 328).   Makes eight 5-ounce soufflés

1¼ pounds fresh chestnuts, peeled (see page 340), or 500 grams frozen or jarred peeled chestnuts, or 1 can (500 grams) unsweetened chestnut puree

2 cups whole milk

1 vanilla bean, split in half lengthwise

2 tablespoons dark rum (optional)

½ cup plus 2 tablespoons (about 4½ ounces) granulated sugar

Butter, for greasing the molds

2 large egg yolks

3 large egg whites

Powdered sugar, for topping

1.   If using peeled fresh chestnuts or frozen or jarred chestnuts, put them in a large saucepan. If using canned chestnut puree, open the can, spoon into a large saucepan, and whisk the puree to loosen.

2.   Add the milk and vanilla bean to the chestnuts and bring to a boil over medium heat. Reduce the heat and simmer the chestnuts until they are tender and the milk has been absorbed. Stir frequently to prevent sticking. Let cool.

3.   Remove the vanilla bean and scrape the seeds back into the chestnuts. Coarsely puree the chestnuts in a blender or food processor. Do this in small batches, as the puree will be quite thick. If using canned puree, warm it to lukewarm. Transfer the puree to a large mixing bowl and add the rum and ¼ cup of the sugar. (*The dessert can be prepared a few hours ahead to this point. Leave at room temperature, covered loosely with plastic.*)

4.   Butter the insides of eight 5-ounce soufflé dishes. Coat these with 2 tablespoons granulated sugar, tapping out any excess. Place the dishes on a baking sheet.

5.   Preheat the oven to 350°F.

6.   Whisk the egg yolks into the chestnut mixture. Put the egg whites into a clean mixing bowl or the bowl of an electric mixer. Mix on low speed until the whites begin to froth, then increase to medium speed and whip until the whites hold soft peaks. Gradually add the remaining ¼ cup sugar in a thin stream. Once all has been added, increase to high speed and whip until the whites are stiff but not dry.

7.   Gently fold half the whites into the chestnut mixture, then fold the chestnuts into the remaining whites. It is all right if there are some streaks of white. Fill the soufflé dishes three-quarters full.

8.   Bake for 20 minutes, or until the soufflés have risen above the rims of the dishes and crusted somewhat on the sides. Meanwhile, set out dessert plates near the oven.

9.   Remove the baking sheet from the oven and place a soufflé on each dessert plate. Dust with powdered sugar. Serve immediately.

Mont Blanc *Mont-Blanc aux marrons*

Mont Blanc is the highest peak in the French Alps and is always snowcapped; this namesake dessert comes from the same region, Savoy. It, too, is white on top, although in this case it is not snow but whipped cream covering a mound of chestnut cream.

You will need a 6-cup ring mold for this. A plastic Tupperware or metal Jell-O–mold ring is perfect. The French use savarin molds.   Makes 8 servings

2 tablespoons butter, softened

2 tablespoons powdered sugar

1½ cups (1 pound) Chestnut Cream with Vanilla (page 339) or canned chestnut puree, very cold

2 cups whipping cream, very cold

¼ cup (1¾ ounces) granulated sugar

Seeds from ½ vanilla bean or ½ teaspoon pure vanilla extract

¼ cup (2 ounces) shelled unsalted pistachios, finely chopped

I.   Generously butter a 6-cup ring mold, then dust it with sifted or strained powdered sugar. Place in the freezer for 30 minutes.

2.   The chestnut cream must be completely smooth, or it will plug the pastry tip. If there are lumps, press the cream through a mesh strainer. Refrigerate the cream for 30 minutes after straining.

3.   Fit a pastry bag with a ⅛-inch plain tip. Fill the bag with chestnut cream and, holding the tip 6 inches above the mold, fill the mold with squiggles of cream. Keep moving around the mold so that it fills evenly. The ring should resemble a nest. Refrigerate the ring for at least 1 hour or up to 24 hours.

4.   Place the bowl and beaters or whisk attachment of an electric mixer in the freezer for at least 30 minutes. Do not use a flat beater. Whisking by hand is preferable to this.

5.   Pour the whipping cream into the chilled bowl and whip on low speed until the cream begins to hold the trails of the beater or whisk. Add the sugar and the vanilla seeds or extract and continue to beat on medium to high speed, until the cream is quite firm but still very smooth. Refrigerate the cream until you are ready to serve.

6.   Invert the chestnut ring onto a serving platter and tap to release. Remove the ring. Pile the cream into the middle of the ring. Using a metal spatula run under hot water and wiped dry, smooth the cream into a dome, so that the cream appears to be a snowcap on the chestnut mountain. Top with chopped pistachios and serve cut into wedges.

Honey Nougat *Nougat au miel*

Not only is Provence the principal herb-growing region in France, it is also the biggest honey-producing region. Beekeepers raise their bees on the flowers of various herbs, which give each of the honeys—and there are as many honeys as there are herbs and flowers, not to mention blends—a distinctive flavor. Try to use a honey with a distinctive flavor for this confection, which resembles almond-studded taffy.

Nougat dates back to a time when honey was the only sweetener known in Provence, before the introduction of cane sugar in the seventeenth century, and certainly before the discovery of sugar prepared from beets during the time of Napoléon Bonaparte. Hot nougat is traditionally poured, cooled, and cut on a thin layer of unleavened bread, a very thin version of the host used during Holy Communion. Called *ostia* in Italian, *Oblaten* in German, this is difficult to find in the United States. If you cannot find sheets of this product, use sheets of the edible rice paper used in Vietnamese cuisine for spring rolls, available in Asian markets. Otherwise, just pour the hot nougat on a baking sheet lined with lightly oiled aluminum foil.   Makes 3 pounds of nougat

> Sheets of edible water paper, edible rice paper, or aluminum foil
>
> Vegetable oil (optional)
>
> 1½ pounds honey
>
> 1½ pounds whole or slivered blanched almonds, lightly toasted

1.   Line a rimmed 16 × 12-inch baking sheet or jelly-roll pan with edible water paper or rice paper or aluminum foil. Smooth the lining. If using foil, grease it with a very thin film of oil spread with a wad of paper towel, not a pastry brush. Grease the sides of the pan.

2.   Pour the honey into a large heavy stainless steel saucepan. Heat over low heat, stirring often with a wooden spoon. As soon as the honey begins to boil, add the almonds. Stir constantly. When the almonds begin to crackle and the honey is deep amber, take the pot off the heat.

3.   Continue to stir for 2 to 3 minutes, then pour the contents of the pot onto the baking sheet. Smooth the nougat with a metal spatula dipped in water. If you have edible water paper or rice paper, cover the top of the nougat. Cool completely.

4.   Turn the cooled nougat onto a cutting board. If foil was used, peel it away. Using a heavy knife, cut the nougat into even or uneven pieces. Wrap individually in small pieces of cellophane, if desired, or store in an airtight container in layers with sheets of foil between. (*The nougat will keep well stored in an airtight container for up to 1 month.*)

THE NEW FRENCH BAKER

Soft Nougat from Provence

Nougat tendre de Provence

It's messy, somewhat complicated, and you may burn yourself, but it's worth it! This soft nougat is chewy and full of nuts. Cut it into small cubes and dip them in tempered chocolate (see page 185). Or cut it into larger pieces and dip one half in chocolate for a lovely addition to a platter of petit fours. Or wrap little pieces in cellophane as part of an assortment of confections, along with Honey Nougat (page 107) and various chocolates. Makes 3¼ pounds of nougat

> 4 large egg whites
>
> 1 cup (¾ pound) honey
>
> 2¼ cups (1 pound) sugar
>
> 2 tablespoons light corn syrup
>
> 2 cups (8 ounces) whole or slivered blanched almonds, toasted
>
> 2 cups (8 ounces) whole blanched hazelnuts, toasted
>
> 1 cup (4 ounces) shelled pistachios, toasted and skins removed
>
> Vegetable oil
>
> Powdered sugar, for cutting

1. Put the egg whites in a clean mixing bowl or the bowl of an electric mixer. Set aside.

2. Put the honey in a small saucepan, with a pouring spout if possible. Heat over a low flame until a candy thermometer registers 240°F.

3. Place 2 cups of the sugar and the corn syrup in a small heavy-bottomed saucepan. If you have an unlined copper caramelizing pot with a pour spout, clean it first with salt and white vinegar, then use it here; this is the ideal pot for caramelizing, as it conducts heat so quickly and evenly. Add ½ cup water to wet all the sugar without dissolving it, or even making it pourable.

4. Begin heating the sugar over low to medium heat. The heat should remain on the bottom of the saucepan; flames should not come up the side of the pan at any time. Wash any crystals clinging to the inside of the pot into the rest of the sugar, using a pastry brush dipped in water. Do this before the pan gets too hot, so that the water from the brush does not simply evaporate against the pan and the brush does not burn. If you notice sugar crystals still clinging to the pan once it heats, try to wash them down with a more generous dose of water on the brush.

108

5.   Heat the sugar without disturbing the pot or stirring until the sugar begins to boil clear. Once the sugar boils clear, swirl it from time to time to distribute the heat within the syrup. When the sugar just begins to take on a light amber color, watch it carefully and swirl the pan often. It will go to deep caramel within just a few minutes.

6.   As soon as the sugar begins to boil clear, start whisking the whites on low speed until they begin to froth. Increase the speed to medium and beat until the whites hold a soft peak. Gradually add the remaining ¼ cup of sugar and beat for 1 minute on high speed.

7.   When the honey is at 240°F, lower the mixer speed and add one-third of the honey to the whites in a thin stream at first and then in a heavier stream with the mixer on medium.

8.   When the sugar is at 316°F, reduce the mixer speed to low and add one-third of the sugar in a thin stream at first and then more rapidly with the mixer on medium. Then whip on high speed for 5 minutes, lower to medium, and continue to whip until the mixture is tepid. Let cool to room temperature. The mixture will be extremely thick and may slow down your mixer considerably.

9.   Line the bottom only of a large, rimmed baking sheet or two smaller ones with aluminum foil. Make sure the foil is very smooth. Place a few drops of oil on the foil and spread it evenly with a wad of paper towel, spreading the oil up the sides of the pan as well, in a very thin coating.

10.   When the nougat has cooled, fold in all the nuts with a rubber spatula. Mix evenly. Spread the nougat onto the pan or pans. Using a wet metal spatula, make the top perfectly flat. Allow the nougat to firm up at room temperature. (*The nougat can be wrapped and stored at room temperature for up to 1 week. Cover the top with a lightly oiled piece of aluminum foil, placing the oiled side against the nougat, then wrap tightly in plastic.*)

11.   When ready to cut, dust a large cutting board with a fine layer of powdered sugar. Unwrap the pan. Remove the top piece of foil and cut around the sides of the pan to release the nougat. Turn the nougat out onto the cutting board and peel away the bottom sheet of foil. With a heavy knife dipped in water, cut squares, rectangles, or whatever shape you want. Wrap immediately; nougat can absorb moisture from the atmosphere.

Neo-Classics

Les Nouveautés

IF YOU WERE TO stick strictly to classic French pastry, it would take years to sample everything—and it is rich in butter, sugar, and eggs. Many desserts are topped with sweet fondant or rolled almond paste. Butter cream makes an appearance in most of the cakes and many of the pastries. Creams and custards hold as many egg yolks as their dairy bases will allow. Besides, the time it takes to execute these recipes in a home kitchen is not available to even the most dedicated baking amateurs these days. Desserts that can be simply prepared, then sliced and plated easily, are the new norm.

Even professional pastry chefs have seen the handwriting on the wall. Their customers are buying fewer butter cream cakes and more fruit mousses. Chefs have discovered phyllo dough and use it to replace the puff pastry called for in many desserts.

This does not mean that all the new desserts are light and airy. Some are so rich that you can serve them only in very thin slices. Others are time consuming, but they consist of elements that can be made ahead and that are less rich than those that inspired their creation. All of the desserts in this chapter are adaptations of classic recipes. They have been lightened and/or made easier so as to be more suitable for a contemporary lifestyle. We Americans are lucky not to be as constrained by tradition as are the French.

Caramelized Pineapple Tart / *Tarte à l'ananas caramelisé*

Raspberry Tart on Puff Pastry / *Tarte feuilletée aux framboises*
   Individual Puff Pastry Tarts / *Tartes feuilletées individuelles*

Mango Napoleons / *Millefeuilles à la mangue*

Phyllo Tulip Shells / *Phyllipes*

Little Chocolate and Raspberry Dacquoises / *Petites dacquoises au chocolat*

   et aux framboises

Caramel Mousse / *Mousse au caramel*

Mosaic of Three Chocolates / *Mosaïque aux trois chocolats*

Roasted Whole Vanilla-studded Pineapple / *Ananas rôti à la vanille*

Gratin of Fresh Fruit / *Gratin de fruits frais*

Caramelized Pineapple Tart

Tarte à l'ananas caramelisé

Fresh pineapple does not find its way into many French desserts. Until recently it was a rare find. Tahitian pineapples, which are quite different from the Hawaiian fruit we find in America, have made an appearance in French markets. This variety has very little citric acid and is much less fibrous than what we are used to, but a Hawaiian pineapple will work fine in this recipe. Besides, fresh pineapple is so readily available here that I am thrilled to give you a wonderful recipe to help you take advantage of our bounty!   Makes one 10-inch tart, for 8 servings

> ¼ recipe (8 ounces) Sweet Short Dough (page 294), chilled but not frozen, or frozen and thawed overnight in the refrigerator, or 1 frozen tart shell, preferably frozen with a layer of Almond Cream (see page 314)
>
> ½ cup Almond Cream (page 314), softened (if shell was not frozen with Almond Cream)
>
> 1 small ripe pineapple (3 to 3½ pounds with crown), peeled, cored, and eyes removed (see page 349)
>
> 1 tablespoon unsalted butter
>
> 1 cup Pastry Cream (page 308) or Mango Cream (page 310), chilled
>
> 1 tablespoon dark rum (optional)

1.   Place the dough on a lightly floured surface and tap it a few times with a rolling pin. Roll it out to a 13-inch circle ⅛ inch thick and fill a 10-inch tart pan. Refrigerate for 1 hour. Or remove the frozen tart shell from the freezer.

2.   Preheat the oven to 375°F.

3.   Spread the Almond Cream, if using, evenly over the bottom of the tart shell and bake for 10 minutes. Check that the bottom of the tart is not puffing up. If it is, prick it with a sharp knife or a skewer. Bake for about 20 minutes more, or until the shell and the Almond Cream are golden brown. Cool on a wire rack.

4.   If the tart pan has 2 parts, remove the ring by holding the bottom with one hand while guiding the ring downward with the other. Place the cooled tart shell on the table and set the ring aside. Either leave the tart shell on the pan bottom or loosen it with a small paring knife and slide it onto a platter.

5.   Lay the pineapple on its side and, using a serrated knife, cut it first into ¼-inch slices, then cut the rings in half.

6. Heat a large, heavy, stainless steel or enameled cast-iron pan over medium heat. Melt the butter. Lay as many pineapple pieces in the pan as will fit and cook until browned, turning once. Remove with tongs and cool on a wire rack with a dish underneath to catch the juices. Pour any juices from the pan into a small stainless steel pot. Without melting more butter (some will cling to the pan), caramelize the remaining pineapple, drain, and cool completely.

7. Take all the collected juices, including those from the dish, and reduce over high heat until very thick. You should not have more than 1 or 2 tablespoons. Cool in a small bowl.

8. Whisk the Pastry Cream or Mango Cream to loosen. Add the reduced pineapple syrup and the rum, if using. Spread the cream evenly over the bottom of the cooled tart shell. Cover the cream with overlapping pieces of pineapple, placing them so the arches curve outward. Serve immediately or refrigerate until ready to serve. (*The tart may be refrigerated for up to 8 hours.*)

You can caramelize the tart just before serving. Sprinkle a thin layer of granulated sugar over the top and caramelize with a blowtorch or under the broiler.

Raspberry Tart on Puff Pastry

Tarte feuilletée aux framboises

This fruit tart, which is made with Puff Pastry rather than short dough, is rather chic, and if you use store-bought pastry, actually quite simple. And if you use whipped cream instead of Pastry Cream, the tart is even simpler. Other fruit can be used in place of the raspberries, although whole berries really do work best. They do not require any glaze, just a sprinkling of powdered sugar.   Makes one 9-inch square tart, for 8 servings

¼ recipe (½ pound) fully turned Puff Pastry (page 296), or 1 sheet (½ package) store-bought pastry, cold

1 large egg yolk mixed with 1 teaspoon water, for egg wash

½ cup whipping cream, chilled, and/or ½ cup Pastry Cream (page 308)

1 tablespoon powdered sugar (optional)

2 teaspoons Kirschwasser, Grand Marnier, or dark rum (optional)

2 cups whole fresh raspberries or blueberries, strawberries, wild strawberries, blackberries, or a combination of some or all

Powdered sugar, for dusting

1.   If using homemade pastry, take it out of the refrigerator at least 2 hours and up to 10 hours before serving. Roll out the dough, still cold, on a lightly floured surface to a large square, ⅛ to ¼ inch thick. Lift the dough to release it from the table and allow it to relax. Place the dough on a parchment-lined baking sheet, cover with plastic, and refrigerate for 1 hour.

2.   If using store-bought pastry, let it rest at room temperature for 5 minutes to prevent cracking, then unfold the sheet and place on a parchment-lined baking sheet. Trim the handmade dough to a 10-inch square; trim ⅛ inch from all edges of the store-bought dough. Using a downward cutting motion, cut a 9-inch square inside the 10-inch square. Leave the ½-inch-wide frame in 1 piece.

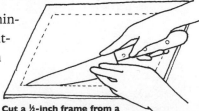

Cut a ½-inch frame from a trimmed square of dough.

3.   Leaving the frame in place, brush the edge of the inner square lightly with water. Lift 1 corner of the frame and, without stretching the dough, lay it on the inner corner of the inner square. Lay the 2 adjacent edges of the frame on top of the square, matching the edges. Before you reach the next 2 corners, twist them by placing the frame corner opposite the first one you placed on the corresponding corner of the solid square, but on the flip side. Think of the inside of the square as a slot, through which you are twisting the opposite

Starting with one corner, begin placing the frame on top of the square of dough, matching the edges.

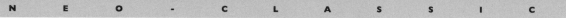

Continue matching 2 adjacent edges, then . . .

. . . flip the corner of the frame opposite where you started . . .

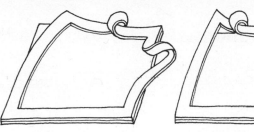

. . . so that the sides of the frame twist. Attach the corner and . . .

. . . move the twists down the sides of the frame, then . . .

corner of the dough. The twisted corners will be raised, and the others will be flush. Brush the frame lightly but evenly with egg wash.

. . . press them into place to form decorative corners.

4.   Using the dull edge of a paring knife, score the sides of the dough. Holding the knife at a 45-degree angle to the baking sheet, mark the dough, without cutting into it, at ¼-inch intervals along all 4 sides of the square but not the corners with the twisted frames on top. Using 2 forks, prick the solid square all over to prevent the dough from puffing during baking. Refrigerate for 15 minutes.

Score the sides lightly with the back of a small knife; prick the base with a fork.

5.   Place an oven rack in the middle of the oven, and preheat the oven to 375°F. Form an 8-inch square pan from aluminum foil to fit inside the pastry frame.

6.   Remove the baking sheet from the refrigerator, place the foil pan inside the pastry frame, and fill the inner pan with a ¼-inch layer of pie weights, rice, or dry beans. Bake for 15 minutes. Remove from the oven and check under the foil pan. The dough should be turning opaque. If not, return it to the oven with the foil pan on top for 5 minutes more. Lift the foil pan with the rice or beans off the tart and return the dough to the oven for 15 to 20 minutes, or until set and golden brown all over. If the center puffs, prick it with a skewer or a sharp knife to allow the steam to escape. Remove the baked shell from the oven and, using 2 metal spatulas, transfer it to a wire rack. Cool completely. (*The pastry can be prepared up to 8 hours before filling and left at room temperature.*)

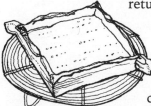

The baked tart shell, cooling

Place a foil pan filled with pie weights in the middle of the unbaked tart.

7.   If you are using whipped cream, whip it with 1 tablespoon powdered sugar until stiff but still very smooth. If you are using Pastry Cream, whisk it to loosen it. Add the liqueur, if desired. If using both creams, gently fold them together. Spread the cream inside the pastry. If the layer is too thick for your taste, reserve some of the cream and serve it on the side. Top with berries placed stem down and very close together. Refrigerate for not more than 1 hour. Just before serving, dust lightly with powdered sugar and transfer to a serving platter. Cut with a heavy or serrated knife.

Individual Puff Pastry Tarts *Tartes feuilletées individuelles*

For individual puff pastry tarts, you will need twice as much dough, and each large square will be cut into 4 smaller ones.

Mango Napoleons *Millefeuilles à la mangue*

Despite its name, this pastry is not made with puff pastry but with phyllo dough. The dessert is easy to prepare and no less Napoleonic in its magnificence than one made with puff pastry—which, of course, you may use instead. Prepare the elements ahead of time and assemble the dessert at the last minute, so that the dough retains its crackle.   Makes 8 pastries

About ⅓ pound (6 sheets) frozen phyllo dough, thawed overnight in the refrigerator

4 ounces (1 stick) unsalted butter, melted and cooled

6 tablespoons (1½ ounces) sliced blanched or unblanched almonds

1 cup whipping cream, cold

2 tablespoons powdered sugar

½ recipe (3 cups) Mango Cream (page 310), chilled

Berries or slices or chunks of fruit, such as kiwi, banana, or mango (optional)

Powdered sugar, for dusting

1 cup Fresh Berry Sauce (page 331)

1.   Preheat the oven to 400°F. Line 2 baking sheets with parchment paper.

2.   Remove the sheets of phyllo from the package, stack them on the work surface, and cover with wax paper and a damp towel. Working with 1 sheet at a time while keeping the others covered, remove 1 sheet and lay it flat. Brush it all over with melted butter and sprinkle evenly with 1 tablespoon of the almonds. Top with another sheet and repeat the process. Top with a third sheet of dough, brush with butter, and sprinkle with 1 tablespoon almonds.

3.   Trim all 4 edges of the rectangle to even it out. Measure the rectangle and cut it into 12 rectangles. Dust with powdered sugar and place the rectangles close together on one baking sheet. Repeat steps 2 and 3 with the remaining 3 sheets of dough.

118

4. Bake one sheet at a time, for 10 to 12 minutes, or until lightly browned and slightly puffed. Cool on the pan. Once cool, place all the rectangles on 1 pan. (*The pastry may be baked ahead and left on the pan, lightly wrapped with plastic, and left at room temperature for up to 12 hours.*)

5. Whip the cream with 2 tablespoons of powdered sugar until firm but still very smooth. Remove the Mango Cream from the refrigerator and whisk it to give it a smooth, even consistency. Gently fold the whipped cream into the Mango Cream using a rubber spatula. (*The filling may be prepared up to 3 hours before assembly, covered with plastic, and refrigerated until just before serving time.*)

6. Place 1 phyllo rectangle on each of 8 dessert plates or on a serving platter. Spoon about ¼ cup of the filling on each one. Place a few pieces of fruit on each, if desired, then top with another phyllo rectangle, pressing down lightly to spread the filling evenly. Spoon another ¼ cup of filling on top of each. Before topping the pastries with the last rectangles, push the tops close together on the baking sheet and dust with powdered sugar. Top the pastries, then spoon 2 tablespoons of berry sauce around them. Serve immediately.

Phyllo Tulip Shells *Phyllipes*

Since these shells are somewhat more neutral in flavor than Tulip Shells (page 168), they lend themselves well to savory as well as sweet fillings. And filled *mini-phyllipes* are a great addition to a platter of hors d'oeuvres. Whatever the filling, be sure to wait until the last minute to garnish the shells. They become soggy rather quickly. However, the shells themselves can be prepared and baked up to 12 hours ahead. **Makes 8 large shells**

About ⅓ pound (6 sheets) frozen phyllo dough, thawed overnight in the refrigerator

4 ounces (1 stick) unsalted butter, melted and cooled

SWEET SHELLS
4 tablespoons honey

Powdered sugar, for dusting

SAVORY SHELLS
6 tablespoons finely grated Parmesan cheese

4 tablespoons hulled sesame seeds

Paprika, for sprinkling

continued

1.　Preheat the oven to 400°F. Lightly butter or spray 8 brioche tins measuring 5 inches across the top or other ovenproof molds that have the shape you want. They need not be the same shape, but they should all be about the same size. Place the molds on 1 or 2 baking sheets.

2.　Remove the sheets of phyllo from the package, carefully reroll the remaining sheets, and wrap them tightly in plastic. Return to the refrigerator. Stack the sheets on the work surface and cover with wax paper and a damp towel. Working with 1 sheet at a time while keeping the others covered, remove 1 sheet and lay it flat. Brush it all over with melted butter. For sweet shells, drizzle with 1 tablespoon honey. For savory shells, sprinkle a fourth of the cheese over the dough sheet. Cover with another sheet of dough and repeat the buttering and sprinkling process. Top with a third sheet of dough and brush evenly with melted butter.

3.　Cut the dough rectangle into 4 more or less square pieces (for exact squares, trim the rectangle). Fit each square into a mold, laying—not pushing—the dough into the bottom of the mold. Be careful not to catch the dough on the edges of the brioche molds. The dough can flop over the rim as long as it doesn't hook on.

4.　Repeat Steps 2 and 3 with the remaining 3 sheets of dough. For sweet shells, dust with powdered sugar. For savory shells, sprinkle with paprika.

5.　Bake 1 pan at a time, for 12 to 15 minutes, or until lightly browned and slightly puffed. Remove from the oven. As soon as the shells are cool enough to handle, carefully lift them out of the molds and cool on a wire rack.

Little Chocolate and Raspberry Dacquoises

Petites dacquoises au chocolat et aux framboises

Classic *dacquoise* layers are thick—crisp on the outside and soft on the inside. They are extremely sweet. The layers are usually filled with chocolate and/or hazelnut butter cream, which brings the finished dessert to the next level of sweetness: unbearably sweet.

In this variation on the theme, thin layers of hazelnut meringue are filled with rosettes of chocolate ganache alternating with fresh raspberries. The contrast in flavors and textures is delightful, and none of the elements is overly sweet. You can make one large dacquoise, but the berries will be cut when the cake is served, and this will take away from the presentation.

These can be made ahead and refrigerated, but not frozen. You can make some additional ganache and serve it warm, surrounding each dacquoise, or serve the pastries with a combination of sauces. By combining sauces, you can paint your dessert plates. The ganache is excellent for this, since it will not bleed into other sauces.   **Makes 10 individual *dacquoises***

½ recipe (twenty 3-inch rounds) Hazelnut Meringue Layers (page 291)

½ recipe (2 cups) Chocolate Ganache (page 318), prepared the day before, left at room temperature

2 pints (3 cups) fresh raspberries

Powdered sugar, for dusting

½ recipe (2 cups) Chocolate Ganache, warmed (optional)

1½ cups Fresh Berry Sauce (page 331) (optional)

½ recipe (1½ cups) Hazelnut Praline Sauce (page 329) (optional)

½ recipe (1½ cups) Crème Anglaise (page 328) (optional)

1.   Lay 10 of the meringue layers in front of you, smooth side down. Fill a large pastry bag fitted with a ⅜-inch open star tip with ganache. Pipe rosettes around the edge of each disk, leaving a space for a raspberry between rosettes. The rosettes should be the same size as the raspberries. Once you have done the edge of each, pipe a few rosettes of ganache over the rest of each disk.

2.   Fill the spaces between rosettes with raspberries, placing the prettiest berries on the outside. Top with the remaining rounds, smooth side up, and press down gently to attach. Serve immediately or cover and refrigerate for up to 24 hours. Remove from the refrigerator 30 minutes before serving so that the ganache softens a bit. Place the pastries on a baking sheet or on a large piece of wax paper. Sift powdered sugar over and place on dessert plates. Serve with the sauce or sauces of your choice.

Caramel Mousse *Mousse au caramel*

This mousse is served in individual dessert cups, with a piece of rum-soaked Walnut Sponge hidden in the middle, and topped with Caramel Sauce. It is extremely rich and fairly sweet. I used to prepare this as a mousse cake, but it needed a lot of gelatin to keep the rather soft mousse from collapsing as the day went on. Since the mousses are prepared in dessert cups, this version requires very little gelatin.

As always when working with caramel, be sure to use a heavy pot holder and not to splash the caramel on your skin. Sugar begins to caramelize at 340°F; sugar that is deep amber in color, almost burnt, may be as hot as 410°F. And, caramelized sugar will cling to your skin. Since you will be whisking the caramel in this recipe, be sure to prepare the sugar in a deep pot so that none of the caramel will splash out.   Makes 8 individual servings

1 recipe Walnut Sponge (page 281), baked in an 8-inch square pan, freshly made or frozen and thawed

½ cup Simple Syrup (page 334)

2 tablespoons dark rum

1 cup plus 2 tablespoons (8 ounces) sugar

1 cup whipping cream, at room temperature

½ cup whole milk

1 vanilla bean, split

4 large eggs, separated

1 teaspoon powdered gelatin, softened in 1 tablespoon cold water and drained

1 cup whipping cream, cold

⅓ recipe (1 cup) Caramel Sauce (page 330)

1.   Using a serrated knife, cut the sponge in half. Freeze or refreeze one half. Cut the other into eight 2-inch squares. Place 1 square in each of eight 8- to 10-ounce dessert cups, preferably made of glass. Combine the syrup and rum, and generously brush each piece of sponge. Set aside.

2.   Place ¾ cup of sugar in a 1-quart heavy-bottomed stainless steel saucepan. Add 3 to 4 tablespoons water to wet all the sugar without dissolving it or even making it pourable.

3.   Begin heating the sugar over low to medium heat. The heat should remain on the bottom of the pot; flames should not be coming up the side of the pot at any time. As soon as you begin heating the sugar, wash any crystals clinging to the inside of the pot into the rest of the sugar, using a pastry brush dipped in water. Do this before the pot gets too hot, so that the water from

122

the brush does not simply evaporate against the pot and the brush does not burn. If you notice sugar crystals still clinging to the pot once it heats, try to wash them down with a more generous dose of water on the brush.

4. Heat the sugar without disturbing the pot until the sugar begins to boil clear. Once the sugar boils clear, swirl it from time to time to distribute the heat within the syrup. When the sugar just begins to take on a light amber color, watch it carefully and swirl the pot often. It will go to deep caramel within just a few minutes.

5. Once the caramel has reached 370°F, turn off the heat and carefully whisk in the room-temperature cream. Use a long-handled whisk and wrap your hand in a towel to protect yourself from splattering caramel. Begin whisking in a thin stream at first, standing back after the first few tablespoons to allow the sauce to settle. Whisk in the rest of the cream.

6. Combine the milk and the vanilla bean in a small saucepan over the heat and bring to a boil. Add to the caramel-cream mixture.

7. Whisk together the egg yolks and ¼ cup of sugar in a medium mixing bowl until the mixture is pale yellow. Pour one-fourth of the caramel-cream mixture into the egg yolks, whisking well. Pour this back into the caramel-cream mixture, and cook over low heat, stirring constantly with a wooden spoon. Cook just until the mixture coats the back of the spoon, at about 175°F, without letting it come to a boil.

8. Immediately pour the mixture through a medium mesh strainer into a large mixing bowl. Add the drained gelatin. Remove the vanilla bean from the strainer and scrape the seeds into the cream. Discard the pod.

9. Place the mixing bowl in a larger bowl filled with ice. Carefully pour cold water between the 2 bowls without splashing. Cool to room temperature, whisking often. This will set up a bit, due to the gelatin.

10. When the caramel custard is cool, whip the cup of cold cream until stiff but still very smooth. Set aside.

11. Put the egg whites in a clean mixing bowl or the bowl of an electric mixer. Using the whisk attachment, mix on low speed until the whites begin to froth, then increase to medium speed and whip until the whites hold soft peaks. Gradually add the remaining 2 tablespoons of sugar in a thin stream. Once all has been added, increase to high speed and whip until the whites are stiff but not dry.

12. Gently fold the caramel custard into the whipped cream. Fold in one-third of the whites without overmixing. It is all right if some streaks of white remain. Fold in another third of the whites. Finally, fold the caramel mixture into the remaining whites.

continued

13. Divide the mousse among the dessert cups, spooning the mixture gently into each one. Gently shake back and forth to level. Refrigerate for at least 2 hours. (*The mousse may be refrigerated for up to 2 days. If refrigerated for more than 2 hours, cover each dish with plastic wrap.*)

14. To serve, slightly warm the Caramel Sauce. Ladle about 2 tablespoons of sauce over each mousse, tilting the bowl as needed to spread the sauce evenly.

Mosaic of Three Chocolates

Mosaïque aux trois chocolats

The sheer decadence of this unbaked chocolate terrine belies the simplicity of its preparation. Three ganaches—bittersweet, milk, and white—are either piped or spooned into a loaf pan, frozen, and sliced. The terrine can be prepared weeks ahead and frozen, then thawed for slicing, and even refrozen. As long as it is well wrapped, it is virtually indestructible.

The ideal mold for this dessert is manufactured by Magic Line and is available in cake decorating stores. It is a straight-sided aluminum pan measuring 11 × 4½ × 2½ inches, with a two-quart capacity. This yields a perfectly rectangular slice that is just the right size. You can also use two one-quart loaf pans measuring 8 × 4 × 2½ inches, which will give you slightly trapezoidal slices. This recipe is easily halved, so you could use just one one-quart pan. Whatever the mold, it should have well-defined, not rounded, angles.

For added richness I have always served thin slices of mosaic with Crème Anglaise. You may prefer a tart berry sauce or just a pile of fresh berries.   **Makes 32 portions**

1 pound plus 1½ ounces (17½ ounces) good-quality bittersweet chocolate

2 pounds plus 1½ ounces (33½ ounces) good-quality milk chocolate

5 ounces good-quality white chocolate

2½ cups whole milk

1 cup minus 2 tablespoons whipping cream

8 ounces (2 sticks) unsalted butter, softened

⅓ recipe (1 cup) Crème Anglaise (page 328) or 1 cup Fresh Berry Sauce (page 331), made with raspberries, strawberries, and blackberries

1 cup berries, preferably raspberries, strawberries, and blackberries

1. Finely chop all the chocolates and place the bittersweet and the milk chocolate each in a medium mixing bowl; place the white chocolate in a small bowl. Bring the milk and ½ cup plus

1 tablespoon of the cream to a boil in a medium saucepan. Measure the milk and cream and pour half over the bittersweet chocolate and half over the milk chocolate. Let stand for 5 minutes to allow the chocolates to melt.

2. Bring the remaining cream to a boil in the same pot and pour it over the white chocolate. Whisk each chocolate until very smooth. Let cool to room temperature.

3. Place the butter in a small mixing bowl and whisk until smooth. It should be at room temperature. Whisk half the butter into the melted bittersweet chocolate and half into the melted milk chocolate. Mix just until no butter streaks remain. The white chocolate needs no butter. Scrape each ganache into another container (glass, plastic, or stainless steel), cool completely, then cover with plastic wrap, and allow them to set up overnight at room temperature.

4. Line the long sides and bottom of an 11 × 4½ × 2½-inch mold or two 8 × 4 × 2½-inch loaf pans with aluminum foil, leaving the ends unlined. Make sure that the foil is very smooth and fits well into the bottom angles. Leave flaps of foil wide enough to cover the top hanging over the sides of the pan.

5. If you have 3 pastry bags, two ½-inch plain tips, and one ¼-inch plain tip, fill the bags with the ½-inch tips with dark and milk ganaches, making sure that there are no air bubbles inside, and the other bag with the white ganache. If you do not have pastry bags, use 3 spoons.

6. If piping, start with the milk ganache and pipe a long tube along each edge and one in the middle, leaving ½ inch between. Fill the spaces with dark ganache. Pipe thin tubes of white ganache along the lines between the two ganaches. Tap the mold flat on the work surface to flatten the ganaches along the bottom and to force out any air. Starting now with the dark ganache, pipe it on top of the milk, then pipe milk ganache on top of the bottom layer of milk chocolate. Pipe with white between these tubes. Continue piping and alternating until the ganaches are used up and/or the mold is filled. Smooth the top of the mold with a small offset spatula or a rubber spatula. Cover with the flaps of foil and freeze for at least 24 hours. (*The terrine may be frozen for up to 1 month.*)

Pipe ganaches into a prepared mold, or . . .

If not piping, drop dollops of ganache into the mold, using equal amounts of dark and milk chocolate ganache, and about one-fourth white ganache. Tap the mold frequently to level the ganaches and force out air bubbles. Continue until the ganaches are used up and/or the mold is filled. Smooth the top of the mold with a small offset spatula or a rubber spatula. Cover with the flaps of foil and freeze for at least 24 hours. (*The terrine may be frozen for up to 1 month.*)

. . . drop the ganaches by heaping spoonfuls.

7. To unmold, run a hot knife along the unlined ends of the frozen terrine and pull the terrine out by tugging on the flaps of aluminum foil. Unwrap this brick of chocolate and place it on a cutting board. Place the board in the refrigerator for 1 hour to allow the terrine to thaw slightly.

continued

8. Using a thin knife dipped in hot water, then dried for each slice, cut as many ⅓-inch slices as you need. Cut straight down each time, so that the slices are of even thickness. Wrap the terrine in plastic and put it back in the freezer or return to the refrigerator if you are going to slice more.

9. Lay each slice in the middle of a chilled dessert plate. Ladle Crème Anglaise or berry sauce around the slice, or heap berries next to it and serve.

- **By scraping the ganaches into other containers, you ensure that any chocolate remaining in the bottom of the bowl gets mixed in.**

- **Since the milk and cream in these ganaches have been boiled and there are no egg products, they can be left to stand at room temperature without risk.**

- **Make the three ganaches for this mosaic the night before you are going to fill your mold(s). The dessert, however, can be made weeks ahead of time. Should you have leftover ganache, freeze and use for another recipe or as chocolate sauce.**

Roasted Whole Vanilla-studded Pineapple *Ananas rôti à la vanille*

At last, a truly fat-free dessert! Fat free, at least, until you scoop some vanilla ice cream on top. Slice the pineapple while it is still warm, top each ring with a scoop of vanilla ice cream, Coconut Ice Cream (page 217), Tropical Sorbet (page 222), or Ginger Ice Cream (page 218), then drizzle caramel syrup over the top. Or, cut the pineapple into chunks and serve them in *tulipes* made from Coconut-Macadamia Tile Cookie batter (page 165) with your favorite sorbet or ice cream. Or, make a caramelized pineapple tart, spreading the bottom of the baked tart shell with a layer of Mango Cream (page 310). Any way you slice it, this is an unusual, simple, and satisfying dessert. Makes **6 to 8 servings**

SYRUP
½ cup plus 1 tablespoon (4 ounces) sugar

2 vanilla beans, split

6 thin slices peeled fresh ginger

One 4-inch stick cinnamon

3 berries whole allspice, crushed

1 cup water

2 tablespoons finely mashed banana (about ¼ to ⅓ banana)

1 tablespoon dark rum

PINEAPPLE
1 barely ripe whole pineapple (about 3 pounds)

5 vanilla beans, split lengthwise, then cut in half crosswise

1. If possible, make the syrup 12 to 48 hours before the pineapple is to be roasted, to allow the flavor of the spices to fully infuse. It can also be prepared just before roasting.

2. Place the sugar in a small heavy-bottomed saucepan. Add 2 tablespoons water to wet all the sugar without dissolving it. Begin heating the sugar over low to medium heat. The heat should remain on the bottom of the pot; flames should not come up the side of the pot at any time. As soon as you begin heating the sugar, wash any crystals clinging to the inside of the pot into the rest of the sugar, using a pastry brush dipped in water. It is important to do this before the pot gets too hot, so that the water from the brush does not simply evaporate against the pot and the brush does not burn. If you notice sugar crystals still clinging to the pot once it heats, try to wash them down with a more generous dose of water on the brush.

3. Heat the sugar without disturbing the pot until the sugar begins to boil clear. Once the sugar boils clear, swirl it from time to time to distribute the heat within the syrup. When the sugar just begins to take on a light amber color, watch it carefully and swirl the pot often. It will go to deep caramel within just a few minutes. When it reaches about 370°F, turn off the heat. Add the 2 split vanilla beans, the ginger, cinnamon, and allspice. Whisk in the water to stop the cooking. Start slowly, as this will spatter quite a bit, then once the caramel calms down, whisk in the rest of the water. Stir in the mashed banana and the rum. Allow the syrup to cool completely. If the syrup is prepared in advance, refrigerate it with all the spices in an airtight container.

4. Adjust the oven rack low in the oven. Preheat the oven to 425°F.

5. Peel the pineapple as described on page 349. Leaving it whole, remove the center with an apple corer. Stand the pineapple in a deep glass pie plate or a glass baking dish. Using a sharp paring knife, stud the pineapple with the 5 quartered vanilla beans, guiding the cut ends of each half into the flesh of the pineapple at random points. Strain the syrup through a medium mesh strainer all over the pineapple, filling the core.

6. Bake for 1 hour, basting with syrup from time to time. The caramel will permeate the pineapple. Remove the pineapple from the oven and let it cool slightly. Remove the vanilla beans. Slice or cut up and serve. (*The pineapple will keep for 1 week in the refrigerator, stored in its syrup in a covered bowl.*)

Gratin of Fresh Fruit *Gratin de fruits frais*

Based on a *crème chiboust*, a mixture of barely sweetened pastry cream and Italian meringue, this is a great do-ahead dessert. It will help you take advantage of whatever fruits are in season: sliced figs, whole or sliced berries, bananas, pineapple. Thinly sliced home-canned or poached fruits, such as peaches or pears, are equally wonderful, especially if combined with berries. These fruits, suspended in the lemony-light *chiboust*, make a great finish to a rich meal.

The addition of gelatin during preparation makes it simple to make these gratins ahead, then transfer them to individual baking dishes for caramelization. If you prefer to omit the gelatin or if you do not have individual ovenproof dishes, the recipe can be assembled in a large gratin dish and refrigerated without risk of collapse.   Makes 8 servings

I cup freshly squeezed lemon juice (5 to 6 large lemons)

½ cup heavy whipping cream

6 large eggs, separated

1¼ cups (8¾ ounces) granulated sugar

2 tablespoons unbleached all-purpose flour

3 sheets leaf gelatin, or 1 tablespoon granulated, softened in cool water and drained (optional)

3 cups sliced fruit and/or berries

Additional ½ cup (3½ ounces) granulated sugar for finishing

I cup Fresh Berry Sauce (page 331), made with any berries, except blueberries (blueberries are okay for the gratin)

1.   Combine the lemon juice and cream in a medium-size, heavy, stainless steel saucepan and bring to a boil over medium heat. Meanwhile whisk the egg yolks and ¼ cup of sugar together in a medium mixing bowl until the mixture is pale yellow. This should take about 1 minute. Strain the flour over the egg mixture and whisk in.

2.   Pour one-third of the boiling liquid over the egg mixture and whisk immediately until smooth. Pour this mixture back into the pot and cook over a low flame, whisking constantly. Bring the contents back to a boil, then continue cooking for 60 seconds. Remove the pot from the heat and whisk in the softened gelatin, if using it. Leave the custard in the pot to keep it warm while preparing the meringue.

3.   Place ¾ cup of the sugar in a small, heavy saucepan with just enough water to wet all the crystals (about 3 tablespoons). Wash down any remaining crystals from the inside of the pot with a wet pastry brush. Place the pot over a medium flame and bring the sugar to a boil without stirring. If you notice any sugar crystals clinging to the inside of the pot, wash them down with a wet pastry brush.

4. When the sugar boils clear, begin whipping your egg whites on low speed until they begin to froth. Increase the speed to medium and whip until the whites hold a soft peak, then gradually add the remaining ¼ cup of sugar and continue whipping.

5. When the sugar measures 240°F on a candy thermometer, increase the mixer speed to high, where it will remain for just a few minutes.

6. When the sugar reaches 243°F, remove it from the heat. On low speed, add one-third of the sugar to the whites in a very thin stream. Avoid hitting the whisk or beaters with the sugar, as it will fly everywhere, except into the whites. Once you have added one-third of the sugar, increase the speed to medium and add the rest, in twice as heavy a stream.

7. When all the sugar has been added, increase the mixer speed and whip on high speed for 30 seconds. Remove the bowl from the mixer and gently fold the custard into the meringue, one-third at a time.

8. If preparing the gratin in a large oval baking (gratin) dish, lightly butter the bottom and halfway up the inside of the dish. Spread half the gratin mixture evenly across the bottom, using a rubber spatula. Cover the mixture with an even layer of fruit, then spread evenly with the remaining gratin mixture. Refrigerate uncovered for 1 hour to set the gratin (even if no gelatin has been used). (*At this point, the large gratin can be covered with plastic wrap and refrigerated for up to 24 hours. Remove from the refrigerator 1 hour before baking to prevent the dish from cracking when placed in the hot oven.*)

9. If you have individual gratin dishes or ovenproof soup plates, and you have enough room in your refrigerator to keep them all, prepare individual gratins as in Step 8, without buttering the dishes. These, too, may be covered and refrigerated for up to 24 hours.

10. If you need to save space, or you need your soup plates for another course, cover 2 baking sheets with parchment or wax paper. (This can actually be done on 1 sheet, but it is easier to work with 2 baking sheets.) Using an inverted bowl or another template, trace eight 4-inch circles on the papers. Invert the papers, then use a metal or rubber spatula to spread the gratin mixture, filling the circle with a ½-inch-thick disk. Top the disk with fruit, going all the way to the edge, then top the fruit with the remaining gratin mixture. This may be slightly mounded. Be sure that the fruit is completely covered. Refrigerate the baking sheets for 1 hour. Once the disks have set up, cut the papers into 8 individual squares, each with a disk of gratin in the middle. These may be stacked up to 3 layers high, wrapped in plastic, and refrigerated for up to 24 hours.

11. Remove the gratin dishes or soup plates 1 hour before serving time. Also 1 hour before, remove the tray of gratin disks and invert each onto an ovenproof soup plate or gratin dish. Peel back the paper and discard. Using your fingertips, spread the tops of the gratins, including the large one, if that is what you've prepared, with granulated sugar. Do this while the gratins are still cold and firm. Let them come to room temperature.

12. Just before serving, heat your oven to 375°F. Bake the gratins for 5 to 7 minutes, or until they just begin to droop. Brown the tops for 1 minute under your broiler, or if you have a blowtorch, pass it rapidly over the tops (the nozzle should be 5 to 6 inches from the surface). Ladle berry sauce around each gratin (inside the dish) or pass it on the side. Serve immediately.

Rolled Yeasted Pastries

Viennoiserie

VIENNOISERIE LITERALLY MEANS THINGS from Vienna, but the term refers to all the rolled yeasted pastries—croissants and *pains au chocolat*, for example—and it comes from the fact that croissants originated in Vienna. It was during the seventeenth century—in 1683, to be exact—when the Turkish Empire attempted to invade Austria. Some Viennese bread bakers, who were, of course, working at night, heard strange noises. They discovered that the Turks were digging a tunnel under the city's ramparts, in an attempt to surprise the Austrians. The bakers alerted the authorities and the attack was thwarted. After the Austrians declared victory, the same bakers created the croissant, or crescent, the symbol of Turkey, to commemorate their role.

Viennoiserie is the job of the *tourier*, or turner, in the pastry shop. This is the person who turns the croissant dough. These days, it is the tourier's job to make all the pastry doughs, and he or she does so with the aid of a rolling machine, called a *laminoir*, or sheeter. This machine resembles a giant pasta maker and works on the same principle. It makes it possible to roll dough, even tough yeasted dough, into sheets of even thickness. If you want to play around with this concept, roll sheets of fully turned puff pastry or croissant dough through a pasta machine, preferably a manual one, so that the dough does not get away from you.

The pastries in this chapter, while delicious at any time, are more what we think of as morning pastries. Personally, I will take a great croissant over just about anything else, at any time of the day.

Croissants

Croissant Dough / *Pâte à croissant*

Chocolate Rolls / *Pains au chocolat*
    Chocolate-Pistachio Rolls / *Exquises*

Cinnamon Twists / *Torsades à la cannelle*
    Cinnamon Elephant Ears / *Oreilles d'éléphant à la cannelle*
    Raspberry Twists / *Torsades à la framboise*

Raisin Buns / *Pains aux raisins*
    Flaky Raisin Buns / *Pains feuilletés aux raisins*

Apple Turnovers / *Chaussons aux pommes*

Croissants

There is arguably nothing more delectable than a perfectly flaky, light, golden brown croissant. It seems simple enough—just cut triangles of dough, roll them up, let them rise, bake them, *voilà*! But alas, this is one of the trickiest pastries to carry off perfectly.

Many bakers seem to believe that butter—more butter—is better. True, the butter separates the layers of dough in the croissant and makes it flaky, but the dough has its limits as to how much butter it can handle. As in most things, balance is very important.

The French make croissants with margarine as well as butter. Even in some of the best pastry shops in France, croissants made with margarine are not only available, they are actually preferred. French pastry chefs have a high-quality margarine for just such a purpose available to them; we do not, or at least not for home use. French law dictates that *croissants au beurre,* or butter croissants, not be curved. *Croissants ordinaires,* or margarine-based croissants, are the curved ones.

Many American croissants seem to be nice and flaky on the outside, but bready or doughy on the inside. A lack of balance is part of the problem here. The other part is that the *détrempe,* or dough, is left to develop too much like a bread dough. This dough should not develop too much gluten before buttering. Take care also not to allow your croissant dough or croissants to overrise. Probably the single most important reason for bready croissants with a low flake quotient, though, is that they are too large. In France, croissants are small and delicate. The triangles of dough are cut and rolled in such a way that the layers of dough are minimized, allowing these layers to inflate properly without pressing on one another and growing together. If you are tempted to make giant croissants, know that they will have to rise too long, and will turn bready.   **Makes about 20 croissants**

> I recipe (2¾ pounds) Croissant Dough (page 136), very cold but not frozen
>
> I large egg plus I large egg yolk
>
> Pinch of salt

I.   Place the dough on a lightly floured work surface. It does not matter which fold is in front of you. Flour the top of the dough and hit it with a rolling pin several times across the dough to spread it. Give the dough a quarter-turn to the right and hit it again, to flatten it further without building up the gluten. Roll the dough, flouring the top and the work surface as needed, to a 17 × 30-inch rectangle ¼ inch thick (or even thinner, if you can). Lift the dough and replace it on the table for 5 minutes to relax the gluten.

2.   Using a long, sharp, heavy knife, cut ½ inch off each of the long sides, to make a rectangle that is 16 inches wide. Cut this into two 8-inch bands. Cut straight through the dough with the knife; do not use the tip or drag the knife, as this will stretch the dough unevenly.

3. Working with one band at a time, cut the bands into triangles, each with a 5-inch base, alternating the orientation of the triangles, so as not to waste any dough. Do not use the very ends, which will not rise or flake properly.

The rolled dough, cut into triangles

4. In the middle of the base of each triangle, perpendicular to the base, make a ½-inch cut. This will make it easier to stretch the dough. Stack the triangles with the wide end closest to you. Working with 1 triangle at a time, roll it up, starting from the wide end and arching your hands slightly outward as you roll. This will stretch the base to longer than 5 inches. Roll gently, without leaving air gaps between the layers. If the croissants are rolled too tight, they will not have room to expand internally. Roll all the croissants.

Snip the bottom of each triangle . . .

- **By snipping the dough in the middle of the base, you make it much easier to stretch the base of the dough. This, in turn, allows for a lesser buildup of dough in the middle of the croissant, which will then expand and bake much more evenly.**

- **The rolled croissants may be frozen for up to 2 weeks. Freeze on a pan until hard, then put the croissants in a zipper bag and freeze for up to 2 weeks. The night before baking, put the croissants on a parchment-lined baking sheet, and thaw in the refrigerator. Let the croissants come to room temperature before baking, about I hour. Let rise as in Step 6, then bake as in Steps 7 and 8.**

. . . then open the flaps and spread the dough outward . . .

5. Place the croissants on parchment-lined baking sheets. As you do so, curve the ends slightly inward, making sure that the tip of what was the triangle is now tucked under the croissant and pointing away from the ends. Place the croissants 3 to 4 inches apart on the baking sheets.

6. Let the croissants rise in a warm, humid spot, such as a turned-off oven with a pan of water in the bottom. When fully risen, the croissants should be puffy but should not deflate when touched; this should take 1½ to 2 hours.

7. For the last 15 minutes of rising, remove the croissants and the pan of water from the oven. Preheat the oven to 425°F.

8. Beat the egg, egg yolk, and salt with a fork or a whisk until evenly mixed. Gently and without poking the dough, evenly brush the tops and sides of the croissants with egg wash without letting the egg wash drip onto the pans. Place the pans in the oven and immediately lower the temperature to 375°F. Bake for about 20 minutes, switching and rotating the pans after 15 minutes if your oven bakes unevenly. Do not switch the pans sooner or the croissants may collapse. They should be golden brown and crisp. Cool on wire racks. Serve within 8 hours.

. . . to form the rolled croissant, tip tucked underneath.

Croissant Dough *Pâte à croissant*

Making croissants at home is a difficult task. You might want to try your hand at a few batches of this dough. The more you do, the more proficient you will become and the flakier and lighter your croissants will be.

Be sure to leave plenty of time—at least nine hours—to prepare the dough. Before you even start buttering the layers, the dough must rise, then cool down and relax. I recommend that you make the dough portion one day, then butter it the following day. Once the dough is made, it must be thoroughly chilled before it can be rolled.   Makes 2¾ pounds of dough, enough for 20 croissants

DÉTREMPE

2 cakes fresh yeast, or 2 packets (1 tablespoon plus 2 teaspoons) active dry yeast

½ cup plus 1 tablespoon lukewarm water (105°F)

4 cups (22 ounces) all-purpose flour

½ cup (3½ ounces) sugar

2 teaspoons salt

3 tablespoons unsalted butter, melted

½ cup plus 1 tablespoon whole milk, cold

BUTTER PACK

12 ounces (3 sticks) dry unsalted butter (see page 2), cold, or (3 sticks) unsalted butter, cold, and
3 tablespoons all-purpose flour

1.   To prepare the détrempe, dissolve the yeast in the water and let the yeast proof until a thin layer of froth forms on top. Combine the flour, sugar, and salt in a large mixing bowl and mix well with your hands. Using a large wooden spoon, stir in the melted butter, the milk, and the dissolved yeast to form a thick paste. Turn this mixture onto a lightly floured work surface and knead for 1 or 2 minutes, just until the dough comes together. It should be somewhat elastic but not necessarily smooth. If the dough seems dry—if pieces of dough are falling off—knead in some more water. This dough should be supple but not wet. Place the dough in a lightly greased mixing bowl, cover it with a damp cloth, and let it rise in a warm spot until double in bulk, 1 to 1½ hours.

2.   Deflate the dough. Flatten it and lay it on a lightly floured baking pan. Cover the dough with plastic and freeze it for 30 minutes, to slow the yeast. Then cover it tightly and refrigerate until the dough is thoroughly chilled, at least 3 hours or up to overnight.

3.   To prepare the butter pack, use dry butter as is. If it is not dry, cut the butter into 1-inch cubes and place it in an electric mixer fitted with the paddle attachment (not a food processor which would warm the butter). Add the flour. Mix the butter and flour until all the flour is incorporated and the consistency is very even. Divide the butter evenly into 2 portions. Wrap and refrigerate 1 portion for 1 hour.

4.   Remove the détrempe from the refrigerator. Roll it into a rectangle, about 36 × 12 inches and about ½ inch thick. Using your fingers or a metal icing spatula, spread the butter as evenly as possible across two thirds of the dough, leaving a 1-inch border around the edges of the dough. Fold the dough in thirds, starting with the unbuttered part, into a folded square of dough with 3 layers of détrempe and 2 of butter. Give the dough a quarter-turn to the right. Hit the dough with a rolling pin, then roll it out again into a rectangle with the same dimensions as the first. Fold it in thirds. The détrempe is not buttered on this turn, but the butter is sealed in. Wrap tightly in plastic. Freeze the dough for 30 minutes, then refrigerate it for 1 hour.

Spread the butter onto two-thirds of the rolled *détrempe*.

5.   About 30 minutes before removing the dough from the refrigerator, remove the second portion of butter from the refrigerator. Repeat the buttering and turning process as in Step 4, making sure that you are always turning the dough in the same direction. If you need to, mark the dough after each turn by poking your finger in at one edge to indicate how many turns, and where the last fold was made. Wrap the dough tightly in plastic. Freeze it for 30 minutes, then refrigerate it for at least 2 hours or, preferably, overnight. The dough is now ready to use.

A Word about Almond Croissants

You may have enjoyed freshly baked almond croissants in America. Made from Croissant Dough (page 136) wrapped around Almond Cream (page 314) and topped with sliced almonds, they are quite delicious. The inspiration for these, however, is something else entirely.

The almond croissants available in most French pastry shops are made of leftovers—day-old croissants that have been cut in half horizontally, dipped in rum syrup to offset their dryness, filled with almond cream, topped with sliced almonds, and baked. Fancier shops glaze these with a transparent *glaçage à l'eau*, or powdered sugar mixed with water and rum. I don't think the patrons know that they are eating yesterday's croissants.

You can make today's croissants into *croissants aux amandes* by filling Croissants (page 134) with Almond Cream before rolling them in Step 4 of the recipe. Place no more than 1 tablespoon of the cream near the wide end of the triangle. Since the cream contains eggs and the croissants will be sitting at room temperature for quite a while before being baked, you might prefer to use store-bought almond paste, which is available in 7-ounce tubes in many supermarkets.

Chocolate Rolls *Pains au chocolat*

Not surprisingly, the French have chocolate sticks that are made especially for filling rolls of crois-sant dough. The chocolate is bittersweet, which, since it's not high in cocoa butter content, holds its shape during baking. You will have to fashion your own chocolate sticks for this recipe. Makes about 30 chocolate rolls

> 1 pound extra bittersweet chocolate
>
> 1 recipe (2¾ pounds) Croissant Dough (page 136), very cold but not frozen
>
> 2 large eggs plus 1 large egg yolk
>
> Pinch of salt

1. Cut rods or slivers of chocolate. Arrange 30 portions on a baking sheet. The piles should be 2½ inches long, so that they show ever so slightly out the ends of the rolls. Set aside.

2. Place the dough on a lightly floured work surface. It does not matter which fold is in front of you. Flour the top of the dough and hit it with a rolling pin several times across the top to spread it. Give the dough a quarter-turn to the right and hit it again, to flatten it further without building up the gluten. Roll the dough, flouring the top and the work surface as needed, to a 26 × 16-inch rectangle ¼ inch thick (or even thinner, if you can). Lift the dough and replace it on the table to relax the gluten.

3. Using a long, sharp, heavy knife, cut ½ inch off each of the sides to make a 25 × 15-inch rectangle. Cut this into five 5-inch bands, and each of the bands into 6 rectangles, each 2½ inches wide. With a pastry brush dipped in water, wet the short end of each rectangle that is farther from you.

4. Divide the chocolate among the pastry rectangles, placing a piece of chocolate at the near short end of each rectangle. Roll each rectangle in thirds, so that the seam is in the middle of the bottom and the dampened dough seals the roll. Press down firmly. Place on parchment-lined bak-ing sheets 2 to 3 inches apart. (*The Chocolate Rolls may be frozen as described on page 135.*)

5. Let the rolls rise covered in a warm, humid spot, such as a turned-off oven with a pan of water in the bottom, 1 to 1½ hours. When fully risen, the rolls should be puffy but should not deflate when touched.

6. For the last 15 minutes of rising, remove the rolls and pan of water from the oven. Preheat the oven to 425°F.

7. Beat the eggs, egg yolk, and salt with a fork or a whisk until evenly mixed. Gently and with-out poking the dough, evenly brush the tops and sides of the rolls with egg wash. Avoid letting egg wash drip onto the pans. Place the pans in the oven and immediately lower the temperature to 375°F. Bake for about 15 minutes, switching and rotating the pans after 10 minutes. The rolls should be golden brown and crisp. Cool on wire racks. Serve within 8 hours.

Chocolate-Pistachio Rolls *Exquises*

These are richer than Chocolate Rolls, if that is possible, and the combination of chocolate and pistachio is quite, well, exquisite.   Makes about 30 rolls

I cup (6 ounces) mini semisweet baking chips or finely chopped semisweet chocolate

½ recipe (½ cup) coarsely ground Pistachio Paste (page 322)

I recipe (2¾ pounds) Croissant Dough, very cold but not frozen

2 large eggs, plus I large egg yolk

Pinch of salt

1.   Combine the chocolate and Pistachio Paste in a small mixing bowl. Set aside.

2.   Prepare and cut the dough as in Steps 2 and 3 of the recipe for Chocolate Rolls.

3.   Using a small spoon, spread about 1 tablespoon of the chocolate-pistachio mixture at the near short end of each rectangle and, leaving a ½-inch border on either end, roll up as described in Step 4 of the master recipe. (*The rolls may be frozen as described on page 135.*)

4.   Continue with Steps 5, 6, and 7 of the recipe for Chocolate Rolls.

Cinnamon Twists *Torsades à la cannelle*

These breakfast pastries are simple and crisp. Their sweetness is tempered by the butter in the dough and the cinnamon. They are perfect with a cup of *café au lait* in the morning or with tea in the afternoon. Makes approximately 40 twists

> 1 recipe (2¾ pounds) Croissant Dough (page 136)
>
> 2 large eggs plus 1 large egg yolk
>
> 1 cup (7 ounces) sugar
>
> 1 tablespoon ground cinnamon

1. Place the dough on a lightly floured work surface. It does not matter which fold is in front of you. Flour the top of the dough and hit it with a rolling pin several times across the dough to spread it. Give the dough a quarter-turn to the right and hit it again, to flatten it further without building up the gluten. Roll the dough, flouring the top and the work surface as needed, to a 40 × 24-inch rectangle ¼ inch thick (or even thinner, if you can). Lift the dough and replace it on the table, to relax the gluten.

2. Beat the eggs and egg yolk with a fork or a whisk until evenly mixed. Combine the sugar and cinnamon in a small bowl and mix evenly. Brush the top of the dough with a thin film of egg wash. Using two-thirds of the cinnamon sugar, very evenly coat two-thirds of the dough the long way, leaving one-third uncoated. Fold the uncoated flap of dough over the middle section, then fold the other on top. Brush with more egg wash, then coat with the remaining cinnamon sugar. You should have a 40 × 8-inch strip.

3. Using a sharp, heavy knife, cut away ½ inch from a short end of the dough. Cut the block into even 1-inch slices, discarding the last ½ inch of dough. (*The strips may be frozen for up to 2 weeks. Place them on a baking sheet and wrap well with plastic. Thaw overnight in the refrigerator. Bring to room temperature, twist the strips, and let them rise.*)

4. Line 2 baking sheets with parchment paper. Pick up a folded strip, give it 2 twists, and place it on a sheet to rise, uncovered, leaving at least 2 inches between strips. Repeat with the remaining strips.

5. Let the twists rise in a warm, humid place, such as a turned-off oven with a pan of water in the bottom, 1½ to 2 hours. When finally risen, the strips should be puffy and somewhat spongy.

6. For the last 15 minutes of rising, remove the strips and pan of water from the oven. Adjust the oven racks to divide the oven into thirds and preheat to 425°F.

7. Place the twists directly in the oven and immediately lower the oven temperature to 375°F. Bake for 15 to 20 minutes, or until the twists are brown and crisp. Cool on the pans. Eat within 8 hours of baking.

Cinnamon Elephant Ears *Oreilles d'éléphant à la cannelle*

Made with the same dough and topping as Cinnamon Twists, these morning pastries resemble palmiers. They take up a lot of room on a baking sheet, so don't try to bake more than 6 per sheet. On the other hand, each pastry uses half the amount of dough as does a twist, yielding a thinner, crisper finished product.   **Makes 24 pastries**

½ recipe (about 1¼ pounds) Croissant Dough (page 136), cold

1 large egg plus 1 large egg yolk

½ cup (3½ ounces) sugar

2 teaspoons ground cinnamon

1. Place the dough on a lightly floured work surface. It does not matter which fold is in front of you. Flour the top of the dough and hit it with the side of a rolling pin several times to spread it. Give the dough a quarter-turn to the right and hit it again, to flatten it further without building up the gluten. Roll the dough, flouring the top and the work surface as needed, into a 10 × 24-inch rectangle, about ¼ inch thick. Lift the dough and place it back on the table, enabling the gluten to relax.

2. Beat the egg and the yolk with a fork or a whisk so that the egg wash consistency is even. Combine the sugar and cinnamon in a small bowl and mix evenly. Brush the top of the dough with a thin film of egg wash. Using three-quarters of the cinnamon sugar, coat the dough evenly. Loosely, but evenly, roll one long edge of the dough toward the middle, then repeat with the opposite edge. Leave a 1-inch space between the two rolls. Brush the tops of the rolls with more egg wash, then coat with the remaining cinnamon sugar. Cut the dough in half, then transfer the two pieces to a parchment-lined baking sheet. Freeze, uncovered, for 30 minutes to firm the dough (do not freeze any longer).

3. Remove the dough from the freezer and place one double roll on a cutting board. Using a sharp, heavy knife, cut away ½ inch from the previously uncut end of dough, then cut the roll into even 1-inch slices. (*If you plan to freeze any of the strips, do it now by wrapping them well on a parchment or foil-lined baking sheet. They may be close together for freezing and may be frozen for up to 2 weeks. Thaw overnight in the refrigerator, then separate the pastries by at least 3 inches and let them rise on parchment-lined baking sheets.*)

continued

4. Place the slices on their sides on parchment-lined baking sheets to rise, leaving at least 3 inches on all sides. Repeat with the remaining double roll.

5. Let the pastries rise in a warm, humid place, such as a turned-off oven with a pan of water in the bottom, 1 to 1½ hours. When finally risen, the strips should be puffy and somewhat spongy.

6. For the last 15 minutes of rising, remove the strips and pan of water from the oven. Adjust the oven racks to divide it into thirds and preheat to 425°F.

7. Place the twists directly in the oven and immediately lower the oven temperature to 375°F. Bake for 15 to 20 minutes, or until the twists are brown and crisp. Cool on the pans. Eat within 8 hours of baking.

Raspberry Twists *Torsades à la framboise*

Prepare the Cinnamon Twists recipe, replacing the egg wash and cinnamon sugar with 1½ to 2 cups of Raspberry Preserves (page 338), spreading them in a thin layer. Continue as per Cinnamon Twists. Dust with powdered sugar to serve.

Raisin Buns *Pains aux raisins*

These coiled breakfast pastries are made from Brioche Dough. The dough must be cold and firm, or you will not be able to roll it up. Traditionally, the rolls are filled with Almond Cream and rum-soaked raisins. They are equally wonderful with chopped dried apricots or pears and walnut pieces.

The buns dry out rather quickly, unfortunately, and so must be eaten within 4 hours of baking. If your dough and Almond Cream have not been previously frozen, you can prepare several rolls and bake them as needed.   Makes 20 buns

½ recipe (about 1 pound) Brioche Dough (page 268)

½ recipe (1½ cups) Almond Cream (page 314), freshly made or cold and softened

1½ cups rum-soaked raisins (see page 14), drained

½ cup (5½ ounces) Apricot Preserves, homemade (page 336) or store-bought, or powdered sugar, for dusting

1. Divide the dough in half, leaving one half in the refrigerator. Roll the dough out on a lightly floured work surface, to a 10 × 6-inch rectangle. Trim the dough and press any scraps into the rectangle. Turn the dough so that a long side is closest to you. Spread evenly with half the Almond Cream, leaving a ½-inch border all around. Sprinkle with half the raisins, then press them gently into the cream. Starting from the long side closest to you, roll the dough tightly. (*The roll may be frozen, whole or cut in half. Wrap well in plastic, then freeze it on a tray. Thaw overnight in the refrigerator. Slice the dough while it is still cold, then place the pieces on a baking sheet to rise.*)

2. Place the roll on a lightly floured baking sheet and refrigerate while repeating this process with the other piece of dough. Allow the rolls to chill until firm before slicing, about 30 minutes.

3. Line 2 or 3 baking sheets with parchment paper. Using a sharp heavy knife, cut the rolls into even 1-inch slices. Lay these flat on the baking sheets, leaving 2 to 3 inches between rolls. If the rolls have become misshapen during cutting, round them again with your fingers. Let the buns rise until puffy and spongy, about 1 hour in a warm, humid spot, such as a turned-off oven with a pan of water in the bottom.

4. For the last 15 minutes of rising, remove the buns and pan of water from the oven. Preheat the oven to 400°F.

5. Bake the buns for 10 to 15 minutes, or until golden brown on top and lightly browned underneath. They should spring back when lightly touched in the middle, and the Almond Cream should feel set. Let the buns cool to room temperature on the pans.

6. Heat the Apricot Preserves, if using, in a small saucepan until they begin to boil and can be brushed. If too thick, add a few drops of water. Brush the tops of the buns and serve. Or omit the preserves and dust the tops of the buns lightly with powdered sugar.

Flaky Raisin Buns *Pains feuilletés aux raisins*

Prepare the recipe for Raisin Buns, replacing the Brioche Dough with fully turned Croissant Dough. Top with powdered sugar rather than Apricot Preserves.

Apple Turnovers *Chaussons aux pommes*

It is not uncommon for French parents to give their children a few extra francs so they may stop at the local bakery and pick up a *chausson aux pommes* en route to school. These turnovers are simple yet satisfying, and equally wonderful as a midafternoon snack with tea.

Whereas the apple filling is classic, you can make your turnovers with any cooked fruit filling. It must be cooked, however, as raw fruit will exude its juices while baking, leaving the crust soggy. Likewise, the cooked filling must be thick and, if necessary, bound with cornstarch or flour to absorb any juices. A thick applesauce needs no binders, however.

Traditionally, chaussons are made by the *tourier* in a French pastry shop. He will roll long bands of puff pastry, then mark the surface of the dough with a row of 4- to 5-inch circles. After dampening the dough slightly, the tourier places a dollop of applesauce in the middle of each circle. He then folds the entire band of dough in half lengthwise and cups his hands around the enclosed filling to force out any air that may have been caught inside. The tourier will then cut away semicircles of dough with a fluted round cutter, placed so that the fold of the dough runs down the middle of the cutter.

This method is very time-efficient, but creates a great deal of scrap dough, which is much more easily used up in a pastry shop than at home. For this reason, I prefer to make my chaussons with square pieces of dough, folded in half to form triangular turnovers.   **Makes 8 turnovers**

½ recipe (1 pound) Puff Pastry (page 296) or 1 package store-bought, thawed

⅔ recipe (2 cups) Buttered Applesauce with Vanilla (page 332), Chunky Applesauce (page 333), or Spicy Applesauce (page 333), cold

1 large egg yolk stirred with 1 teaspoon cold water

1.   On a lightly floured surface, roll the homemade Puff Pastry into a rectangle, about 10×20 inches and ⅛ to ¼ inch thick. Lift the dough up to detach it from the table, then replace it. If using store-bought dough, unwrap and unfold carefully so that it does not crack. Trim ¼ inch from all edges of either dough, using a sharp, heavy knife.

2.   Cutting straight down with your knife (not dragging the tip, which will stretch the dough), cut the dough into 8 squares, about 4 inches each. Separate the squares slightly. Brush 2 adjacent edges of each square very lightly with cold water.

3.   Remove the filling from the refrigerator and stir to loosen. Place about ¼ cup of applesauce in the middle of each square, then fold the square into a triangle, placing the undampened edges over the dampened ones. As you fold the dough, press out any air surrounding the filling. This will prevent the turnovers from exploding during baking. Match the dough's edges as best as you can, then press to seal.

4.   Place the turnovers on a parchment-lined baking sheet, leaving at least 1½ inches between pastries. Brush evenly with egg wash, avoiding puddling at the edges. Refrigerate, uncovered, for 1 hour before baking. (*After 1 hour, the turnovers can be covered completely with plastic and refrigerated overnight, or frozen for up to 2 weeks. If freezing, trim and decorate as in Step 5 before freezing; when ready to bake, place the frozen turnovers directly in a hot oven.*)

5.   Heat your oven to 375°F. Remove the turnovers from the refrigerator and, with a single, downward motion, cut away about ⅛ inch from each cut edge to make them even, and remove any egg wash that may have dripped down. Using a small, sharp paring knife, lightly cut through the top ¹⁄₁₆ inch of dough to form a featherlike pattern that will appear as the dough bakes. Take care not to cut all the way through to the filling.

6.   Bake the turnovers for 20 to 25 minutes, or until puffed and golden brown. If your oven is uneven, turn the pan halfway through the baking time. Use a wide metal spatula to transfer the piping hot turnovers to warmed salad plates and serve immediately, or cool on wire racks and serve at room temperature. The turnovers may be rewarmed in a 400°F oven for about 5 minutes. These will keep, wrapped and refrigerated, for up to 24 hours. Reheat before serving.

Cookies

Petits fours secs

I RECALL THAT AT PÂTISSERIE Hardel in the Sixteenth Arrondissement of Paris, Monday was *petits fours secs* day. That was the day we used up all the egg whites left from the ice creams and custards we had prepared during the week before, turning them into cookies. Each recipe—and there were many—was pretty simple to prepare. Several were transformed into two or three different cookies, just by changing the shape or a topping. Some were tedious to execute, once the batter was made. But by the end of my stay at that particular pastry shop, Monday had become my favorite day of the week.

You, too, will be creating a fair amount of egg whites by making the recipes in this book.

You can save them and freeze them (see page 4) for your cookie-making days. These recipes for *petits fours secs*, literally dry little baked things, will help diminish your supply, though not all the recipes are based on egg whites, of course. And believe it or not, some are actually fairly low in fat. Of course, that does not matter when one consumes them 100 grams at a time (which is how they are sold in France).

Many of these recipes will help you hone your technique with a pastry bag. In fact, if you feel that you need practice in that area, start by making *Éponges* or *Duchesses* (see pages 156 and 163). These are relatively easy recipes that call for regularly sized cookies.

Most of these cookies will keep for at least several days at room temperature. If you are planning a dessert buffet or a tea, or if you plan to make cookies for the holidays, you can make several types of cookies over a few days' time.

Three Puff Pastry Cookies
     Palm Leaf Cookies / *Palmiers*
     Straws / *Pailles*
     Pinwheels / *Spirales*

Two Chewy Meringue Cookies / *Éponges et miroirs*
     Sponges / *Éponges*
     Mirrors / *Miroirs*

French Macaroons / *Macarons*
     Hazelnut Macaroons / *Macarons aux noisettes*
     Coffee Filling / *Garniture au café*

Chocolate-spread Hazelnut Wafers / *Biarritz*
     Hazelnut Sandwich Cookies / *Duchesses*
     Rum-soaked Raisin Wafers / *Palets aux raisins*

Almond Tile Cookies / *Tuiles d'amandes*
     Coconut-Macadamia Tile Cookies / *Tuiles tropicales*

Rolled Cigarette Cookies / *Cigarettes*
     Tulip Shells / *Tulipes*

Madeleines
     Chocolate-Orange Madeleines / *Madeleines au chocolat*

Cat Tongues / *Langues de chat*

Rolled Butter Cookies / *Sablés*
     Raspberry Ring Cookies / *Couronnes aux framboises*

Almond Shortbread Cookies / *Zéphyrs*
     Chocolate Almond Shortbread Cookies / *Zéphyrs au chocolat*

Spritz Cookies, Paris Style / *Sablés viennois*

Florentines / *Florentins*

Three Puff Pastry Cookies

The texture and flavor of Puff Pastry can only be improved by the addition of sugar, carmelized by baking. Here are three recipes that emphasize the pure and simple qualities of this versatile pastry.

Palm Leaf Cookies *Palmiers*

A perfect *palmier* is a thing of beauty. Graceful swirls of crisp, flaky dough enclose sugar that has caramelized in the dough's butter. While palmiers require Puff Pastry, they are quite simple to prepare, and a single batch has a high yield. Store-bought pastry works just fine.

There is one very important trick worth noting here: Once you have rolled and sugared the dough, it is crucial not to cut it along its long edges before folding it into the palm shape. These edges must remain folded and closed. If they are cut, and consequently opened, they will spread apart like fingers during baking, causing the palmiers to buckle, unfurl, and lose their shape. This is true only for palmiers and pinwheels (see page 154); all other cookies and savory pastries made from *feuilletage* should be cut along the edges so that they do spread and open (see page 300).   Makes about 72 cookies

½ recipe (1 pound) Puff Pastry (page 296), preferably at 4 turns, or 1 package store-bought pastry, cold

2 cups (14 ounces) sugar

I.   If using homemade pastry, give the dough its last 2 turns in granulated sugar, whether it was frozen after 4 turns or made fresh. Dust the work surface with sugar. When you roll the dough, spread a thin, even layer of sugar on top before folding and turning the dough. Repeat. Wrap the dough completely in plastic and refrigerate for 1 hour.

2.   Roll out the homemade dough on a lightly sugared work surface to a width of 10 inches and a thickness of ¼ to ⅛ inch. For homemade dough, the length will be about 20 inches; store-bought dough will measure half that length and requires no rolling. Spread a thin, even layer of sugar over the dough. Fold one long edge (for store-bought dough, this should be an edge of folded dough, not dough that has been cut) evenly toward the middle to form a 2-inch flap. Repeat this with the opposite edge. Taking care not to curl the edge of the first flap, fold in another flap on each side. These flaps will be slightly wider than the first and will leave a strip about 1 inch wide in the middle. Make sure that the flaps are equal in width

Fold the sugared dough evenly, leaving a space down the middle.

along the length of the dough. Gently lay one flap on top of the other, so that all the edges are even, taking care not to stretch the dough that runs between the 2 flaps. Repeat, if using store-bought dough. If necessary, cut the roll or rolls into 2 or 3 pieces, for ease in handling. Wrap the rolls individually in plastic and freeze for at least 1 hour. (*The pastry may be frozen for up to 1 month. It may be sliced and baked 1 roll at a time. Thaw for 1 hour in the refrigerator before slicing.*)

3.   Adjust the oven racks to divide the oven into thirds and preheat the oven to 400°F. Line 2 baking sheets with parchment paper.

4.   Remove one of the rolls from the freezer. If the dough has been frozen for more than 1 hour, thaw it slightly in the refrigerator. The pastry must be quite firm when cut; this will make slicing it thin much easier. Using a sharp, heavy knife, cut the roll into even ¼-inch slices. Cut the entire roll at once, in case it starts to thaw. Lay 12 to 15 palmiers flat on each baking sheet, spacing them evenly at least 2 inches apart. They will resemble books. Open the books about ½ inch to allow for even spreading without buckling. Bake for 10 minutes, or just until the edges start to turn golden.

5.   Meanwhile, if you plan to bake more palmiers, cut and lay them on parchment paper that has been cut to the size of the baking sheets.

6.   Carefully remove the baking sheets from the oven and flip each palmier over with a metal spatula. As you flip each, flatten it with the spatula. Return the baking sheets to the oven for 5 to 10 minutes more, or until golden. Watch carefully, as the sugar can burn quickly. Remove from the oven and carefully slide the paper onto a flat surface to let the palmiers cool. It is not necessary to cool these on a rack, only to remove them from the hot baking sheets. Cool the baking sheets slightly, then slide on another batch and bake.

7.   Once they are completely cooled, serve immediately or store the palmiers in an airtight container at room temperature. These will lose their crispness when exposed to humidity, since both the caramel and the pastry are quite absorbent, so keep them under wraps. (*The palmiers may be stored in an airtight container for up to 5 days.*)

Straws *Pailles*

I'm not quite sure why these sandwiches of caramelized puff pastry and raspberry preserves are called *pailles*, or straws, but I can tell you this: If you're looking for a small pastry that is more delicious and even simpler than *palmiers*, this is it. The raspberry filling is classic, but you can create your own variation on a theme by filling your puff pastry wafers with Chocolate Ganache (page 318), Caramelized Hazelnut Paste (page 320), or Chocolate-Hazelnut Paste (page 322). Makes about **36 sandwiched pastries**

½ recipe (1 pound) Puff Pastry (page 296), preferably at 4 turns, or I package store-bought cold

2 cups (7 ounces) sugar

½ cup Raspberry Preserves, homemade (see page 338) or store-bought, at room temperature, for filling

Powdered sugar, for dusting (optional)

1. If using homemade pastry, give the dough its last 2 turns in granulated sugar, whether it was frozen after 4 turns or made fresh. Dust the work surface with sugar. When you roll the dough, spread a thin, even layer of sugar on top before folding and turning the dough. Repeat. Wrap the dough completely in plastic and refrigerate for 1 hour.

2. Roll out the homemade dough on a lightly sugared work surface to a width of 10 inches and a thickness of ¼ to ⅛ inch. For homemade dough, the length will be about 20 inches; store-bought dough will measure half that length and requires no further rolling. Trim ¼ inch from each of the long (closed) edges, to allow the dough to spread evenly as it bakes. Spread a thin, even layer of sugar over the dough. Measure the width of the dough, then cut 3 strips of equal width along the length of the dough. Stack these strips one on top of the other, keeping the edges as flush as possible. If using store-bought dough, repeat stacking with the second piece. If necessary, cut the stack or stacks into 2 or 3 pieces, for ease in handling. Wrap the stacks individually in plastic and freeze for at least 1 hour. (*The pastry may be frozen for up to 1 month. It may be baked 1 stack at a time. Thaw for 1 hour in the refrigerator.*)

3. Adjust the oven racks to divide the oven into thirds and preheat the oven to 400°F. Line 3 baking sheets with parchment paper.

4. Remove one of the strips from the freezer. If the dough has been frozen for more than 1 hour, thaw it slightly in the refrigerator. The pastry must be quite firm when cut; this will make slicing it thin much easier. Using a sharp, heavy knife, cut the dough into even ¼-inch slices. Cut the entire strip at once, in case it starts to thaw.

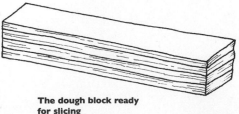

The dough block ready for slicing

Lay 12 to 16 pailles flat on each baking sheet, spacing them evenly at least 3 inches between the long edges and 1 inch between the short edges. Bake for 10 minutes, or just until the edges start to turn golden.

5. Meanwhile, if you plan to bake more pailles, cut and lay them on parchment paper cut to the size of the baking sheets. If the layers of dough begin to separate, put them back where they belong, and they will stick during baking.

6. Carefully remove the baking sheets from the oven and flip each paille over with a metal spatula. Return the baking sheets to the oven for 5 to 10 minutes more, or until golden. Watch carefully, as the sugar can burn quickly. Remove from the oven and carefully slide the paper onto a flat surface to let the pailles cool. It is not necessary to cool these on a rack, only to remove them from the hot baking sheets. Cool the baking sheets slightly, then slide on another batch and bake.

7. Once completely cooled, place a dab of preserves in the middle of half the baked wafers (¼ to ½ teaspoon per cookie, depending on how runny the preserves are). Place another wafer on top and press down gently to spread the filling evenly. Dust with powdered sugar, if desired, and serve immediately or store in an airtight container at room temperature. (*The pailles may be stored in an airtight container for up to 3 days.*)

Baked pailles, sandwiched with raspberry preserves

When dusting with powdered sugar, lay the cookies edge-to-edge on a paper-lined baking sheet so as to not waste any sugar. If you wish, you can lay doilies or strips of paper randomly on top of the sandwiched cookies to make patterns.

Pinwheels *Spirales*

This will show you what Puff Pastry can really do! This is a variation on the *palmier*, but because it is formed like a pinwheel, then folded in half before baking, it spreads out along the folded edge, making it a rather whimsical addition to a cookie platter. As with *palmiers*, it is important not to trim the long, folded edges. If you do, these edges will open during baking, and the pinwheels will lose their nice shape.   Makes about 72 cookies

½ recipe (1 pound) Puff Pastry (page 296), preferably at 4 turns, or 1 package store-bought pastry, cold

2 cups (14 ounces) granulated sugar

¾ cup Raspberry Preserves, homemade (page 338) or store-bought

Powdered sugar (optional)

1.   If using homemade pastry, give the dough its last 2 turns in granulated sugar, whether it was frozen after 4 turns or made fresh. Dust the work surface with sugar. When you roll the dough, spread a thin, even layer of sugar on top before folding and turning the dough. Repeat. Wrap the dough completely in plastic and refrigerate for 1 hour. If using store-bought pastry, lay each sheet of pastry on a sugared work surface. Spread the top with a thin, even layer of sugar. Fold the dough in thirds. Repeat with the other sheet of dough. Wrap in plastic and refrigerate for 15 minutes.

2.   Roll out the dough on a lightly sugared work surface to a width of 10 inches and a thickness of ¼ to ⅛ inch. For homemade dough, the length will be about 20 inches; store-bought dough will measure half that length. Turn the dough so that a long, uncut edge is facing you. Spread a thin layer of preserves on the dough, leaving a ½-inch border along the far edge; use only half the preserves if using store-bought dough, as you will be repeating this process with the other piece. Starting with the edge nearest you, roll the dough tightly, making sure that there are no gaps. If necessary, cut the roll or rolls into 2 or 3 pieces, for ease in handling. Wrap the rolls individually in plastic and freeze for at least 1 hour. (*The pastry may be frozen for up to 1 month. It may be baked 1 roll at a time.*)

3.   Adjust the oven racks to divide the oven into thirds and preheat the oven to 400°F. Line 2 baking sheets with parchment paper.

4.   Remove one of the rolls from the freezer. If the dough has been frozen for more than 1 hour, thaw it slightly in the refrigerator. The pastry must be quite firm when cut; this makes slicing it thin much easier. Using a sharp, heavy knife, cut the roll into even ¼-inch slices. Cut the entire roll at once, in case it starts to thaw. Fold each pinwheel in half and place 12 to 15 on each baking sheet, spacing them evenly about 2 inches apart. Bake for 10 minutes, or until the pinwheels just begin to brown.

5. Meanwhile, if you plan to bake more pinwheels, cut and lay them on parchment paper cut to the size of the baking sheets.

6. Carefully remove the baking sheets from the oven and flip each pinwheel over with a metal spatula. Return the baking sheets to the oven for 5 to 10 minutes more, or until golden. Watch carefully, as the sugar and preserves can burn quickly. Remove from the oven and carefully slide the paper off onto a flat surface to let the pinwheels cool. It is not necessary to cool these on a rack, only to remove them from the warm baking sheets. Cool the baking sheets slightly, then slide on another batch and bake.

7. Once completely cooled, dust lightly with powdered sugar. Serve immediately or store the pinwheels in an airtight container at room temperature. These will lose their crispness when exposed to humidity, since both the caramel and the pastry are quite absorbent, so try to limit exposure to the elements. (*The pinwheels may be stored in an airtight container for up to 5 days.*)

Two Chewy Meringue Cookies

Éponges et miroirs

Both of these cookies are made from the same batter, so you can easily make a half batch of each. The *éponges*, or sponges, are almond-coated meringues, sandwiched together with dabs of raspberry preserves. If the meringues are piped out properly, they will form hemispheres. When two are sandwiched together, they become little almond-studded balls—perfect light mouthfuls of chewy meringue.

The *miroirs*, or mirrors, are circles of meringue batter, covered with almonds and baked with Almond Cream centers. The cookies are then glazed with apricot preserves. These are quite elegant, yet extremely simple to prepare.

Sponges *Éponges*

When you make this batter, put the almonds in the sieve first. If you put the sugar in first, it will fall through the sieve before you have a chance to put anything else in. Makes about 45

½ cup plus 1 tablespoon (4 ounces) granulated sugar

1 cup (5 ounces) packed ground blanched almonds

2 level tablespoons unsifted all-purpose flour

4 large egg whites, at room temperature

2 cups (8 ounces) chopped, slivered, or sliced blanched almonds

¼ cup Raspberry Preserves, homemade (page 338) or store-bought

Powdered sugar, for dusting

1. Position the oven racks to divide the oven into thirds. Preheat to 375°F.

2. Set aside 2 tablespoons of the sugar. Put the ground almonds, the flour, and the remaining sugar in a medium mesh sieve and sift them together onto a sheet of wax paper. Set aside.

3. Put the egg whites in a clean mixing bowl or the bowl of an electric mixer. Using the whisk attachment, mix on low speed until the whites begin to froth, then increase to medium speed and whip until the whites hold soft peaks. Gradually add the 2 tablespoons sugar in a thin stream. Once all has been added, increase to high speed and whip until the whites are stiff but not dry.

4.   Pick up the wax paper with the sifted dry ingredients by the long ends, in one hand. Shake the dry mix in a constant thin stream over the whites, folding with a rubber spatula as you do so. Place the bowl on a coiled towel to keep it from spinning. Make sure to dip the spatula to the bottom of the bowl, to pick up any dry ingredients that sink. Handle this batter carefully so that it will retain its lightness.

5.   Fill a pastry bag fitted with a ⅜-inch plain tip. Use nonstick baking sheets or line them with foil or parchment paper. Pipe out thick, quarter-size mounds of batter onto the pans. Keep the size even by touching the tip to the pan, squeezing until you have the right size, then lifting the tip quickly and moving on to the next position on the pan. These will not spread much, so they can be as close as ¾ inch on the pans.

6.   Pipe out all the batter, then sprinkle evenly with the almonds. If the piped cookies are close together, be careful not to connect them with an almond.

7.   Bake for 7 to 10 minutes, or until the nuts are lightly browned and the meringues feel set when lightly touched. Let cool on the pans. Loosen the cookies by carefully running a metal spatula underneath.

8.   Turn half the meringues flat side up. Using a small metal spatula or a pastry bag fitted with a ¼-inch plain tip, dab about ¼ teaspoon of preserves onto the inverted cookies. Top each with another cookie, rounded side up. Press to attach well.

9.   Sift a light film of powdered sugar over the tops of the cookies. (*The cookies can be stored in an airtight container at room temperature for up to 4 days. Sift more powdered sugar over the tops before serving.*)

Mirrors *Miroirs*

Makes approximately 40 miroirs

> 1 recipe batter for Sponges (page 156)
>
> ¼ recipe (¾ cup) Almond Cream (page 314), softened
>
> ¼ cup Apricot Preserves, homemade (page 336) or store-bought

1.   Preheat the oven to 375°F. Line baking sheets if necessary.

2.   Prepare the batter as in Steps 2, 3, and 4 of the recipe for Sponges.

3.   Using a pastry bag fitted with a ⅜-inch plain tip, pipe circles of batter, 1½ inches in diameter, about ¾ inch apart. Do not wash out the pastry bag.

4.   Top the meringue circles with chopped, slivered, or blanched almonds.

5.   Fill the pastry bag with the Almond Cream. Place the tip down into the middle of each circle of meringue, and fill the circle with about 1 teaspoon of the cream. It should be at about the same level as the meringue.

6.   Bake for 10 to 12 minutes, or until the nuts are lightly browned and the meringues and almond centers feel set when lightly touched. Let cool on the pans. Loosen the cookies by carefully running a metal spatula underneath.

7.   Warm the preserves in a small pan over low heat. If necessary, add a few teaspoons of water to thin out the preserves to be able to brush them on the cookies. Using a small pastry brush, brush just the center, almond-cream portion of each cookie with warm preserves. Let the glaze dry. (*The cookies can be stored at room temperature in an airtight container with wax paper between the layers for up to 4 days.*)

French Macaroons *Macarons*

Classic French macaroons are light, smooth, and shiny-surfaced sandwich cookies, filled with *ganache*, coffee cream, lemon curd, or preserves, depending upon the flavor of the macaroon. The cookie is based on ground almonds, not coconut, and properly executed, it will make you the most popular baker around. There are pastry shops in France known for their macaroons alone.

This particular recipe comes from Jean Néret, who is a master pastry chef and former president of the *Confédération des Pâtissiers* in France. Monsieur Néret has his shop in Loches, in the Touraine region where fruit trees are plentiful; he buys his almonds from a local grower. They are loaded with flavor and yield outstanding pastries without the addition of other flavorings. This recipe, unlike others I've tried, is fairly foolproof. Whereas other recipes would have you very gingerly fold ground almonds, sugar, and flavorings into stiffly beaten egg whites—a tricky proposition under the best of circumstances—this one calls for lightening the almond-sugar mix with raw egg whites. This added step makes it much easier to incorporate the dry ingredients without causing the egg whites to collapse due to overmixing.   **Makes about 120 small sandwich cookies**

2 cups (8 ounces) whole blanched almonds

3½ cups (1 pound) powdered sugar

1 tablespoon instant coffee or 3 tablespoons unsweetened cocoa powder

6 large egg whites

2 tablespoons granulated sugar

1¼ cups Coffee Filling (page 161) or 1 cup Chocolate Ganache (page 318), at room temperature

1.   Start with a cold oven, so that no moisture from a previously baked product remains. Position the oven racks to divide the oven into thirds. Preheat the oven to 450°F.

2.   Grind the almonds as fine as possible in a food processor. To avoid bringing out the oil in the nuts, grind them in small batches, pulsing the on-off switch. Add a small amount of the powdered sugar with each batch to help avoid clumping. If you are making coffee macaroons, grind the instant coffee with the last batch of almonds.

3.   Using a medium-fine mesh sieve, sift together the almonds, the sugar, and the cocoa, if using, 3 times, removing any pieces of almond that remain in the strainer. If you have a large amount left, grind those pieces again. Transfer the mixture to a large mixing bowl.

4.   Put half the egg whites in a clean mixing bowl or the bowl of an electric mixer. Using the whisk attachment, mix on low speed until the whites begin to froth, then increase to medium speed and whip until the whites hold soft peaks. Gradually add the granulated sugar in a thin stream. Once all has been added, increase to high speed and whip until the whites are stiff but not dry.

5.   Stir the remaining whites into the dry ingredients. Mix evenly and thoroughly, but do not overmix. This mixture should remain light.

6.   Gently fold one-third of the beaten whites into the almond mixture. Fold another third of the beaten whites into the mixture. Some streaks of white may remain. Fold this mixture into the remaining whites, mixing gently but thoroughly.

7.   Fit a pastry bag with a ⅜-inch plain tip, twist the bag just above the tip, and stuff this twist into the top of the tip itself. Fill the open end of the bag with 1 or 2 cups of batter. Line four 16 x 12-inch baking sheets with parchment paper. Pipe out sixty quarter-size dollops on each sheet, spacing them evenly about 1 inch apart.

8.   As soon as you have filled 2 baking sheets, place them in the oven and lower the temperature to 400°F. Bake for 5 to 7 minutes. Just as the cookies begin to form a crust and rise from the pan, prop the oven door ajar with the handle of a wooden spoon. Bake for 10 minutes more, or until the cookies feel completely set.

9.   Fill a measuring cup with about ½ cup of water and leave it next to your sink.

10.   Remove both pans from the oven and close the door immediately to allow the temperature to rise back to 400°F. Wearing an oven mitt, carefully tilt 1 corner of the pan into the sink while holding the paper in place with your thumb. With your other hand, flip back 1 corner of the parchment, with the macaroons still stuck to it. Drizzle about half of the water from the measuring cup onto the pan, put back the paper, and level the pan so that the water spreads evenly over it but still runs under the paper. This dampening will help the macaroons release from the parchment when cooled. Repeat this process with the other pan. Let the pans cool on racks. You may lose a couple of macaroons to water damage, but they will still be tasty, though too soggy to fill.

11.   Bake the remaining pans of macaroons.

12.   Once all the macaroon halves have cooled, turn half of them over on a dry surface (not the baking pan). Fill a pastry bag fitted with a ⅜-inch plain tip with filling. Pipe about 1 teaspoon of filling onto the middle of each inverted cookie, spreading the filling slightly as you go. Match these cookies with unfilled cookies of the same size and shape. (*The cookies can be stored, but not stacked too high, in an airtight container at room temperature for up to 4 days.*)

Hazelnut Macaroons *Macarons aux noisettes*

You can substitute blanched hazelnuts for the blanched almonds. The hazelnuts should not be toasted, so buy raw blanched nuts. Omit the coffee or cocoa. Proceed as for almond macaroons. Traditionally, these are filled with Caramelized Hazelnut Paste (page 320), but you can fill them with Chocolate Ganache (page 318) or Chocolate-Hazelnut Paste (page 322). Chocolate and hazelnuts are a wonderful pair.

Coffee Filling *Garniture au café*

Many pastry shops use a coffee cream that is custard based to fill coffee macaroons. The macaroons should not be refrigerated, and I am not comfortable leaving this filling at room temperature, even if the eggs have been cooked. The following almond paste–based filling has no eggs. Like the macaroons, it comes from Monsieur Néret. This filling can be flavored with anything: coffee extract, cocoa powder, or vanilla extract. In fact, if you do not have ganache on hand, you can make this filling and flavor it with cocoa powder.   Makes about 1¼ cups

> ½ cup (3½ ounces) good-quality almond paste
>
> 3½ ounces (⅞ stick) cold unsalted butter, cut into pieces
>
> Coffee Flavoring (page 342) or sifted cocoa, to taste

I. Put the almond paste in the bowl of an electric mixer and beat on medium speed until very light and quite smooth. Add the butter, piece by piece, and continue beating. Once all the butter has been added, beat the mixture on high speed for 1 minute. Scrape down the inside of the bowl from time to time with a rubber spatula.

2. Add the flavoring or cocoa at low speed and mix just until evenly blended. Use immediately; the filling will be at the right consistency for piping.

> • **In the pastry shop, macaroons are baked on doubled steel sheet pans covered with a thin layer of plywood (for insulation), which is then covered with parchment. This is hardly practical for home baking, not to mention that it is not necessary, since home ovens have racks and in professional pastry ovens, the pans are placed directly on the oven bottom. The racks provide for good air circulation around the pans and lower the risk of burning. I recommend pans that are doubled with a thin layer of air between the sheets of metal. Macaroons, and most other cookies, will bake perfectly on them.**
>
> • **Good-quality almond paste is available in supermarkets under the brand name Odense. It comes in a 7-ounce plastic-covered roll, and it is far superior to the domestic type available in cans in the States.**

Chocolate-spread Hazelnut Wafers

Biarritz

A *Biarritz* is a thin hazelnut wafer coated on the bottom with dark chocolate. These cookies are ideal with coffee or tea, ice cream or sorbet. The wafers can be made with ground almonds, instead of hazelnuts. They keep very well at room temperature in an airtight container. They may lose a bit of their snap, but still taste good.

For directions for tempering chocolate, see page 185.   **Makes about 90**

1 cup (5 ounces) packed ground hazelnuts

½ cup plus 1 tablespoon (4 ounces) sugar

3 tablespoons unsifted all-purpose flour

4 large egg whites

2 tablespoons plus 2 teaspoons unsalted butter, melted and cooled

8 ounces dark couverture chocolate, tempered (see page 185)

1. Position the oven racks to divide the oven into thirds. Preheat to 375°F. Use nonstick baking sheets or line uncoated sheets with parchment paper.

2. Combine the nuts, sugar, and flour in a small mixing bowl. Stir with a wire whisk to mix evenly. Stir in the egg whites, blending very evenly. Add the butter and mix very well.

3. Fill a pastry bag fitted with a ⅜-inch plain tip with the batter. Pipe even rows of quarter-size rounds onto the baking sheets, about 1½ inches apart.

4. Bake the cookies for 5 to 7 minutes, or until the edges are golden and the centers are barely colored. Turn the pans and switch them on their racks halfway through the baking time. Cool completely on the pans.

5. Temper the couverture and place the bowl in front of you. Running a metal spatula carefully underneath, loosen the wafers from the pans or paper. Using a small metal spatula, place a small dab of chocolate about the size of 2 chocolate chips on the bottom of a wafer, then spread it thinly and evenly. Lay the cookie on its rounded side to allow the chocolate to set. Repeat with all the wafers. Let the chocolate set. (*These cookies can be stored, stacked, in an airtight container at room temperature for up to 1 week.*)

Hazelnut Sandwich Cookies *Duchesses*

Biarritz wafers without the chocolate can be sandwiched with a small amount of Caramelized Hazelnut Paste. Then these bite-size cookies are called *Duchesses*, or duchesses. They are crunchy and creamy at the same time.

You can also sandwich the wafers with Raspberry Preserves (page 338) or softened Chocolate Ganache (page 318), though they won't have a classic name. If you really want to go over the top, dip them halfway in tempered chocolate.   **Makes 45 sandwich cookies**

1 recipe Chocolate-spread Hazelnut Wafers (page 162), without the chocolate

¼ recipe (¼ cup) Caramelized Hazelnut Paste (page 320), blended until smooth

1.   Prepare and bake the wafers as in Steps 1 through 4 of the recipe for Biarritz.

2.   Pair off cookies of equal size and shape. Place 1 wafer of each pair flat side up, the other flat side down.

3.   Fill a pastry bag fitted with a ¼-inch plain tip with the hazelnut paste. Pipe about ¼ teaspoon onto each flat side, then top with its mate. You can also apply the paste with a small spatula. Press together to spread the filling. (*These cookies may be stored in an airtight container at room temperature for up to 1 week.*)

Rum-soaked Raisin Wafers *Palets aux raisins*

The raisins on top of these wafers will lose most of their alcohol during baking, but they will remain moist. Because the raisins retain much of their moisture, however, the cookies themselves will not remain crisp when stored. They will still taste delicious, but if you want crisp wafers, eat them right away!   **Makes 90 wafers**

1 recipe Chocolate-spread Hazelnut Wafers (page 162), without the chocolate

1½ cups rum-soaked raisins, well drained

1.   Prepare the batter and pipe out wafers as in Steps 1 through 3 of the recipe. Place 3 raisins on top of each, distributed evenly.

2.   Bake as in Step 4. Cool completely. (*These will keep for up to 1 week stored in an airtight container.*)

Almond Tile Cookies *Tuiles d'amandes*

These classic, delicate, wafer-thin curved cookies, named for the clay roof tiles they resemble, are the perfect accompaniment to ice cream or sorbet. They are also a great addition to a tray of flat cookies.

The French use a metal tray with five troughs to shape these cookies. As they come out of the oven, the chef removes the cookies from the pans and inverts them in these troughs. If you have one of these pans, use it. If not, you can make perfect *tuiles* by placing the hot wafers on a rolling pin.

If you do not want to make all the cookies at once, you can refrigerate or freeze part of the batter.   Makes about thirty-six 4-inch curved wafers

¾ cup (5½ ounces) sugar

1 cup (4 ounces) sliced blanched almonds

⅓ cup (scant 1½ ounces) all-purpose flour, sifted or strained after weighing

4 large egg whites

2 tablespoons unsalted butter, melted

1 teaspoon pure vanilla extract

1.   Combine the sugar, almonds, and flour in a small mixing bowl. Stir in the egg whites with a wooden spoon. Add the butter and vanilla and stir well. (*The batter may be prepared ahead and refrigerated for up to 1 week or frozen for up to 1 month. Thaw in the refrigerator, then stir with a wooden spoon.*)

2.   Place a rack in the middle of the oven. Preheat the oven to 375°F. Use a nonstick or lightly greased baking sheets. Wedge a rolling pin on the work surface in such a way that it cannot roll.

3.   Using 1 heaping tablespoon of batter for each cookie, place 6 dollops on the baking sheet. Flatten each mound with the bottom of a fork, dipping the fork in a glass of water between cookies. Keep the cookies as round as possible. Prepare several pans at once.

4.   Bake 1 pan at a time for 7 to 10 minutes, or until the wafers are an even golden brown. Remove the pan from the oven and immediately replace it with another. Using a metal spatula, lift each wafer off the hot pan and lay it on top of the rolling pin. The cookies will cool quickly. Once cooled and crisp, transfer the cookies to a serving platter or an airtight container. Serve immediately. These will become soft if left at room temperature for more than 8 hours. You can crisp them in a turned-off oven for 30 minutes. If you have an electric oven, turn it on to the lowest setting for 10 minutes, then turn it off for 15 minutes before putting the cookies inside. (*The cookies may be stored for up to 5 days at room temperature in an airtight container.*)

Coconut-Macadamia Tile Cookies *Tuiles tropicales*

While almond tiles are as classic a *petit four sec* as you'll ever see, this variation is as contemporary. These cookies are the perfect accompaniment to an assortment of tropical sorbets and ice creams, such as Mango Sorbet (page 221) or Coconut or Ginger Ice Cream (pages 217–218).

The coconut and macadamia nuts add a great deal of richness to the original recipe and, by their nature, these ingredients maintain a certain crunch but not necessarily a lot of crispness. Therefore, these cookies should be made the day they are to be served. They do not fare well if reheated in an attempt to restore crispness. Makes about thirty-six 4-inch curved wafers

¾ cup (5 ounces) granulated sugar

½ cup (2 ounces) finely chopped unsalted raw or roasted macadamias

½ cup (about 1½ ounces) sweetened flaked coconut

⅓ cup (scant 1½ ounces) all-purpose flour, sifted or strained after weighing

4 large egg whites

2 tablespoons unsalted butter, melted

1 teaspoon pure vanilla extract

Follow the directions for Almond Tile Cookies (page 164).

Rolled Cigarette Cookies *Cigarettes*

Until I learned to make these ethereal rolled wafers, also called *cigarettes russes*, which must be rolled while they are still hot, they were one of my favorite treats. Now that I know how time consuming they are to make, I take the time to savor each one. There is still nothing like a fresh crisp cigarette.

    This is a great project for two. Either one can roll while the other pipes and cleans pans, or both of you can roll so that you can finish more cookies before they harden. Be prepared to get your fingers hot.

    You may want to pipe a filling, such as Hazelnut Praline Butter Cream (page 317), into the middle of the cigarettes, then dip the ends in tempered chocolate (see page 185) or chopped hazelnut croquant (see page 320) to seal them. Leave these at room temperature for up to 2 hours. Do not refrigerate the wafers; they will absorb moisture from the refrigerator, and the result will be less than wonderful.

    The same batter is used for Tulip Shells (page 168).   **Makes about 36 rolled wafers**

½ cup (1¾ ounces) powdered sugar

2½ tablespoons unsalted butter, softened

2 large egg whites, lightly beaten to loosen

¼ teaspoon pure vanilla extract

⅓ cup (1¼ ounces) all-purpose flour

1.   Place the oven rack in the middle of the oven and preheat to 375°F. Using softened butter on a pastry brush or pan spray, lightly grease 2 baking sheets. Even if you are using nonstick cookie sheets, grease them slightly, to help the wafers brown and release from the pan more easily.

2.   Sift or strain the powdered sugar over the 2½ tablespoons of butter in a medium mixing bowl. Whisk the two together until smooth and very pale yellow, about 60 seconds.

3.   Whisk in the egg whites. The mixture may start to break; this is normal. Add the vanilla.

4.   Sift or strain the flour over the bowl and whisk until smooth. This will bind the batter again. (*The batter can be used immediately or refrigerated, covered with plastic wrap placed directly on the batter's surface, for up to 4 days. If chilled, leave the batter at room temperature for 30 minutes, then stir before using.*)

5.   Fill a pastry bag fitted with a ⅓-inch plain tube with the batter. Or drop the batter by the teaspoonful. In either case, place no more that 6 teaspoons of batter on each pan, leaving at least 4 inches between dollops and making the dollops as round as possible. Bake the pans, one at a time, for 5 to 7 minutes, or until the edges of the wafers just begin to brown. Remove the cookies from the oven and put the other pan inside.

6. Working on a surface that will retain the heat (metal, not tile or marble), remove 1 wafer at a time with a spatula and flip it onto the work surface. Quickly roll the wafer around the handle of a wooden spoon, pressing down as you roll the last edge to seal the cookie. Slide the rolled wafer off the handle, set it aside where it won't get crushed, and roll the next. If the wafers start to harden before you have a chance to roll them all, place the pan back in the oven for 1 minute to soften the wafers. Or work with 4 wafers per pan until you have your system down.

7. Let the baking sheet cool completely. Wipe it dry with a dry cloth, or paper towel, regrease it, and put more batter on the pan. If the pan is still warm, the butter will melt and separate, changing the consistency of the wafers. After regreasing, pipe or place more batter on the pan and bake and roll until all the cigarettes are done. (*The cigarettes may be stored in an airtight container for up to 5 days at room temperature.*)

Tulip Shells *Tulipes*

It's an ice cream dish. It's a cookie. It's an ice cream dish *and* a cookie. These impressive receptacles are nothing more than Rolled Cigarettes in another form. They are fragile and delicious and can turn store-bought ice cream into an ice cream creation. Or place a dollop of Pastry Cream (page 308) or lightly Whipped Cream (page 307) in the bottom of the shell and pile fresh fruit on top. Be sure to place the shell on its serving dish before filling. Once filled, the tulip will be difficult to move.

Make your tulips not more than a few hours before serving. They are difficult to store because they are so fragile and odd-shaped, and they will absorb moisture from the air. **Makes 8 to 10 large tulips**

1 recipe Rolled Cigarette Cookies (page 166)

1. Determine the shape you would like for your tulips and prepare your forms. These can be large cereal bowls with smaller bowls that fit inside or very clean brioche tins, measuring 5 inches across the top, which can be stacked one inside another, to give the shells fluted sides. Have at least 2 sets of forms ready.

2. Proceed as in Steps 1 through 4 of the Cigarette recipe.

3. Prepare only 2 tulips at a time. Place 2 dollops of batter, about 1½ tablespoons each, on a baking sheet. The dollops should be at least 8 inches apart and placed so that they can be spread into 8-inch rounds. Spread the batter, using a small offset icing spatula. Repeat with the second pan.

4. Bake one pan for 7 to 10 minutes, or until the wafers are golden. Remove from the oven and, working quickly with a metal spatula and a pair of tongs, place 1 wafer over a cereal bowl or brioche tin. Quickly place the inner bowl or tin on top and gently press down. These harden quickly, so be careful. Repeat with the other wafer. Allow the wafers to set for 2 minutes, then carefully remove them from the molds and place them on a wire rack to cool completely.

5. Bake the second pan and form the tulips. Once the first pan has cooled, wipe it with a paper towel to remove any burned butter or pieces of wafer. Regrease and apply more batter. Continue to bake and form tulips until all the batter has been used.

Madeleines

For such simple little cakes, Madeleines have quite a long history. They were originally produced in the town of Commercy, in Lorraine, under the tutelage of Stanislas Leszczynski. In 1730, Stanislas brought some of these shell-shaped cakes to the Court of France, to his daughter, Marie Leszczynska, who was the wife of Louis XV. When asked the name of the delicious treats, Stanislas could only think of the name of one of the girls who had helped prepare them, and answered, "Madeleine."

Madeleines are still so revered in Commercy that every July 22 there is a meeting of the *Compagnons de la madeleine*, or Fellows of the Madeleine.

The shells, baked in special molds called Madeleine pans, are like little pound cakes. They are ideal dippers in coffee or tea. While they can be stored in an airtight container, I think that Madeleines are best when eaten within an hour of baking. At this point, they still have a sort of crust, and the center is moist and tender. Afterward, they almost have to be dipped, as they dry out a bit.

Makes twenty-four 2-inch shells

1½ cups (8 ounces) unbleached all-purpose flour

1 teaspoon baking powder

8 ounces (2 sticks) unsalted butter, melted and cooled

5 large eggs

¾ cup (5½ ounces) sugar

Finely grated zest of 1 lemon

1.   Sift the flour with the baking powder onto a sheet of wax paper and set aside.

2.   Preheat the oven to 425°F. Use 2 tablespoons of the butter to thoroughly grease the shell molds. Make sure to brush in all the grooves.

3.   Combine the eggs and sugar in a large mixing bowl and begin whisking immediately. The mixture should become very light and frothy, and the sugar should dissolve. If the bowl is heat-proof, you can very carefully whisk this mixture directly over low heat. Do not heat it past tepid, or the eggs will partially cook and make dry Madeleines.

4.   Still whisking, add the sifted dry ingredients in a steady stream. Pick up the wax paper by the long edges and shake it over the mixing bowl with one hand, while whisking with the other. Place the bowl on a towel to keep it from spinning. Once smooth, stir in the remaining 6 tablespoons of butter and the lemon zest. (*At this point, half the batter can be refrigerated for up to 3 days or frozen for up to 1 month. Thaw in the refrigerator overnight.*)

5.   Fill a pastry bag fitted with a ½-inch plain tip with batter. Or drop the batter by large spoonfuls. Whatever your method, fill the shells about seven-eighths high; these will rise quite a bit.

6.   Bake for 8 to 10 minutes, or until the Madeleines have peaked, spring back when lightly touched, and are lightly browned. Do not overbake, or they will dry out. Immediately invert onto a clean towel or a cooling rack. If they stick, loosen them with a small, sharp knife. Cool completely or eat while still somewhat warm. (*Madeleines may be stored in an airtight container with wax paper between the layers for up to 3 days at room temperature.*)

Chocolate-Orange Madeleines *Madeleines au chocolat*

Substitute ¼ cup of unsweetened cocoa powder for ¼ cup of the flour and the finely grated zest of 1 orange for the lemon zest. Sift the cocoa together with the flour and baking powder. Proceed as directed.

Cat Tongues *Langues de chat*

The name may be unfortunate, but this crunchy butter wafer remains a classic. You must use a pastry bag for this recipe, and that may require some practice. The cookies are an excellent accompaniment to sorbets, ice creams, and custards.

If you want, you can pipe out 6-inch strips, bake, then wrap the still-hot cookies in a spiral around the handle of a wooden spoon. **Makes 30 to 36 long wafers**

3½ tablespoons unsalted butter, softened

About ⅓ cup (1¾ ounces) powdered sugar

1 large egg

1 large egg yolk

¼ teaspoon pure vanilla extract

⅔ cup (3½ ounces) all-purpose flour

1.   Place the oven racks to divide the oven into thirds. Preheat to 375°F. Using softened butter on a pastry brush, lightly grease 2 baking sheets. Even if you are using nonstick cookie sheets, grease them slightly, to help the wafers brown and release from the pan more easily.

2.   Place the remaining butter in a medium mixing bowl and whisk until smooth. Sift or strain the powdered sugar over the butter and vigorously whisk the two together until very smooth and pale yellow, about 60 seconds. Add the egg and the egg yolk and whisk until completely incorporated. Whisk in the vanilla extract.

3.   Sift or strain the flour over the mixture in the bowl and whisk just until smooth. Do not overmix. Fill a pastry bag fitted with a ¼-inch plain tip with batter. Pipe out straight strips about 2½ inches long and 1½ inches apart.

4.   Bake for about 7 minutes, rotating the pans if necessary, until the edges are golden and the centers of the strips are pale brown. Cool completely on the pans, then carefully remove with a metal spatula. (*These cookies may be stored in an airtight container at room temperature for up to 2 weeks.*)

Rolled Butter Cookies *Sablés*

Every pastry shop in France makes these cookies, and they are as satisfying as they are simple. While many of these shops consider these little wonders a good way to fill a slot in the pastry case, I consider them great cookies to make with my kids, to serve with tea, or to decorate for any holiday. If you want to get really fancy, dip half of each cookie in tempered bittersweet chocolate (see page 185). Or sandwich two cookies together with some Chocolate Ganache (page 318), Caramelized Hazelnut Paste (page 320), or Raspberry Preserves (page 338).   **Makes about thirty-six 1½-inch cookies**

½ recipe (1 pound) Sweet Short Dough (page 294), chilled

2 large egg yolks (optional)

1.   Position the oven racks to divide the oven into thirds. Preheat the oven to 375°F. Use non-stick baking sheets or line uncoated sheets with parchment paper.

2.   On a lightly floured work surface, roll the dough to a thickness of ¼ inch. Use a 1½-inch fluted cookie cutter and cut out as many rounds as possible. Gather the scraps and reroll them once. You may need to refrigerate the scraps before rolling. Place the rounds on the baking sheets, about ½ inch apart.

3.   For shiny tops, refrigerate the pans for 15 minutes. Stir the egg yolks with 2 teaspoons of water and evenly brush the tops of the firm cookies. If you wish, you can run the tines of a fork over each cookie, to make a crosshatch pattern in the glaze.

4.   Bake the cookies for 10 to 12 minutes, until lightly browned all over, reversing the pans if necessary to ensure even browning. Cool on the pans or on wire racks. (*The cookies may be stored in an airtight container at room temperature for up to 1 week. They can be stored exposed to the air as well, but they will lose their crispness.*)

Raspberry Ring Cookies *Couronnes aux framboises*

These are considerably fancier than *Sablés*, but not much more difficult. You can fill the holes with any type of preserves or even a rosette of Chocolate Ganache (page 318).   **Makes about 2 dozen cookies**

1 recipe Rolled Butter Cookies (page 172)

Powdered sugar, for dusting

¼ cup Raspberry Preserves, homemade (page 338) or store-bought

1.   Prepare the dough and roll it out as described in Steps 1 and 2 of the master recipe.

2.   Use a 2-inch *plain* cookie cutter and cut out as many rounds as possible. Place all the rounds on a baking sheet and refrigerate. Gather and reroll the scraps once.

3.   Count the total number of rounds. Using a 1-inch plain or fluted cookie cutter, cut a hole in the center of half the disks that were rolled from fresh dough, not from scraps. Reroll scraps and make more rings and disks. Brush the rims of the solid disks with a barely dampened pastry brush. Top with rings and press down slightly. Place the disks on the baking sheets about ½ inch apart.

4.   Bake for 12 to 15 minutes, or until golden. Cool completely on the pan.

5.   Push the cookies close together on the pan and sift powdered sugar lightly over the tops. Fill the centers with Raspberry Preserves, using about ½ teaspoon for each. Serve flat on a pastry dessert tray.

- **If you use a fluted cutter for the *Couronnes*, the edges may be difficult to match when topping the disks with rings. A fluted cutter does make a somewhat prettier cookie, however, so if you are up to the challenge, use one.**

- **By dusting the cookies with powdered sugar before filling them with preserves, you create cookies with a white ring and red center, since the preserves will not be topped.**

Almond Shortbread Cookies *Zéphyrs*

The simplicity of these rich cookies makes them seem that much more sinful. They are small, thick, and fragile, and rimmed by a thin sugar crust. The dough is shaped into rolls—like refrigerator cookies—then sliced. In pastry shops, several rolls are placed on a *guitare*, or cutter, which has a lever that is strung with evenly spaced wires. Lower the lever onto the rolls, *et voilà!* individual slices.

You can easily vary these cookies by adding chopped pecans or pistachios. Add these to the recipe, but do not omit any of the ground almonds, which give the cookies their sandy texture. You can also roll the dough in crystallized sugar, cinnamon sugar, or more ground nuts.   Makes dough rolls for 140 cookies

1 cup (4 ounces) whole, sliced, or slivered blanched almonds

2 cups (11 ounces) unsifted unbleached all-purpose flour

7 ounces (1¾ sticks) cold unsalted butter, cut into small pieces

2 large yolks

½ cup (3½ ounces) sugar

1 teaspoon pure vanilla extract

1 large egg

Additional sugar, for glazing

1.   Grind the almonds as fine as possible, using a food processor or a nut grinder. Press the nuts through a mesh sieve or strainer, to break up any lumps. Do not discard any larger pieces that remain in the strainer, but regrind them and add them to the others.

2.   Place the ground nuts in a medium mixing bowl or the bowl of an electric mixer. Add the flour and the butter and, using the paddle attachment, mix on low speed. Stop mixing when the butter is completely broken up and the mixture resembles coarse cornmeal. The mixture should not come together. If it does, stop the mixer. The cookies will be somewhat less delicate due to overmixing.

3.   Whisk together the egg yolks, the sugar, and the vanilla until pale yellow, about 60 seconds. Add the yolk mixture to the nut mixture and mix on low speed until the dough comes together and is smooth. Turn the dough out onto a lightly floured surface and knead a few times. Avoid incorporating any air.

4.   Divide the dough into 4 parts and roll each into a log about 1¼ inches in diameter, with no air gaps in the rolls, which would cause the cookies to fall apart. Refrigerate the rolls for at least 1 hour.

5.   Remove all the rolls from the refrigerator. Wrap any you want to freeze in plastic. (*The rolls may be frozen for up to 3 weeks. Thaw overnight in the refrigerator.*)

6.   Adjust the oven racks to divide the oven into thirds. Preheat the oven to 375°F. Line 2 baking sheets with parchment paper or aluminum foil.

7.   Whisk the whole egg until very loose. Sprinkle the extra granulated sugar in a straight line in front of you. Brush the rolls evenly with egg wash, then roll them evenly in the sugar. Once these are done, either reuse the sugar immediately in another dough or discard it.

8.   Cut the rolls, one or several at a time, into even ¼- to ⅓-inch slices. Place the slices on the baking sheets, 1 inch apart.

9.   Bake for 7 to 10 minutes, or until the edges of the cookies are lightly golden and the centers are barely colored. Cool on the pans. (*These cookies may be stored in an airtight container at room temperature for up to 5 days.*)

Chocolate Almond Shortbread Cookies *Zéphyrs au chocolat*

Substitute ¼ cup of sifted or strained unsweetened cocoa powder for ¼ cup of the flour. The cocoa needs to be sifted because the lumps may not break up during baking. Proceed as directed.

Spritz Cookies, Paris Style *Sablés viennois*

The French would never refer to these melt-in-your-mouth wonders as spritz cookies, but that is what they are. If you have a spritz press, use it. If not, pipe these with a pastry bag fitted with a star tip. Because this recipe has no egg yolks, the cookies will come out very crisp.

These are made with real vanilla beans, which will give the cookies a delicate and unusual flavor and little black specks, setting them light-years apart from your grandmother's spritz cookies. Split the vanilla bean lengthwise with a small knife, then scrape out the seeds. Experiment with other spices, such as cinnamon, nutmeg, and ginger. For a recipe of this size, do not use more than one teaspoon, one-quarter teaspoon, and one-half teaspoon, respectively. A little bit of these spices goes a long way.   **Makes about 72 little cookies**

1½ cups (about 8 ounces) unsifted unbleached all-purpose flour

¾ cup (about 3½ ounces) unsifted powdered sugar

7 ounces (1¾ sticks) unsalted butter, at room temperature

1 large egg white

Seeds from 1 vanilla bean

1. Position the oven racks to divide the oven into thirds. Preheat the oven to 375°F. Lightly grease 2 baking sheets or line them with parchment paper.

2. Sift or strain the flour and set it aside. Sift the powdered sugar into a medium mixing bowl or the bowl of an electric mixer. Add the butter to the bowl and cream until light. Add the egg white and the vanilla seeds and beat until evenly mixed. On low speed, add the flour in 3 parts, beating only until incorporated each time. Do not overmix, or the cookies will be tough. Finish mixing with a wooden spoon or rubber spatula.

3. Using a rubber spatula, fill a spritz press or a pastry bag fitted with a ⅜-inch open star tip (this dough will not go through a closed star tip). Make sure that there are no air bubbles in either. Pipe shapes of your choice—squiggles, S-shapes, stars, rosettes—about 1½ inches apart.

4. Bake 2 sheets at a time for 12 to 15 minutes, or until golden. Turn the pans if necessary to ensure even browning. Remove the cookies from the baking sheets and cool on wire racks. (*The cookies may be stored at room temperature in an airtight container for up to 1 week.*)

Traditionally in the United States, spritz cookies make an appearance around Christmas. They are a favorite in holiday baskets. However, they are often colored (the green spritz Christmas tree) or decorated with sprinkles or glazed fruit (the spritz wreath). Finely chopped walnuts or pecans, sprinkled on the piped cookies before baking, will add texture and flavor as well as your own signature. Dust the baked cookies with powdered sugar.

Florentines *Florentins*

More a confection than a cookie, these *petits fours* are especially popular at Christmastime. Traditionally, the flat part of each Florentine is spread with tempered chocolate (see page 185), which is then rippled with a decorating comb. A simpler way to add chocolate is to sandwich two wafers together with a dab of Chocolate Ganache.

As the name implies, Florentines are of Italian culinary ancestry, and they have several ingredients typically found in Italian pastries: almonds, glazed fruit, and candied orange rind. Be sure to use good-quality fruit, available in many nut and gourmet shops. You can vary the glazed fruit, depending on your taste and even on the season.

You will need a candy thermometer for this recipe.   **Makes ninety 3-inch single cookies or 45 sandwich cookies**

> 5 tablespoons honey
>
> 1½ cups whipping cream
>
> 1½ cups (10½ ounces) sugar
>
> ½ cup light corn syrup
>
> 8 ounces glazed fruit, chopped into ¼-inch pieces
>
> 8 ounces chopped Candied Orange Peel, homemade (page 361) or store-bought
>
> 3 cups (12 ounces) sliced blanched almonds
>
> ⅔ cup (3½ ounces) all-purpose flour, sifted or strained after measuring
>
> 8 ounces tempered bittersweet chocolate (see page 185) (optional), or about ¼ recipe (1 cup) Chocolate Ganache (page 318), at room temperature

1.   Combine the honey, cream, sugar, and corn syrup in a medium-sized heavy saucepan. Cook over medium heat, stirring constantly, until a candy thermometer reads 240°F.

2.   Place the orange peel, almonds, and flour in a large mixing bowl and mix well, so that the fruit and peel are coated with flour and everything is evenly distributed.

3.   Pour the honey mixture over the dry ingredients and mix well with a wooden spoon. Allow the mixture to cool to the point where it can be handled. Turn the dough out onto a very lightly floured surface and knead slightly to mix.

4.   If you have a scale, weigh out six 10½-ounce pieces of dough. If not, divide the dough into 6 even pieces as best you can. Roll each piece into a log 1 inch in diameter. Using a heavy knife, cut each log into 15 pieces.

continued

5. Position the oven racks to divide the oven into thirds. Preheat the oven to 375°F. Roll each dough piece into a ball and place 12 to 15 balls on two or more nonstick baking sheets. If nonstick sheets are not available, line baking sheets with aluminum foil and lightly grease the foil; do not use parchment paper, which will wrinkle and make it difficult to remove the wafers. Leave 3 inches between balls. Flatten the balls slightly with your hand, dampened if necessary to keep them from sticking. Using a flat-bottomed glass, flatten all the dough pieces evenly, dipping the bottom of the glass in water to prevent sticking.

6. Bake 2 sheets at a time for about 7 minutes, or until the cookies begin to bubble. Remove from the oven and bake 2 more sheets, allowing the first two to cool a bit. Bake all of the cookies once, then bake again for 7 minutes, or until the cookies begin to bubble again. Cool on the pans on wire racks. If using tempered chocolate, prepare it now.

7. Carefully remove the cooled cookies with a metal spatula.

8. If spreading the bottoms with chocolate, use a small icing spatula to do so. Spread an even layer of chocolate on each cookie, letting any excess drip back into the chocolate bowl. Place the cookies on a flat surface, chocolate side up, to allow the chocolate to cool. (*These cookies may be stored in an airtight container at room temperature for up to 5 days.*)

9. If sandwiching cookies with ganache, place half the cookies flat side up on a work surface. Place 1 teaspoon of ganache in the middle of each cookie, then top with a cookie of similar size and shape. Gently press down to spread the filling evenly. Store as you would chocolate-coated Florentines.

> **As these bake, the edges will become jagged and lacy. If you want perfectly round cookies with smooth edges, use a 3-inch cookie cutter to trim the edges while the Florentines are still warm in Step 6. In France, pastry chefs use a small tart ring to gather the edges of the cookies inside the ring, resulting in perfectly round cookies. These are great for spreading with chocolate, but more important, they look good in a pastry case, and even more important, there is no waste (and since the dough for each cookie is weighed before baking, food cost is strictly controlled). I prefer the lacier, homier version. The cookies are more delicate and require much less work.**

Chocolates

Les Chocolats

CHOCOLATE MAY NOT BE the first word that every child learns, but it probably becomes a part of every human's vocabulary, no matter what the native tongue, within the first five years of life. Can you ever remember a time when you did not know what chocolate was?

The quality of any chocolate depends on where the chocolate comes from and how it is processed. The type of chocolate best suited to a particular recipe or use depends on the proportions of cocoa liqueur and cocoa butter as well as sugar and milk, if used. Chocolates that taste wonderful in fillings may not be good for surrounding those fillings. As the name implies, an extra bittersweet chocolate, for example, is not sweet. It makes a wonderful ganache, but it will not melt down to a thin coating for dipping. A couverture chocolate—usually semisweet—is needed for dipping.

Choose your chocolate carefully. For interiors, choose a chocolate that tastes great to you. I like extra bittersweet, because its strong taste stands up to such other ingredients as cream, caramel, and alcohols. For dipping, be sure to use a chocolate with a high cocoa-butter-to-sugar ratio. Read the ingredients label, but more than anything, taste the chocolate—it should not coat the roof of your mouth or feel greasy.

As a rule of thumb, you will need the equivalent in couverture of about half the weight of a chocolate center to enrobe it. Most of the recipes in this book make centers that weigh about 10 grams (⅓ ounce). Each chocolate will need about 5 grams of couverture. To put it another way, if you have a batch of centers that weighs 1 pound, that is, all the ingredients weigh a pound, you will need to temper ½ pound of couverture to dip the chocolate. Add a bit extra so you are not scraping the bowl to dip your last chocolate.

The recipes in this chapter provide a variety of fillings as well as many different ways in which to shape and decorate them.

A Few Simple Chocolate Decorations / *Quelques simples décors au chocolat*

Hazelnut Praline Truffles / *Truffes pralinées*

Muscadines

Rochers

Chocolate-dipped Caramelized Hazelnuts / *Noisettes*

Raspberry-filled Chocolates / *Framboises*

Jamaicans / *Jamaïcains*

Brazilians / *Brésiliens*

Chocolate-covered Caramels / *Perlias*

Chocolate-covered Nougat / *Nougats au chocolat*

Chocolate-covered Orange Peel / *Aiguillettes d'oranges au chocolat*

Dried Fruit and Nut Bark / *Mendiants*

A Few Simple Chocolate Decorations *Quelques simples décors au chocolat*

Something as simple as a single chocolate curl can turn an unadorned dessert or cake into an elegant one. There are decorations that require tempered chocolate, and those that simply require a bar of chocolate. French pastry chefs have at their fingertips a battery of tools and contraptions to help them create chocolate curls and other decorations, but even at home you need no longer rely on the vegetable peeler run across a bar of chocolate as your sole decorating tool. Here are a few items to have on hand that will make your job easier:

A heavy chef's knife, preferably with a 10- or 12-inch blade, for chocolate cigarettes

A 2-inch plain (not fluted) round cookie cutter, for chocolate curls

At least one very heavy, very flat steel (not aluminum) pan for chocolate ruffles. This must not be warped at all, or your scraper will not run across it evenly. It must be made of steel, as a softer metal will scrape away with the chocolate

A long offset spatula (at least a 12-inch blade), for spreading chocolate on pans

A wide, triangular putty knife, for making chocolate ruffles

A thin-bladed, flexible knife, such as a fish-fillet knife, with a 9-inch blade, for making chocolate bands

A small offset spatula (4-inch blade), for spreading chocolate on acetate bands

A few sheets of thin acetate, available at art supply stores, which can be cut into bands of various lengths and widths

Parchment paper, for decorating cones

Chocolate Curls

Whether they are perfect cigarettes laid side by side or random feathers piled high, chocolate curls are the most common of all chocolate decorations. You may certainly continue to create these by running a vegetable peeler over a small bar of chocolate. A large bar of commercial dark, milk, or white couverture will broaden your horizons considerably. These bars weigh ten or eleven pounds each, depending on whether they were manufactured in America or in Europe. I prefer European—and particularly French—chocolate. Store the chocolate at room temperature. Once you have removed the wrapper, wrap the block in plastic. Try to keep the block intact.

Lay the block in front of you, with a short side closest to you and the smooth, undecorated side up. There are two methods for making curls:

• For cigarettes or wide rolls, use a long, heavy chef's knife. Hold the knife handle in one hand, the tip in the other. Rest the knife on the chocolate's surface with the top of the blade tilted very slightly toward you. Draw the knife firmly toward you. The harder you press down onto the chocolate, the wider and thicker your cigarettes will be. Set the

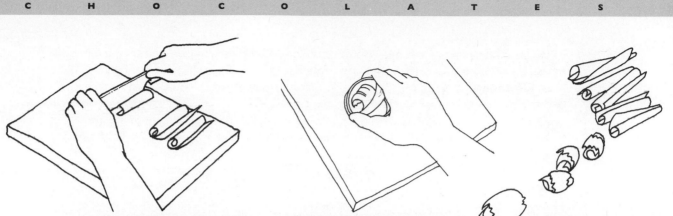

Form long rolls by pulling a knife toward you, across a large block of chocolate.

Form barrel-shaped curls by pulling a round cookie cutter across the chocolate.

Long and barrel-shaped curls

cigarettes aside on a plate or pan or directly on the cake or dessert as you create them. If you do set them aside, transfer them later with a wide metal spatula.

- For rounded, featherlike curls, use a 2-inch plain round cookie cutter. Hold the cutter with one edge resting on the chocolate's surface. Make sure that the cutter's seam is not touching the chocolate. The cutter should be angled at about 30° to the chocolate. Draw the cutter toward you and a curl will follow. Transfer these to a plate or a tray, using a wide metal spatula, or place them directly on whatever you are decorating.

Chocolate Ruffles

These are best with dark chocolate, which is the easiest to temper and spread. Also, when you make chocolate ruffles and curls, they look lighter in color, so ruffles made of milk chocolate may appear too light. Do not make these with white chocolate; it is too difficult to temper. Since ruffles are made with tempered chocolate, they can be used on cakes served at room temperature as well as cold cakes.

- For ruffles or fans, use a long offset spatula to spread an extremely thin layer ($\frac{1}{32}$ inch) of tempered chocolate (see page 185) on a marble slab or an extremely flat steel tray. Let the chocolate set. Use the putty knife to create chocolate ruffles by scraping away from you. Gather the band on one side to create a ruffle or a fan. Store these on a tray in the refrigerator or place directly on whatever you are decorating.

- For a band of chocolate, spread another tray with tempered chocolate and let it set up. Hold the thin flexible knife at a 30° angle, the blade facing you. Have as much of the blade in contact with the pan as possible. Draw the knife toward you, pulling up a band of chocolate as you do so. Pick up the band and quickly wrap it around a waiting cake. Be careful: This may melt in your hands. It helps to hold one end up with the knife blade.

Chocolate Bands

These are for cold cakes only. Cut acetate strips that are the same width as the cake you are wrapping is high. The length of the strip should be $\frac{1}{2}$ inch greater than the perimeter of the cake, for a slight overlap. Measure the perimeter of a square or rectangular cake by taking the sum of its sides. Measure around a round cake with a measuring tape.

Lay the strips on a very flat surface. Using a small offset spatula, spread a thin layer of melted—this need not be tempered—chocolate. If you are preparing several bands at once, place the strips side by side on the flat surface. The layer of chocolate should be 1/32 inch thick and very even. Make sure that no chocolate gets on the other side of the strips, or you will not be able to remove the acetate. Pick up the strip and wrap it around the cake, without overlapping completely. As the chocolate hits the cold cake, it will set up. Peel away the first inch of acetate, then overlap the other end. Peel away all the acetate when the chocolate has set up. Make sure that the bottom edge of the band matches up to the bottom of the cake, all the way around.

Piped Chocolate Decorations

For three-dimensional decorations, prepare a decorating cone by cutting a parchment triangle 12 × 12 × 17 inches. Make sure that all the edges are perfectly straight and clean. Hold one corner in one hand with the right angle facing up. Then flip that right angle so that it points downward, and with your other hand, pull the other corner around so that the longest edge

A filled paper cone, rolled away from the seam. Use one hand to squeeze, the other to guide.

A few simple designs, including fans, continuous line decorations, one design with beads, and one beaded border.

forms into a pointed cone. Tuck this last corner inside the open end of the cone and fold it down. The right angle will be pointing away from the cone. Fill the cone two-thirds full with tempered, strained (use a fine mesh tea strainer) couverture, then with the seam facing you and the right angle away, fold the opening down over the couverture. Make sure not to trap any air inside. Once you have closed the cone, roll the top down like a tube of toothpaste, making sure that you're rolling away from the seam. This will keep the seam taut. Snip the tip of the cone to form a small, round hole for thin, even piping.

Pipe out fans, or whatever design you want, onto a parchment-lined baking sheet. Let the decorations set up at room temperature or in the refrigerator. Lift the decorations off the paper and stand them on your cake or dessert.

The same decorations can be done flat on top of cakes or pastries. For this, strain melted chocolate into a decorating cone and draw the designs directly on the cake.

Tempering Chocolate

In an ideal world, chocolate bonbons—homemade or otherwise—would be stored at room temperature, below 80°F. At room temperature, dipped chocolates are shiny and pliable, never grainy or spotty, and never gray or cloudy. The reason for this is tempering.

Any chocolate that is to remain at room temperature—that is, when its hardness will not be maintained by refrigeration—must be tempered. This includes couverture into which chocolate centers will be dipped for bonbons, as well as all chocolate decoration that is either free-standing or to be used on nonrefrigerated cakes and pastries. (Chocolate used for writing or flat decoration on room-temperature cakes need not be tempered. In the case of chocolate ruffles, tempering is absolutely necessary, since untempered chocolate would simply melt onto the cake at room temperature. Chocolate curls that are simply scraped from bars of chocolate need not be tempered, since the bars themselves are already tempered.)

Tempering is the process in which couverture, or coating chocolate, is melted thereby spreading all its component molecules are spread apart. The chocolate is then cooled very evenly—and even cooling is key—and then evenly melted again, this time to the optimal temperature so that it sets up quickly and evenly at room temperature. When solid, it reflects light, it breaks in an even crack, and it has an even finish that is never streaky. Here's how to temper chocolate:

1. Place all or half the chocolate in a stainless steel or glass bowl that fits snugly inside a pot, with no gaps around the rim. Choose a bowl whose rim will come as close as possible to that of the pot. Fill the pot with hot water to a level that, when the bowl is set inside, the water will come up to the level of the chocolate. The chocolate should be completely jacketed in water. Place the pot over medium heat and melt the chocolate to the desired temperature, (see page 187). Since the bowl will continue to conduct heat, you can take it off the heat before it is completely melted, then stir to melt without risk of having the chocolate burn. (If you have any couverture left over from a previous tempering job, chop it and add it to the bowl for melting.)

2.   When the chocolate has been completely melted, it must be cooled to bind it again. This can be done in one of several ways:

- Add finely chopped chocolate of the same type (half the total amount needed) to the melted chocolate. Stir with a wooden spoon until the added chocolate is completely melted. The mixture should thicken considerably. If the temperature has not dropped sufficiently and the chocolate is not beginning to solidify on the sides of the bowl or on a small metal spatula dipped in the chocolate, perform the next step, which can be done as the only cooling step.

- Twist a towel, turn it into a circle, and place it in the bottom of a larger bowl. Fill the bowl halfway with ice, then with cold water. Set the chocolate bowl inside, on top of the towel, which will keep the bowl from rocking and lower the risk of having ice water get inside the chocolate bowl. Stir the chocolate constantly, taking it out of the ice bath from time to time, so that the temperature lowers evenly.

- Pour the melted chocolate onto a large marble slab. Using a large metal spatula or scraper, keep lifting the chocolate in the air and spreading it back on the marble. Do this until the chocolate has the consistency of a smooth paste.

3.   Place the cooled chocolate back in the hot water bath. Stir constantly with a wooden spoon. Take the bowl out of the water bath from time to time. The bowl will continue to conduct heat.

4.   If you heat the chocolate beyond the recommended temperature, let it cool and start over.

5.   Once the chocolate has been tempered, you must maintain its temperature within a few degrees, or it will begin to set up in the bowl. Do not keep it in a water bath, as the chocolate may become overheated or, even worse, water may somehow splash out of the bath into the chocolate and cause it to seize. Instead, stir the chocolate frequently to distribute the temperature evenly, bearing in mind that whatever you are dipping will change the temperature of the couverture. After you have dipped about ten centers, check the temperature of the couverture, either with a thermometer or by dipping your finger in the chocolate and quickly touching it to your lip; it should feel like body temperature. If the temperature has dropped by more than 2 degrees, place the bowl back in the hot water bath for just a few seconds. Stir constantly, and remember that the bowl will continue to conduct the heat even after it has been removed from the water bath. Continue working with the tempered chocolate. Once you have done this a few times, you will begin to recognize the signs of cooling chocolate. You can then dispense with the thermometer and go for longer stretches without reheating the couverture.

There are several things you can do to keep your chocolates from having a temper tantrum:

- Have centers at room temperature when you dip them. The coating will cool and set evenly. Also, be sure to stir the couverture frequently, since the centers will cool it down, and unevenly at that. Place the bowl of couverture back in the hot water bath from time to time, but do not overwarm it.

- Take care not to let any moisture get in the dipping chocolate. This will cause the chocolate to seize right away, or bloom later on. (Bloomed chocolate has little white spots that are caused by the sugar separating from the rest of the chocolate.)

- Do not mix any liquids directly into melted chocolate. If you want alcohol or any other flavors in the chocolates, either mix them into a ganache for centers or in the case of herbs and whole spices, infuse them in the milk that will go into the ganache.

- If you are dipping centers that have a lot of fat, such as Hazelnut Praline Truffles, some of the fat may melt into the dipping chocolate. Keep stirring the chocolate. When you have finished dipping, cool the dipping chocolate and use it only for the interior of another chocolate or for baking. Do not temper this chocolate again; it will never shine.

- On the other hand, if you add something to your couverture, such as chopped almonds for Rochers, you can temper that chocolate again and use it for the same recipe or another like it.

- If you are using chocolate molds, have them at room temperature and very clean (wipe clean with cotton balls and cotton swabs; do not wash or use anything abrasive).

- Get a set of dipping forks and loops. These are specially designed to help shake off excess chocolate, as well as to place designs on the tops of dipped chocolates that have not yet set.

Use a dipping fork that is suited to the shape you are dipping.

Tempering Temperatures

TYPE OF COUVERTURE	MELT TO	COOL TO	WARM TO
Dark chocolate	122° to 131°F	80.6° to 82.4°F	86° to 87.8°F
Milk chocolate	113° to 122°F	80.6° to 82.4°F	84.2° to 86°F

NOTE: White chocolate does not appear in this table or in the discussion of tempering. White chocolate is not really chocolate, because it contains no cocoa liqueur. It is difficult to temper, and it burns easily. Personally, I never use it in chocolate candies. If you want to dip centers in white chocolate, just melt it at a low temperature and stir until evenly mixed. You may have to refrigerate chocolates dipped in white couverture.

Hazelnut Praline Truffles *Truffes pralinées*

If you are expecting huge, dense, chocolate cream–filled bonbons here, you are in for a surprise but, hopefully, not a disappointment. These cocoa-covered treasures are filled with an extremely creamy, airy, and rich hazelnut-chocolate mixture. The centers are piped and may be irregular in shape. They are then dipped in chocolate and rolled in strained cocoa while the chocolate is still wet, so that the cocoa layer is rather thick. This is a great dipping job for two: one dips while the other rolls the chocolates in cocoa. Because the centers are cold when dipped and the chocolates are covered in cocoa, it does not matter if the tempering is a little off. Do not, however, use this couverture again for tempering; it will surely have traces of the truffle centers mixed in.   **Makes about 90 pieces**

I recipe (I cup) Caramelized Hazelnut Paste (page 320)

10 ounces (2½ sticks) unsalted butter, left at room temperature for I hour

¼ cup light corn syrup

10 ounces extra bittersweet chocolate, melted and cooled

2 pounds dark couverture

2 to 3 cups (8–12 ounces) sifted unsweetened cocoa powder

I.   Beat the hazelnut paste with an electric mixer until very smooth. Gradually beat in the butter until completely incorporated, scraping down the bowl with a rubber spatula from time to time. The mixture should become very light and fluffy. Beat in the corn syrup.

2.   With the mixer on low speed, gradually add the melted and cooled chocolate. Be sure to scrape down the mixing bowl from time to time. The mixture should be thick enough to pipe. If not, refrigerate for 1 hour, stirring from time to time with a rubber spatula to ensure an even consistency.

3.   Line 2 baking sheets with parchment paper. Work with 2 cups of filling at a time. More than this may melt in your hands while piping. Fill a pastry bag fitted with a ⅜-inch plain tip. Hold the tip ½ inch above the pan. The bag should be perpendicular to the pan. Holding the bag steady, pipe out a ½-inch ball. This will shape itself as it comes out of the bag. When the ball is the right size, stop squeezing and move to the next position on the pan. These can be close together. Do not worry if the shapes are irregular. Use up all the filling, then refrigerate the centers for at least 1 hour. (*The centers may be refrigerated for up to 3 days, covered loosely with plastic.*)

4.   Temper the couverture (see page 185) and place the bowl in front of you. If you are right-handed, place a shallow pan filled with sifted cocoa to your right and have the centers on your left. If you are left-handed, switch these positions. Place another shallow container next to the cocoa.

5.   Remove 1 tray of centers from the refrigerator and unwrap. Gently press down any points left by the pastry tip with the palm of your hand. Do not overhandle these centers, as they melt easily. Drop the centers, one at a time, into the chocolate. With a dipping loop, turn the center around in the chocolate so that it is completely covered. Lift out the truffle with the loop and tap off any excess couverture. Drop the truffle into the cocoa. Do this with several centers, making sure not to drop the dipped chocolates onto one another. Maintain the temperature of the tempered chocolate within a few degrees as directed on page 186. Put down the dipping fork and roll the still-wet truffles around in the cocoa with a small spatula or spoon. Roll these off to the side to harden. If you have someone to help you with this, you can dip one center at a time and your assistant can keep rolling. As hardened truffles accumulate, shake off any excess cocoa and place in the other container.

6.   When all the centers have been dipped and rolled, pour any leftover couverture into a small bowl and let it harden. Do not reuse this couverture for dipping, as these centers tend to streak the chocolate. It may be used for ganache. Strain the cocoa to remove any chocolate pieces, store in an airtight container, and reuse. (*The truffles may be stored, refrigerated or in a cool spot, in an airtight container for up to 2 weeks. Remove from the refrigerator 30 minutes before serving to allow the centers to soften. Tap off any excess cocoa and place the truffles in foil-lined candy cups, or simply pile them on a serving plate.*)

> In America, truffle has come to mean a huge dipped chocolate, filled with a flavored ganache and decorated with just about anything. In France, appellations of this sort are not taken lightly. A *truffe*, or truffle, is always somewhat irregular in shape. No matter what the filling is and whether the center is dipped or not, truffes are always rolled in cocoa. They are meant to resemble the irregular, soil-covered fungus for which they are named.

Muscadines

The day I arrived in France in 1981, I fell and broke my leg. I was in the hospital for three weeks, and there I met Pascaline Simar, who remains one of my closest friends. Pascaline's grandmother visited us regularly, and one day she brought with her a bag of these chocolates.

Muscadines are long, wrinkled chocolates—they look like giant raisins—that are rolled in powdered sugar. Inside, they are a smooth blend of hazelnut paste, chocolate, finely chopped candied orange peel, and Cointreau, an orange brandy. They melt in the mouth.   **Makes about 120 pieces**

2 ounces extra bittersweet chocolate, chopped

¾ cup whipping cream

2 tablespoons Cointreau

¼ cup finely minced Candied Orange Peel, homemade (page 341) or store-bought

2 recipes (2 cups) Caramelized Hazelnut Paste (page 320)

2 ounces (½ stick) unsalted butter, left at room temperature for 1 hour

1½ pounds dark couverture

3½ cups (1 pound) powdered sugar, sifted

1.   Put the bittersweet chocolate in a small mixing bowl. Combine the cream and Cointreau in a small saucepan and bring to a boil over medium heat. Pour the liquid over the chocolate. Let stand for 3 minutes to allow the chocolate to melt, then whisk until smooth. Pour this ganache into a shallow pan or bowl and allow it to cool completely. Fold in the orange peel.

2.   Beat the hazelnut paste on high speed with an electric mixer until very smooth. Add the butter in 4 parts, beating well and scraping down the bowl with a rubber spatula after each addition. On low speed, add the cooled ganache, mixing only until incorporated. If there are any streaks, finish mixing with a rubber spatula. This fragile mixture could curdle if overbeaten.

3.   Line 1 or 2 baking sheets with parchment, wax paper, or aluminum foil. Work with 1½ cups of the filling at a time, as this filling will melt in your hands and may separate. Place it in a a pastry bag fitted with a ½-inch plain tip and pipe out ½-inch-thick sausages along the entire length of the pan or pans. Keep these as straight and even as you can. Resting the tip on the pan will help guide you. Refrigerate the pan or pans until firm, at least 1 hour. (*At this point, the pan or pans can be wrapped in plastic and refrigerated for up to 1 week.*)

4.   Temper the couverture (see page 185) and place the bowl in front of you. Place a shallow pan next to the chocolate and sift or strain powdered sugar into it. Place another shallow container next to this.

5.   Remove 1 tray of centers from the refrigerator and unwrap. With a long, sharp knife, cut the sausages into 1-inch pieces and leave them on the pan.

6.   If you have somebody to help with this, it will make the job easier, but it is still feasible to do it alone. Drop the centers, one at a time, into the chocolate. With a dipping fork, turn the center over until it is completely coated. Lift out the center with the fork and tap off any excess couverture. Drop the dipped chocolate into the powdered sugar, then roll it around in the sugar while it is still wet. Dip and drop several chocolates, then pick up a fork (not the dipping fork) and push them around in the sugar. Have the tines of the fork parallel to the chocolate, so that the outside wrinkles a bit. Stir the chocolate often, as the cold centers will lower the temperature of the couverture in spots. Maintain the temperature of the tempered chocolate within a few degrees as directed on page 186. Put the finished chocolates off to the side. Once the chocolates have hardened, scoop them up with a wire skimmer, shake off the excess sugar, and place them in the other container.

7.   When all the centers have been dipped and rolled, pour any leftover couverture into a small bowl and let it harden. Use this chocolate in a ganache or another filling, but not for dipping. Strain the powdered sugar to remove any pieces of chocolate, and reuse. (*Muscadines may be stored at room temperature in an airtight container for up to 2 weeks. If it appears that the powdered sugar has melted, dust the muscadines lightly with more sugar, then tap off the excess before presenting them in elongated foil candy cups.*)

> **Muscadines, like truffles, are rolled in something—powdered sugar in this case—after they are dipped. Both of these chocolates have centers that are cold when dipped, and those cold centers will make the chocolate coating dull. The cocoa and powdered sugar act as camouflage. With this in mind, do not fret if your tempering is not perfect.**

Rochers

Little round bonbons, filled with *gianduja*, a combination of chocolate and hazelnut paste, these are simple and fabulous. They can be dipped in dark or milk chocolate, mixed with toasted chopped almonds. Rochers are produced commercially by Suchard and Lindt, among others, but you can make them easily at home.   Makes about 90 pieces

> 2 recipes (4 cups) Chocolate-Hazelnut Paste (page 322)
>
> Sifted cocoa, for dusting the work surface and your hands
>
> 1½ pounds dark or milk chocolate couverture
>
> 1 cup (4 ounces) slivered blanched almonds, toasted, cooled, and chopped, at room temperature

1.   Pound the Chocolate-Hazelnut Paste with a rolling pin to soften it, then knead to an even consistency. Lightly dust the work surface with cocoa, then roll the spread into a large disk, ½ inch thick. To do this evenly, place 2 rods or dowels, each ½ inch thick, about 12 inches apart, parallel to each other, as guides. Roll out the spread between the guides. Use a 1-inch plain round cutter to cut out as many disks as you can. Knead the scraps into a ball, reroll it, and cut more disks. Repeat until all the spread has been cut. Lightly coat your hands with cocoa and roll each disk into a ball. All the balls should be the same size. Place them on a baking sheet.

2.   Line 2 baking sheets with foil or parchment. Temper the couverture (see page 185) and place the bowl in front of you. Stir in the almonds. If you are right-handed, place the balls to the left of the bowl and a baking sheet to the right. Switch if you are left-handed.

3.   Using a chocolate dipping loop or your fingers, drop a ball into the tempered chocolate. With the other hand, loop in hand or not, move the ball around so that it is completely coated. Pick up the ball and tap or shake off any excess. Drop it onto the pan. Repeat this until all are coated. Maintain the temperature of the tempered chocolate within a few degrees as directed on page 186. When all the balls have been dipped, pour any leftover couverture into a small bowl and let it harden. You may temper this chocolate and use it again for coating more Rochers. (*Rochers may be stored for up to 2 weeks in a covered container, not necessarily airtight, at room temperature. Place sheets of wax paper between the layers of chocolates, as the almonds can nick the coatings of adjacent chocolates. Present on a platter, in a decorative box or tin, or in cellophane bags. These need not be placed in candy cups.*)

Chocolate-dipped Caramelized Hazelnuts *Noisettes*

This chocolate is a study in contrast. Toasted hazelnuts are coated with caramelized sugar, then stuck together with a bit of chocolate ganache. Finally, they are dipped in dark or milk chocolate couverture. If you like the combination of hazelnuts and chocolate, this could be your own private nirvana. Use your fingertips to dip these.

As always when working with caramel, be sure to use a heavy pot holder and not to splash the caramel on your skin. Sugar begins to caramelize at 340°F; sugar that is deep amber in color, almost burnt, may be as hot as 410°F. And, caramelized sugar will cling to your skin.   Makes about 60 pieces

½ cup minus 1 tablespoon (3 ounces) sugar

2 cups (8 ounces) lightly toasted blanched whole hazelnuts, still warm

1 tablespoon unsalted butter, at room temperature

½ to ¾ cup Chocolate Ganache (page 318), at room temperature, softened

1½ pounds dark or milk chocolate couverture

I.   Line a baking sheet with aluminum foil. Set aside.

2.   Place the sugar in a low heavy-bottomed saucepan. Add 2 tablespoons water to wet all the sugar without dissolving it, or even making it pourable.

3.   Begin heating the sugar over low to medium heat. The heat should remain on the bottom of the pot; flames should not come up the side of the pot at any time. As soon as you begin heating the sugar, wash any crystals clinging to the inside of the pot into the rest of the sugar, using a pastry brush dipped in water. It is important to do this before the pot gets too hot, so that the water from the brush does not simply evaporate against the pot and the brush does not burn. However, if you notice sugar crystals still clinging to the pot once it heats, try to wash them down with a more generous dose of water on the brush.

4.   Heat the sugar without disturbing the pot until the sugar begins to boil clear. Once the sugar boils clear, swirl it from time to time to distribute the heat within the syrup. When the sugar just begins to take on a light amber color, watch it carefully and swirl the pot often. It will go to deep caramel within just a few minutes. Cook the caramel to 365°F. Turn off the heat.

5.   Add the hazelnuts. Stir with a wooden spoon to coat all the nuts. Add the butter; the nuts will separate. Pour the nuts onto the baking sheet, keeping them as separate as possible. Cool completely.

continued

6.   Count the caramelized hazelnuts. You will need 4 for each chocolate piece. Form groups of 3 hazelnuts, setting aside 1 nut for each group of 3.

7.   If the ganache is not soft enough to pipe, put it in a heatproof bowl and warm it directly over a flame for just a few seconds. Stir the ganache with a spoon to even out the consistency. Spoon the ganache into a pastry bag fitted with a ¼-inch plain tip. Pipe about ½ teaspoon of ganache into the middle of each nut triangle. You may need to hold them together to prevent the ganache from pushing the nuts apart. After completing all the triangles, press another caramelized nut in the middle of each, to form a pyramid. Put the pyramids on a baking sheet.

8.   Line a baking sheet with aluminum foil or parchment paper. Temper the couverture (see page 185) and place the bowl in front of you. Maintain the temperature of the tempered chocolate as directed on page 186. Drop pyramids into the couverture with one hand and swirl them in the chocolate with the other. Lift out the dipped pyramids, shake off any excess couverture, and place on the lined baking sheet to set up. Pour any leftover couverture into a small bowl and let it harden. You may temper this chocolate and use it again for coating. (*These may be stored for up to 2 weeks in an airtight container at room temperature. Place sheets of wax paper between the layers of chocolates, as the hazelnuts can nick the coatings of adjacent chocolates. Present these on a platter with cookies and small pastries.*)

Raspberry-filled Chocolates *Framboises*

Few fruits are as enhanced by chocolate as the raspberry. These sumptuous centers are not made with fresh raspberries, but they will give you a triple hit: a ganache made with Raspberry Preserves, black raspberry liqueur, and raspberry eau-de-vie that is dipped in dark chocolate. The seeds are wonderful in the otherwise smooth center. You will need a pan that will give you a ½-inch-thick layer of ganache when it is poured in.   Makes 160 pieces

1¼ pounds extra bittersweet chocolate, finely chopped

½ cup whipping cream

½ cup Chambord (black raspberry liqueur)

¼ cup framboise (raspberry brandy)

½ cup plus 2 tablespoons (6½ ounces) Raspberry Preserves, homemade (page 338) or store-bought, with seeds

Sifted cocoa, for dusting the cutting board

1½ pounds dark couverture

194

1. Put the chocolate in a medium mixing bowl. Combine the cream, Chambord, framboise, and preserves in a small saucepan and bring to a boil over medium heat. Stir frequently, to prevent the preserves from sticking to the bottom of the pan. Pour the liquid over the bittersweet chocolate in a large mixing bowl and let stand for 5 minutes to allow the chocolate to melt. Whisk until smooth.

2. Line a 12 × 10 × 1-inch pan with aluminum foil. This must be perfectly smooth, or it will be difficult to remove the foil. Pour the ganache into the pan and smooth it with a metal spatula, for a ½-inch-thick even layer all over. Place the pan on a level surface. Let the ganache set up at room temperature until it is quite firm, about 2 hours. (*The centers can be made ahead, wrapped well in plastic, and refrigerated for up to 2 weeks. Before cutting, leave the tray at room temperature for 30 minutes, to allow the ganache to soften slightly. This will prevent crumbling.*)

3. Lightly dust a cutting board with cocoa powder. Turn the pan over onto the board. Lift off the pan and peel away all the foil, checking in the corners for wrinkles. Fill a tall jar with very hot water for dipping a thin knife and have a towel at hand to dry the knife after each cut. Line 2 baking sheets with parchment paper or aluminum foil.

4. Trim about ¼ inch from each side of the ganache and discard. Using a ruler to guide you, mark 1 × ¾-inch rectangles on the surface (160 of them), then cut these with the hot knife. Place the pieces on the baking sheets. Let stand at room temperature while you temper the couverture (see page 185).

5. Line 2 baking sheets with parchment paper or aluminum foil. Place the bowl of tempered couverture in front of you. Have the centers on one side, the baking sheets on the other. Drop the centers, one by one, into the couverture. Using a 2- or 3-tine dipping fork, turn each piece around in the couverture. Lift the pieces out with the fork going only about two-thirds across the bottom of the chocolate. Tap off any excess couverture. Set one edge of the piece on the baking sheet, then slide the fork out from under. Lay the fork across the top of the chocolate, allowing the tines to mark the top. Lift the fork away. Repeat with the remaining centers. Maintain the temperature of the tempered chocolate as directed on page 186.

6. When the chocolates are set, lift them off the pan. If they have any feet, or excess chocolate spread from the bottoms of the bonbons, cut the feet away and scrape the excess chocolate into the bowl of tempered chocolate. Pour any leftover couverture into a small bowl and let it harden. You may temper this chocolate and use it again for coating. (*These may be stored for up to 2 weeks in a covered container, not necessarily airtight, at room temperature. Place sheets of wax paper between the layers of chocolates. Present on a platter or in candy cups.*)

Jamaicans *Jamaïcains*

French pastry nomenclature associates Jamaica with pastries, chocolate, and desserts made with dark rum. These dark chocolate bonbons are no exception. Rum-soaked raisins are chopped and added to a dark ganache, along with the rum itself. The ganache is then formed into balls and dipped in more dark chocolate. These pack quite a punch but are nonetheless very balanced and not too sweet.

You will need a very small (¼-ounce) ice cream scoop to form these balls. A melon baller will work, but it can be difficult to tap the fillings out. The ganache can also be piped out through a ½-inch plain tip. The centers may then be irregular in shape and size. If that doesn't matter to you, pipe away. Have a toothpick handy, just in case the raisins plug the pastry tip. Or replace the raisins with dried currants to help in this regard.

Plan ahead for these little bonbons. Their confection requires two overnight processes. **Makes about 110 pieces**

1 cup (5 ounces) raisins or currants

1¼ cups dark rum

13 ounces extra bittersweet chocolate, finely chopped

13 ounces milk chocolate, finely chopped

¾ cup whipping cream

1¼ pounds dark couverture

1. Combine the raisins or currants and the rum in a small bowl, cover loosely with plastic, and let soak overnight at room temperature.

2. If you have used raisins, drain them, reserving all the rum. Chop them, at least in half if not smaller, then put them back in the rum. If you are piping the chocolates, drain and chop the currants as well.

3. Put the bittersweet and milk chocolates in a large bowl. Combine the cream, raisins or currants, and rum in a small saucepan over medium heat and bring to a boil. Pour the liquid over the chocolate and let stand for 5 minutes to allow the chocolates to melt. Whisk until the chocolates have melted evenly. Pour the ganache into a bowl or plastic container to set up at room temperature overnight. Once cool, cover loosely with plastic wrap. Do not refrigerate.

4. Line 2 baking sheets with parchment or wax paper. Using a small ice cream scoop, a melon baller, or a pastry bag fitted with a ½-inch plain tip, form balls, leaving them on the covered pans. If using a bag, see Step 3 of the recipe for Hazelnut Praline Truffles (page 188), but do not refrigerate. If scooping, avoid getting air into the centers. Scrape down the bowl or container and use all the ganache.

5. Line 2 baking sheets with parchment paper or aluminum foil. Temper the couverture (see page 185) and place the bowl in front of you. Have the chocolate centers on one side and the baking sheets on the other. Drop a center into the couverture with one hand and turn it over in the couverture with a dipping loop. Lift out the bonbon, tap off any excess, and turn it onto the baking sheet. Repeat this with all the centers, placing them close together but not touching. When you have filled one pan, dip your fingertips into the couverture and then flick thin strands of chocolate over the dipped bonbons to decorate. Maintain the temperature of the tempered chocolate as directed on page 186. Pour any leftover couverture into a small bowl and let it harden. You may temper this chocolate and use it again for coating. (*These may be stored for up to 2 weeks in a covered container at room temperature. Place sheets of wax paper between the layers of chocolates. Present on a platter or in candy cups.*)

Brazilians *Brésiliens*

Just as the French associate rum-flavored sweets with Jamaica, they attribute coffee-flavored ones,
for the most part, to Brazil. Here is a small square chocolate filled with a coffee-flavored ganache.
The French have coffee-flavored chocolate available to them, and if you can find that, use it here.
Make sure that what you get is not a filled chocolate bar, which would make the ganache too loose.
If you find the coffee-flavored chocolate, use half the amount of instant coffee called for below.
Makes about 120 pieces

> 18 ounces extra bittersweet or coffee-flavored chocolate, chopped
>
> 18 ounces milk chocolate, chopped
>
> ¾ cup whole milk
>
> 2 cups minus 2 tablespoons whipping cream
>
> ¼ cup (2 ounces) instant coffee
>
> 4 ounces (1 stick) unsalted butter, at room temperature
>
> Sifted cocoa, for dusting the work surface
>
> 28 ounces (1¾ pounds) dark couverture
>
> 120 chocolate coffee beans, for decoration

1.   Put the bittersweet and milk chocolates in a large bowl. Combine the milk and cream in a
small saucepan over medium heat and bring to a boil. Dissolve the instant coffee in this mixture.
Pour the liquid over the chopped chocolates. Let stand for 5 minutes to allow the chocolates to
melt, then whisk until smooth. Cool to room temperature.

2.   Whisk the butter in a small bowl until smooth. Whisk it into the ganache, mixing only until
no butter streaks remain.

3.   Line a 12 × 10 × 1-inch baking pan with aluminum foil. Make sure that the foil is smooth all
over. Pour the coffee ganache into the pan and spread evenly with a metal spatula. The layer will
almost reach the top of the pan. Refrigerate until firm, about 1½ hours. (*Once the ganache is firm,
the pan may be covered and refrigerated for up to 2 weeks.*)

4.   Lightly dust a cutting board with cocoa powder. Turn the pan over onto the cutting board.
Lift off the pan and peel away the foil, checking in the corners for wrinkles. Fill a tall jar with very
hot water for dipping a thin knife and have a towel at hand to dry the knife after each cut. Line 2
baking sheets with parchment paper or aluminum foil.

5.   Trim about ¼ inch from each side and discard. Using a ruler to guide you, mark 1-inch squares on the surface (120 of them), then cut these with the hot knife. Place the squares on the baking sheets. Let stand at room temperature while you temper the couverture (see page 185).

6.   Place the bowl of tempered couverture in front of you. Have the centers on 1 side, the baking sheets on the other. Drop the centers, one by one, into the couverture. Using a 2- or 3-tine dipping fork, turn the cubes around in the couverture. Lift the piece out with the fork going only about two-thirds across the bottom of the chocolate. Tap off any excess couverture. Set 1 edge of the piece on the baking sheet, then slide the fork out from under. Place a coffee bean on top of the piece, crease side up. Repeat with the remaining centers. Maintain the temperature of the tempered chocolate as directed on page 186.

7.   When the chocolates are set, lift them off the pan. If they have any feet, or excess chocolate spread from the bottoms of the squares, cut the feet away and scrape the excess chocolate into the bowl of tempered chocolate. Pour any leftover couverture into a small bowl and let it harden. You may temper this chocolate and use it again for coating. (*These may be stored for up to 2 weeks in a covered container at room temperature. Place sheets of wax paper between the layers of chocolates. Present on a platter or in candy cups.*)

Chocolate-covered Caramels *Perlias*

These luscious chocolate-flavored soft caramels are dipped in dark or milk chocolate. You can make the centers ahead and refrigerate them. Cut them while still cold, but be sure to let them come to room temperature before dipping.

As always when working with caramel, be sure to use a heavy pot holder and not to splash the caramel on your skin. Sugar begins to caramelize at 340°F; sugar that is deep amber in color, almost burnt, may be as hot as 410°F. And, caramelized sugar will cling to your skin. Since you are going to whisk the caramel, be sure to prepare the sugar in a deep pot, so that none of the caramel splashes out.   **Makes about 120 pieces**

> 1½ cups whipping cream
>
> ¾ cup (5¼ ounces) sugar
>
> 3 tablespoons light corn syrup
>
> 10 ounces extra bittersweet chocolate, finely chopped
>
> 6½ ounces milk chocolate, finely chopped
>
> 3 tablespoons unsalted butter, at room temperature
>
> Sifted cocoa, for dusting the cutting board
>
> 1½ pounds dark or milk couverture

1. Bring the cream to a boil in a small saucepan. Cover and set aside.

2. Put the sugar in a deep, heavy-bottomed stainless steel saucepan. Add the corn syrup and 2 tablespoons of water, then stir with a wooden spoon to wet all the sugar without dissolving it, or even making it pourable.

3. Begin heating the sugar over low to medium heat. The heat should remain on the bottom of the pot; flames should not come up the side of the pot at any time. As soon as you begin heating the sugar, wash any crystals clinging to the inside of the pot into the rest of the sugar, using a pastry brush dipped in water. Do this before the pot gets too hot, so that the water from the brush does not simply evaporate against the pot and the brush does not burn. However, if you notice sugar crystals still clinging to the pot once it heats, try to wash them down with a more generous dose of water on the brush. Heat the sugar without disturbing the pot until the sugar begins to boil clear. Once the sugar boils clear, swirl it from time to time to distribute the heat within the syrup. When the sugar just begins to take on a light amber color, watch it carefully and swirl the pot often. It will go to deep caramel within just a few minutes. Once the caramel has reached 370°F, turn off the heat and quickly but carefully whisk in the hot cream. Use a long-handled whisk and wrap a towel around your hand to protect yourself from splattering caramel. Avoid standing directly over the pot until the eruption has subsided.

4. Put the bittersweet and milk chocolates into a large mixing bowl, then pour the caramel-cream mixture over. Let stand for 5 minutes to melt the chocolates, then whisk until smooth. Cool to room temperature.

5. Whisk the butter in a small bowl until smooth. Whisk it into the cooled ganache, mixing only until no butter streaks remain.

6. Line a 12 × 10 × 1-inch baking pan with aluminum foil. Make sure that the foil is smooth all over. Pour the ganache into the pan and smooth it evenly with a metal spatula. Refrigerate until firm, about 1 hour. (*Once the ganache is firm, the pan may be covered and refrigerated for up to 1 week.*)

7. Lightly dust a cutting board with cocoa powder. Turn the pan over onto the cutting board. Lift off the pan and peel away the foil, checking in the corners for wrinkles. Fill a tall jar with very hot water for dipping a thin knife and have a towel at hand to dry the knife after each cut. Line 2 baking sheets with parchment paper or aluminum foil.

8. Trim about ¼ inch from each side and discard. Using a ruler to guide you, mark 1-inch squares on the surface (120 of them), then cut these with the hot knife. Place the squares on the baking sheets. Let the centers come to room temperature while you temper the couverture (page 185).

9. Place the bowl of tempered couverture in front of you. Have the centers on one side, the baking sheets on the other. Drop the centers, one by one, into the couverture. Using a 2- or 3-tine dipping fork, turn the square around in the couverture. Lift the square out with the fork going only about two-thirds across the bottom of the chocolate. Tap off any excess couverture. Set one edge of the square on the baking sheet, then slide the fork out from under. Lay one tine of the fork on a diagonal across the top of the chocolate, then lift off the fork, leaving a mark. Repeat with the remaining centers. Maintain the heat of the tempered chocolate as described on page 186.

Tap the fork on the side of the bowl to remove excess chocolate; keep the chocolate close to the tip of the fork.

Lay one tine diagonally on top of the still-wet chocolate, then lift the fork to leave a peak for decoration.

10. When the chocolates are set, remove them from the pan. If they have any feet, or excess chocolate spread from the bottoms of the squares, cut the feet away and scrape the excess chocolate into the bowl of tempered chocolate. Pour any leftover couverture into a small bowl and let it harden. You may temper this chocolate and use it again for coating. (*Perlias may be stored for up to 1 week in a covered container at room temperature. Place sheets of wax paper between the layers of chocolates. Present on a platter or in candy cups.*)

Chocolate-covered Nougat

Nougats au chocolat

These are like miniature candy bars that have just the right amount of chocolate. They are rectangles of soft nutty nougat dipped in a thin layer of chocolate. Chewy, crunchy, and sweet—exactly what candy bars should be! Nougat bars are the perfect addition to a tray of petit fours. Makes about 100 pieces

> 1 recipe (3¼ pounds) Soft Nougat from Provence (page 108), prepared on a 16 × 12-inch pan
>
> 2¼ pounds dark couverture
>
> ¼ cup (1 ounce) finely chopped unsalted pistachios

1. Line 2 or more baking sheets with aluminum foil. Cut the nougat into 2 × 1-inch pieces. Separate the pieces and place them on the baking sheets.

2. Line 2 other baking sheets with parchment paper or aluminum foil. Temper the couverture (see page 185). Place the pans of nougat on one side of the bowl and the lined baking sheets or a large piece of parchment or foil on the other. With one hand, drop a piece of nougat into the couverture. Turn the nougat over in the couverture with a wide dipping fork. Lift the nougat out of the couverture so that the nougat is perpendicular to the fork, and the tines of the fork extend about three-fourths of the way underneath the chocolate. Tap off any excess chocolate, then set 1 long end of the bar on the baking sheet or paper. Release the bar and slide the fork out from under. Immediately drop a few pieces of chopped pistachio onto the chocolate. Repeat with all the chocolates. Maintain the temperature of the tempered chocolate as described on page 186.

3. Once the chocolates have set, remove them from the pan or paper. If they have any feet, or excess chocolate spread from the bottoms, cut the feet away and scrape the excess chocolate into the bowl of tempered chocolate. Pour any leftover couverture into a small bowl and let it harden. You may temper this chocolate and use it again for coating. (*These may be stored for up to 1 week in a covered container at room temperature. Present on a platter alone or with assorted cookies and petit fours.*)

Chocolate-covered Orange Peel

Aiguillettes d'oranges au chocolat

These are the simplest of all chocolate confections, since you need not fuss with centers. Of course, if you make your own candied orange peel, the results will be even better. If the peels have syrup clinging to them, pat them dry with paper towels. If they still seem to be oozing, place the peels in a strainer and rinse them in warm water. Pat them dry thoroughly; any water would ruin your tempered chocolate.

Make this confection for a tray of petit fours. You can roll the dipped peels, while they are still wet, in chopped toasted almonds, if you wish.

You should temper more chocolate than you need. The extra ensures that you have enough chocolate for all the peel and that you don't have to scrape the bottom of the bowl.   **Makes about 1 pound**

> 1 recipe (8 ounces) Candied Orange Peel, homemade (page 341) or store-bought, at room temperature
>
> ¾ pound dark couverture

1.   If using homemade orange peel, cut the pieces into 2- to 3-inch strips. Keep these as regular as possible for a good presentation.

2.   Temper the couverture (see page 185). Line a baking sheet with parchment paper or aluminum foil. Smooth the foil. Drop the orange peel, one piece at a time, into the couverture and turn it over in the chocolate with a dipping fork. Lift out the peel and tap off any excess chocolate. Lay the peel on the baking sheet, turning it upside down and dropping it from the fork. Continue with all the orange peel. Maintain the temperature of the tempered chocolate as directed on page 186. Pour any leftover couverture into a small bowl and let it harden. You may temper this chocolate and use it again for coating. *(These may be stored for up to 1 month in a covered container at room temperature. Place wax paper between the layers. Present on a platter or beside individual cups of tea.)*

This is a great way to practice tempering and coating with couverture—no need to worry about chocolate centers. Purchase good-quality candied orange peel—make sure that the pieces are regular in length and not crystallized—and dip away.

Dried Fruit and Nut Bark *Mendiants*

In French candy-making, *Mendiant* is the term used to describe a classic mix of dried fruits and nuts, namely, almonds, figs, hazelnuts, and raisins. Over time, the mix has changed, but when you see the term *Mendiant,* you can be assured that a dried fruit and nut mixture is involved.

Many shops make their Mendiants in rounds. They look stunning in a pastry case and equally so in a candy box, but they are a nuisance to make, and unless you have a use for the scraps, which contain fruits and nuts, they are wasted. This bark is made on a cookie sheet, then cut into squares with a knife. It can also be broken into random pieces.   **Makes 2 pounds**

A total of ¾ pound of any or all of the following:

Whole blanched toasted almonds

Whole blanched toasted hazelnuts

Whole blanched unsalted pistachios

Dark raisins

Chopped Candied Orange Peel (page 341)

1 pound extra bittersweet chocolate

¾ recipe (¾ cup) ground Caramelized Hazelnut Paste (page 320)

1.　Cover a very flat work surface or an inverted baking sheet with a large piece of aluminum foil. Stir together the nuts and fruits, mixing very evenly.

2.　Temper the bittersweet chocolate (see page 185) and stir in the Caramelized Hazelnut Paste. Pour the chocolate mixture onto the prepared work surface, spreading it to a thickness of about ¼ inch. Before the chocolate sets, cover the top evenly with the mixture of dried fruits and nuts. Using your fingertips, press these lightly into the chocolate. Cover with a sheet of parchment or wax paper, and lightly roll over the paper with a rolling pin, to make sure that the topping is set into the chocolate. Do this quickly; the chocolate sets up fast. As soon as the chocolate sets up, cut the bark into 2-inch squares using a sharp, heavy knife. Or break it into uneven chunks. *(These may be stored for up to 1 month in a covered container at room temperature. Place wax paper between the layers as the nuts may nick adjacent pieces. Present a few pieces in cellophane bags or on a platter, or pile the bark on a platter.)*

Since extra bittersweet chocolate has a relatively low percentage of cocoa butter, it is difficult to use as a dipping chocolate because it is not terribly fluid when tempered. You can use extra bittersweet chocolate in this recipe, however, since it doesn't require a thin coating of chocolate. Bittersweet chocolate will complement the dried fruits and nuts beautifully.

Simple Chocolate Desserts

Simples desserts au chocolat

THERE ARE A FEW criteria that must be met before I will call a dessert simple.

- It must not take more than 30 minutes to prepare (excluding baking time).

- A child old enough to use the oven must be able to carry out the recipe (it is all right if the child takes more than 30 minutes to do so).

- The end result must belie the time needed to prepare the dessert.

By coincidence, the recipes in this chapter are all for chocolate desserts. Perhaps this is because chocolate is so satisfying in itself that one need not do much to it. If only life—and all pastry baking—were always this simple!

Ulysse's Chocolate Cake / *Gâteau au chocolat d'Ulysse*

Warm Chocolate Cakes / *Gâteaux tieds au chocolat*
    Warm Chocolate Cake / *Gâteau tied au chocolat*

Four-tiered Chocolate Mousse / *Mousse aux quatre chocolats*

Ulysse's Chocolate Cake *Gâteau au chocolat d'Ulysse*

When I returned to France to do research for this book, I went to visit one of my closest friends, Pascaline Simar. Her son, Ulysse, then twelve years old, presented me with this chocolate cake. This was truly a surprise, as Ulysse had never shown any particular interest in baking. Even more thrilling was the confidence with which this rather shy child presented me with the cake, which he had prepared using a hand mixer in a kitchen—typically Parisian—the size of a postage stamp and equipped with only a tabletop convection oven. I will always treasure the copy of Ulysse's recipe, written in his own hand (complete with misspelled words).

The cake is a rich torte, composed of the simplest of ingredients. You can prepare this just before your guests arrive and serve it warm with some lightly whipped cream, fresh berries, or a drizzle of Chocolate Ganache (page 318) on the side. Never serve it cold, as this will obscure the subtleties of the flavors.   Makes one 9-inch cake, for 6 to 8 servings

Butter, for greasing the pan

Fine dry bread crumbs, flour, or cornstarch, for dusting the pan

5 ounces bittersweet chocolate, chopped

4 ounces (1 stick) unsalted butter, cut into small pieces

½ cup plus 1 tablespoon (4 ounces) sugar

4 large eggs, separated

2½ tablespoons cornstarch

1.   Preheat the oven to 400°F. Lightly butter a 9-inch cake pan or springform pan. Line the bottom with parchment paper. Butter the paper, then dust the entire pan with bread crumbs, flour, or cornstarch.

2.   Combine the chocolate and butter in a bowl or in the top of a double boiler. Set the bowl in simmering water, with the part of the bowl containing the chocolate surrounded by water, not sitting above it. The bowl should seal the pot, to prevent steam from coming out and getting into the chocolate. Melt the chocolate and butter together, then remove the bowl from the heat and whisk the mixture until smooth.

3.   Stir in ½ cup of sugar, reserving 1 tablespoon for the egg whites. Whisk in the egg yolks, one at a time, stirring thoroughly after each addition. Sift or strain the cornstarch over the chocolate mixture. Mix well.

continued

4. Put the egg whites in a clean mixing bowl or the bowl of an electric mixer. Using a whisk attachment, mix on low speed until the whites begin to froth, then increase to medium speed and whip until the whites hold soft peaks. Gradually add the reserved tablespoon of sugar in a thin stream. Once all has been added, increase to high speed and whip until the whites are stiff but not dry.

5. Carefully fold the chocolate mixture into the whites. Do not overmix. Pour the batter into the pan.

6. Bake for 25 to 30 minutes. The cake should just begin to rise and will form a crust. A toothpick inserted into the middle of the cake should come out dry.

7. Cool the cake on a rack until it begins to come away from the pan. Gently invert the cake onto another rack, remove the pan and the paper, and invert it again onto a serving platter. Serve the cake warm or at room temperature.

Warm Chocolate Cakes *Gâteaux tieds au chocolat*

This dessert is not for the faint of heart. The richness of a flourless chocolate cake is intensified by serving it warm. The recipe is, however, so incredibly simple that you can top off a fancy meal with a dessert that will enthrall your guests. And you will not have to spend more than half an hour preparing it. Not that you need the added richness, but I recommend serving each cake with a dollop of barely sweetened, lightly whipped cream for the contrast in flavors and temperatures.

I prefer to make the dessert in individual ramekins, which make it much easier to serve hot. If you want to make one large cake (see the following recipe), you have to wait for the cake to cool to lukewarm before unmolding and cutting it. Makes 10 individual cakes

I pound bittersweet chocolate, coarsely chopped

8 ounces (2 sticks) unsalted butter, cut into large pieces

6 large eggs

¼ cup plus 2 tablespoons (2½ ounces) sugar

Finely grated zest of I orange

I cup (4 ounces) whole unsalted pistachios, lightly toasted (optional)

I cup whipping cream

1. Place an oven rack in the middle of the oven, with no racks above it. Preheat the oven to 400°F. Boil a kettleful of water and set aside.

2. Combine the chocolate and butter in a bowl. Set the bowl in simmering water with the part of the bowl containing the chocolate surrounded by water, not sitting above it. The bowl should seal the pot, to prevent steam from coming out and getting into the chocolate. Melt the chocolate and butter together, then remove the bowl and whisk the mixture until smooth. Set aside to cool. This mixture should be tepid when used. Turn off the heat, leaving the simmering water in the pot.

3. Place the eggs in a large mixing bowl or the bowl of an electric mixer and whisk to mix. Add ¼ cup sugar and whisk immediately. Place the bowl in the warm water in the pot and whisk the eggs and sugar until the mixture is tepid and the sugar is dissolved. Beat the eggs with an electric mixer until they have tripled in volume. This mixture will not attain the thickness of a *génoise*. Add the orange zest at the end of the mixing time.

4. Using a rubber spatula, fold the warm chocolate mixture into the eggs. About halfway through, the mixture will come together and sink a bit. Be sure to scrape all the chocolate out of the bowl. Fold in the pistachios, if using.

5. Spoon the batter into ten 5-ounce ungreased ramekins. Fill to ¼ inch from the top. Place these in a large roasting pan or baking dish, leaving one out for the moment. Fill the pan with hot water from the kettle, pouring into the space left by the last ramekin. Take care not to splash water into the chocolate. The water should reach three-quarters the depth of the batter. Place the last ramekin in the pan. Carefully slide the pan into the oven, still being careful not to splash any water.

6. Bake for 12 to 15 minutes, or until the tops of the cakes are set, slightly risen, and still jiggle when touched. Remove the pan from the oven and let the cakes cool slightly in the water.

7. Whip the cream and 2 tablespoons sugar together until the cream holds the trail of the whisk or beaters.

8. As soon as they can be touched, lift the molds out of the water and wipe them dry. Serve immediately, in the ramekins, with the whipped cream passed in a bowl. Or let the cakes cool, then refrigerate. (*The ramekins may be refrigerated for up to 4 days. To reheat, let the cakes come to room temperature. Preheat the oven to 400°F, set them in another hot water bath, and heat for 5 minutes. Serve immediately.*)

Warm Chocolate Cake *Gâteau tied au chocolat*

If you prefer a large cake, use the same ingredients as for the Warm Chocolate Cakes, but make the following changes in the directions.

I. In Step 1 of the master recipe, line the bottom of an 9-inch cake pan with a parchment circle.

2. Prepare the batter as in Steps 2, 3, and 4.

3. Pour the batter into the pan and place it in a large roasting pan. Pour hot water into the roasting pan, coming about halfway up the cake pan. Slide the pan into the oven.

4. Bake for 20 minutes. Cool the cake in the water bath for 10 minutes, then on a wire rack for 1 hour, at most. Unmold the cake by running a thin knife or a small metal spatula around the edge. Turn the cake onto a serving platter and remove the pan. Peel away the paper. Serve with lightly whipped cream, passed in a bowl. This cake may be served slightly warm or at room temperature. If it is too hot, it will be difficult to serve in attractive wedges.

Four-tiered Chocolate Mousse

Mousse aux quatre chocolats

I used to make this dessert when I was the pastry chef at 72 Market Street in Venice, California. At the time, I would make forty-eight servings at once, all in individual molds or rings that I would remove before serving. The dessert is very soft and creamy, and frankly, it was a pain to unmold. But the patrons loved it, and I could not take it off the menu.

Fortunately, you can now make this same mousse with ease. Simply layer the four components into clear dessert glasses. White-wine glasses with a six-ounce capacity are ideal because the stem brings the dessert closer to eye level, and the richness of the mousses begs for small portions.

Use the best-quality imported chocolate you can find. If you do not want to prepare Gianduja yourself, buy a bar of milk chocolate filled with hazelnut cream or hazelnut truffle. All of these chocolates are available in supermarkets under the brand names Tobler, Lindt, and Suchard, and in gourmet shops under the name Valrhona.   Makes 8 servings

2 ounces white chocolate, finely chopped

2 ounces milk chocolate, finely chopped

2 ounces *Gianduja* (page 322), finely chopped

2 ounces bittersweet chocolate, finely chopped

3 cups whipping cream, 2 cups very cold

Tuiles d'amandes (page 164) or *Cigarettes* (page 166)

Chocolate Curls (page 182) or *Crème Chantilly* (page 307)

1.   Place the chocolates in 4 separate small mixing bowls. Bring 1 cup of the cream to a boil in a small saucepan over medium heat. Divide it evenly among the 4 chocolates, pouring about ¼ cup into each bowl. Let the chocolates stand for 5 minutes to melt, then whisk each until smooth, moving from the lightest to the darkest chocolate and tapping off the excess as you go. Let cool to room temperature.

2.   Place a large mixing bowl or the bowl of an electric mixer in the freezer, along with the mixer's beaters or whisk attachment. Freeze for 15 minutes.

3.   Whip the remaining 2 cups of cream, starting on low speed and gradually increasing to medium as it thickens, until it holds a shape but is not completely stiff. Measure the volume of the whipped cream.

4.   Starting with the white chocolate and working with 1 color at a time, fold one-fourth of the cream into the ganache and mix lightly, but thoroughly. By the time you get to the bittersweet chocolate, it may be too cold to mix in the whipped cream. Warm the ganache slightly by placing the bowl in a large bowl with 1 inch of hot tap water in it for a few seconds.

5.   Using a pastry bag fitted with a large plain tip or an oval spoon that fits inside the top of the glass, divide the white mousse between 8 stemmed white-wine glasses. Tap each glass lightly on the table to level the mousse. Repeat this mixing procedure with the milk chocolate, Gianduja, and bittersweet chocolate mousse, in that order, tapping each time to fill in any gaps and level the mousse. Top with *Tuiles d'amandes* or *Cigarettes* and Chocolate Curls or *Crème Chantilly*. Refrigerate for at least 2 hours or up to 24 hours. Serve cold.

Ice Cream and Sorbets

La Glacerie

I **HAVE NEVER REALLY** understood the connection between climate and the popularity of ice creams and sorbets. During the summer months, I can think of many different ways to cool off other than by eating ice cream. In the winter, I enjoy ice cream with equal verve, even if it is cold outside. After all, I am inside, where it is warm and cozy.

Perhaps it is the connection between the availability of certain fruits and summer that is the key. Frankly, with the availability of fruits year-round these days, there is no excuse for depriving oneself of homemade ice cream or sorbet. It is so incredibly easy to make ice cream and sorbets at home that you should run out right now and buy an ice cream maker.

The principle is simple: a cold mixture is poured into a freezing chamber that has a revolving paddle in the middle. The turbine keeps the mixture moving, and as it comes in contact with the walls of the chamber, it freezes. If the mixture has the right balance—not too much sugar or too much cream—it will freeze in very tiny crystals, which form a compact mass. As long as it is not overchurned, it will not take in too much air and will remain smooth.

When preparing ice cream, it is crucial that the base be cold before it is poured into the ice cream maker. Otherwise, the butterfat in the mix will separate out.

Ice creams and sorbets should be churned only to the consistency of soft-serve ice cream. Churned any more and ice creams will turn buttery, and sorbets will not benefit at all. The final hardening occurs in the freezer. Once ice cream, and particularly sorbet, has been in the freezer for a long time, its consistency changes. Sorbet can be thawed and rechurned, but ice cream cannot. Generally speaking, ice creams and sorbets are at their peak within 8 hours of churning. They should not be scooped directly out of the ice cream maker; they do need some time in the freezer.

What kind of ice cream maker to buy for home use? I have had great results with several types. It really depends on the mix and truly following the manufacturer's directions on how to use the device. An ice cream maker that has a container in which you can store the ice cream after it is churned is a definite plus. Make sure to freeze the container first; this renders the ice cream maker more efficient. I have also had excellent results with the type of ice cream maker that freezes the mix for several hours but only requires one turn of the crank every quarter-hour.

If you are adding anything chunky, such as nuts or rum-soaked raisins, to ice cream or sorbet, do so only when the mix is almost done churning. Large chunks added to the mix early on will keep the base mix away from the walls of the freezing chamber, and the base will not freeze evenly, with fine crystals.

Sorbets are an excellent way to use up fruit that no longer looks great but still tastes good. They are perfect for cleansing the palate between courses, especially the more neutral sorbets, such as those made from citrus juices. Note that alcohol lowers the freezing temperature of sorbets and ice cream. They don't freeze at the same temperature as a nonalcoholic product. A sorbet or ice cream with a great deal of alcohol may stay mushy. This may be an advantage with certain ice creams, as they will remain very creamy, never hard. But if you are looking for the perfect scoop, keep the alcohol at a minimum.

There are a few basic formulas that you can use as rules of thumb. They will enable you to create your own frozen fantasies.

- For fruit sorbets made from fruit puree, use equal volumes of puree and Simple Syrup (page 334) and add three-quarters that volume in water.

- Enhance the flavor, or compensate for sweetness, with a small amount of freshly squeezed lemon juice.

- For citrus sorbets, take the weight of the juice and use 30 percent sugar. For example, for 1 quart of grapefruit juice, which weighs 32 ounces, add 9.6 ounces (about 1¼ cups) of sugar. This sorbet will be somewhat icy, since there is no syrup to even out the crystals. Make sure that the sugar dissolves completely in the juice.

• For ice cream, start with 3 cups Crème Anglaise (page 328) and add flavorings while the Crème Anglaise is still warm. You can also infuse the milk and cream with such ingredients as ground coffee, unsweetened coconut, and fresh herbs.

Of course, you are the ultimate judge. If you taste an ice cream or sorbet mix before it is churned and you feel that it needs something, be creative. As long as you keep to the basic principles, there is very little that can go wrong.

Coconut Ice Cream / *Glace à la noix de coco*

Ginger Ice Cream / *Glace au gingembre*

Green Apple Sorbet with Basil / *Sorbet à la pomme verte au basilic*

Chocolate Sorbet / *Sorbet au chocolat*

Chocolate-Mint Sorbet / *Sorbet chocolat-menthe*

Mango Sorbet / *Sorbet à la mangue*

Tropical Sorbet / *Sorbet éxotique*

Pear Sorbet / *Sorbet à la poire*

Raspberry Sorbet / *Sorbet aux framboises*

Coconut Ice Cream *Glace à la noix de coco*

Technically speaking, this is an ice milk, since it contains no cream. Nor does it contain eggs. The fat content of the coconut itself gives this a creamy texture. Do not leave it in the freezer too long, though, or the coconut oil will become grainy.

The beauty of this sorbet, besides its flavor, which complements a variety of tropical flavors, as well as chocolate, is its stark white color. It provides a great contrast with brightly colored sorbets.

Makes about 5 cups

3 cups whole milk

2 cups (7 ounces) unsweetened flaked or shredded coconut

1 tablespoon light corn syrup

1¼ cups Simple Syrup (page 334), cold

1. Combine the milk and coconut in a large stainless steel pot over medium heat and bring to a boil. Turn off the heat, cover the pot, and let steep for 1 hour.

2. Puree the infusion in a food processor or blender, or with a handheld blender, until fine. Press the puree through a fine mesh strainer, extracting as much of the milk as possible. The mixture should be light and creamy, similar in consistency to very lightly whipped cream. Stir in the corn syrup. Chill the mixture in an ice bath or in the refrigerator.

3. Whisk the Simple Syrup into the mixture. It may have separated somewhat while chilling, so be sure to mix well.

4. Pour the mixture into the container of an ice cream maker and churn according to the manufacturer's instructions to the consistency of soft ice cream. Transfer to a freezer container and freeze until firm, 2 to 3 hours, depending on the size and depth of the container.

Ginger Ice Cream *Glace au gingembre*

A fascination with Asian cuisine has broadened the horizons of the French chef and the pastry chef as well. This subtle ice cream captures the spiciness of ginger with both fresh and crystallized ginger.

Ginger goes well with exotic fruits and the sorbets made from those fruits. However, served solo or with a Coconut-Macadamia Tile Cookie (page 165), Ginger Ice Cream is perfect after an Asian-influenced meal.

I recommend making the base a day before churning the ice cream, in order to give the flavors a chance to meld. The flavor of the ice cream itself will mellow—even fade—after two days, so try to serve the ice cream within twenty-four hours of preparing it.   **Makes about 3 cups**

½ cup (3½ ounces) sugar

3 tablespoons (packed) grated or finely minced fresh ginger

1 cup whole milk

2 tablespoons minced crystallized ginger

4 large egg yolks

1 cup whipping cream, very cold

½ to 1 teaspoon freshly squeezed lemon juice

1.   Heat ½ cup water with ¼ cup of the sugar in a small, stainless steel saucepan over medium heat. When the sugar dissolves, add the fresh ginger. Bring this mixture to a boil, then reduce the heat and simmer for 5 minutes. Turn off the heat and leave the syrup in the pan.

2.   Heat the milk with 1 tablespoon of the crystallized ginger in a medium stainless steel saucepan over medium heat, until fine bubbles form around the edge of the milk's surface, just to scald it. Turn off the heat. Using a rubber spatula, stir in the ginger syrup, scraping in all the pieces of ginger. Cover the saucepan and let steep for 20 minutes.

3.   Fill a large bowl with ice cubes. Place a medium bowl in the ice bath and set a medium mesh strainer over the inner bowl.

4.   Uncover the saucepan of infused liquid and bring to a boil over medium heat. Meanwhile, take care that the mixture does not boil over.

5.   In a medium mixing bowl, whisk the egg yolks with the remaining ¼ cup of sugar until the mixture is thick and pale yellow. This should take about 60 seconds. Pour all the liquid over the eggs, whisking constantly, then pour this mixture back into the pot.

6. Cook the custard over low to medium heat, stirring constantly with a wooden spoon and touching the bottom of the pot with the spoon at all times until the custard coats the back of the spoon, 1 to 2 minutes. The mixture must not come to a boil, or the egg yolks will curdle.

7. Pour the custard through the strainer into the inner bowl. Carefully pour cold water between the bowls, over the ice, without adding so much water that the inner bowl bobs up and down, causing water to splash into the custard. Press the liquid through the strainer. Stir the cream into the custard. Chill the custard thoroughly in the ice bath. Stir often but do not whisk. Once the custard is cold, refrigerate it overnight.

8. Just before churning, taste the custard and adjust the sweetness with lemon juice. Pour the mixture into the container of an ice cream maker and churn according to the manufacturer's instructions to the consistency of soft ice cream. Add the remaining 1 tablespoon minced preserved ginger and churn for 1 minute more. Transfer to a freezer container, and freeze for at least 2 hours before serving.

Green Apple Sorbet with Basil

Sorbet à la pomme verte au basilic

A scoop of this beautiful and delicious sorbet is a great topper to a summer fruit salad. Serve the sorbet almost immediately after churning; if not, it will become icy and the basil will turn black. This sorbet is equally wonderful, albeit somewhat less daring, with fresh mint.   Makes about 3 cups

1¼ cups (9 ounces) sugar

1 large Granny Smith apple, peeled, cored, and cut into small cubes (1¼ cups)

Finely grated zest of 1 orange

8 large leaves of basil

1 cup less 2 tablespoons freshly squeezed lime juice (about 7 limes)

1. The night before serving, place 1¼ cups water and the sugar in a medium stainless steel saucepan. Add the apple and the orange zest and bring to a boil over low heat. Turn off the heat. Chop 3 basil leaves and add them. Cover the saucepan or transfer the mixture to another container and let cool. Refrigerate for 8 to 12 hours to let the mixture steep.

2. The next day, puree the mixture in a blender or food processor until fine. Strain through a medium mesh strainer, preferably stainless steel. Add the lime juice. Pour the mixture into the container of an ice cream maker and churn according to the manufacturer's instructions. When the sorbet is almost ready, chop the remaining basil leaves. Churn for just a few minutes more, then serve.

Chocolate Sorbet *Sorbet au chocolat*

This sorbet is composed of only five ingredients—water, sugar, cocoa powder, extra bittersweet chocolate, and a dash of vanilla extract—that work in perfect harmony to produce an intense chocolate flavor. The sorbet will freeze very hard, because of all the chocolate with no fat to soften it, so use it the day you prepare it.

Cocoa powder makes the sorbet extremely dark—almost black. This is quite dramatic next to a white ice cream or sorbet, such as pear or coconut, or with brightly colored sorbets, such as mango or raspberry. A Tulip Shell (page 168) filled with three sorbets is always an elegant finale.   Makes I quart

½ cup less I tablespoon (3 ounces) sugar

2 tablespoons unsweetened cocoa powder, sifted or strained

I pound extra-bittersweet chocolate, chopped

I teaspoon pure vanilla extract

I.   Combine 1½ cups water, the sugar, and cocoa in a medium saucepan and bring to a boil over medium heat. Remove from the heat. Add the chocolate and whisk until completely smooth. Whisk in the vanilla extract. Transfer the mixture to a bowl and place it in a larger bowl surrounded with ice. Pour cold water over the ice, taking care not to splash any into the sorbet mix. Chill the chocolate mixture thoroughly, whisking often. This can be prepared several hours ahead and refrigerated.

2.   Pour the mixture into the container of an ice cream maker and churn according to the manufacturer's instructions to the consistency of soft ice cream. Transfer to a freezer container and freeze until firm.

Chocolate-Mint Sorbet *Sorbet chocolat-menthe*

Crème de menthe keeps this chocolate sorbet very soft. It is also quite sweet. The combination of chocolate and mint, however, is hard to beat and makes up for the sweetness.   Makes about 5 cups

½ recipe (2 cups) Simple Syrup (page 334)

I cup sifted unsweetened cocoa powder

5 tablespoons plus I teaspoon crème de menthe

I.   Bring the syrup to a boil, add the cocoa, and whisk. Whisk in 2 cups cold water. Transfer the mixture to a bowl and place it in a larger bowl surrounded with ice. Pour cold water over the ice, taking care not to splash any into the sorbet mix. Chill thoroughly, whisking often. (*This mixture can be prepared several hours ahead and refrigerated.*)

2.   Just before churning, stir in the crème de menthe. Pour the mixture into the container of an ice cream maker and churn according to the manufacturer's instructions to the consistency of soft ice cream. Transfer to a freezer container and freeze until firm.

Mango Sorbet *Sorbet à la mangue*

This may be the smoothest sorbet ever. Mango is considered to be *gras*, or fat, by pastry chefs. This is a matter of texture, not fat content. Pureed and strained mango has a very smooth texture; when mixed with syrup, it will remain smooth even after churning. This sorbet scoops easily and actually glistens.

The color of the sorbet is as rich as its texture. In an assortment of fruit sorbets, the mango both stands out and complements the others. A scoop can stand alone in a chilled bowl, with nothing but a Rolled Cigarette Cookie (page 166) by its side.   Makes about I quart

1½ cups mango puree (see page 350)

1½ cups Simple Syrup (page 334)

I to 2 teaspoons freshly squeezed lemon juice

I.   Whisk together the puree, syrup, and 1 cup plus 2 tablespoons cold water. Adjust the flavor with lemon juice. If the mix is too tart, add a bit more syrup in very small increments. Transfer the mixture to a bowl and place it in a larger bowl surrounded with ice. Pour cold water over the ice, taking care not to splash any into the sorbet mix. Chill thoroughly, whisking often. (*This mixture can be prepared several hours ahead and refrigerated.*)

continued

2.   Pour the mixture into the container of an ice cream maker and churn according to the manufacturer's instructions to the consistency of soft ice cream. Transfer the sorbet to a freezer container and freeze until firm. This sorbet will not become extremely hard.

Tropical Sorbet *Sorbet éxotique*

Do not feel obliged to use all the fruits listed below, nor in the same proportions, though they will yield a very balanced sorbet in terms of flavor and texture. Be sure to mix fruits that oxidize easily, such as banana and apricot, with lime juice as soon as the fruits are pureed. This will keep them from turning brown. Puree all the fruits in a food processor or blender. For very fibrous fruits, such as pineapple and mango, press the puree through a medium mesh strainer before measuring.

This sorbet is beautiful in a Tulip Shell (page 168), topped with sliced tropical fruits and a few passionfruit seeds.   Makes about 1 quart

½ cup (one 5-ounce banana) banana puree

½ cup (4 ounces pulp) pineapple puree

½ cup (one 8-ounce mango) mango puree

½ cup (4 passionfruits) passionfruit puree

¾ cup (4 apricots) fresh apricot puree

¼ cup freshly squeezed lime juice (about 2 limes)

1 cup (7 ounces) sugar

¼ teaspoon ground cinnamon

Pinch of ground cloves

1.   Prepare all the fruit purees, adding lime juice as needed. Combine them in a large mixing bowl. Blend the sugar and the spices, then add this mixture to the fruit purees. Mix until the sugar is dissolved. Transfer the mixture to a bowl and place it in a larger bowl surrounded with ice. Pour cold water over the ice, taking care not to splash any into the sorbet mix. Chill thoroughly, whisking often. (*This mixture can be prepared several hours ahead and refrigerated.*)

2.   Pour the mixture into the container of an ice cream maker and churn according to the manufacturer's instructions. This sorbet may remain somewhat slushy in the churn. Transfer to a freezer container and freeze for 3 to 4 hours. Serve slightly soft.

Pear Sorbet *Sorbet à la poire*

Pear sorbet is extremely versatile. It is made from poached pears (see pages 18–19). It can also be made from canned pears. It has a beautiful creamy color and a very subtle flavor that make it an excellent partner for other sorbets with more intense color and flavor.

For the puree, drain poached or canned pear halves and pieces and puree them in a food processor or blender until extremely fine, with no chunks whatsoever.   Makes about 1 quart

1½ cups (3 to 4 poached or canned pear halves) pear puree

1½ cups Simple Syrup (page 334)

1 cup plus 2 tablespoons cold water

1 to 2 teaspoons freshly squeezed lemon juice

1.   Combine all the ingredients and whisk to mix. Transfer the mixture to a bowl and place it in a larger bowl surrounded with ice. Pour cold water over the ice, taking care not to splash any into the sorbet mix. Chill thoroughly, whisking often. (*This mixture can be prepared several hours ahead and refrigerated.*)

2.   Pour the mixture into the container of an ice cream maker and churn according to the manufacturer's instructions to the consistency of soft ice cream. Transfer to a freezer container and freeze until firm. Serve within 24 hours or thaw at room temperature and rechurn.

Raspberry Sorbet *Sorbet aux framboises*

Whenever I have a surplus of raspberries, especially those that are a bit crushed but not at all moldy, I puree, strain, and freeze them. That way, I have puree ready when I need to make a mousse, a coulis, or this wonderful sorbet. Frozen raspberries are also good for this purpose. These are often sweeter and cheaper than the fresh ones.   Makes about 1 quart

1½ cups strained (10 ounces) raspberry puree

1½ cups Simple Syrup (page 334)

1 to 2 teaspoons freshly squeezed lemon juice

1.   Whisk together the puree, syrup, and 1 cup plus 2 tablespoons cold water. Adjust the flavor with lemon juice. If the mix is too tart, add a bit more syrup in very small increments. Transfer the mixture to a bowl and place it in a larger bowl surrounded with ice. Pour cold water over the ice, taking care not to splash any into the sorbet mix. Chill thoroughly, whisking often. (*This mixture can be prepared several hours ahead and refrigerated*.)

2.   Pour the mixture into the container of an ice cream maker and churn according to the manufacturer's instructions to the consistency of soft ice cream. Transfer the sorbet to a freezer container and freeze until firm. Serve within 2 days, or the sorbet will become icy. If this happens, thaw the sorbet at room temperature and rechurn.

> **Use this recipe for raspberry, blackberry, or strawberry sorbet. I hesitate to make strawberry sorbet in America because the fruit in this country tends to be large, hollow, and waterlogged. If you find deep red, intensely flavored strawberries, puree, strain, and freeze a whole flat to have on hand for sorbet, mousses, and sauces. Blueberries, on the other hand, must be cooked, pureed, and strained before turning into a sorbet. Most of their color and much of their flavor comes from the skins. If you puree and strain the berries without cooking them, they will lose a lot of their flavor and color.**

Savory Pastries

Pâtisseries salées

THE RECIPES IN THIS chapter, while not numerous, demonstrate the versatility of neutral doughs such as puff pastry and phyllo. These doughs lend themselves not only to classic desserts but to their savory counterparts as well. While a classic Napoleon consists of crisp layers of puff pastry filled with lightened pastry cream, a savory variation consisting of layers of smoked salmon and herbed cream cheese sandwiched between delicate phyllo layers redefines the term.

Wrapping a filling inside pastry will transform that filling from something that needs to be spooned up into something self-contained. The finished product is far greater than the sum of its parts.

Take these recipes and let your imagination run with them. Change the ingredients to fit your needs and taste, but be sure to follow the tips within each recipe for perfectly cooked fillings surrounded by properly baked pastry.

Smoked Salmon Napoleons / *Millefeuilles au saumon fumé*
Tuna Sashimi Napoleons / *Millefeuilles à la japonaise*

Three Savory Puff Pastry Hors d'Oeuvres
Parmesan Palm Leaves / *Palmiers au Parmesan*
Roquefort Pinwheels / *Spirales au Roquefort*
Smoked Salmon and Puff Pastry Sandwiches / *Pailles au saumon fumé*

Nice-style Pizza / *Pissaladière niçoise*

Alsatian Onion Tart / *Tarte alsacienne*

Pear and Roquefort Tarts / *Feuilletés de poires au Roquefort*

Spinach Turnovers / *Chaussons aux épinards*

French-style Pigs in Blankets / *Saucisses en brioche*

Smoked Salmon Napoleons
Millefeuilles au saumon fumé

Over the years, many French chefs have broken away from classic culinary doctrine and modernized elements of their rich culinary history. This savory pastry is an excellent example. Twenty years ago, phyllo dough was unheard of in France, and giving the name *millefeuilles* to a pastry made without puff pastry would have been tantamount to treason. Culinary parameters have broadened considerably since then to accommodate different tastes, a broader cross section of society, time constraints, and ingredients that are more readily available.

Smoked salmon is available at every *traiteur*, or delicatessen, in France. This is the case more and more in the United States as well. Besides smoked salmon, you can use halved cooked shrimp between the layers or foie gras or sautéed scallops. You can make it vegetarian with an artichoke mousse or Mediterranean with thin layers of hummus or baba ganoush. Whatever you use, just make sure that it is not tough or sinewy, like prosciutto.

The phyllo pastry rectangles can be prepared ahead, but the cream filling should be spread on the layers as soon as it is prepared—and this should be shortly before serving—as it becomes too firm under refrigeration.   **Makes 8 pastries**

About ⅓ pound (6 sheets) frozen phyllo dough, thawed overnight in the refrigerator

4 ounces (1 stick) unsalted butter, melted and cooled

6 tablespoons (1½ ounces) sliced blanched or unblanched almonds

8 ounces (1 large package) cream cheese

1 cup sour cream

1 tablespoon chopped shallot

1 tablespoon chopped chives

1 tablespoon chopped dill

1 teaspoon freshly ground pepper

Zest of 1 lemon

4 ounces sliced smoked salmon, cut into small pieces

Sprigs of dill, for garnish

1. Preheat the oven to 400°F. Line 2 baking sheets with parchment paper.

2. Remove the sheets of phyllo from the package, stack them on the work surface, and cover with wax paper and a damp towel. Working with 1 sheet at a time while keeping the others covered, remove 1 sheet and lay it flat. Brush it all over with melted butter and sprinkle evenly with 1 tablespoon of the almonds. Top with another sheet and repeat the process. Top with a third sheet of dough, brush with butter, and sprinkle with 1 tablespoon almonds.

3. Trim all 4 edges of the rectangle to even it out. Measure the rectangle and cut it into 12 rectangles. Place them close together on the baking sheet. Repeat Steps 2 and 3 with the remaining 3 sheets of dough.

4. Bake, one pan at a time, for 10 to 12 minutes, or until lightly browned and slightly puffed. Cool on the pans. Once they are cool, place all the rectangles on 1 pan. (*The pastry may be baked ahead and left on the pan, lightly wrapped with plastic, at room temperature for up to 12 hours. Or they can be prepared and refrigerated for up to 24 hours before baking.*)

5. Just before serving, combine the cream cheese and sour cream in a mixing bowl or food processor and whip or process until smooth and light. Add the shallot, chives, dill, pepper, and lemon zest and mix until evenly incorporated.

6. Place a dab of cream filling in the middle of each of 8 salad plates to keep the pastry from sliding around on the plate as you serve it. Press the first phyllo stack onto the cream. Spread a thin layer of filling, about 1 tablespoon, on each layer, taking care not to press too hard. Cover the cream with smoked salmon. Top with another phyllo stack, pressing down lightly to spread the filling evenly. Spoon another tablespoon of filling on top and cover with salmon. Top with a third phyllo stack. If there is any filling left, spoon a dollop next to each Napoleon. Place a sprig of dill on or next to it and serve.

Tuna Sashimi Napoleons *Millefeuilles à la japonaise*

The special ingredients for this Japanese-inspired Napoleon—unhulled sesame seeds, sushi ginger, and wasabi—are available in Japanese markets and some grocery stores.   **Makes 8 pastries**

About ⅓ pound (6 sheets) frozen phyllo dough

4 ounces (1 stick) unsalted butter, melted and cooled

6 tablespoons (3 ounces) unhulled sesame seeds, toasted

3 ounces (1 small package) cream cheese

½ cup sour cream

1 tablespoon Japanese soy sauce

2 tablespoons sushi ginger, drained and finely chopped

1 teaspoon grated fresh ginger

1 tablespoon wasabi

6 to 8 ounces very fresh sashimi-grade albacore or ahi tuna, preferably a loin piece, cut across the grain into ¼-inch slices

Sunflower sprouts or another green, for garnish (optional)

1.   Prepare and bake the phyllo rectangles as in Steps 1 through 4 of the recipe for Smoked Salmon Napoleons (page 228), replacing the almonds with sesame seeds.

2.   Beat or process the cream cheese and sour cream until smooth and light. Add the soy sauce and continue beating. Stir in the sushi ginger and fresh ginger.

3.   Combine the wasabi with 2 teaspoons water to form a paste. Lay the slices of tuna on a cold plate in a single layer. Spread each with a very thin layer of wasabi paste. Cut the tuna into pieces no larger than the rectangles, patching as necessary.

4.   Fill as in Step 6 of the recipe for Smoked Salmon Napoleons, spreading the phyllo stacks with about 2 teaspoons of filling and placing a slice of tuna on top. Repeat the layering process, finishing with a phyllo rectangle. Surround each Napoleon with a few sunflower sprouts, if desired, and serve immediately.

Three Savory Puff Pastry Hors d'Oeuvres

Like their sweet counterparts (see pages 150–155), these pastries are simple and delectable, a far cry from cheese straws and bread sticks.

Parmesan Palm Leaves *Palmiers au Parmesan*

Use freshly grated, best-quality Parmesan for these treats. Poppy seeds add texture and subtle flavor, not to mention those black dots. Sesame seeds are equally wonderful. Makes about 72 wafers

½ recipe (1 pound) fully turned Puff Pastry (page 296) or 1 package store-bought pastry, cold

2 egg yolks mixed with 2 teaspoons cold water, for egg wash

1 cup (5 ounces) finely grated Parmesan cheese

2 teaspoons ground cayenne (optional)

Freshly ground black pepper (optional)

¼ cup poppy seeds or ¼ cup hulled sesame seeds (optional)

1. Roll out the dough on a lightly floured work surface to a width of 10 inches and a thickness of ¼ to ⅛ inch. For homemade dough, the length will be about 20 inches; store-bought dough will measure half that length per piece. Brush the top of the dough with egg wash. Spread the grated cheese evenly over the top of the dough and press it in gently with the rolling pin. Sprinkle evenly with one or more of the optional toppings and press into the cheese. Fold one long edge (for store-bought dough, this should be a folded edge of dough, not dough that has been cut) evenly toward the middle to form a 2-inch flap. Repeat this with the opposite edge. Taking care not to curl the edge of the first flap, fold in another flap on each side. These flaps will be slightly wider than the first and will leave a strip about 1 inch wide in the middle. Make sure that the flaps are equal in width along the length of the dough. Gently lay one flap on top of the other, so that all the edges are even, and taking care not to stretch the dough that runs between the 2 flaps. Repeat, if using store-bought dough. If necessary, cut the roll or rolls into 2 or 3 pieces, for ease in handling. Wrap the rolls individually in plastic and freeze for at least 1 hour. (*The pastry may be frozen for up to 1 month. It may be baked 1 roll at a time.*)

2. Adjust the oven racks to divide the oven into thirds and preheat the oven to 375°F. Line 2 baking sheets with parchment paper.

continued

3. Remove one of the rolls from the freezer. If the dough has been frozen for more than 1 hour, you may thaw it in the refrigerator. The pastry must be quite firm when cut; this will make slicing it thin much easier. Using a sharp, heavy knife, cut the roll into even ¼-inch slices. Cut the entire roll at once, in case it starts to thaw. Lay 12 to 15 palmiers flat on each pan, spacing them evenly at least 2 inches apart. They will resemble books. Open the edges of the books about ½ inch to allow for even spreading without buckling. Bake for 10 minutes, or just until the edges start to turn golden.

4. Meanwhile, if you plan to bake more palmiers, cut and lay them on parchment paper that has been cut to the size of the baking sheets.

5. Carefully remove the baking sheets from the oven and flip each palmier over with a metal spatula. As you flip each, flatten it with the spatula. Return the baking sheets to the oven for 5 to 10 minutes more, or until the palmiers are golden. Watch carefully, as the cheese can burn quickly. Remove from the oven and carefully slide the paper onto a flat surface to let the palmiers cool. It is not necessary to cool these on a rack, only to remove them from the hot baking sheets. Cool the baking sheets slightly, then slide on another batch and bake.

6. Once they are completely cooled, serve immediately or store the palmiers in an airtight container at room temperature. These will lose their crispness when exposed to humidity. (*The palmiers may be stored in an airtight container for up to 3 days.*)

Roquefort Pinwheels *Spirales au Roquefort*

These pinwheels are quite rich, but the amount of cheese in each is minuscule compared to the flavor it lends. These are a fabulous addition to a cheese tray, but they're also wonderful on their own.
Makes about 72 crackers

> 4 ounces Roquefort or other blue cheese, at room temperature
>
> 2 ounces (½ stick) unsalted butter, at room temperature
>
> ½ recipe (1 pound) fully turned Puff Pastry (page 296) or 1 package store-bought pastry, cold
>
> ½ cup (2¼ ounces) finely chopped walnuts

1. Beat the cheese and butter together with a wooden spoon or an electric mixer so that the consistency is even and spreadable. Set aside.

2.   Roll out the dough on a lightly floured work surface to a width of 10 inches and a thickness of ¼ to ⅛ inch. For homemade dough, the length will be about 20 inches; store-bought dough will measure half that length per piece. Turn the dough so that a long, uncut (in the case of store-bought dough) edge is facing you. Using an offset spatula, spread an even layer of cheese on the dough, leaving a ½-inch border along the far edge; use only half the cheese if using store-bought dough, as you will be repeating this process with the other piece. Sprinkle evenly with walnuts. Starting with the edge nearest you, roll the dough tightly, making sure that there are no gaps. If necessary, cut the roll or rolls into 2 or 3 pieces, for ease in handling. Wrap the rolls individually in plastic and freeze for at least 1 hour. (*The pastry may be frozen for up to 1 month. It may be baked 1 roll at a time.*)

3.   Adjust the oven racks to divide the oven into thirds and preheat the oven to 375°F. Line 2 baking sheets with parchment paper.

4.   Remove one of the rolls from the freezer. If the dough has been frozen for more than 1 hour, thaw it in the refrigerator. The dough must be quite firm when cut; this makes slicing it thin much easier. Using a sharp, heavy knife, cut the roll into even ¼-inch slices. Cut the entire roll at once, in case it starts to thaw. Fold each pinwheel in half and place 12 to 15 on each baking sheet, spacing them evenly about 2 inches apart. Bake for 10 minutes, or until the pinwheels just begin to brown.

5.   Meanwhile, if you plan to bake more pinwheels, cut and lay them on parchment paper that has been cut to the size of the baking sheets.

6.   Carefully remove the baking sheets from the oven and flip each pinwheel over with a metal spatula. Return the pans to the oven for 5 to 10 minutes more, or until golden. Watch carefully, as the cheese can burn quickly. Remove from the oven and carefully slide the paper onto a flat surface to let the pinwheels cool. It is not necessary to cool these on a rack, only to remove them from the warm baking sheets. Cool the baking sheets slightly, then slide on another batch and bake.

7.   Once they are completely cooled, serve immediately or store the pinwheels in an airtight container. These will lose their crispness when exposed to humidity. (*The pinwheels may be stored in an airtight container for up to 3 days. The high temperature during baking will prevent the cheese from spoiling.*)

Smoked Salmon and Puff Pastry Sandwiches

Pailles au saumon fumé

These are incredibly rich. You can cut back by using a reduced-fat garlic cheese spread or by replacing the smoked salmon with trimmed prosciutto. Or use other fillings that inspire you.

Because of the filling, these hors d'oeuvres have to be refrigerated until serving. Since refrigeration can make the baked pastry lose some of its crispness, do not make these too far in advance. Or make the crackers ahead and fill them at the last minute.   Makes about 36 sandwiched pastries

½ recipe (1 pound) fully turned Puff Pastry (page 296) or 1 package store-bought pastry, cold

2 egg yolks mixed with 2 teaspoons water, for egg wash

1 package (5.2 ounces) Boursin cheese or another creamy cheese spread

6 ounces sliced smoked salmon, cut into 1-inch squares

Dill sprigs, for decoration (optional)

1.   If using homemade pastry, roll it out on a lightly floured surface to 3 times as long as it is wide and about ¼ inch thick. If using store-bought pastry, lay both sheets in front of you on a very lightly floured surface. Brush the top of the dough with egg wash. Trim ¼ inch from each of the long edges (or the folded edges, in the case of store-bought dough), then measure the length. Cut 3 equal strips across the length of the dough. Stack these strips one on top of the other. If necessary, cut the stacked strips into 2 or 3 pieces. Wrap well in plastic and freeze for at least 1 hour. (*The pastry may be frozen for up to 1 month. You may bake 1 strip at a time.*)

2.   Adjust the oven racks to divide the oven into thirds and preheat the oven to 375°F. Line 3 baking sheets with parchment paper.

3.   Remove one of the strips from the freezer. If the dough has been frozen for more than 1 hour, thaw it slightly in the refrigerator. The pastry must be quite firm when cut; this will make slicing it thin much easier. Using a sharp, heavy knife, cut the dough into even ¼-inch slices. Cut the entire strip at once, in case it starts to thaw. Lay 12 to 16 pailles flat on each baking sheet, spacing them evenly and leaving at least 2 inches between the long edges and 1 inch between the short edges. Bake for 10 minutes, or just until the edges start to turn golden.

4.   Meanwhile, if you plan to bake more pailles, cut and lay them on parchment paper cut to the size of the pans. If the layers of dough begin to separate, put them back where they belong, and they will stick during baking.

5. Carefully remove the baking sheets from the oven and flip each paille over with a metal spatula. Return baking sheets to the oven for 5 to 10 minutes more, or until golden. Watch carefully, as the pailles can burn quickly. Remove from the oven and carefully slide the paper off onto a flat surface to let the pailles cool. It is not necessary to cool these on a rack, but do remove them from the hot baking sheets. Cool the baking sheets slightly, then slide on another batch and bake.

6. Place the cheese in a bowl and beat it with a wooden spoon to soften. Once the wafers are completely cooled, spread about ½ teaspoon of cheese in the middle of each half of the wafers. Place a piece or two of smoked salmon and a small sprig of dill, if desired, on top. Cover with another wafer and press down gently. Serve immediately or refrigerate for up to 3 hours. Bring to room temperature 30 minutes before serving.

> **Boursin cheese, a cream cheese blended with herbs, spices, and garlic, is widely available in supermarkets and gourmet shops. You can create your own spread by blending cream cheese with one or more of the following: garlic, chopped fresh herbs, cracked pepper, sun-dried tomatoes, capers, or pesto. You can substitute prosciutto, sardines (leave the tail sticking out), smoked Gouda, or grilled marinated eggplant for the smoked salmon.**

Nice-style Pizza *Pissaladière niçoise*

This appetizer resembles a pizza in name and layout, but it is far more delicate. The crust can handle a variety of toppings and lots of them as long as they are not wet.

Traditionally, the crust is spread with a layer of *confit d'oignons*, onions that have been cooked down so that their juices have evaporated, leaving behind a sweet, flavor-packed spread. The *pissaladière* is then topped with other Provençal ingredients: anchovy fillets, pitted black olives, and strips of sun-dried tomatoes. Of course, you can top your pissaladière with whatever you choose, including cheese, sautéed sausage, grilled eggplant, or roasted red peppers.

Use Puff Pastry scraps, not fresh Puff Pastry, for this recipe. It would be far too fragile to support the toppings. Freeze scraps according to the guidelines on page 349, so that they roll out evenly.

Makes one 10-inch tart, for 8 servings

8 ounces Puff Pastry scraps, thawed but cold

CONFIT D'OIGNONS
1 tablespoon pure olive oil

2 large onions, peeled and thinly sliced (about 4 cups)

¼ teaspoon salt

½ teaspoon freshly ground black pepper

2 teaspoons fresh thyme leaves or 1 teaspoon dried thyme

1 teaspoon minced fresh garlic

TOPPINGS
8 anchovy fillets, drained

16 pitted black olives, such as kalamata

¼ cup oil-packed sun-dried tomatoes, drained and cut into ¼-inch strips

Extra virgin olive oil, for drizzling

2 tablespoons shredded basil leaves

1. Form the dough into a disk and pound it several times in each direction to flatten it. Roll out the dough on a lightly floured work surface, as thin as possible—preferably to a thickness of ⅛ inch. Lift the dough and put it back on the table a few times to relax it. The round of dough should be about 13 inches in diameter. Line a tart ring with a removable bottom, taking care to lay the dough well into the bottom and corners of the pan without stretching the dough. Let any excess dough hang over the sides of the pan, without trimming, or the dough may shrink. Refrigerate for 1 hour.

2.   Heat a large sauté pan over medium heat. Add the olive oil and heat it through. Put the onions in the pan and sauté, stirring constantly, until the onions are translucent and just begin to take on color, about 10 minutes. Season with salt, pepper, and thyme and continue to cook for 5 minutes. Add the garlic. Cook until the onions are golden brown and no liquid remains in the pan, about 10 to 15 minutes more. Transfer to a plate or shallow bowl to cool completely.

3.   Preheat the oven to 400°F.

4.   Remove the tart pan from the refrigerator and trim the excess dough by running your rolling pin over the top. Discard the scraps. Prick the dough all over with a fork. Spread the onions evenly over the bottom of the tart shell. Arrange the anchovies like the spokes of wheel on top of the onions. Scatter the olives and the tomatoes all over, then drizzle with a very thin stream of olive oil.

5.   Bake for 30 to 40 minutes, or until the crust is well browned. Check for doneness by removing the tart from the oven and carefully removing the bottom from the ring. With a metal spatula, gently lift the bottom slightly. If the crust is not golden brown, replace the tart bottom in the ring and bake for 10 minutes more.

6.   Remove the tart from the oven, then remove the ring. Using a wide metal spatula, carefully slide the pissaladière from the tart bottom onto a cutting board or a flat serving platter. Sprinkle with shredded basil, cut into wedges, and serve.

Alsatian Onion Tart *Tarte alsacienne*

A thin layer of ricotta cheese and sautéed onions baked on top of an even thinner, crisp, lightly yeasted crust, this is a simple and delicious appetizer, whether shaped into a round and cut into wedges or shaped into a rectangle and cut into rectangles and squares of any size. If you like, add browned *lardons*, or cooked pieces of thick-cut smoked bacon, or disks of sautéed smoked sausage. Strips of smoked salmon can be laid atop the tart after baking. Vary the herbs to complement the topping: Parsley and chervil go well with smoked meats; dill is ideal with smoked salmon.

You can top this dough with your favorite pizza toppings or give it a Provençal twist with black olives, anchovies, and sun-dried tomatoes.   Makes two 8-inch round tarts or one 12 × 8-inch rectangle

DOUGH

1 teaspoon active dry yeast or ⅓ cake (6 grams) compressed yeast

½ teaspoon sugar

⅔ cup lukewarm water (105 to 110°F)

2 cups (11 ounces) unbleached all-purpose flour

¾ teaspoon salt

2 tablespoons pure olive oil or vegetable oil

TOPPING

1 tablespoon pure olive oil or butter

1 large red onion, peeled and thinly sliced (about 2 cups)

Salt and freshly ground pepper

1½ cups ricotta cheese

1 tablespoon all-purpose flour

1 egg, lightly beaten

Pinch of salt

½ teaspoon freshly ground black pepper

2 tablespoons chopped fresh parsley

Oil, for baking pan

2 tablespoons chopped parsley or chives, for topping

1.   To prepare the dough, dissolve the yeast and sugar in the water and let the yeast proof (until a thin layer of froth forms on top).

2.   Place the flour and salt in a medium mixing bowl or in the bowl of an electric mixer fitted with a dough hook. Stir to mix. Add the yeast mixture and the oil to the flour and mix with a wooden spoon or the dough hook until the dough begins to come together.

3.   Continue kneading with the dough hook or turn the dough out onto a lightly floured surface and knead by hand. Knead until the dough is smooth and elastic. The dough will not be stiff. Place the dough in a lightly oiled bowl and turn it over in the bowl so that it is oiled all over. Cover loosely with a damp cloth or with plastic wrap and let rise in a warm spot until the dough has doubled in bulk, 45 minutes to 1 hour.

4.   To prepare the topping, heat a large sauté pan over medium heat and add the olive oil or butter. When it is heated through, add the sliced onion and sauté until translucent. Season with salt and pepper, and continue to cook until the onion is lightly colored and no longer gives off any liquid, about 15 minutes. Transfer to a plate or shallow bowl and let cool completely.

5.   If the ricotta has liquid on top, pour it off. Transfer the ricotta to a medium mixing bowl, and whisk in the flour. Add the egg and whisk until smooth. Season lightly with salt and pepper and add the parsley.

6.   When the dough has risen sufficiently, preheat the oven to 400° F.

7.   Deflate the dough and turn it out onto a lightly floured work surface. If you are making round tarts, cut the dough in half with a knife, then form each half into a ball. Let the dough rest for 10 minutes. For a 12 × 8-inch rectangular tart, roll the dough into as large a rectangle as possible (at some point, the gluten will cause it to bounce back each time you roll it), then place it on a greased baking sheet. Let the dough rest for 10 minutes, then press it to its final size with your fingertips.

8.   Roll each ball of dough into an 8-inch round. Place the rounds on a large lightly greased baking sheet or 2 lightly greased pizza pans. Allow the dough to rest for 10 minutes. Once the dough has relaxed, press it to its final size with your fingertips.

9.   Using a large icing spatula or a rubber spatula, spread the ricotta mixture over the dough, leaving a ½-inch border all around. Top with the onions, distributing them evenly over the cheese with your fingers.

10.   Bake for 30 minutes, or until the topping begins to bubble and the edges of the dough are well browned. Lift the dough with a metal spatula to check that the dough has browned underneath.

11.   Remove the tart or tarts from the oven and cut into wedges, rectangles, or squares with a long heavy knife or a pizza cutter. Sprinkle with chopped herbs and serve immediately.

Pear and Roquefort Tarts

Feuilletés de poires au Roquefort

The combination of sweet and salty foods is somewhat uncommon in France, but the combination of poached pears and Roquefort cheese is a delightful exception. They often find themselves in a Belgian endive salad, along with toasted walnuts and a light walnut vinaigrette, particularly in mid-autumn. This recipe adds the richness of puff pastry and makes for a wonderful first course or an unusual cheese course.

Traditionally, these tarts are prepared with an upper and lower crust, with the Roquefort oozing from between the two. This type of presentation is great for a restaurant, as the feuilletés can be prepared ahead of time and warmed, without any risk to the aesthetics of the filling. At home, however, I prefer to prepare the tarts ahead of time and refrigerate them raw, then present them bubbling hot out of the oven, showing off the beautifully fanned pears. This approach also enables you to add the Roquefort toward the end of the baking time to prevent it from running.

Use any recipe to poach your pears (see pages 18–19). Do not use canned pears, however, as they tend to be too sweet and soft. Do not use fresh pears either, as they will not bake evenly and may exude their juices, making the dough underneath soggy.   Makes 4 individual tarts

¼ recipe (½ pound) Puff Pastry (page 296) or ½ package store-bought, thawed and chilled

2 halves poached pears, well drained and patted dry with paper towels

1 large egg yolk, stirred with 1 teaspoon water

½ cup (2 ounces) walnut pieces

½ cup (about 2½ ounces) Roquefort or any other blue cheese, crumbled

1.   On a lightly floured surface, roll homemade Puff Pastry into a 9-inch square ⅛ to ¼ inch thick. Lift the dough off the table to release any parts that are sticking and to relax the dough slightly. If using store-bought dough, simply unfold 1 sheet, but do so carefully to prevent it from cracking.

2.   Use a heavy, sharp knife to cut away ½ inch from all 4 sides of the dough, then cut the dough into 4 squares, about 4 inches each. Transfer the squares to a parchment-lined baking sheet. Prick the center of each square several times with the tines of a fork, leaving a ½-inch unpricked border on each edge. Set aside.

3.   Cut the pear halves lengthwise into ¼-inch slices. Place a quarter pear (half of a half) on each square of dough, fanning the slices out at the broad end, but keeping them together at the narrow (stem) end as you do so. Place the narrow part of the pear so that it points to one of the corners of the dough square, then fans across the rest of the square.

4. Brush the pears and the surrounding dough lightly with egg wash; do not let any egg drip down the sides of the dough. Cover lightly with plastic wrap and refrigerate the tarts for at least 30 minutes or up to 8 hours. *(The tarts can be prepared to this point, then wrapped well in plastic on the pan, and frozen for up to 2 weeks. There is no need to thaw them before baking.)*

5. Preheat your oven to 375°F. Remove the tarts from the refrigerator and peel away the plastic. Sprinkle each tart with one-quarter of the walnuts, placing them on top and around the pears. Bake for 20 minutes, or until the dough is puffed and golden brown. Remove from the oven and sprinkle each tart with one-quarter of the Roquefort, then return to the oven for 2 to 3 minutes, or until the cheese is just melted.

6. Remove the tarts with a wide metal spatula and slide them onto warmed salad plates. Serve immediately or at room temperature up to 2 hours after baking. These can also be baked up to 8 hours ahead and warmed at 375°F for 5 minutes. In this case, do not add the Roquefort until the reheating stage.

Spinach Turnovers *Chaussons aux épinards*

Not only are these individual savory pastries simple to prepare, they illustrate a few very important guidelines to follow when baking anything in puff pastry:

- If wrapping anything that may exude its juice during baking, as will spinach or fish, combine the filling first with a roux-based sauce, such as a béchamel. This sauce will absorb the excess juices and keep the dough from becoming soggy.

- Any filling must be thoroughly chilled before it is placed on the puff pastry. A warm filling will soften the dough and make it very difficult to work with.

- Avoid placing raw ingredients, such as fish or meat, and most vegetables, in puff pastry. Not only will these fillings exude their liquids but the baking time may not be sufficient to thoroughly cook the filling. In other words, the pastry may be cooked, and the fish or meat inside may not.

Spinach Turnovers are an excellent addition to a buffet table, or as a simple but filling first course. They can be prepared ahead and frozen for up to 2 weeks, allowing you to bake as many or as few as you need at a time. They are best served piping hot or at room temperature.

Like the Apple Turnovers on page 144, these are traditionally made from a long band of dough, which is then folded in half and cut into filled semicircles. For this recipe, I have modified the classic to form triangular turnovers, thereby eliminating all dough scraps. Prepare the filling at least 8 hours or up to 1 day before assembling the turnovers. If you have a favorite creamed spinach recipe, use it here, or make these turnovers from leftover creamed spinach.   **Makes 8 turnovers**

FILLING

2 tablespoons butter

1½ tablespoons all-purpose flour

1 cup whole milk

Salt

Pinch of freshly grated nutmeg

Freshly ground black pepper

2 tablespoons (about ½ ounce) freshly grated Parmesan cheese (optional)

¼ yellow onion (about ¼ cup), peeled and finely minced

1 package frozen chopped spinach, thawed

½ recipe (1 pound) Puff Pastry (page 296) or 1 package store-bought, thawed

1 large egg yolk stirred with 1 teaspoon cold water

1.   Melt 1 tablespoon of butter in a very small saucepan over a low flame. Whisk in the flour and cook this *roux*, whisking constantly, for 2 minutes, or until the mixture is frothy but not at all browned. Remove the pan from the heat and set aside.

2.   In a separate, small saucepan, combine the milk and ¼ teaspoon salt and bring to a boil over medium heat. Whisk in the roux (scrape it out of the smaller pan with a rubber spatula) and continue heating the milk mixture, whisking constantly. Once the sauce has come to a boil, continue cooking for 1 minute, still whisking. Remove from the heat and stir in the nutmeg, ¼ teaspoon pepper, and the Parmesan, if desired. Pour the sauce into a glass or stainless steel bowl and let cool. The sauce will develop a skin on its surface; do not worry, as this will be stirred in later.

3.   Heat a medium-size frying pan over medium heat. Add the remaining butter and let it melt. Add the minced onion and sauté for 1 minute, or until translucent. Place the spinach in the pan and sauté for 2 to 3 minutes, or until just cooked. Season lightly with salt and pepper. Transfer the cooked spinach to a colander or mesh strainer placed over a bowl, and let it drain and cool. Once it is cooled, press out as much liquid as possible, then stir the spinach into the cooled sauce. Refrigerate the filling for at least 2 hours, or up to 24 hours, in a covered bowl.

4.   On a lightly floured surface, roll the homemade Puff Pastry into a rectangle, about 10 × 20 inches and ⅛ to ¼ inch thick. Lift the dough up to detach it from the table, then replace it. If using store-bought dough, simply unwrap and unfold it, but do so carefully so that it does not crack. Trim ¼ inch from all edges, using a sharp, heavy knife.

5.   Cutting straight down with your knife (not dragging the tip, which will stretch the dough), cut the dough into 8 squares, about 4½ inches each. Separate the squares slightly. Brush 2 adjacent edges of each square very lightly with cold water.

6.   Remove the filling from the refrigerator and stir to loosen. Place about 3 tablespoons of filling in the middle of each square, then fold the square into a triangle, placing the undampened edges over the dampened ones. As you fold the dough, press out any air surrounding the filling. This will prevent the turnovers from exploding during baking. Match the dough's edges as best you can, then press to seal.

7.   Place the turnovers on a parchment-lined baking sheet, leaving at least 1½ inches between pastries. Brush evenly with egg wash, avoiding puddling at the edges. Refrigerate, uncovered, for 1 hour before baking. *(After 1 hour, the turnovers can be covered completely with plastic and refrigerated overnight, or frozen for up to 2 weeks. If freezing, trim and decorate as in Step 8 before freezing, then place the frozen turnovers directly in a hot oven.)*

continued

8. Heat your oven to 375°F. Remove the turnovers from the refrigerator and with a single, downward motion, cut away about ⅛ inch from each cut edge to make them even and remove any egg wash that may have dripped down. Using a small, sharp paring knife, lightly cut through the top 1/16 inch of dough to form a featherlike pattern that will appear as the dough bakes. Take care not to cut all the way through to the filling.

9. Bake the turnovers for 20 to 25 minutes, or until puffed and golden brown. If your oven is uneven, turn the pan halfway through the baking time. Use a wide metal spatula to transfer the piping hot turnovers to warmed salad plates and serve immediately, or cool on wire racks and serve at room temperature. The turnovers may be rewarmed at 400°F for about 5 minutes. These will keep, wrapped and refrigerated, for up to 24 hours. Reheat before serving.

French-style Pigs in Blankets *Saucisses en brioche*

It may seem sacrilegious to refer to these savories as pigs in blankets, especially considering the delicacy of brioche dough and the gourmet sausages available today, but the name certainly conjures up an image that is not far from reality.

As with puff pastry, wrapping anything in brioche dough, or any other yeasted dough, requires adhering to a few very important guidelines:

- Any meat, fish, or poultry filling must be completely cooked before it is encased in dough. If not, the filling will be left at a warm temperature for however long it takes for the dough to rise, during which time any bacteria that may be in the filling will also be multiplying. Furthermore, raw meat may not have enough time to cook completely before the pastry crust is finished. Also, a cooked filling has less of a tendency to shrink away from its surrounding crust during baking.

- The filling, whether it is a forcemeat or a solid piece, must be cold when wrapped. Otherwise, its heat will cause the dough to rise unevenly.

- A filling other than one made with meat should be mixed into a *roux*-based sauce, such as a *béchamel* or *velouté*, so that any juices exuded by the filling ingredients will be absorbed by the sauce, thus preventing the dough from becoming soggy.

By following these guidelines, you can vary the fillings as well as the dough to make such classics as *coulibiac* of salmon (poach and chill the salmon, then drain and surround it with mushroom *duxelles* before wrapping in brioche or puff pastry); beef Wellington (sear and chill beef tenderloin, then wrap in duxelles and brioche or puff pastry); or Brie in brioche (trim some of the outer rind of a whole Brie before wrapping in brioche dough).   Makes 8 servings

> ¾ recipe (1½ pounds) Brioche Dough (page 268), cold
>
> 3 tablespoons Dijon mustard (optional)
>
> 8 sausage links (about 3 ounces each, 4 to 5 inches in length), fully cooked and chilled, casings peeled away
>
> 1 large egg yolk stirred with 1 teaspoon water

1. On a cool, floured surface, roll the Brioche Dough into a 12- × 16-inch rectangle, about ¼ inch thick. Trim about ¼ inch from each edge and reserve the scraps. Cut the large rectangle into 8 smaller ones, each 4 × 5 inches. If desired, spread a thin layer of mustard on top of each rectangle, leaving a ½-inch border all around.

2. Lay a piece of scrap down the middle of each rectangle. With a lightly dampened pastry brush, wet one long edge of each.

3. Place a sausage along the dry edge of each dough rectangle. Roll up, sealing with the dampened edge. Stretch the dough over the ends of each sausage and pinch shut. Place the wrapped sausages, seam side down, on a parchment-lined baking sheet, leaving at least 2 inches between pieces. At this point, the sausages can be covered with plastic wrap and refrigerated for up to 4 hours. If refrigerating, allow for an extra 10 to 15 minutes of rising time.

4. Brush the tops of the sausage rolls with egg wash. Place the baking sheet, uncovered, in a warm, draft-free place to allow the dough to rise until puffy. The dough should not be so risen that it begins to droop onto the pan. This should take 45 minutes to 1 hour.

5. Bake in the middle of a 375°F oven for about 20 minutes, or until the dough is golden brown and feels set when squeezed lightly. Serve immediately with mustard and other condiments on the side or cool on a wire rack and serve at room temperature.

Breads

Les Pains

THE MOST APPARENT DIFFERENCE between breads made in France and those made in the United States is the crust. Why do French breads have that perfect, crackly crust that is sometimes thick, sometimes thin, never too chewy, and always perfectly colored? The answer lies, for the most part, in the oven. Most bread baked in France is baked directly on the stone hearth bottom of a hot, steam injected oven. These ovens are specially designed to provide the optimum conditions for baking bread.

This does not mean that you should give up on the whole idea of baking French breads at home. There are things you can do that will help you achieve the crust you want. For crusty breads you should:

- Get a baking stone. This will mimic the live hearth bottom of a bread oven. Heat the stone for at least a half hour before placing the bread in the oven. Even if you are baking your bread in a pan and not directly on the stone, the baking stone will help keep the heat even.

- Buy a bread peel to slide the bread on and off the stone.

- Bake at a high temperature. Preheat the oven to 450°F, unless the recipe notes otherwise.

- Place a shallow pan of water in the bottom of the oven to create steam inside the oven—very important when you first place the dough inside. Do not use the old trick of throwing ice cubes into your oven while baking. They can ruin the lining of many home ovens.

- About 10 minutes after putting the dough in the oven, carefully remove the pan of water. By then the bread should have risen as much as it is going to; it's time to start baking that crust. Do this quickly, since the oven temperature will drop dramatically while you have the oven door open.

- About 10 to 15 minutes before the bread is done, prop the oven door open with the handle of a wooden spoon. This will vent the steam and allow the crust to dry out.

- Test the bread to see if it's done. It should sound hollow when rested on three fingers of one hand and tapped on the bottom with the other. If it does not sound hollow, return it to the oven at a lower temperature to prevent the crust from browning any further.

- Always cool bread on a wire rack, not on or in the pan. This allows any moisture trapped in the bread to evaporate, leaving the crust crisp.

In order to perfect your bread-baking techniques, you need to understand what is going on inside the dough. Basic bread dough consists of flour—composed mostly of carbohydrates—mixed with water and yeast. When yeast comes in contact with carbohydrates, it multiplies, giving off gas in the form of carbon dioxide. It is this gas that makes the dough expand. While the yeast multiplies, it ferments the carbohydrates on which it is feeding. These ferments give bread its distinctive flavor. A dough that is made with a very small amount of yeast but is allowed to rise slowly over a long period of time develops more flavor than a dough that starts with a higher proportion of yeast and rises quickly.

Other flavor components are sugar and salt. Sugar added to a dough will excite the yeast, while salt will inhibit its growth. The key is to strike a balance between flavor and rising times. A word of caution: Since salt inhibits yeast growth, it is important not to place these two ingredients in direct contact with each other, but rather to blend salt into the flour separately.

The protein component in flour, gluten, is what gives bread its stretchy, supple quality or body.

Body develops through the mechanical kneading of the dough, which lengthens and strengthens gluten strands. It is important to work the gluten sufficiently during the kneading process in order to obtain a bread that browns properly, that slices cleanly, and whose slice bends but does not break. To test the gluten's development, pull off a walnut-size piece of kneaded dough. Stretch it into a rectangle between your thumbs and forefingers. When your hands are 3 inches apart, the dough should be stretched into a thin sheet; it should not break apart before that point.

Temperature also plays a role in the development of a bread dough. The higher the temperature, the faster the dough will rise. This may not be desirable, as a dough that has risen too quickly may not have had time to develop enough body or enough flavor through fermentation. For this reason, I recommend using fresh cake (compressed) yeast, which does not require dissolving in tepid water like active dry yeast, or a starter whenever possible, then proceeding with *cold* water to form the dough. The cold water will retard the dough, even if it has been made with active dry yeast, and yield a bread with more flavor and body, and large pores, which are formed by carbon dioxide during a slow rise.

Clearly, the water in France is different from ours in its mineral composition. More to the point, however, is the difference between the water in New York and that in Los Angeles, not to mention the extent of chemical treatment of city waters. For these reasons and for the sake of consistency, I recommend making bread doughs with bottled spring water.

A yeasted dough may be made by adding fresh or activated yeast; it may be made from a yeasted starter; or it may be made by adding a sponge that contains natural yeasts. Yeasted starters have their roots in Poland, where bakers cultivated their own starters. This type of starter is called *poolish* in French. Every time the Polish bakers removed a certain quantity of starter, they would replace the same weight in water and flour, thus feeding the starter. This practice was abandoned when commercially produced yeast became cheaper and more plentiful. But it has become popular again over the years, because the breads produced from starters are very flavorful, have large holes, wonderful texture, and thick, crisp crusts. Breads from starters also keep very well. Once you have an active starter, you can keep it in the refrigerator (covered; it has a strong odor). Stir it every so often to keep it active, and be sure to replace whatever starter you remove with water and flour.

French bread bakers do not enjoy the luxury of kneading bread dough by hand. Even a small batch, ten loaves, is too large to knead outside of a spiral mixer. At home, however, I love to knead by hand, to feel the dough developing. Having stated that, I can also wholeheartedly recommend a sturdy stationary mixer with a dough hook for the job. I do not recommend making bread in a food processor, however. The action of this machine will shred, not knead, your dough. The motor, located right under the work bowl, will heat up, and this heat will transfer to the dough.

As for bread machines, I think they are good because they encourage people to make fresh bread at home. The recipes in this book, however, require hands-on techniques and knowledge. Bread machines are great, but not for these recipes.

It is crucial to use a scale when making bread. Flour and water can be measured with cups, and the resulting doughs can be adjusted by feel, but many of the recipes in this chapter also call for quantities of starter, old dough, and other ingredients that must be in proportion to the flour, yeast, and water in the recipe. It is impossible to measure accurately with a cup, since you have no way of knowing if the starter, for example, is at an inflated or deflated stage. For that reason, certain ingredients in these bread recipes are given in weight measurements only.

Tradition dictates that the French buy or bake their bread fresh daily. Storing bread is not part of their worldview. It is ours, however, and this can be done without adding chemicals or destroying the quality of the bread. Barley malt powder, a great natural preservative, is available in most health food stores and by mail order (see page 360). Many of the recipes in this chapter call for it. Since it is not necessary for the flavor, omit the malt if you cannot find it easily.

Every French home has a cloth *sac à pain*, or bread bag. This long bag hangs in the kitchen and is just the right size for one or two baguettes. The tightly woven fabric is perfect for keeping out air without letting the bread get soggy or chewy. Wrap your homemade bread in several tea towels or in foil. Avoid using plastic, as it will keep moisture inside and cause the crust to get chewy.

Three Crusty Loaves / *La Baguette, le pain, et le bâtard sur poolish*
    Crusty Rolls / *Petits pains croustiants*

Country Bread / *Pain de campagne*

Normandy Sourdough Apple Bread / *Pain aux pommes*
    Apple Starter / *Levain de pommes*

Mariner's Bread from Normandy / *Pain brié*
    Yeasted Sponge / *Levain levure*
    Old Dough / *Vieille pâte*

White Pullman Loaf / *Pain de mie*
    Hamburger Buns / *Petits pains au lait*

Caraway Rolls / *Petits pains au cumin*

Walnut Bread / *Pain aux noix*
    Walnut Rolls / *Petits pains aux noix*

Brioche Dough / *Pâte à brioche*

Fluted or Parisian Brioche / *Brioche à tête dite "parisienne"*

Brioche Loaf / *Brioche Nanterre*
    Little Brioches / *Brioches individuelles*

Three Crusty Loaves

La Baguette, le pain, et le bâtard sur poolish

Here are three loaves made from the same dough. One is long and thin, a *baguette;* or stick; another, referred to simply as a *pain*, or bread, is long and thick; the third, a *bâtard*, or bastard, is short and thick.

These loaves are based on a yeasted sponge that is made from scratch. This so-called *poolish*, which has its roots in Poland, allows for a very long, slow rise. It produces a loaf that has large holes, a thick crisp crust, and a fairly long shelf life. The bread itself has a lovely, nutty flavor. This is in contrast to a classic Parisian baguette, which rises quickly and has a relatively sweet flavor, as well as a more uniform, tighter texture.

If you decide to double the recipe, be sure that the mixer can hold that amount of dough and still mix efficiently. Double all the ingredients except the yeast in the sponge and the dough, however—that stays the same.   Makes one 1½-pound pain, two ¾-pound bâtards, or two ¾-pound baguettes.

POOLISH
½ cake of compressed fresh yeast, crumbled, or 1¼ teaspoons (½ packet) active dry yeast

1 cup minus 2 tablespoons cool spring water (75 to 80°F)

1½ cups (8 ounces) bread flour

DOUGH
All the poolish

1 cup minus 2 tablespoons tepid spring water (95 to 100°F)

3 cups (1 pound) bread flour, preferably organic

½ cake of compressed fresh yeast, crumbled, or 1¼ teaspoons (½ packet) active dry yeast, dissolved in some of the water

1 tablespoon salt

1. To make the poolish, dissolve the yeast in the water in a large mixing bowl. Stir in the flour. Mix for 5 minutes with a wooden spoon. Let the sponge ferment in a warm, draft-free spot, lightly covered with a damp cloth, for 3½ to 4 hours. It is ready when the sponge has risen, then collapsed in the middle.

2. To make the dough, pour the water over the collapsed sponge, reserving some water if using dry yeast. Gently pour this mixture into the bowl of an electric mixer. Add the flour and the yeast to the mixing bowl and stir to blend.

3. Knead the dough for about 10 minutes on low speed, then increase the speed to medium and knead for 10 minutes more. Add the salt during the last 5 minutes of kneading. The dough should be smooth and elastic. Check the dough for gluten development (see page 249).

4. Place the dough in a lightly greased bowl and cover the bowl with a damp tea towel. Let rise for about 2 hours in a warm, humid spot, such as a turned-off oven with a pan of warm water in the bottom. After 1 hour of rising time, pick up the dough and turn it over, to deflate it somewhat.

5. When the dough has doubled in bulk, turn it out onto a very lightly floured work surface. Handle it gently to avoid pressing out all the air.

6. For a *pain*, roll out the dough to a 18 × 10-inch rectangle. Roll up the rectangle, starting from a long end. Press it as you roll, without pounding it.

    For 2 *bâtards*, cut the dough in half, then roll each to a 12 × 8-inch rectangle. Roll up each rectangle, starting from a long end and pressing as you roll.

    For 2 *baguettes*, cut the dough in half, then roll each to a 16 × 6-inch rectangle. Roll up each rectangle, starting from a long end and pressing as you roll.

7. Place the bread, seam side down and ends tucked underneath, on a lightly floured bread peel or baking pan. Cover lightly with a damp tea towel and let rise in a warm draft-free spot until doubled in bulk, 1½ to 2 hours.

8. About 30 minutes before the loaves are fully risen, put a baking stone in the oven and place a shallow pan of water near the bottom of the oven. Preheat the oven to 450°F.

9. When the bread has risen, cut several ½-inch-deep diagonal slashes across the top of the pain or baguettes or 1 long slash down the bâtards. Put the bread in the oven and remove the pan of water after 5 minutes. Bake for 20 to 30 minutes, depending on the size of the bread, propping the oven door ajar with the handle of a wooden spoon for the last 5 to 10 minutes. The crust should be brown and somewhat rough.

10. Remove the bread from the oven and test for doneness by tapping the bottom of the loaf. It should sound hollow. If done, place the bread immediately on a wire rack or racks to cool. (*These breads will keep 2 days, wrapped in several tea towels or in foil.*) If not done, lower the oven temperature to 400°F and return to the oven to bake for 5 minutes more.

Crusty Rolls *Petits pains croustiants*

While individual rolls are fairly untraditional in the French home or restaurant, they are certainly a part of our tradition in America. The best part of these particular rolls is their crust, which is thick and crunchy and surrounds just enough bread to spread with butter or dip in olive oil. Makes twelve 2-ounce rolls

1.   Follow the recipe for Three Crusty Loaves through Step 4.

2.   When the dough has doubled in bulk, turn it out onto a lightly floured work surface. Weigh twelve 3-ounce pieces of dough, and roll them lightly into balls, taking care not to force the air out of the dough. Place the balls on a lightly floured or parchment-lined baking sheet, leaving 3 to 4 inches between. Cover the rolls with a damp tea towel and let rise in a warm draft-free spot until doubled in bulk, 1 to 1½ hours.

3.   About 30 minutes before the rolls are fully risen, place a rack in the upper third of the oven and place a pan of water near the bottom. Preheat the oven to 425°F.

4.   When the rolls have risen, snip points on the tops with a pair of kitchen shears dipped in water so that they do not stick to the dough. These cuts should be about ½ inch deep. Place the baking sheet in the oven and remove the pan of water.

5.   Bake the rolls for 15 to 20 minutes, propping the door ajar with the handle of a wooden spoon for the last 5 minutes. When done, the rolls should be golden brown and the crust should look rough. Cool completely on a wire rack.

Country Bread *Pain de campagne*

Pain de campagne is a bit of a misnomer, since this bread was born in the city. It is a copy, though, of the hearty country loaf that country people would enjoy with a hunk of cheese, sausage, or ham, or just a layer of home-churned butter after early-morning chores. The return-to-country-life ideal associated with this bread has been accompanied by a return to a love of things natural, and consequently, a turning away from anything with preservatives or marked with the French equivalent of "lite."

This dough has both wheat and rye flours and a starter of old bread dough. It is an even-textured, slightly gray bread with a thick, dense crust that keeps for days. This can be replaced by a sourdough starter, such as an Apple Starter. If you have a coiled-willow rising basket, canvas lined or not, use it here. The dough will rise slowly and keep its shape beautifully.

Pain de campagne comes in many different shapes: rounds with different markings, wreathlike rings of small balls of dough, long loaves, and the cloverleaf. All are permitted under French law. The law is strict, however, on the weight of the rye flour, which must be at least 10 percent that of the wheat flour.

In Province (everywhere outside of Paris), bread dough was prepared and shaped at home, then brought to the local bakery for completion in a wood-fired oven. To distinguish their loaves from those of the other local people, farm wives would place a baking tile with a unique design in the middle of the bottom of their loaves—a sort of bread "brand." Once the bread was baked, the image on the tile remained and the baker could give the loaf back to its rightful owner, along with the tile, to be used for future loaves.   Makes one 1-pound loaf

1½ cups (8 ounces) bread flour

2 tablespoons (1 ounce) dark rye flour

½ teaspoon barley malt powder (optional)

1 teaspoon salt

½ cup plus 2 tablespoons tepid spring water (105°F; use cool water—75 to 80°F—with compressed yeast)

1 tablespoon unsalted butter, softened

½ cake of compressed fresh yeast, crumbled, or 1¼ teaspoons (½ packet) active dry yeast, dissolved in some of the water

4½ ounces old dough (page 257), fermented for at least 12 hours, or Apple Starter (page 258)

continued

1.   Combine the bread flour, rye flour, barley malt, if using, and salt in the bowl of an electric mixer and stir to mix. Add the water, butter, and crumbled compressed yeast or dissolved yeast and mix for 5 minutes. Using the dough hook, add the old dough, and knead until smooth and elastic. This may take as long as 18 to 20 minutes. The dough will be somewhat loose. Test that the gluten has developed (see page 249).

2.   Place the dough in a lightly greased bowl and cover it with a damp tea towel. Let the dough rise in a warm, humid spot, such as a turned-off oven with a pan of water in the bottom, until double in bulk, 2 to 2½ hours. This dough rises slowly. After 1 hour of rising, punch down the dough (this will put the yeast back in contact with the flours).

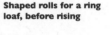

3.   If you have a *banneton,* or rising basket, flour it generously. Otherwise, flour a bread peel or baking sheet. Turn the dough out onto a lightly floured work surface, deflating it as you do so. Gently work the dough into a large ball and place it in the basket, on the peel, or on the floured pan. Or cut the dough into 8 equal-size pieces, roll each into a ball, and place the balls in a circle on the baking sheet, leaving ½ inch between pieces; they will touch as they rise. Or shape the dough into 4 equal balls and place them, barely touching, on a pan. Cover the shaped loaf with a damp towel and let it rise in a draft-free spot until doubled in bulk, about 1½ hours. Do not let this dough overrise, or it will lose its shape during baking.

Shaped rolls for a ring loaf, before rising

4.   During the last 30 minutes of rising, preheat the oven to 450°F. If using a baking stone, put it in the oven to heat. Place a shallow pan of water in the bottom of the oven.

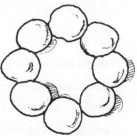

The risen ring loaf, before baking

5.   If the dough is in a banneton, gently turn it over onto a floured bread peel or a floured baking sheet. Using a very sharp blade, slash a few ¼-inch-deep arches or crosshatches or a spiral on top. Slide the dough onto the baking stone and close the oven.

If the dough is on a baking sheet, sift flour over the top of the loaf. Slash the large round loaf in ¼-inch-deep arches or crosshatches or a spiral. The ring does not need to be slashed. Place the bread in the oven.

If the dough is on a peel, sift flour over the top and slash as above. Slide the dough onto the stone.

Whatever shape you choose, lower the oven temperature to 425°F as soon as you place the bread inside.

The baked ring loaf, cooling

6.   Bake the bread for a total of 35 to 45 minutes. After the first 10 minutes, remove the pan of water. During the last 10 minutes, prop the door ajar with the handle of a wooden spoon. When the bread is deep brown, remove it from the oven. Tap the bottom to test for doneness. If ready, cool completely on a wire rack. If not, return to the oven to bake for 5 minutes more at 400°F.

Use a sharp blade to slash a cloverleaf loaf or a round one.

Old Dough

The old dough can be the equivalent of 1 large roll prepared, but not baked, the day before. Refrigerate the dough overnight, then take it out 1 hour before beginning to make this bread. The dough may smell really fermented, but this will impart a wonderful flavor to the loaf and increase its shelf life.

Baked loaves, cooling

Normandy Sourdough Apple Bread
Pain aux pommes

Normandy is famous for its apples, among other things. This bread is made from a fruit starter based on apples, but since the starter is not a powerful one, there is a small amount of yeast in the bread recipe. The bread has a crisp, crackly crust and lovely holes inside. The addition of sautéed apples and the use of the starter give the bread staying power. It is delicious with cheese or sausage.

      Plan ahead to make this bread. If you need to prepare the starter from scratch, you are in for a two-week wait for the bread.   **Makes one 14-ounce round bread**

1¼ cups (6¾ ounces) bread flour

3 tablespoons (1½ ounces) rye flour

Pinch of barley malt powder (optional)

1 teaspoon salt

5 ounces Apple Starter (page 258)

3 fluid ounces spring water, cool or lukewarm if you are using it to dissolve the yeast

⅓ cake (0.2 ounce) of compressed fresh yeast, crumbled, or 1 scant teaspoon active dry yeast dissolved in some of the water

1 tart apple, cored, chopped into ¼-inch cubes, sautéed in 1 tablespoon butter until translucent, and cooled

continued

1. Combine the bread flour, rye flour, barley malt, if using, and salt in a large mixing bowl or in the bowl of an electric mixer and stir to mix. Add the starter, water, and crumbled compressed yeast or dissolved yeast and mix with a paddle for 5 minutes. Using the dough hook, knead for about 10 minutes, or until the dough is smooth and elastic. Test that the gluten has developed (page 249). Knead in the apple by hand.

2. Place the dough in a lightly greased bowl and cover with a damp tea towel. Let the dough rise in a warm, humid spot, such as a turned-off oven with a pan of warm water in the bottom, until double in bulk, about 3 hours. After 1 hour of rising, punch down the dough and let it continue to rise.

3. Without pressing out all the air, gently but firmly form the dough into a large ball. Or shape a free-form loaf about 8 inches in length. For the latter, roll the dough out into a rectangle about 10 inches long, then roll the rectangle up, starting with a long edge. Place the loaf, seam side down and folded edges underneath, on a lightly floured pan or baking peel. Cover with a damp tea towel and let rise until double in bulk, 1 to 2 hours. Pieces of apple will show on the surface of the loaf.

4. During the last 30 minutes of rising, preheat the oven to 450°F. If using a baking stone, put it in the oven to heat. Place a shallow pan of water in the bottom of the oven.

5. Place the bread in the oven and immediately lower the temperature to 425°F. Bake the bread for a total of 35 to 45 minutes. After the first 10 minutes, remove the pan of water. During the last 10 minutes, prop the oven door ajar with the handle of a wooden spoon. Tap the bottom to test for doneness, and cool on a wire rack.

Apple Starter *Levain de pommes*

Use this starter for Normandy Sourdough Apple Bread (page 257) or any sourdough bread that calls for a yeast-free starter. Once the starter is active, it can be stored in a cool spot in a covered container. Check the contents from time to time to make sure that they are still bubbling, and stir, to keep the natural yeasts fed. If the starter seems to be dying, refresh it by following the last step of the recipe.

You can make your own fruit starter from any overripe fruit. Use organically grown fruit, as the chemicals on conventionally grown fruit may become toxic during the fermentation. Leave all the peels on; the acids in the peels will enhance the fermentation and the flavor of the starter. Make bread from the starter at least once a week. This will force you to keep feeding and refreshing the starter. Some starters last for years.

The starter takes close to two weeks to prepare. Once you have your starter, you will see that it was worth the wait.   Makes 4 pounds of starter, enough for 12 loaves of bread

One 3-ounce tart apple, cored and cut into chunks

2 tablespoons sugar

About 4½ cups (1½ pounds) bread flour, preferably organic

1 teaspoon barley malt powder (optional)

About 4 cups lukewarm spring water (105 to 110°F)

Pinch of salt

1.   Mix the apple, sugar, and a few drops of water in a 1-quart jar. Cover and leave the jar in a warm spot.

2.   After 8 to 10 days, the mixture will begin to give off carbon dioxide gas and bubble quite a bit. Weigh a large mixing bowl or the bowl of an electric mixer and write down the weight. Pour the contents of the jar into the bowl and crush the apple with a fork. Stir in 1 heaping cup of the flour, ½ teaspoon of the malt, and enough lukewarm water to obtain a thick dough. Knead the dough by hand or with the dough hook of the mixer for 5 minutes, or until smooth. Cover with a damp tea towel. Let ferment for 10 hours in a warm, humid spot, such as a turned-off oven with a pan of warm water in the bottom.

3.   Weigh the contents of the bowl by weighing the full bowl and subtracting the weight of the empty bowl. Add an equivalent weight of water, the remaining ½ teaspoon of malt, salt, and enough flour to obtain a thick dough, probably another cup. Stir to mix, by hand or with a mixer, and let the starter ferment for another 10 hours in the turned-off oven.

4.   Repeat Step 3, allowing the starter to ferment for only 8 hours.

5.   If the starter does not seem active, repeat Step 3 again, fermenting the starter for only 2½ to 3 hours. Store, covered, checking for activity from time to time.

6.   Each time you remove a given weight of starter, replace it with half that weight in flour, half in lukewarm water. Stir to obtain a smooth dough.

Mariner's Bread from Normandy *Pain brié*

With its thick crust and dense texture, this Mariner's Bread is ideal for the traveler who does not expect to find a bakery any time soon. The dough for the bread is beaten before the loaf is shaped. This removes all the air bubbles from inside.

This recipe is based on a *levain levure*, or yeasted sponge, and some previously prepared white bread dough that has already risen for at least two hours. If you've made too much white bread dough, refrigerate it and make this bread to use up the leftovers.

Unlike most bread doughs, this one only gets one rise, and this is after the loaf is shaped. This is why the dough is so dense. Most breads develop their flavor during the long first rise, but this one does not have a chance to do so. Flavor comes from the levain and the old dough.   Makes one 1-pound loaf

> 5 ounces Yeasted Sponge (page 261)
>
> 7 ounces Old Dough (page 261)
>
> ¾ cup (4 ounces) bread flour
>
> 1 to 2 tablespoons spring water, at room temperature or tepid (105 to 110°F) if using with dry yeast
>
> 1 tablespoon unsalted butter, at room temperature
>
> ½ cake (0.3 ounce) compressed fresh yeast, crumbled, or 1¼ teaspoons (½ package) active dry yeast, dissolved in some of the water
>
> 1 teaspoon salt

1.   Combine all the ingredients in a large bowl or in the bowl of an electric mixer and mix with a paddle for 5 minutes. Using the dough hook, knead for 10 minutes more, then switch back to the paddle and knead the dough until smooth, elastic, and extremely stiff. Test for gluten development (see page 249). Beat the dough for 10 minutes on low speed. Or place the dough on a lightly floured work surface and beat it with a rolling pin. There should be no visible air bubbles.

2.   Allow the dough to rest in the bowl for 10 minutes. Roll it out into an oval, about 8 inches long, then roll it up very tightly into a football-shaped loaf. Place the loaf on a lightly floured bread peel or baking pan, seam underneath, then cover it lightly with a damp tea towel. Allow the loaf to rise in a draft-free spot until double in bulk, 45 to 60 minutes. Halfway through the rising time, slash the bread 4 or 5 times with a sharp razor blade along the entire length of the bread. The slashes should be ½ inch deep, to allow moisture to escape during baking.

3.   During the last 30 minutes of rising, preheat the oven to 450°F. If using a baking stone, put it in the oven to heat.

4.   Slide the loaf onto the baking stone or place the pan in the oven. Immediately lower the oven temperature to 425°F. Bake for about 40 to 45 minutes, lowering the temperature to 375°F after 25 minutes, to allow this extremely dense loaf to bake through.

5.   Remove from the oven and test for doneness by tapping the bottom lightly. When done, it will have a deep hollow sound. The crust will be yellow, not brown, since the dough had only one rise. Cool on a wire rack. (*The loaf will keep for 1 week, wrapped in aluminum foil or plastic.*)

Yeasted Sponge *Levain levure*

When making a batch of white bread, remove a 3½-ounce piece (the amount you would use for a dinner roll), and let it rise in a cool draft-free spot for 8 to 10 hours. Or refrigerate it overnight in a loosely covered bowl. After the dough has fermented, add 2 tablespoons flour and 1 tablespoon water. Knead until the dough is quite firm. Let it rise again until doubled, for 3 to 4 hours before adding it to a recipe.

Old Dough *Vieille pâte*

Refrigerate leftover white bread dough as soon as you have decided not to bake it. Keep it in a covered plastic container in the refrigerator, and punch it down every few days for up to 5 days. This will keep the yeast alive. Use some of the dough from the White Pullman Loaf (page 262) or the Three Crusty Loaves (page 252) for Old Dough.

White Pullman Loaf *Pain de mie*

The *croûte* is the crust of the bread; the *mie* is the center. Here is a bread meant to have a negligible crust and a lot of white center. It is baked in a straight-sided loaf pan with a slide-on lid. The lid keeps the bread from rising too much and gives the mie a very dense texture. The bread is ideal for sandwich slices and perfect for morsels that require very regular slices. Remove the crusts and slice the loaf very thin, then cut the slices into rounds or other shapes for canapés.

This is a perfect example of a dough with a relatively large proportion of yeast. It rises quickly and does not develop a great deal of flavor. As plain loaves go, it is the antithesis of the Three Crusty Loaves (page 252). The dough is versatile, however, as it can easily be made into round or long rolls that will not develop a thick crust, even with steam. Leftover dough makes good Old Dough (page 261). **Makes one 1½-pound loaf**

3 cups (1 pound) unbleached all-purpose or bread flour, preferably organic

1 teaspoon salt

2 tablespoons unsalted butter, softened, or 2 tablespoons vegetable oil (not olive oil)

½ cup milk

½ cup lukewarm spring water (105°F)

1 cake (0.6 ounce) of compressed fresh yeast, crumbled, or 2½ teaspoons (1 packet) active dry yeast, dissolved in some of the water

1. Combine all the ingredients in a large bowl or in the bowl of an electric mixer and mix with a paddle for 5 minutes. Using the dough hook, knead on low speed for about 10 minutes, or until extremely smooth and elastic but not tough. Or knead by hand for about 15 minutes. Test the dough for gluten development (see page 249).

2. Place the dough in a lightly greased bowl and cover with a damp tea towel. Let the dough rise in a warm spot until double in bulk, 45 minutes to 1 hour.

3. Generously grease an 11 × 4 × 3½-inch pullman loaf pan and its lid. Flour the pan and the lid, tapping out the excess.

4. When the dough has doubled, punch it down to deflate it completely. Turn the dough out onto a lightly floured work surface and let it rest for 5 minutes. Roll out the dough to a rectangle, 12 × 10 inches, about 1 inch thick. Roll up the rectangle starting with a long end, pounding the dough as you roll to ensure that it is sealing as you go and that there are no air bubbles. Place the dough into the pan, seam side down, tucking the ends under the roll as you do so. Let rise in a warm spot, until the top of the dough barely reaches the top edge of the pan, 30 to 45 minutes.

5. Preheat the oven to 400°F.

6. When the dough has risen sufficiently, slide the lid on and put the pan in the oven. Bake for 40 to 45 minutes. Check the bread by sliding the lid back a few inches. The crust should be light to medium brown, no darker. Remove the bread from the oven, carefully slide off the lid, and slide the bread onto a cooling rack. Tap the bottom of the bread to test for doneness. If it does not sound hollow, place the bread on a baking sheet and bake it for a few minutes more. Cool completely on a wire rack. (*This bread will keep for several days, wrapped in plastic. Since a crisp crust is not crucial for this bread, it can be safely wrapped in plastic.*)

Hamburger Buns *Petits pains au lait*

If you wish, you can brush your buns with an egg wash or milk. Milk will give the buns a shine, without darkening them; the egg will give them a golden sheen. Then sprinkle with sesame or poppy seeds. Do this just before baking the rolls.

You can also make long rolls by rolling each 3½-ounce piece into an oval, then rolling the oval up starting with a long side. Bake in the same manner.   **Makes eight 3½-ounce buns**

I recipe White Pullman Loaf (page 262)

I large egg yolk mixed with I teaspoon water (optional) or 3 tablespoons milk, for brushing (optional)

4 teaspoons sesame or poppy seeds (optional)

I. Prepare Steps 1 and 2 of the recipe for White Pullman Loaf.

2. Weigh 8 pieces of dough, 3 to 3½ ounces each. Roll each tightly into a ball. Using a rolling pin, flatten each ball into a 4-inch disk. Place the disks on a lightly floured or parchment-lined baking sheet. Let rise uncovered in a warm spot until doubled in size, about 30 minutes.

3. Place an oven rack in the middle of the oven. Preheat the oven to 400°F.

4. When the buns have risen, brush them with egg wash or milk and also sprinkle seeds over the top, if desired. Bake for 15 to 20 minutes, or until lightly browned or golden, if you used egg. The buns may be lighter in color on the sides, toward the bottoms. Cool on wire racks.

Caraway Rolls *Petits pains au cumin*

These diamond-shaped rolls are rustic and hearty, wonderful with soups and salads. They are made with all-purpose flour, do not require a long rising time, and bake quickly. Plan for a bit of time to shape the rolls, however. Before baking, each diamond is dusted with flour and topped with caraway. The rolls are a nice addition to a bread basket and an excellent choice for a cheese platter.   Makes about 15 rolls

3 cups (1 pound) unbleached all-purpose flour

½ cup plus 2 tablespoons whole milk

½ cup plus 2 tablespoons lukewarm water (105°F)

1 cake (0.6 ounce) compressed fresh yeast, crumbled, or 1 packet active dry yeast, dissolved in some of the water

1 tablespoon unsalted butter, at room temperature

1½ teaspoons salt

1 teaspoon barley malt powder (optional)

2 tablespoons whole caraway seeds

Flour, for dusting

1. Combine the flour, milk, water, yeast, butter, salt, and barley malt in a large bowl or in the bowl of an electric mixer and mix with a paddle for 3 to 5 minutes. Using the dough hook, knead for about 10 minutes, or until the dough is smooth and elastic. This dough will be soft. Or knead by hand for 15 minutes. Reserve 2 teaspoons of the caraway seeds for topping and add the rest during the last minute of kneading. Place the dough in a lightly greased bowl and cover with a damp tea towel. Let rise in a warm draft-free spot until double in bulk, about 1 hour. After 30 minutes, punch down the dough.

2. Turn the dough out onto a lightly floured work surface. Weigh about 15 pieces of dough, about 2 ounces each, and roll them into balls. Let the dough balls rest for 10 minutes, to relax the gluten. Line 2 baking sheets with parchment paper and lightly dust with flour.

3. Roll out each ball into a 4-inch disk, then fold the flaps of each disk inward, to form a diamond shape. The flaps will overlap. Place the rolls on the baking sheets, flap side up, 3 inches apart. Place the rolls in rows, not randomly. Cover with a barely dampened tea towel and let rise in a warm, draft-free spot until double in bulk, 45 to 60 minutes.

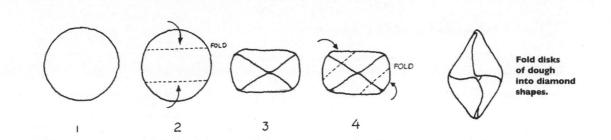

FOLD

1   2   3   4

FOLD

Fold disks of dough into diamond shapes.

4. During the last 30 minutes of rising, preheat the oven to 425°F and place a shallow pan of water in the bottom of the oven. Cut a 12 × 1½-inch strip of parchment, wax paper, or aluminum foil.

5. When the rolls are risen, lay the paper strip over the middle of the rolls in 1 row, going across the width of each diamond. Sift flour over, then lift the strip, leaving the dough underneath naked. Repeat this across all the rolls.

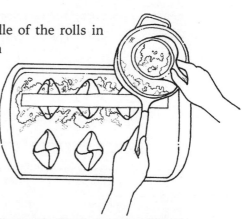

6. Dip a pastry brush in water, shake off the excess, and gently brush the unfloured part of each roll. Do not press down with the brush, as it could deflate the rolls. Sprinkle a few of the remaining caraway seeds across the dampened part of each roll and in the depression in the middle.

Place a strip of paper down the middle of a row of risen rolls, then sift flour over the row.

7. When you place the rolls in the oven, remove the pan of water. Bake for 10 minutes, then prop the door ajar with the handle of a wooden spoon. Bake for 5 to 8 minutes more, or until the rolls are deep brown in color and well rounded. Cool the rolls on wire racks.

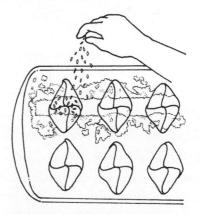

Sprinkle caraway seeds over unfloured dough.

Walnut Bread *Pain aux noix*

Le Dauphiné, a region in the southeast of France with a rich culinary history, is famous for its walnuts, among other things. This triangular loaf—or the rolls made from the same dough—will be no less wonderful made with California walnuts. The crust is thick and the interior tightly textured. Made with a combination of whole wheat and white flours, the bread is perfect with winter soups or an assortment of cheeses. This bread can also be baked in a loaf pan (see color insert); bake 10 to 15 minutes longer.

French folklore has it that if one eats something resembling a part of one's body, the food will have an effect on that body part. Hence, eating kidney beans was thought to keep the kidneys healthy, and eating walnuts, loosely resembling the brain (at least in shape), was thought to aid the memory.   **Makes two 10-ounce loaves**

1¼ cups plus 1 tablespoon (6½ ounces) bread flour

1¼ cups plus 1 tablespoon (6½ ounces) whole wheat flour

1 cup tepid spring water (105°F)

2 tablespoons unsalted butter, softened, or 2 tablespoons walnut oil

1 cake (0.6 ounce) compressed fresh yeast, crumbled, or 2½ teaspoons (1 packet) active dry yeast, dissolved in some of the water

1 teaspoon salt

¾ cup (3½ ounces) ground walnuts

¼ cup (1 ounce) walnut halves and pieces

Flour, for dusting

1.   Combine the flours, water, butter or oil, yeast, and salt in a large bowl or in the bowl of an electric mixer and mix with a paddle for 5 minutes. Using the dough hook, knead on low speed for about 15 minutes. Add the ground walnuts and knead for 2 minutes more. Or knead the dough by hand for 20 minutes. The dough will be moderately stiff but not especially smooth. Test the dough by squeezing it; it will resist when ready.

2.   Place the dough in a lightly greased bowl and cover with a damp tea towel. Let the dough rise in a warm, humid place, such as a turned-off oven with a pan of water in the bottom, until fully double in bulk, 45 to 60 minutes.

3.   Punch down the dough and turn it out onto a lightly floured work surface. Divide it into 2 even pieces and form each into a ball, pressing all the air out. Let the dough balls rest for 10 minutes. Roll out each ball piece into a large disk, 1 inch thick. Sprinkle half the walnut pieces in the middle of each, then fold in 3 flaps to meet in the middle, forming a triangle. Turn the triangles over onto a lightly floured baking sheet or peel. Cover the breads with a damp tea towel and let rise until double in bulk, about 1 hour.

4. During the last 30 minutes of rising, preheat the oven to 450°F. If using a baking stone, put it in the oven to heat. Place a shallow pan of water in the bottom of the oven.

5. When the dough has risen, sift flour over each loaf. Place the pan in the oven or slide the bread from the peel onto the stone and immediately lower the temperature to 425°F. After 10 minutes, remove the pan of water from the oven.

6. Bake the bread for 30 to 35 minutes. During the last 10 minutes, prop the oven door ajar with the handle of a wooden spoon. The breads should be dark brown under the flour. Test for doneness by tapping the bottoms, taking care not to shake off the flour. Cool on wire racks. This bread is best when eaten within 24 hours of baking.

Walnut Rolls *Petits pains aux noix*

Makes ten 2-ounce rolls

1 recipe Walnut Bread (page 266)

1. Prepare Steps 1 and 2 of the recipe for Walnut Bread.

2. Turn the dough out onto a lightly floured work surface. Weigh 10 pieces of dough, about 2½ ounces each, and roll into balls. Let rest for 5 minutes. Roll out the balls into 4-inch disks, then place 1 or 2 walnut pieces in the middle of each. Fold into triangles by bringing 3 flaps to meet in the middle. Place on a lightly floured sheet pan, cover with a damp tea towel, and let rise until double in bulk, about 30 to 40 minutes.

3. During the last 30 minutes of rising, preheat the oven to 425°F. If using a baking stone, put it in the oven to heat. Place a shallow pan of water in the bottom of the oven.

4. Place the pan of rolls in the oven, removing the pan of water immediately. Bake for 12 to 15 minutes. Prop the oven door ajar with the handle of a wooden spoon for the last 5 minutes. The rolls are done when their crust is deep brown and they sound hollow when tapped underneath. Cool on wire racks.

Brioche Dough *Pâte à brioche*

Is it a cake or a bread? It is yeasted, so it could certainly be considered a bread, but it has the texture of cake. Brioche cannot be pigeonholed. It may well be the ultimate pastry. Classic brioche dough has the maximum amount of butter and eggs that flour can absorb. The dough is beaten at length to incorporate these ingredients, thereby building up a great deal of gluten in the flour, so the mass is lightened with yeast. Since brioche is only slightly sweet, it is incredibly versatile in both the sweet and savory realms. It puts the fancier stuff to shame. It takes a bit more work than other breads, but it is worth it.

Brioche Dough must be prepared the day before it is to be baked. Because of all the butter, the dough is only workable when it is thoroughly chilled. Prepared dough will keep for up to three days in the refrigerator, after which it begins to ferment. You can also freeze the dough once it has stopped rising, as long as it is very well wrapped.

I do not recommend making Brioche Dough by hand. An electric mixer with a dough hook is ideal. Not the food processor, however. The heat from the processor could melt the butter. **Makes about 2 pounds of dough, enough for 2 large brioches or 16 small brioches**

3 cups (1 pound) all-purpose flour

½ teaspoon salt

1 cake of compressed fresh yeast, crumbled, or 2¼ teaspoons (1 packet) active dry yeast

¼ cup warm milk (110°F)

3 tablespoons sugar

5 large eggs

10 ounces (2½ sticks) unsalted butter, left at room temperature for 1 hour

1. Place the flour and salt in the bowl of an electric mixer. Stir to distribute the ingredients. Dissolve the yeast in the milk, then stir in the sugar. Allow the yeast to proof until thickened. Add to the mixing bowl.

2. Add 2 of the eggs to the bowl and begin mixing with the dough hook at low speed. Add the remaining eggs, one at a time, scraping down the bowl with a rubber spatula between additions. Wait until the dough is smooth before adding each egg. Once all the eggs have been added, increase the speed to medium and continue mixing for 5 minutes. The dough should be extremely smooth and elastic and should begin to pull away from the bowl.

3.   Using a rolling pin, pound the butter lightly between 2 pieces of wax paper to an even consistency. Remove 1 sheet of wax paper and cut or break up the butter into walnut-size pieces.

4.   With the mixer on low speed, add the butter, 1 piece at a time, waiting only a few seconds between additions. Once all the butter has been added, mix the dough on medium speed until no butter lumps remain. Stick your hand into the dough to feel for butter lumps.

5.   Cover the bowl with a slightly dampened tea towel or very loosely with plastic wrap. You may leave the dough hook in the dough. Allow the dough to double in volume, 1 to 1½ hours.

6.   Deflate the dough by reattaching the dough hook and giving it a few turns on the mixer or by beating it down with a wooden spoon. The dough should be extremely smooth and shiny, and quite loose.

7.   Pour the dough into a plastic container just large enough to hold it with a tight-fitting lid. Weigh down the top of the container with a plate and some full jars. Refrigerate the dough for at least 8 hours. (*The dough may be refrigerated for up to 3 days.*) If the dough is warm, place it in the freezer for 1 hour to chill it down faster. This dough will grow if not checked. Once chilled, however, it will stop rising. If not baking all the dough at once, divide it in half and freeze one portion. (*The dough may be frozen, well wrapped in plastic, for up to 3 weeks. Thaw overnight in the refrigerator.*)

Fluted or Parisian Brioche

Brioche à tête dite "parisienne"

Brioche comes in many shapes and sizes, but the *brioche à tête* is probably the most recognizable. You may have already attempted to make these two-part breads at home with less than perfect results. Perhaps the head fell off, or maybe the head and shoulders merged.

This can happen in professional bakeries as well, and I certainly had my share of brioche decap-itations. That is, until I learned a favorite trick of Gérard Rever, who owned a pastry shop in the Parisian suburb of Fontenay-aux-Roses. He would anchor the head with a foot, which was stuck under the body of the brioche. The result was a brioche with a perfectly centered head, surrounded by shrugging shoulders, all in perfect balance. Even individual brioches, which are formed differently, always managed to keep their heads.   **Makes one 1-pound round brioche**

> Soft unsalted butter, for the mold
>
> ½ recipe (1 pound) cold Brioche Dough (page 268)
>
> 1 large egg, for glaze

1.   Generously butter an 8-inch brioche tin.

2.   On a lightly floured surface, divide the dough into 2 parts, one slightly larger than the other, and roll them into large balls. Flatten the larger ball slightly, then poke your finger through the middle to make a hole. Open this hole to about 2 inches, then even out the dough around it so that it looks like a giant doughnut. Press down on the second ball of dough with the side of your hand, placing your hand off center. Move your hand back and forth in a sawing motion, creating a lopsided dumbbell out of the second ball. The larger end should be twice the size of the smaller one, and the thin part between the two should be the size of the hole in the other piece. Push the smaller end of the dumbbell through the doughnut and pull it out the other side. Set the dough inside the tin so that the smaller dumbbell end is firmly anchored on the bottom and the larger end is in the middle of the top.

Form half the dough into a doughnut, half into an uneven dumbbell.

Fit the dumbbell into the doughnut.

3.   Beat the egg until completely blended. Brush the brioche all over, without letting any egg wash collect around inside the tin or in the crease between the head and the shoulders. Let rise in a warm, draft-free place until the brioche just reaches the top of the mold and feels loose but not so loose that it would easily deflate, 1 to 1½ hours.

4. Preheat the oven to 375°F.

5. Carefully brush the brioche with egg wash, again avoiding the inside of the tin and taking care around the head. Dip the tips of a pair of kitchen shears in the egg wash and make vertical cuts 1 inch deep in 4 spots on the shoulders of the brioche.

Snip the risen dough with scissors.

6. Bake for 35 to 45 minutes, or until the brioche has risen well above the mold and is deep brown in color. A toothpick or wooden skewer inserted into the thickest part of the loaf should come out clean. Let cool for 5 minutes. As soon as you can handle the brioche, loosen it from the tin and lift it out. Put it back in the tin at an angle, so that the tin acts as a cooling rack. This will give the brioche a bit more support than a wire rack, while still allowing the brioche to cool without steaming in the pan.

Brioche Loaf *Brioche Nanterre*

While a Parisian brioche makes a dramatic presentation and shows off your baking talents, a *Brioche Nanterre*, named for a suburb of Paris, is more workaday, giving you very even slices. You can easily bake two loaves at a time and freeze one. If you have any brioche left over, use it for bread pudding (see page 101). Makes one 1-pound loaf

> Butter, for the pan
>
> ½ recipe (1 pound) cold Brioche Dough (page 268)
>
> 1 egg, for glaze

1. Butter the inside of an 8½ × 4-inch loaf pan. Line it with parchment paper, letting the paper hang over the sides of the pan. Butter the parchment.

2. Divide the dough into 6 even pieces. Roll the pieces tightly into balls, then flatten each slightly. Stand these disks in the pan. They should be barely touching and just reach the top of the pan. Beat the egg until completely blended and brush the top of the dough. Let rise in a warm, draft-free place until double in bulk, 1 to 1½ hours.

3. Preheat the oven to 375°F with no steam.

4. When the dough has risen, brush it with egg again. Dip the tips of a pair of kitchen shears in the egg wash and snip through each section of dough, cutting perpendicular to the seams and ½ inch deep.

5. Bake for 30 to 40 minutes, or until the loaf has stopped expanding and is golden brown. A toothpick or wooden skewer inserted into the thickest part of the loaf should come out clean. Remove the brioche from the oven and slide it out of the pan, onto a cooling rack. Cool the brioche upright. Remove the parchment when the loaf is cooled.

Little Brioches *Brioches individuelles*

Once you make these for a Sunday brunch, you will spoil your guests forever.   **Makes eight 2-ounce brioches**

Soft butter, for the molds

I pound Brioche Dough (page 268)

I egg, for glaze

1.   Thoroughly brush eight ⅓-cup tins with butter.

2.   Weigh eight 2-ounce pieces of dough and place them on a lightly floured work surface. Working with 2 pieces of dough at a time, with lightly floured hands, press down on 1 piece of dough with each hand. Begin rolling the dough around, slowly curling your fingers around the dough as you do so. As soon as you have formed 2 small balls, set them aside and roll 2 more, until you have formed 8 balls.

3.   Flour the side of your hand and press down, slightly off center, moving your hand back and forth in a sawing motion, to form a lopsided dumbbell, with one end 3 times as large as the other and the thin part about ½ inch thick. Shape all the pieces in this way.

4.   Pick up a dumbbell by holding the smaller end, destined to become the head, with the tips of your thumb and fingers. Press this inside one of the molds, and as you do so, create an indentation in the bigger end of the dumbbell with your thumb and fingertips, setting the head inside. Repeat this with all the pieces of dough.

5.   Flour your forefinger and poke it into the thicker part of the dough, just below and to the side of the head, aiming toward the middle of the mold. Repeat this all around the head, flouring your finger as needed. This method will create a deep crease between the head and the shoulders, without cutting the head off. Repeat with all the little brioches.

continued

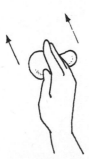

Form each dough ball into an uneven dumbbell.

Set the dough into the buttered tin.

Press the dough in, gripping the "head."

With a floured forefinger, dig into the dough just beneath the head.

273

6.   Beat the egg until completely blended. Brush the brioches all over, without letting any egg wash collect inside the tins or in the crease between the heads and the shoulders. Put the brioches in a warm, draft-free place. Let rise until the brioches just reach the tops of the molds and feel loose but not so loose that they will easily deflate, 45 to 60 minutes.

7.   Preheat the oven to 375°F.

8.   Carefully brush the brioches with another layer of egg wash, again avoiding the inside of the molds and taking care around the heads. Be careful not to poke the dough with the brush, or the dough might deflate. Place the brioches on a baking sheet.

9.   Bake for 20 to 25 minutes, or until the brioches have risen well above the molds and are golden brown. Let cool for 5 minutes in the tins. As soon as you can handle the brioches, loosen them from the tins and lift them out. Cool on a wire rack.

The Basics

Les Recettes de base

IF YOU WERE TO walk through the back of a French pastry shop and look in the refrigerators, freezers, and cupboards, you would probably not see many finished cakes or pastries. Instead, you would see wrapped doughs, creams, fillings, flavoring, and dry mixes, which, when combined according to the house recipes, go into making all the magnificent cakes, tarts, pastries, cookies, chocolates, and breads that you just passed in the front of the shop.

Many high-quality shops are run by a chef and two assistants. They do it all. The keys are organization and preparation. If they have all the components they need, ready to go, all that is left is assembly and decoration.

This chapter has a fraction of the recipes that are considered basic, but it does have all those you will need to create the recipes in this book and, even more important, to create your own pastries and desserts. With just a few of the basics, you can create a whole pastry menu just by changing a few ingredients, such as a fruit or a flavoring. Many of these basics can be made in advance, so that not every complex recipe need be started from scratch.

You need not make every one of these recipes. If, for example, you like to make and eat tarts, concentrate on the tart components: *pâte sucrée, crème d'amandes, crème pâtissière*, and a fruit glaze. If mousse cakes are your preference, concentrate on the different sponge bases: *génoise, fonds de succès,* and *joconde*. If you like to dress up simple desserts, expand your sauce repertoire.

Whatever path you take, know your basics. That is the difference between merely following recipes and creating them.

Sponge and Meringue Bases *Les Fonds*

Basic Sponge Cake / *Génoise nature*
    Chocolate Sponge / *Génoise au chocolat*

Ladyfingers / *Biscuits à la cuillère*
    Ladyfinger Rounds / *Fonds de biscuit à la cuillère*

Walnut Sponge / *Biscuit aux noix*

Hazelnut-Chocolate Sponge / *Biscuit noisettes-chocolat*

Almond Sponge Sheets / *Biscuit Joconde*

Almond Sponge / *Biscuit aux amandes*

Three Meringues
    Italian Meringue / *Méringue italienne*
    French Meringue / *Méringue française*
    Swiss Meringue / *Méringue suisse*

Almond Meringue Layers / *Fonds de succès*
    Hazelnut Meringue Layers / *Fonds de progrès*

Basic Sponge Cake *Génoise nature*

Called *génoise* by pastry chefs in France and the world over, this is the most basic of sponge layers. It is made by heating the eggs with sugar first, then folding in the flour. The recipe is a basic formula, and as long as the ratios are respected, the recipe can be multiplied or divided as needed. The ratios are:

- Equal weights of flour and sugar
- The weight of the eggs equals that of the flour and sugar combined

This is one recipe for which measuring cups really will not do; if you were ever unsure about buying a kitchen scale, get one now. While it is one of the simplest recipes used in French pastry making, it does require a light hand for folding.   Makes one 9-inch cake

4 large eggs

½ cup plus 1 tablespoon (4 ounces) sugar

Scant ¾ cup (4 ounces) all-purpose flour, sifted or strained after measuring or weighing

1. Adjust an oven rack to divide the oven in half. Preheat the oven to 375°F. Lightly grease a 9-inch round or square cake pan (spray grease is fine; a thin layer of softened butter will produce a slightly better crust). Dust the pan with flour, tapping out any excess. Line the bottom of the pan with parchment paper.

2. Place the eggs and the sugar in the mixing bowl of an electric mixer and whisk immediately. Place the bowl over a low flame, or if you have an electric range or are using a glass bowl, place it in a pot with about 1 inch of barely simmering water. Whisking constantly, heat the egg mixture until the sugar is completely dissolved and the mixture begins to froth. It should be tepid.

3. Using the whisk attachment, beat the egg mixture on high speed until it triples in volume and the beaters leave trails in the mix. Using a rubber spatula, gently fold the flour into the egg mixture. Be sure to dip the spatula all the way to the bottom of the bowl to catch and break up any clumps of flour. Carefully pour the batter into the prepared pan and level the top with a spatula. Lightly tap the pan on the table to knock out any large air bubbles.

4. Bake until the sponge is golden and the top springs back when lightly touched, 15 to 20 minutes.

5. Cool the sponge completely on a wire rack. Run a small metal spatula or knife around the edge to release it. Remove the parchment circle. (*The génoise, well wrapped in plastic, can be frozen for up to 2 weeks.*)

Chocolate Sponge *Génoise au chocolat*

Replace 1 tablespoon of the flour with 2 tablespoons unsweetened cocoa powder. Sift the cocoa and flour together and proceed as above.

> **If you are planning to cut the sponge into layers and fill it, try to bake it a day ahead. Store it at room temperature, wrapped in plastic. It will be easier to cut.**

Ladyfingers *Biscuits à la cuillère*

There are probably as many ways to make Ladyfingers, a necessary component of charlottes, as there are pastry shops in France. This method is, I believe, the easiest. In more traditional recipes, the sugar is first whipped with the egg yolks, the egg whites are whipped separately, then both masses are folded together with the flour—risking total collapse at any moment, due to the fragile nature of the egg whites. In the following method, you whip the whites first and gradually add the sugar, giving the whites more strength. The yolks are barely mixed in, followed by the flour. It is virtually foolproof. Whatever the method, the formula for ladyfingers is the same. The ratios are:

- **Equal weights of flour and sugar**
- **The weight of the eggs equals that of the flour and sugar combined**

  Makes about 30 pieces

5 large eggs, separated

½ cup plus 2 tablespoons (4¼ ounces) sugar

¾ cup plus 1 tablespoon (4¼ ounces) all-purpose flour, sifted after weighing

Powdered sugar, for dusting

1. Adjust the oven racks to divide the oven into thirds. Preheat the oven to 375°F. Grease 2 baking sheets or use 2 nonstick sheets. Do not line the pans with paper or aluminum foil. These pastries bake better directly on the pans.

2. Put the egg whites in a clean mixing bowl or the bowl of an electric mixer. Using the whisk attachment, mix on low speed until the whites begin to froth. Gradually add one-fourth of the sugar, increase the speed to medium, and whip until the whites hold soft peaks. Gradually add the remaining sugar in a thin stream. Once all has been added, increase the speed to high and whip until the whites are stiff but not dry. Change the speed to its lowest setting, then scrape in the egg yolks all at once. Give the mixture just a couple of turns of the whisk. Remove the bowl from the mixer. Gently fold in the sifted flour with a rubber spatula. Do not overmix.

3. Fill a large pastry bag fitted with a ½-inch plain tip. Pipe out 3- to 3½-inch fingers about 1½ inches apart on the baking sheets. When you have piped out all the batter, sift powdered sugar generously over the tops. This will give the ladyfingers a nice glaze and crust when baked.

4. Bake both pans of pastry at once. Switch the trays from top to bottom and rotate, if necessary, to ensure even baking. Bake until just lightly browned and firm to the touch, 8 to 12 minutes.

5. Cool the trays on wire racks, then remove the ladyfingers with a metal spatula. Use immediately or store in an airtight container with wax paper between the layers.

Ladyfinger Rounds *Fonds de biscuit à la cuillère*

Layers of this sponge mixture can be piped out for use in charlottes. This helps break up the richness of the mousse, while giving the charlotte an even bottom. Pipe rounds of batter onto parchment-lined pans as you would Almond Meringue Layers (page 290). These need not be dusted with powdered sugar. Bake until lightly browned and springy, 10 to 12 minutes. This is a great way to use up Ladyfingers batter that has deflated and will not produce good ladyfingers. (The layers can be baked ahead of time and frozen, well wrapped in plastic, for up to 2 weeks.)

Walnut Sponge *Biscuit aux noix*

Adding ground nuts to a *génoise* batter turns an ordinary sponge into a cake that can stand on its own. Toast the nuts first for extra crunch and extraordinary flavor. The nuts may cause your sponge to fall. Not to worry: A denser sponge will be no less delicious.   **Makes one 9-inch round or 8-inch square cake**

4 large eggs

Scant ½ cup (3½ ounces) sugar

½ cup (2¾ ounces) all-purpose flour, unsifted

½ cup (about 2 ounces) walnuts, toasted and ground

1.   Adjust an oven rack to divide the oven in half. Preheat the oven to 375°F. Lightly grease a 9-inch round or 8-inch square pan (spray grease is fine; a thin layer of softened butter will produce a slightly better crust). Dust the pan with flour, tapping out any excess. Line the bottom of the pan with parchment paper.

2.   Place the eggs and the sugar in the mixing bowl of an electric mixer and whisk immediately. Place the bowl over a low flame, or if you have an electric range or are using a glass bowl, place it in a pot with about 1 inch of barely simmering water. Whisking constantly, heat the egg mixture until the sugar is completely dissolved and the mixture begins to froth. It should be tepid.

3.   Using the electric mixer fitted with the wire whip or beaters, whisk the egg mixture on high speed until it triples in volume and the beaters leave trails in the mix.

4.   Sift or strain the flour onto a large piece of wax paper. Combine the walnuts with the flour, breaking up any lumps of nuts. The mixture should be very even. Using a rubber spatula, gently fold the flour-nut mixture into the egg mixture. Be sure to dip the spatula all the way to the bottom of the bowl to catch and break up any clumps of dry ingredients. Carefully pour the batter into the prepared pan and level the top with a spatula. Lightly tap the pan on the table to knock out any large air bubbles.

continued

5. Bake the sponge until it is golden and the top springs back when lightly touched, 15 to 20 minutes.

6. Cool the sponge completely on a wire rack before running a small metal spatula or knife around the edge to release. Remove the parchment liner. (*The sponge, well wrapped in plastic, can be frozen for up to 2 weeks.*)

- **Let toasted nuts cool completely, then grind in a food processor. Take care not to grind the nuts into a paste. Walnuts will never grind as fine as almonds, because of the walnuts' higher oil content.**

- **If you are planning to cut the sponge in layers and fill it, try to bake it a day ahead. Store it at room temperature, wrapped in plastic. It will be easier to cut.**

Hazelnut-Chocolate Sponge

Biscuit noisettes-chocolat

While a chocolate *génoise* always comes in handy and can be transformed into just about any sort of filled cake, the sponge itself is rather plain and often dry. This is no accident: It is meant to be moistened with a syrup that complements the filling.

The following recipe is considerably more interesting. The cake is moister and thus will not require being brushed with syrup, although you may certainly choose to do so. It is denser than a génoise and slices beautifully into horizontal layers without crumbling. The whole hazelnuts give it a lovely flavor and contrast in texture, but they make the cake considerably less neutral. This cake is wonderful when filled with ganache as in *L' Alhambra* (see page 69).   Makes two 9-inch cakes

I cup (5½ ounces) all-purpose flour, unsifted

2 tablespoons unsweetened cocoa powder

½ cup (2 ounces) hazelnuts, toasted and skins removed (see page 10)

8 large eggs, separated

I cup plus 2 tablespoons (8 ounces) sugar

4 ounces (1 stick) unsalted butter, melted and still warm

1. Adjust an oven rack to divide the oven in half. Preheat the oven to 350°F. Line two 9 × 2-inch round cake pans with parchment paper. Butter or spray-grease the pan and the paper.

2. Slft or strain the flour and cocoa together, then mix in the hazelnuts. Set aside on a piece of wax paper or in a bowl.

3. Place the egg yolks and 1 cup sugar in a medium mixing bowl or the bowl of an electric mixer. Using the whisk attachment if available, whip at high speed until the mixture is pale yellow and forms a ribbon when the beater is lifted.

4. If you do not have an extra mixer bowl, scrape the yolk mixture carefully into a medium mixing bowl. Thoroughly wash the mixer bowl and whisk and dry with a clean towel. If you are using a handheld mixer, wash the beaters.

5. Put the egg whites in the clean bowl and mix on low speed until the whites begin to froth, then increase to medium speed and whip until the whites hold soft peaks. Gradually add the remaining 2 tablespoons sugar in a thin stream. Once all has been added, increase to high speed and whip until the whites are stiff but not dry.

6. Gently fold the dry ingredients into the yolk mixture, mixing only until incorporated. Fold one-third of the egg whites into the yolk mixture, mixing very gently. Fold in another third. Fold the yolk mixture into the remaining whites, mixing only until no streaks of white remain. Gently fold in the melted butter. Divide the batter evenly between the 2 prepared pans.

7. Bake both pans on the same rack until the tops of the cakes spring back when lightly pressed, 25 to 30 minutes.

8. Cool completely on wire racks before unmolding. Remove the parchment circles from the bottoms before using. (*The cakes, well wrapped in plastic, can be frozen for up to 2 weeks.*)

Make two of these at a time and freeze one. You will need 2 mixing bowls. If your electric mixer has 2 bowls, use both.

Almond Sponge Sheets *Biscuit Joconde*

In the French art world, La Joconde refers to the Mona Lisa. In the pastry world, it refers to a thin sponge layer made of almonds, whole eggs, and egg whites. The layer is very light yet sturdy enough to hold up under a lot of butter cream and ganache, even when thoroughly soaked with coffee syrup.

These ingredients make up the classic Opera Cake (page 66), but this sponge need not be limited to that pastry alone. Use it for any mousse cake that calls for sponge layers that are heavily soaked with Simple Syrup, fruit juice, liqueur, or a combination. Even left unbrushed, the sponge will remain moist and springy.

This recipe requires an electric mixer. Two mixing bowls will make life easier. The recipe does not divide well. If you do not need both sheets of sponge, bake two and freeze one, either on a baking sheet or rolled up.   Makes two 16 × 12-inch sheets

1½ packed cups (7½ ounces) ground blanched almonds

1 cup plus 2 tablespoons (8 ounces) sugar

5 large eggs

5 large egg whites, at room temperature

3 tablespoons (1 ounce) all-purpose flour, unsifted

3 tablespoons unsalted butter, melted and cooled

1.   Adjust the oven racks to divide the oven into thirds. Preheat the oven to 450°F. Line two 16 × 12-inch baking sheets with parchment paper. Generously butter or spray-grease the paper in an even layer.

2.   Place the almonds, 1 cup of the sugar, and the whole eggs in the bowl of an electric mixer. Using the paddle attachment, beat on high speed until the mixture is pale yellow and has tripled in volume. Remove from the mixer. If you do not have an extra mixer bowl, gently scrape the mixture into a mixing bowl, taking care to not deflate the mixture. Thoroughly wash the mixer bowl (and beaters, if you have no other attachment) and dry with a clean towel.

3.   Put the egg whites in the clean mixing bowl and, using the whisk attachment (or the clean beaters), mix on low speed until the whites begin to froth, then increase to medium speed and whip until the whites hold soft peaks. Gradually add the remaining 2 tablespoons sugar in a thin stream. Once all has been added, increase to high speed and whip until the whites are stiff but not dry.

4.   Sift the flour over the almond mixture and gently fold it in. Fold one-third of the egg whites into the almond mixture, without mixing in completely. Fold in another third of the whites, then fold the almond mixture back into the remaining whites. Always fold gently; this mixture is fragile. Mix only until there are no streaks of white. Finally, fold in the melted butter.

5.   Divide the batter between the 2 prepared pans and spread evenly. Using a long, narrow offset spatula, spread to the corners first, then spread the center, to ensure that the batter is not thicker in the middle than at the sides. The layers should be about ¼ inch thick. Run your finger through the batter around all the edges to help release the baked layers.

6.   Bake until the tops of the sponges spring back when lightly touched, 3 to 4 minutes. They should be barely colored.

7.   Remove the pans from the oven and immediately cut around the edge of each sheet. Use a spatula to slide the sheets, still attached to the parchment, onto wire racks to cool. Do not cool these in the pans, as they will continue to bake and will dry out. (*The sheets, well wrapped in plastic, can be frozen for up to 2 weeks.*)

Almond Sponge *Biscuit aux amandes*

These extremely fragile sheets are similar in formula to French Macaroons (page 159). Based on egg whites and almost devoid of flour, the pastry will melt in your mouth. It is perfect for layering delicate mousses or light butter creams. Since the sheets may become crisp, they cannot be used for rolled pastry logs.   Makes two 16 × 12-inch sheets

I cup minus 2 tablespoons (6½ ounces) sugar

2 heaping teaspoons all-purpose flour

I cup (5 ounces) finely ground blanched almonds

4 large egg whites, at room temperature

1.   Adjust the oven racks to divide the oven into thirds. Preheat the oven to 425°F. Line two 16 × 12-inch baking sheets with parchment paper. Butter or spray-grease the paper in an even layer.

2.   Divide the sugar in half. Set one half aside. Sift or strain the remaining sugar together with the flour and the ground almonds (be sure to put the sugar in the strainer *last*). Mix any almond pieces that remain in the sifter into the sifted ingredients. Set aside on a piece of wax paper.

3.   Put the egg whites in a clean mixing bowl or the bowl of an electric mixer. Using the whisk attachment, mix on low speed until the whites begin to froth. Increase the speed to medium, and whip until the whites hold soft peaks. Gradually add the remaining sugar in a thin stream. Once all has been added, increase the speed to high and beat until the whites are stiff but not dry. Remove the mixing bowl from the mixer.

4.   Gently shake the sifted dry ingredients over the egg whites while folding them in with a rubber spatula. Mix only until incorporated. Divide the batter evenly between the 2 prepared pans. Using a long, narrow offset spatula, spread the batter quickly and evenly.

5.   Bake both pans at once until the sponge springs back when lightly touched and is just beginning to color, 5 to 7 minutes. If your oven is uneven, switch and rotate the pans when half-baked.

6.   Remove the pans from the oven and, running a small, sharp knife around the edge of the biscuit, pull each sheet of pastry off with its parchment attached. Cool completely on wire racks or on a cool surface. Do not cool in the pans, or the sheets will dry out. These will cool quickly.

7.   If using the sheets immediately, turn each over and peel away the parchment paper, which should release easily. If not using the sheets immediately, cool completely and stack on a clean baking sheet. Cover with plastic, wrapping it all around the pan. These will keep at room temperature for 24 hours. The parchment may be more difficult to remove at that time than when fresh. Do not freeze these sponge sheets.

Three Meringues

Meringues fall into three categories: Italian, French, and Swiss. Each has a specific use or uses, and they can rarely be used interchangeably. Such complexity from a product that has only two ingredients—egg whites and sugar. All these meringues have the following in common:

- All meringues are based on a two-to-one ratio of sugar to egg whites. While it is true that this ratio results in a very sweet product, it is always a light one. This is the ratio for traditional meringues; not all recipes call for meringue with these proportions.

- Old egg whites give the best results. Some pastry chefs leave their whites at room temperature for days, but I do not recommend this. The whites should, however, be at room temperature before you begin.

- Frozen egg whites make perfectly acceptable meringues. Just make sure that you know the weight of the whites you are using. Weigh them either before or after freezing, then use double that weight of sugar.

- If you are using a free-standing mixer, such as a KitchenAid with a 5-quart bowl, do not attempt to make more than 8 egg whites' worth of meringue. The volume will increase tremendously and the meringue will overflow.

- Always put the whites in a very clean bowl. A few drops of water in the bowl will not hurt the egg whites. It is better to have a little water than to wipe out the bowl with a towel that may have some grease on it.

Italian Meringue

This meringue is actually cooked when you add boiling sugar to egg whites as you beat them. Once the sugar is added, the meringue is cooled by continued beating. Italian meringue is rarely used alone, except on a tart (page 20) or a dessert like baked Alaska, which the French call *omelette norvégienne*. It is added to creams, usually egg based, to lighten them and turn them into mousses. In this case, the quantity of sugar used in the cream component is reduced. This meringue is rarely added to anything that will be baked, since the egg whites are already cooked and will not add much lift, which is the reason for adding the egg whites.

French Meringue

This is one of the baked meringues. Egg whites are beaten with twice their weight in sugar, then piped or dropped onto parchment paper for slow baking. The meringues are puffy, crunchy, and extremely fragile. French Meringue is often combined with ground nuts, as in the Almond Meringue Layers (page 290) and baked to make crisp layers for classic desserts, such as *dacquoise* (see page 121).

Swiss Meringue

If you want to make a perfectly white, dense, crisp shell, also called a vacherin, for ice cream or fresh fruit, this is the meringue to use. While a French Meringue may puff and crack during baking and will be extremely fragile and crumbly, Swiss Meringue remains dense, crack-free, and quite sturdy. And this after less baking. If you have a gas oven, you can leave the meringues in overnight, and they will dry beautifully. For these meringues, the egg whites and sugar are combined, then heated until the sugar dissolves. The mixture is then beaten until completely cool and quite stiff. This meringue is ideal for piping out shapes that will remain as such, not to mention shiny and white. It is perfect for meringue mushrooms and other decorations.

Italian Meringue *Méringue italienne*

Makes about 3 cups (18 ounces)

1½ cups plus 2 tablespoons (11½ ounces) sugar

4 to 6 tablespoons water

5 large egg whites, at room temperature

1. Put 1½ cups of the sugar in a small heavy saucepan with just enough water to wet all the crystals. Wash down any crystals from the inside of the saucepan with a wet pastry brush. Place the saucepan over medium heat and heat, without stirring, until the sugar begins to boil. When the sugar boils clear, begin beating the egg whites on low speed until they begin to froth. Increase the speed to medium and beat until the whites hold a soft peak. Gradually add the remaining 2 tablespoons sugar and continue beating.

2. When the sugar reaches 244°F on a candy thermometer (between the soft ball and hard ball stages), increase the mixer speed to high. When the sugar reaches 248°F (hard ball stage), remove it from the heat.

3. On low speed, add one-third of the sugar to the whites in a very thin stream. Avoid hitting the whisk or beaters with the sugar. Once you have added one-third of the sugar, increase the speed to medium and add the rest, in twice as heavy a stream. When all the sugar has been added, beat on high speed for 5 minutes. Lower the speed to medium—the meringue will have increased quite a bit in volume—and beat until the meringue is at room temperature. The meringue may be left at room temperature for up to 4 hours. Lay a piece of plastic wrap directly on the surface.

> There will be times when you will mix Italian Meringue into creams, as in *crème chiboust* (see page 312), while the meringue is still warm. It is very fragile while warm, since it has not completely cooked and the whites are not completely set. Note that warm meringue will deflate somewhat when mixed with a cream.

French Meringue *Méringue française*

Makes about 3 cups (18 ounces)

5 large egg whites, at room temperature

1½ cups plus 2 tablespoons (11½ ounces) sugar

1. Put the egg whites in a clean mixing bowl or the bowl of an electric mixer. Using the whisk attachment, mix on low speed until the whites begin to froth. Gradually add 3 tablespoons of the sugar, then increase the speed to medium. Gradually add the remaining sugar in a thin stream. Once all has been added, increase the speed to high and whip until the whites are stiff but not dry.

2. Adjust the oven racks to divide the oven into thirds. Preheat the oven to 200°F. Line 2 baking sheets with parchment paper. Do not use any grease.

3. Pipe out shapes, such as small rosettes, or drop meringues with a spoon, which will yield more cloudlike meringues. Bake for at least 3 hours, then turn off the oven and leave the meringues inside to dry completely. The meringues will puff and crack a bit and may take on a bit of color. (*If possible, store in a turned-off oven, as these will absorb a lot of moisture from the air. Otherwise, store in airtight containers with wax paper between the layers.*)

Swiss Meringue *Méringue suisse*

Makes about 3 cups (18 ounces)

5 large egg whites, at room temperature

1½ cups plus 2 tablespoons (11½ ounces) sugar

1. Place the egg whites and the sugar in a large stainless steel mixing bowl or the bowl of your electric mixer. Whisk immediately by hand.

2. Place the bowl directly over a low flame and, whisking constantly, heat the mixture until tepid (about 105°F), to ensure that the sugar dissolves. The mixture should become thick. Whip on high speed until extremely thick and voluminous. Continue beating until the meringue is at room temperature.

3. Adjust the oven racks to divide the oven into thirds. Preheat the oven to 200°F. Line 2 or 3 baking sheets with parchment paper.

continued

4. Pipe the meringue onto the baking sheets. To make individual vacherins, trace six to nine 4-inch circles, 2 inches apart, on sheets of parchment paper cut to fit the baking sheets. Place the paper on the pans, ink side down. Fit a large pastry bag with a ⅜-inch star or plain tip and fill it with about 2 cups of meringue. Hold the bag straight up, with the tip ½ to 1 inch above the pan. Starting from the middle of each circle, pipe spirals of meringue to form rounds, stopping just inside each tracing. Stop squeezing and quickly lift the tip up to stop the flow of meringue. Pipe a single circle of meringue around the perimeter of each round to form a slight ridge. Pipe another circle on top of that. Continue piping, refilling the bag as necessary.

Hold the bag vertically and pipe a spiral.

For a large vacherin, trace an 8-inch circle and pipe a round of meringue, as for individual vacherins. Pipe a circle of meringue around the perimeter of the round, then another just inside that so that they are barely touching. Pipe another pair of circles on top of the first two. Top these with rosettes of meringue. If you wish, pipe a few rosettes of meringue on the same pan, but not touching the large vacherin. Once baked, these can be used as decoration for an ice cream and fruit vacherin, or they may be stuck between scoops of ice cream or rosettes of whipped cream.

Pipe a rim on top of the disk, or . . .

5. Bake at 200°F for 2 hours. Or leave in a turned-off gas oven with a pilot light overnight. Be sure the oven is not hotter than 200°F, or the meringues will inflate and be too fragile when removed from the oven, or they may deflate and take on a wrinkled appearance. If leaving meringues in the oven overnight to dry out from the heat of the pilot light, make sure that the oven is completely cool except for the heat of the pilot. Meringues that are exposed to too much heat become fragile and lose their whiteness.

. . . form a rim with teardrops of meringue.

Almond Meringue Layers *Fonds de succès*

These layers lose their crispness quickly but are still quite delicious when chewy. They do become difficult to cut, however, so if you are planning to serve many guests and you are making the cake ahead of time, you may want to consider individual pastries, and leave the cutting to your guests.

Makes four 8-inch round layers or about forty 3-inch layers

½ cup plus I tablespoon (4 ounces) sugar

I cup (5 ounces) ground almonds

I tablespoon all-purpose flour

5 large egg whites, at room temperature

1. Adjust the oven racks to divide the oven into thirds. Preheat the oven to 300°F. Line 2 baking sheets with parchment paper. Use the bottom of an 8-inch cake pan or a glass with a 3-inch bottom to trace circles on the paper, 1 inch apart. Turn the paper over so that you do not bake directly on the ink or pencil marks.

2. Set aside 2 tablespoons of the sugar. Combine the remaining sugar, the ground almonds, and the flour in a medium mesh strainer and press through onto a piece of wax paper. Pick up the paper by 2 opposite sides, then strain the mixture again onto another piece of paper. Set aside.

3. Put the egg whites in a clean mixing bowl or the bowl of an electric mixer. Using the whisk attachment, mix on low speed until the whites begin to froth. Increase to medium speed and whip until the whites hold soft peaks. Gradually add the reserved 2 tablespoons sugar in a thin stream. Once all has been added, increase to high speed and whip until the whites are stiff but not dry.

4. Gently shake the dry ingredients over the whites while folding them in with a rubber spatula. Be sure to go all the way to the bottom of the bowl with the spatula, as clumps of nuts may sink.

5. Fill a pastry bag fitted with a ⅜-inch plain tip. Starting from the center of each circle and holding the tip 1 inch above the paper, pipe out a spiral of batter so that there are no gaps. If you come across any air bubbles, just fill them in with more batter. If the tip gets clogged with nuts, pull them through with a toothpick.

6. When you have finished all the circles, bake until the layers are lightly browned and crisp, 45 to 50 minutes (somewhat less for smaller circles). Cool on wire racks. If you are storing the layers for later use, peel away the parchment. This becomes more difficult as the layers sit at room temperature and absorb moisture. (*These layers will keep at room temperature for 3 days and will remain crisp. Store with sheets of wax or parchment paper between the layers.*)

Hazelnut Meringue Layers *Fonds de progrès*

Replace the almonds with an equal weight of toasted, blanched, and ground hazelnuts. Bake as directed.

> **Unlike other pastry and sponge layers, these meringue layers are baked for a long time at a relatively low temperature. This prevents the whites from rising, leaving thin, crisp layers that still have a good deal of body.**

Doughs

Les Pâtes

Flaky Pastry Dough / *Pâte brisée*

Sweet Short Dough / *Pâte sucrée*

Choux Paste / *Pâte à choux*

Puff Pastry / *Pâte feuilletée*

Three Puff Pastry Shells
    Feuilletés
    Bouchées
      Vol-au-vent
    Mini Bouchées

Flaky Pastry Dough *Pâte brisée*

This dough, the traditional shell for a quiche, is very fragile. *Briser,* **in fact, means to break or to shatter. In its raw form, however, it has enough body to make working with it easy. Once baked, it is flaky but still gives you something to bite into. It has a lovely, buttery, balanced flavor.** Makes about 2 pounds of dough, enough for four 10-inch pastry shells

> 3 cups (1 pound) unsifted unbleached all-purpose flour
>
> 1 teaspoon salt
>
> 1 tablespoon sugar
>
> 10 ounces (2½ sticks) cold unsalted butter, cut into ½-inch cubes
>
> 2 large egg yolks
>
> 7 tablespoons cold water

1. Sift the flour, salt, and sugar together into the bowl of an electric mixer or a large mixing bowl. Add the butter. Using the paddle attachment or a pastry blender, mix the ingredients together until no large chunks of butter remain and the mixture resembles coarse cornmeal.

2. Whisk the egg yolks and water together and add to the flour-batter mixture. Mix with the paddle or a heavy wooden spoon only until the dough begins to come together.

3. Turn out the dough onto a lightly floured surface and knead by pushing small pieces of dough away from the rest with the heel of your hand. This will form a second mass of dough pieces. Pull these pieces together and repeat the process, which the French call *fraisage.* This will yield an evenly mixed but flaky dough. Gather the pieces together and form them into four 7-inch disks, 1 inch thick. Wrap individually in plastic and refrigerate for at least 1 hour or up to 1 week. (*The disks may also be frozen for up to 1 month. Thaw in the refrigerator overnight before rolling the dough.*)

Sweet Short Dough *Pâte sucrée*

Not only does this foundation dough make the perfect, delicate crust for a fruit tart, it is also the incredibly simple base for Rolled Butter Cookies (page 172) and many other traditional French cookies. The recipe is another of those classic formulas that can be multiplied or divided by any number. Just be careful not to multiply to a point where you are no longer able to mix the ingredients evenly or where you end up overmixing the dough in order to achieve even blending. Makes about **2 pounds of dough, enough for about four 10-inch pastry shells**

3 cups unbleached all-purpose flour, unsifted

1¾ cups (8 ounces) powdered sugar, unsifted

8 ounces (2 sticks) cold unsalted butter, cut into ½-inch cubes

1 large egg

1 large yolk

½ teaspoon vanilla extract

1.   Sift or strain the flour and powdered sugar together into the bowl of an electric mixer or into a large mixing bowl. Add the butter. Using the paddle attachment or a pastry blender, mix the ingredients together until no large chunks of butter remain and the mixture has the consistency of fine cornmeal.

2.   Beat the egg with the vanilla extract by hand and add to the other ingredients. Mix with the paddle, a heavy mixing spoon, or your hands just until the dough comes together.

3.   Turn out the dough onto a lightly floured surface and knead lightly a few times. Divide the dough in 4 portions and form each portion into a disk about 6 inches in diameter. Make sure that there are no air holes in the disks. Wrap each in plastic and refrigerate for at least 1 hour before rolling. (*The disks may be refrigerated for up to 5 days. They may also be frozen. Thaw frozen dough in the refrigerator overnight to ensure even thawing and easier rolling.*)

> **Always roll chilled dough. If it is too soft, it will be very difficult to roll and even more difficult to transfer to a tart pan.**

Choux Paste *Pâte à choux*

Choux Paste, an easy dough that is the base for cream puffs and éclairs, Paris-Brest (page 34), and countless hors d'oeuvres, is prepared following a simple formula:

- The weight of the liquid (water, milk, or a combination) equals the weight of the eggs.
- The combined weight of the flour and butter also equals the weight of the liquid.

Using only water results in a crisper texture, while using only milk gives a softer shell, good for cream puffs. I like to use half water and half milk for cream puffs and éclairs, so that there is just enough resistance before you bite in.

You can also adjust the amounts of sugar and salt in the recipe, or even eliminate one or the other entirely, depending upon the filling you plan to use. A small amount of both produces a lovely, neutral shell with a good deal of versatility.   **Makes 24 ounces of dough**

I cup milk

I cup water

7 ounces (1¾ sticks) unsalted butter, cut into small pieces

½ teaspoon salt

I tablespoon sugar

2 cups minus 2 tablespoons (9 ounces) all-purpose flour, sifted or strained after weighing

12 large eggs

1.   Place the milk, water, butter, salt, and sugar in a large saucepan and bring to a simmer. The butter should melt completely. Turn off the heat, but leave the pot on the stove.

2.   Pour all of the flour into the liquid and mix it in thoroughly with a wooden spoon. Turn the heat back on to medium and, stirring constantly, cook the mass until it is smooth and slightly shiny and pulls away from the side of the pot.

3.   Pour the dough into a large mixing bowl or the large bowl of an electric mixer. It should come out of the pot as a single mass.

4.   Using a paddle or beaters, start mixing the dough on low speed. Add the eggs, one at a time. Mix the dough until it is smooth before adding the next egg. Be sure to scrape down the bowl with a rubber spatula between additions.

5.   Before adding the last 2 eggs, check the consistency of the dough. It is ready when, just as you turn off the mixer, it spreads about ¼ inch away from the beater and then stops. If the dough is at this stage, do not add any more eggs. If it is stiffer, add 1 egg and check again. You might not need the last egg. If not using immediately, divide into four 6-ounce portions. Place each in a container and place a piece of plastic wrap directly on the surface of the dough to prevent a crust from forming. Seal the container and refrigerate for 24 hours. (*Choux Paste can be frozen for up to 1 month. Thaw the dough in the refrigerator overnight before piping.*)

PASTRY	TIP SIZE	PIPED DIMENSIONS
Large éclairs / *Éclairs*	¾ inch	5 inches long
Mini-éclairs / *Carolines*	⅜ inch	3 inches long
Large puffs / *Choux*	¾ inch	2 inches in diameter
Small puffs / *Petits choux*	⅜ inch	1 inch in diameter

Puff Pastry *Pâte feuilletée*

Puff Pastry is a miracle of pastry engineering. Through a process of ordered rolling and folding, paper-thin layers of a simple dough (the *détrempe*) are alternated with equally thin layers of butter—729 layers of each. The result is an explosion—the dough may rise up to eight times its original thickness—of thin buttery layers with nothing but air in between. As the pastry bakes, the layers of butter melt into the pastry, leaving layers of leaves, hence the French terms *pâte feuilletée* and *feuilletage*, or leafy dough. Puff Pastry can be made with or without sugar, depending on whether the end product will be sweet or savory.

This recipe, properly executed under perfect conditions, will yield fantastic puff pastry. What are those conditions?

- A space in which to work that is consistently cool.

- A cool work surface, such as marble, is a real plus, though not crucial.

- Plenty of room to roll out the dough.

- A way to roll your dough very evenly without heating it up.

• **A dough sheeter, which looks like a giant pasta maker, is not a must, but it makes rolling a lot easier.**

You can make the dough when you have the time, giving it four of the six required turns, and freeze it for up to one month. This lesser number of turns keeps the dough portion thicker than the layers of butter, and these thicker layers are not apt to melt together with the butter when frozen. Thaw the nearly completed dough in your refrigerator overnight, then give it two turns one hour before the final rolling. The final product will be every bit as high and airy as one made with fresh dough.

If you've tried without success to make Puff Pastry or if you don't want to attempt it at all, there are alternatives. Store-bought puff pastry, which can be found in the frozen-food section of your supermarket, is great. It comes in evenly rolled sheets, ready to bake. And for some recipes that call for Puff Pastry, such as Napoleons (page 41), you may be able to substitute phyllo dough, which is also available in the frozen-food section.   **Makes about 2 pounds of dough**

DOUGH PORTION (DÉTREMPE)
3 cups (1 pound) all-purpose flour, unsifted

1½ teaspoons salt

1 tablespoon sugar (optional)

2 ounces (½ stick) chilled unsalted butter, cut into small chunks

1 cup cold water

BUTTER PACK
12 ounces (3 sticks) cold dry unsalted butter (see page 2) or ¾ pound (3 sticks) cold unsalted wet butter and 3 tablespoons all-purpose flour

1.   To prepare the dough portion (détrempe), sift together the flour, salt, and sugar, if using, and place the mixture in the large bowl of an electric mixer or in a large mixing bowl. Add the butter chunks and mix with the paddle attachment on low speed or your hands until the butter is completely incorporated and no chunks are visible.

2.   Still mixing on low speed or with a wooden spoon, drizzle the water over the dough. Mix only until the dough begins to come together. Turn out the dough onto a work surface, preferably wood or marble, and knead very lightly to form into a ball. The consistency of the dough might look uneven at this point—that is fine. Take care not to overwork the gluten in the flour through too much kneading. Wrap the dough in plastic and refrigerate for at least 1 hour or up to overnight.

continued

3. To prepare the butter pack with dry butter, pound the sticks together with the side of a rolling pin. Fold the butter over several times and continue pounding until it is of an even consistency. Form the butter into a 6-inch square and place it on a piece of wax paper for easy handling.

Pound the block of butter to give it a uniform consistency.

To prepare the butter pack with wet butter, cut the butter into 1-inch cubes and place it in an electric mixer, not a food processor. Add the flour and using the paddle attachment, mix until all the flour is incorporated and the consistency is very even. Turn out the butter onto a lightly floured surface and form it into a 6-inch square.

While pounding, form the butter into a 6-inch block, 1 inch thick.

4. Unwrap the chilled détrempe and place it on a large, cool, lightly floured surface, leaving yourself plenty of room. Using a large, sharp knife, cut an X through the top half of the dough ball. Pull the dough out from the X. (Pulling the dough rather than rolling it helps avoid overrolling and building up too much gluten.) With some imagination, the dough should resemble a four-leaf clover. With a light hand, gently roll the "leaves" of the clover to an even thickness of about ½ inch. Roll the center of the clover to form an even pad, about 7 inches square and ¾ inch thick.

Cut an X halfway through the ball of dough.

Pull the dough apart at the cuts.

Roll out the *détrempe*, with a thick pad in the middle.

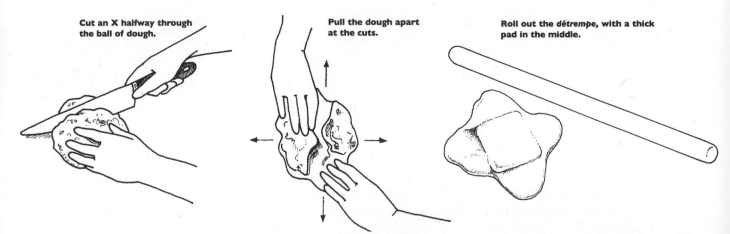

5. Place the butter pack on the dough pad so that the corners of the butter are pointing to the depressions between the dough leaves. Fold the dough over the butter, starting with 1 leaf and working clockwise, making sure that the leaves overlap and no butter is showing. Seal the leaves and the corners over the butter by pressing the dough together at all seams.

Seal the butter completely in the dough.

6. Place 1 edge of the square of dough so that it is parallel with the edge of the table closest to you. Holding a rolling pin perpendicular to the table edge, evenly hit the dough 6 times across the top, starting from the middle of the dough square and working outward. This will spread the dough, which is too thick to roll, without building up the flour's gluten.

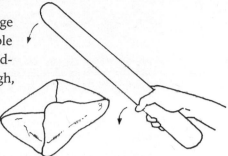

7. Rotate the dough one quarter turn to the right. Roll the dough evenly until it is about 1 inch thick and 3 times as long as it is wide. Fold the top third down toward you and the bottom third up to meet it and form a square.

Hit the dough with a rolling pin . . .

8. Tap the dough again with the rolling pin to begin to spread it. Rotate the dough one quarter turn to the right and roll it out until it is 3 times as long as it is wide. Fold the top third down and the bottom third up to meet it and form a square. Wrap the dough tightly in plastic and refrigerate for at least 1 hour or up to 4 hours.

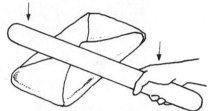

. . . and spread it without toughening.

9. Lightly flour the work surface and place the unwrapped dough on top with the last fold you made parallel to the edge of the table nearest you. Hit the dough with the rolling pin and give the dough 2 more rolls and turns as in Steps 7 and 8. Wrap and refrigerate the dough for 1 hour. (*The dough, well wrapped in plastic, may be frozen for up to 1 month. Thaw in the refrigerator overnight.*)

Fold the rolled dough into thirds before turning.

10. Give the dough 2 more turns to finish it, making sure to start with the last fold you made parallel to you and always to rotate in the same direction. Wrap the dough in plastic and let it rest in the refrigerator for at least 1 hour but no more than 4 hours before rolling it out for use in a recipe.

- **Whether you rotate your dough to the right or to the left is unimportant. What is crucial is to rotate it always in the same direction for the turns. Equally important is to fold in the same pattern (top flap first, for example). This way, the dough is always pulled and rolled evenly and will rise evenly when baked.**

- **If for some reason you are not sure that you will be able to keep track of the number of turns you've given your dough, mark the dough before refrigerating it. Make 2, 4, or 6 finger indentations on top of the dough to indicate the number of turns that have been performed.**

- **German or Austrian puff pastry, called *Blätterteig*, is often made with a bit of lemon juice or vinegar. The acid makes the détrempe less permeable to the layers of butter, keeping them more distinct. It also adds a bit of flavor. To try this, replace 1 tablespoon of the water in the dough portion with an equal amount of freshly squeezed lemon juice or cider vinegar.**

Three Puff Pastry Shells

You can change the most everyday dish into a dramatic gourmet presentation by serving it in a flaky shell of Puff Pastry. Here are three classic shells that will show you how very versatile this dough is.

Feuilletés

Feuilletés, the simplest of the three crusts, are the perfect vehicle for asparagus in cream sauce or berries with whipped cream. They are not unlike two-layer Napoleons. Remember to split the shells in half horizontally while they are still hot and scoop out the inevitable raw dough. You will be left with nothing but lighter-than-air flakes of dough to complement whatever you are serving.   Makes 12 individual shells

¼ recipe (½ pound) fully turned Puff Pastry (page 296) or 1 sheet (½ package) store-bought pastry, cold

2 large egg yolks

1.   If using homemade Puff Pastry, roll it out into a 9- or 10-inch square, ¼ to ⅛ inch thick, then refrigerate for at least 1 hour to allow the gluten to relax and thus minimize shrinkage. Leave store-bought dough at room temperature for 5 minutes before unfolding, to keep it from cracking. It will require no further rolling. Cut either type of pastry while cold, working quickly so that all the pieces are the same size.

2.   Stir the egg yolks with 2 teaspoons water. Remove the dough from the refrigerator and lay it flat on a lightly floured work surface. Brush the dough evenly with egg wash. Using a heavy, sharp knife, cut about ¼ inch off each edge of the dough sheet and discard these scraps. Using a ruler to guide you, cut the dough into three 3-inch strips. Cut each of these strips into 4 even pieces. Line a baking sheet with parchment paper and place 4 ovenproof cups or rings in the corners of the pan. Place the 12 pieces on the pan ½ inch apart. If any are touching, use 2 pans. Refrigerate for 30 minutes, or until the dough is quite firm.

3.   Preheat the oven to 400°F.

4.   Remove the pan from the refrigerator, leaving the second pan, if using, in the refrigerator. Using the tip of a small sharp knife, cut a feather shape on the top few layers of the dough. As the pastries bake, the dough will split at the top layers and the feather will be visible. Do not cut through the dough. Place a rectangular wire cooling rack, supported at the corners by the cups, over the feuilletés.

5.   Bake until the feuilletés are puffed and deep brown on top and the sides are golden and set, 15 to 20 minutes. Remove from the oven and immediately lift off the rack. Cool for 5 minutes on the pan.

6.   While the feuilletés are still hot, cut each in half horizontally. Flip the top over, then use the tip of a small knife to pull away any soft, unbaked dough from both halves of each rectangle. Turn the cleaned tops over again and cool completely on a rack or on the pan.

7.   Use the shells within 8 hours of baking. You can reheat them for 5 minutes at 350°F, if desired, for a warm appetizer, main course, or dessert.

Bouchées

When you say *bouchée*, you've said a mouthful. Literally. These round shells were originally meant to be eaten in one mouthful. They have grown over time, so that now, a Bouchée up to four inches in diameter is still called a Bouchée; anything larger is a *Vol-au-vent* (page 303).

Bouchées have raised sides, unlike *Feuilletés*, and thus can hold the sauciest of savory or sweet specialties without overflowing. Traditionally, they have a little cap, cut from the center, which tops the filling.

Bouchées lend themselves well to being served on a platter for a buffet, not just on individual plates. Many French pastry shops that are also *traiteurs*, or delicatessens, serve savory specialties. These shops load their cases with four-inch Bouchées, filled with chicken and sweetbreads in cream sauce or veal in white wine and cream. On Ash Wednesday, the first day of Lent, you might find Bouchées filled with *brandade de morue*, a rich mixture of salt cod, potatoes, and garlic. All of these hold up quite well when refrigerated and can be transported easily, although the shells will lose some of their crispness when chilled.   **Makes four to five 4-inch cases**

About ½ recipe (1 pound) fully turned Puff Pastry (page 296) or 1 package store-bought pastry, cold

2 large egg yolks

1.   If using homemade Puff Pastry, roll it out into a 10 × 20-inch rectangle, ¼ to ⅛ inch thick, then refrigerate it for at least 1 hour to allow the gluten to relax and thus minimize shrinkage (fold the sheet of dough in half with a sheet of parchment between the layers, then wrap on a parchment-lined baking sheet). Leave store-bought dough at room temperature for 5 minutes before unfolding, to keep it from cracking. It will require no further rolling. Cut either type of pastry while cold, working quickly so that all the dough pieces are the same size.

2.   Remove the dough from the refrigerator and lay it flat on a lightly floured work surface. Prick half the dough (1 sheet of store-bought pastry) all over with a fork. Brush the dough lightly with water. On the other half of the dough, mark as many 4-inch circles as you can, using the blunt side of a fluted or plain round cookie cutter. Do not overlap and do not cut through the dough.

3.   Stir the egg yolks with 2 teaspoons water. Brush the marked half of the dough evenly with egg wash. Cut a hole in the center of each circle, using a 3-inch plain or fluted cookie cutter. Set the centers aside. Carefully pick up the second half of the dough and lay it on the dampened first half. Using the cutting side of the 4-inch cookie cutter, cut through both layers of dough.

4.   Line a baking sheet with parchment. Place 4 ovenproof cups or rings in the corners of the pan. Using a metal spatula, place the rings of dough on the baking sheet, ½ inch apart. Refrigerate for 30 minutes, or until the dough is firm.

If baking the caps, line a second baking sheet with parchment. Place 4 ovenproof cups or rings, shallower than the ones for the rings, in the corners of the pan. Using a metal spatula, place the disks on the baking sheet, ½ inch apart. Refrigerate for 30 minutes, or until the dough is firm.

If not baking the caps, either make them into mini *bouchées* and freeze them on a baking sheet, then transfer them to a zipper-type plastic freezer bag, or add them to the scraps.

5.   Pick up the scraps and layer them one on top of the other. Wrap tightly in plastic. (*Scraps may be frozen for up to 1 month. If the dough was previously frozen, however, freeze only up to the total freezer life of the dough. Thaw overnight in the refrigerator.*)

6.   Preheat the oven to 400°F. Remove the pan with the rings from the refrigerator.

7.   Place a wire cooling rack over the bouchées, supported at the corners by the cups.

8.   Bake until the bouchées are puffed and deep brown on top and the sides are golden and set, 20 to 30 minutes. Remove from the oven and immediately lift off the rack. Cool the bouchées on the pan on a wire rack. If baking caps, bake and cool them in the same manner.

9.   The baked caps may have toppled over. Not to worry: They are for decoration only. Pull away the top third and use this to top your filling, discarding the rest. Cool on a wire rack.

10.   If the insides of the Bouchées have not baked all the way through, use a small sharp knife to pull away the unbaked layers while still warm. These can be baked up to 8 hours before filling and serving.

Vol-au-vent

A *Vol-au-vent* is a large shell that is cut exactly the same way as individual bouchées. Use an 8- or 9-inch round cake pan as a template for cutting the circle. Cut crosshatches, or any other design, in the egg-glazed top for decoration. Bake the Vol-au-vent for 35 to 45 minutes, depending on the size. Check for puffing in the middle of the Vol-au-vent during that time. If it is puffing, prick it with a sharp knife to deflate and ensure thorough baking. Cool on a wire rack.

Mini Bouchées

A _Mini Bouchée_ is just one bite, ideal on an hors d'oeuvre platter as well as with an assortment of petit fours. Fill Mini Bouchées with a savory delicacy or pipe a rosette of whipped cream inside each and top with a fresh berry. They are prepared with one layer of Puff Pastry. Makes about thirty-six 1½-inch cases

> About ¼ recipe (½ pound) fully turned Puff Pastry (page 296) or 1 sheet (½ package) store-bought pastry, cold
>
> 2 large egg yolks

1. If using homemade Puff Pastry, roll it out into a 9- or 10-inch square, ¼ to ⅛ inch thick, then refrigerate it for at least 1 hour to allow the gluten to relax and thus minimize shrinkage. Leave store-bought dough at room temperature for 5 minutes before unfolding, to keep it from cracking. It will require no further rolling. Cut either type of pastry while cold, working quickly so that the pieces are the same size.

2. Stir the egg yolks with 2 teaspoons water. Remove the dough from the refrigerator and lay it flat on a lightly floured work surface. Brush the dough evenly with egg wash. Cut out 1½-inch rounds with a fluted or plain cookie cutter. Using a 1-inch plain cutter, cut through just the top few layers of dough. This will split away during baking. Line a baking pan with parchment paper. Place 4 ovenproof cups or rings in the corners of the pan. Place the rounds on the baking pan and refrigerate for 30 minutes.

3. Preheat the oven to 400°F.

4. Place a wire cooling rack, supported at the corners by the cups, over the rounds.

5. Bake until the rounds are puffed and deep brown on top and the sides are golden and set, 15 to 20 minutes. Remove from the oven and immediately lift off the rack. Cool for 5 minutes on the pan.

6. Using a small sharp knife, pick off the caps that have separated from the rest of the crust. Set these aside. Since these pastries are so small, it will be difficult to pull out unbaked dough. Simply push it down with the handle of a wooden spoon. Cool completely on a wire rack or on the pan.

> • **Glazing with egg wash before cutting ensures that the egg wash does not run down the sides of the cut pastry. That would keep the pastry from rising evenly by sealing the sides of the dough.**

- Placing a wire cooling rack over the pastries prevents them from rising unevenly, since once they hit the rack, they stop rising. For that reason, the cups or rings supporting the rack must all be of the same depth. Choose cups that are about 1¼ inches deep for *Feuilletés* and *Mini Bouchées,* 1½ to 2 inches deep for larger *Bouchées.* These can be made of metal, ceramic, or glass, although ceramic or glass cups will need a small amount of water in each to keep them from cracking, and this water will put steam—however little—in your oven.

Creams, Fillings, Toppings, and Glazes

Les Crèmes, les garnitures, les glaçages, et les nappages

Whipped Cream / *Crème Chantilly*

Pastry Cream / *Crème pâtissière*
    Chocolate Pastry Cream / *Crème pâtissière au chocolat*
    Hazelnut Praline Pastry Cream / *Crème pâtissière pralinée*
    Coffee Pastry Cream / *Crème pâtissière au café*

Mango Cream / *Crème de mangues*

Crème Mousseline

Meringue-lightened Pastry Cream / *Crème chiboust*

Almond Cream / *Crème d'amandes*

Lemon Cream / *Crème au citron*

Butter Cream / *Crème au beurre*
    Coffee Butter Cream / *Crème au beurre au café*
    Chocolate Butter Cream / *Crème au beurre au chocolat*
    Hazelnut Praline Butter Cream / *Crème au beurre pralinée*
    Caramel Butter Cream / *Crème au beurre au caramel*

Chocolate Ganache / *Ganache au chocolat*

Almond Brittle / *Nougatine*

Caramelized Hazelnut Paste / *Praliné aux noisettes*

Chocolate-Hazelnut Paste / *Gianduja*

Pistachio Paste / *Pâte de pistaches*

Chocolate Glaze I and II / *Glaçage au chocolat I et II*

Glaze for Fruit Tarts and Desserts / *Nappage*

Streusel

Whipped Cream *Crème Chantilly*

The French call whipped cream Chantilly, a town just north of Paris, which is known for its rich culinary history. This cream has countless uses. I prefer whipped cream very lightly sweetened, so that it does not detract from whatever it is topping or accompanying.

The cream should be whipped to various degrees of stiffness, depending on the purpose:

- For rosettes or other piped decorations, it should be stiff enough to pipe out smoothly without breaking and to hold its shape.
- For dollops, it should be stiff enough to hold a soft shape.
- For mousses, it should barely hold a soft shape, so that further mixing does not cause it to break.
- A good rule of thumb is that the cream should be slightly thicker than what is being folded in.
- For passing in a bowl at table, it should barely hold trails of the beater or whisk.

For best results, start with very cold cream, and a chilled mixing bowl and beaters or whisk.

Makes about 2 cups

1 cup whipping cream, cold

1 tablespoon granulated or powdered sugar

¼ teaspoon vanilla extract or the seeds from ¼ vanilla bean

Place the cold cream, sugar, and vanilla in a chilled bowl. With cold beaters or a cold whisk, start whipping the cream on low speed until it begins to thicken. Gradually increase the speed and whip the cream until stiff enough for your purposes but still very white and smooth. Use immediately. (*The cream can be kept refrigerated in a covered container for up to 2 hours. Give the cream 2 or 3 turns of the whisk to even its consistency.*)

Pastry Cream *Crème pâtissière*

This custard is used to fill fruit tarts, Napoleons (page 41), and many other classic desserts. It is also the base for *Crème Mousseline* (page 311). I make it with a vanilla bean instead of vanilla extract for a more subtle flavor. However, you can omit the vanilla entirely and flavor the cream with Grand Marnier, Kirschwasser, or another brandy or liqueur, depending on the cream's final use.   Makes about 6 cups

4 cups whole milk

1 cup plus 2 tablespoons (8 ounces) granulated sugar

1 vanilla bean, split lengthwise (optional)

8 large egg yolks

½ cup (2¼ ounces) cornstarch

¼ cup (about 1½ ounces) all-purpose flour

2 teaspoons vanilla extract (optional)

2 tablespoons Grand Marnier, Kirschwasser, or other brandy or liqueur (optional)

3½ ounces (7 tablespoons) unsalted butter, softened

Powdered sugar, for dusting

I.   Bring the milk, half the sugar, and the vanilla bean, if using, to a boil in a medium stainless steel saucepan.

2.   Meanwhile, whisk the egg yolks with the remaining sugar in a medium mixing bowl until the mixture is a light, pale yellow. Sift or strain the cornstarch and flour over the egg mixture. Whisk them in, making sure there are no lumps.

3.   When the milk begins to boil, reduce the heat and carefully pour half the liquid into the egg mixture. Place the pot back on the stove over very low heat. Whisk the egg mixture immediately and thoroughly to temper the eggs. Whisking constantly, pour the egg mixture into the simmering milk. Quickly scrape any remaining egg mixture into the pot with a rubber spatula. Continue to whisk the custard over low heat just until it begins to boil. Let it boil for 10 seconds to kill any microbes that might have been in the yolks.

4.   Immediately pour the custard into a large bowl. Use a rubber spatula to scrape out any that remains in the pot, although if the cream is cooked thoroughly, it should release from the pot in a large mass. Be careful working with the custard at this point: Not only is it extremely hot, it will stick to your skin.

5.   If you have used a vanilla bean, pull it out of the cream with tongs, scrape out the seeds, and whisk them back into the cream. If you are flavoring the cream with vanilla extract or liqueur, whisk it in now. Thoroughly whisk in the softened butter.

6.   Dust the top of the cream evenly with powdered sugar, either with a sugar shaker or through a fine mesh strainer. Let the cream cool to room temperature. Whisk in the melted powdered sugar. Refrigerate until ready to use. (*Pastry Cream will keep in an airtight container in the refrigerator for up to 5 days.*)

Chocolate Pastry Cream *Crème pâtissière au chocolat*

Make the Pastry Cream without vanilla. When you pour the cream into the bowl to cool, whisk in ½ cup Chocolate Ganache (page 318) or 3 ounces chopped bittersweet chocolate. Sprinkle the top of the cream with powdered sugar and cool completely. Ganache will make a slightly creamier custard.

Hazelnut Praline Pastry Cream *Crème pâtissière pralinée*

Blend Caramelized Hazelnut Paste (page 320) thoroughly and measure out 2 to 4 tablespoons, to taste. Whisk the paste into 1 recipe of cooled vanilla-flavored Pastry Cream. Wait until the cream is cooled, or it will cause the oil in the hazelnut paste to separate. This is a fantastic filling for éclairs.

Coffee Pastry Cream *Crème pâtissière au café*

Although this can be prepared by infusing ground coffee in hot milk, adding coffee flavoring to prepared Pastry Cream is simpler and produces a better-tasting cream. Dissolve 2 tablespoons instant coffee in 1 tablespoon hot water and let the mixture cool. Whisk this into 1 recipe of vanilla-flavored Pastry Cream. Or whisk 2 to 3 teaspoons Coffee Flavoring (page 342) into 1 recipe of Pastry Cream.

Mango Cream *Crème de mangues*

This Mango Cream can be used as a replacement for pastry cream in a tropical fruit tart. It has the texture of a thick pudding and can stand on its own as a dessert, served with Coconut-Macadamia Tile Cookies (page 165) on the side. This recipe can be multiplied or divided as long as the proportions are not changed.   Makes about 6 cups

¾ cup whipping cream

3 cups mango puree (see page 350)

1 cup (7 ounces) granulated sugar

8 large egg yolks

½ cup (2¼ ounces) cornstarch

Powdered sugar, for dusting

1. Bring the cream, mango puree, and half the sugar to a boil in a medium stainless steel saucepan, stirring frequently with a wooden spoon. Take care: The fruit puree can stick to the bottom of the pan.

2. Meanwhile, in a medium mixing bowl, whisk the yolks with the remaining sugar, until the mixture is a light, pale yellow. Sift cornstarch over the egg mixture and whisk until smooth.

3. When the cream mixture begins to boil, reduce the heat and carefully pour half into the egg mixture. Place the pot with the remaining cream on the stove over very low heat. Whisk the egg mixture immediately and thoroughly to temper the eggs. Whisking constantly, pour the egg mixture into the simmering cream mixture. Quickly scrape any remaining egg mixture into the pot with a rubber spatula. Continue to whisk the custard over low heat just until it begins to boil. Let it boil for 10 seconds to kill any microbes that might have been in the yolks.

4. Immediately pour the custard into a large bowl. Use a rubber spatula to scrape out any that remains in the pot, although if the cream is cooked thoroughly, it should release from the pot in a large mass. Be careful working with the custard at this point: Not only is it extremely hot, it will stick to your skin.

5. Dust the top of the cream evenly with powdered sugar, either with a sugar shaker or through a fine mesh strainer. This will melt and form a protective layer on top of the cream, and will keep a skin from forming. Let the cream cool to room temperature. Whisk in the melted powdered sugar. Refrigerate until ready to use. (*The cream may be refrigerated in an airtight container for up to 5 days.*)

Crème Mousseline

Unimaginable though it may seem, this cream filling, which appears in many classics, is Pastry Cream lightened with butter. The key here is to whip butter until it is begging for mercy, then add cold Pastry Cream. The result is a mousselike filling that holds its shape under refrigeration without gelatin.

The classic recipe is a formula: four parts Pastry Cream to one part butter. Fortunately, a smaller proportion of butter will still hold the cream up, so you can adjust the amount if you like.

Makes about 4½ cups

6 ounces (1½ sticks) unsalted butter, at room temperature

½ recipe (3 cups) chilled Pastry Cream flavored with vanilla or brandy (page 308)

1. Beat the butter with an electric mixer until it is extremely light in texture and in color. Add the cold Pastry Cream, ¼ cup at a time, mixing thoroughly after each addition, on medium to high speed.

2. When all the Pastry Cream has been added and evenly mixed, use it immediately. It will keep for 5 days in a pastry. (*Crème mousseline does not store well.*)

Meringue-lightened Pastry Cream

Crème chiboust

This is an incredibly versatile mixture that consists of barely sweetened Pastry Cream folded together with Italian Meringue. *Chiboust* is a component in such classics as Normandy Apple Tart (page 90), in yellow fruit mousses, such as the one in Pear Charlotte (page 82), and in very light fruit gratins (page 128). Gelatin can be incorporated in the pastry cream portion, so that the chiboust will maintain its height, without losing its lightness, when refrigerated. You can use either granular or sheet gelatin.

You can create your own "classic" version by adapting your pastry cream with fruit puree, as in the Mango Cream (page 310). Use just enough sugar to keep the cream smooth, using the rest of the sugar in the meringue component. Otherwise, you will end up with a light but cloyingly sweet dessert.   **Makes about 6 cups**

2 cups whole milk

4 large eggs, separated

½ cup plus 2 tablespoons (4½ ounces) sugar

¼ cup (1 ounce) cornstarch

2 tablespoons (¾ ounces) all-purpose flour

1 teaspoon vanilla extract (optional)

1 tablespoon Grand Marnier, Calvados, or other brandy or liqueur (optional)

2 teaspoons (or 2 sheets) gelatin, softened in cold water and drained (see page 8)

1¾ ounces (3½ tablespoons) unsalted butter, softened

1.   Bring the milk to a boil in a medium stainless steel saucepan.

2.   Meanwhile, whisk the egg yolks with 3 tablespoons sugar in a medium mixing bowl until the mixture is a light, pale yellow. Sift the cornstarch and flour over the egg mixture. Whisk them in, making sure there are no lumps.

3.   When the milk begins to boil, reduce the heat and carefully pour half the liquid into the egg mixture. Place the pot back on the stove over very low heat. Whisk the egg mixture immediately and thoroughly to temper the eggs. Whisking constantly, pour the egg mixture into the simmering milk. Quickly scrape any remaining egg mixture into the pot with a rubber spatula. Continue to whisk the custard over low heat just until it begins to boil. Let it boil for 10 seconds to kill any microbes that might have been in the yolks. Whisk in the vanilla or liqueur, if using, the gelatin, and the butter.

4.   Immediately pour the custard into a small mixing bowl. Use a rubber spatula to scrape out any cream that remains in the pot, although if the cream is cooked thoroughly, it should release from the pot in a large mass. Be careful working with the custard at this point: Not only is it extremely hot, it will stick to your skin. Do not stir the cream; it should remain warm while you are preparing the meringue.

5.   Put the egg whites in a large clean mixing bowl or the bowl of an electric mixer and set aside. Put 6 tablespoons of the remaining sugar in a small saucepan with just enough water to wet the crystals (no more than 2 to 3 tablespoons). Wash down any remaining crystals from inside the pot with a wet pastry brush. Place the pot over a low flame and heat, without stirring, until the sugar begins to boil.

6.   When the sugar boils clear, begin whisking the egg whites on low speed until they begin to froth. Increase the speed to medium and whip until the whites hold a soft peak. Gradually add the remaining tablespoon of sugar and continue to whip.

7.   When the sugar measures 244°F on a candy thermometer (between the soft ball and hard ball stages), increase the mixer speed to high. When the sugar reaches 248°F (hard ball stage), remove it from the heat.

8.   On low speed, add one-third of the sugar to the whites in a very thin stream. Avoid hitting the whisk or beaters with the sugar. Once you have added one-third of the sugar, increase the speed to medium and add the rest in twice as heavy a stream.

9.   When all the sugar has been added, beat on high speed for 2 minutes, just to stabilize the whites. Remove the whites from your mixer, and gently fold in the cream in thirds. Use immediately, or refrigerate. *(Chiboust can be refrigerated in an airtight container for up to 2 days. It will become firm. To use leftover chiboust, either let it stand at room temperature for 30 minutes to soften slightly, then spread it with a spatula, or give it 2 to 3 turns with a whisk and pipe the cream though a pastry bag fitted with a plain or star tip.)*

Almond Cream *Crème d'amandes*

Have you ever wondered how pastry chefs confidently make a tart in the morning and serve it in the evening without fear of the crust becoming soggy? Easy—before baking, they spread the bottom of the tart shell with a thin layer of this cream, which, when baked, forms a crisp layer that absorbs any juices that leak down. In addition, Almond Cream is used to fill many classics, including *Gâteau de Pithiviers* (page 32), Raisin Buns (page 142), and the little almond meringue cookies called *Miroirs* (page 158).

Although Almond Cream spreads very easily at room temperature, it is not recommended that you leave it out of the refrigerator long enough for it to soften completely because of the raw eggs. Rather, take a small amount of chilled cream and beat it with a wooden spoon to a uniform consistency. It will then spread like whipped cream.

Almond Cream also pipes easily through a pastry bag, adding little spots of crunchy texture to otherwise uniform doughs. The cream can be refrigerated for up to one week, or frozen for up to one month.   **Makes about 3 cups**

½ cup plus 1 tablespoon (4 ounces) sugar

¾ cup (4 ounces) ground blanched almonds

4 ounces (1 stick) cold unsalted butter, cut into pieces

2 large eggs

¼ teaspoon almond extract (optional)

2 teaspoons dark rum (optional)

1.   Place the sugar, almonds, and butter in a mixing bowl and beat with an electric mixer until smooth. Add the eggs, one at a time, beating until smooth after each addition. Scrape the bowl with a rubber spatula with each addition. Add the almond extract and rum, if desired.

2.   Use immediately; this is the perfect consistency for piping. (*Almond Cream will keep in an airtight container for up to 5 days in the refrigerator or for up to 1 month in the freezer.*)

Ground blanched almonds are available in some specialty food stores. While this is a very convenient way to purchase this product and while it has a very even consistency because it is produced commercially, it often lacks flavor. I recommend that you purchase whole or slivered blanched almonds, which are available in most supermarkets, and grind them in a food processor. Do so in small batches, pulsing on and off. Grind a pound or more at a time and store the almond meal in airtight containers (zipper bags are ideal for this) in the freezer.

Lemon Cream *Crème au citron*

This simple Lemon Cream makes a great filling for a Lemon Tart (page 20). Since the eggs in this custard cream are fully cooked, you can also use it as a spread, like lemon curd.

Unlike other recipes, this does not need to be prepared in a double boiler. You must, however, use a stainless steel pan; the acid from the lemons will react with anything else. Mix the ingredients in the order listed—if not, the consistency of the cream will be different.   Makes about 3 cups

6 large eggs

1½ cups (10½ ounces) sugar

Zest of 2 lemons

Juice of 6 large lemons (1½ cups)

3 tablespoons (1½ ounces) unsalted butter, cut into 3 pieces

I.   Put the eggs in a 1-quart stainless steel saucepan. Whisk until blended. Add the sugar and whisk immediately. Add the lemon zest and the juice and whisk well. Cook over medium heat, whisking constantly. After about 5 minutes, the mixture will begin to thicken and the froth created by whisking will begin to subside. Watch carefully: As soon as all the froth subsides and you see the first big bubble, remove the pan from the heat. Whisk in the butter.

2.   Pour the cream through a medium mesh strainer and use immediately. Or cool to room temperature and refrigerate, covered. (*The cream will keep in an airtight container for 1 week in the refrigerator.*)

Most custards without starch should not be allowed to boil. However, in this preparation the acidity of the lemon juice stabilizes the eggs so that they don't curdle when boiled.

Butter Cream *Crème au beurre*

Classic Butter Cream is made from butter, cooked sugar, and egg yolks, and when well executed it is smooth and rich. Large pastry shops use frozen pasteurized yolks; however, these yolks are not available at retail, and even if they were, I prefer the following yolkless recipe. It is lighter and easier to make.

While this recipe includes volume measurements, I strongly recommend using scale measurements here. The balance between sugar and butter is very important.   Makes about 3 cups

4 large egg whites

1 cup plus 2 tablespoons (8 ounces) sugar

1 tablespoon corn syrup

8 ounces (2 sticks) unsalted butter, left out of the refrigerator for 1 hour and cut into small pieces

1. Put the egg whites in the bowl of an electric mixer and set aside. If the mixer has a whisk, attach it. Place 1 cup of the sugar and the corn syrup in a small pot, preferably with a pouring spout. Add just enough water to wet the sugar (about ¼ cup). Brush down any crystals clinging to the side of the pot with a wet pastry brush. Cook the sugar until it measures 248°F on a candy thermometer (the hard ball stage).

2. When the sugar begins to boil clear, start whisking the whites on low speed to break them up. As soon as they begin to froth, increase the speed and whip until soft peaks form. Slowly add the remaining 2 tablespoons of sugar. Whip on high speed until the cooking sugar is ready.

3. Remove the sugar from the heat. With the mixer on low speed, add one-third to the egg whites in a very thin stream. Make sure that the stream is reaching the egg whites; if it hits the whip it will simply splatter around the inside of the mixing bowl. Increase the speed to medium and add the remaining sugar in a heavier stream. Once all the sugar has been added, whip on high speed for 5 minutes. Decrease the speed to medium and whip the meringue until it is at room temperature.

4. With the mixer on low speed, quickly add the butter in small pieces. Once it has all been added, increase the speed to high and beat until there are no butter chunks, however small, remaining. Stick your hand in and feel for lumps.

5. Flavor and use immediately or refrigerate until ready to use. (*Butter Cream may be frozen in an airtight container for up to 1 month. Thaw in the refrigerator, then bring to room temperature. Or thaw in the microwave on low power in 1-minute increments. Rewhip until smooth.*)

• **It is important that the butter be neither cold nor too soft. If too cold, it will not blend well into the meringue. If too soft, it may separate and cause the butter cream to** break. It is also important to add the butter only after the meringue has cooled completely. Warm meringue will cause the butter to separate.

- If your Butter Cream looks broken or curdled, whip it on high speed until it comes together again. This works even after the Butter Cream has been refrigerated or frozen, then rewhipped.

- This Butter Cream is made from Italian Meringue (page 288) mixed with butter in the classic proportion: equal weights of sugar and butter. Since meringues are composed of egg whites and sugar with the weight of the sugar twice that of the egg whites, the butter is equal to two-thirds the weight of the meringue. This fact will come in handy when you want to use up leftover meringue you have after preparing, for instance, a mousse that has already achieved the optimum lightness. Simply weigh the leftover meringue, take two-thirds of that weight in butter, and beat the butter into the meringue. You can then freeze the Butter Cream—be sure to mark the total weight or volume and the date—for later use.

Coffee Butter Cream *Crème au beurre au café*

Dissolve 2 tablespoons instant coffee in 1 tablespoon boiling water and let cool. Just before using, whisk into the Butter Cream. You may also use 2 to 3 teaspoons Coffee Flavoring (page 342).

Chocolate Butter Cream *Crème au beurre au chocolat*

Melt ½ cup (4 ounces) unsweetened chocolate and let cool to 95 to 100°F. Make sure that the Butter Cream is at room temperature and that the chocolate is not so warm that it will break it. Whisk the chocolate into the cream.

Hazelnut Praline Butter Cream *Crème au beurre pralinée*

Stir ⅓ cup Caramelized Hazelnut Paste (page 320) or ½ cup ground hazelnut croquant into the Butter Cream. For a smooth butter cream with an even color, use the paste; for a butter cream with crunch and speckles, use croquant.

Caramel Butter Cream *Crème au beurre au caramel*

Prepare the Butter Cream recipe, but instead of cooking the sugar until it reaches the hard ball stage, continue to cook it until it reaches a deep amber color. Begin beating the egg whites when the sugar reaches 293°F (hard crack stage). Before pouring the sugar into the egg whites, dip the pot into a bowl of ice water to stop the cooking of the sugar. Otherwise, it will continue cooking from the heat of the pot. Wipe the bottom of the pot dry before pouring. Continue as in the master recipe.

Chocolate Ganache *Ganache au chocolat*

Chocolate Ganache is one of those items you should always have on hand. It has many uses:

Warm, it is the ultimate chocolate sauce.

Melted and mixed with a small amount of corn syrup (for shine), it is a perfect glaze for a cake or pastry.

At room temperature, it is a rich and silky filling for French Macaroons (page 159), Duchesses, or as a substitute for Chocolate Butter Cream in Opera Cake (page 66).

Whatever you're using ganache for, be sure to prepare it with a high-quality bittersweet chocolate. Valrhona Extra-Bitter is becoming more available in specialty markets, but Tobler Excellence will do just fine, and it is widely available in supermarkets.

This ganache contains butter, which gives it a silky texture and added richness. It is important that the butter be at room temperature and whisked to the consistency of softly whipped cream before it is added to the ganache, which should also be at room temperature at this point. **Makes about 4 cups**

1¼ cups whole milk

¼ cup whipping cream

1 pound bittersweet chocolate, chopped

4 ounces (1 stick) unsalted butter, at room temperature and whisked until smooth

1. Boil the milk and cream together in a small saucepan. Watch carefully to prevent overboiling.

2. Place the chocolate in a large mixing bowl. Pour the boiling milk and cream over the chocolate and let stand for 10 minutes. This will enable the chocolate to melt evenly and prevent overmixing, which can produce a grainy ganache. After 10 minutes, whisk the chocolate mixture until smooth. Let cool to room temperature.

3. Using a rubber spatula, scrape all the butter into the chocolate mixture. Whisk just until the butter is completely incorporated. There should be no streaks. If using the ganache for a piped filling, such as for macaroons, place a piece of wax paper or plastic wrap directly on the surface to prevent a crust from forming and let stand at room temperature overnight. Or refrigerate in a covered container. (*Ganache will keep well in the refrigerator for up to 1 week or in the freezer for up to 1 month. Thaw in the refrigerator.*)

Almond Brittle *Nougatine*

The pastry shops of a generation ago would use large cut pieces of this confection as decoration, or even as a large base for a *pièce montée* or presentation cake. Standing in front of the blasting hot oven and working on the hot metal surface in order to keep the *nougatine* pliable, the chef would roll and cut the nougatine. Not only were burns commonplace but also injuries from trying to cut through hardening toffee with a cookie cutter. These days, decoration with nougatine is all but a lost art, and quite frankly, good riddance to it, as it was rarely carried out with a light touch. On the other hand, nougatine itself is quite tasty, and shards of chopped nougatine add a caramel-nut crunch to an otherwise dull chocolate or dessert.

Because this nut brittle must remain as dry as possible, the sugar is caramelized without the addition of any water, except for that in the corn syrup. The glucose in the corn syrup, however, is necessary to stabilize the sugar and keep it from recrystallizing.

As always when working with caramel, be sure to use a heavy pot holder and not to splash the caramel on your skin. Sugar begins to caramelize at 340°F; sugar that is deep amber in color, almost burnt, may be as hot as 410°F. And, caramelized sugar will cling to your skin.   Makes about I pound

Vegetable oil

I cup plus 2 tablespoons (8 ounces) sugar, divided into 4 portions

2 teaspoons light corn syrup

2 cups (8 ounces) slivered or sliced blanched almonds, chopped into ⅛-inch pieces

I.   Cover a baking sheet with aluminum foil, making sure that it is very smooth. The foil need not go up the sides of the pan. Grease the foil lightly and evenly with a few drops of oil.

2.   Place about one-fourth of the sugar and all the corn syrup in a medium heavy-bottomed saucepan. If you have an unlined copper caramelizing pot with a pour spout, clean it first with salt and white vinegar, then use it here; this is the ideal pot for caramelizing, as it conducts heat so quickly and evenly.

Begin heating the sugar over a low heat and stir with a wooden spoon. After about 3 minutes, the sugar will melt and become light amber in color. Add another portion of sugar, and continue stirring. The sugar will dissolve and color after 1 or 2 minutes. Repeat this step twice, using all the sugar. Continue stirring until the sugar is medium amber in color and registers 360 to 365°F on a candy thermometer.

3.   Remove the caramel from the heat and immediately stir in the almonds. They will take on some color from the heat of the caramel. Stir to distribute the almonds evenly.

continued

4. Pour the hot nougatine onto the baking sheet, spreading it as thin as possible. Cool completely. Be careful: The pan will be hot.

5. Break the nougatine into chunks by hand or by pounding it with a hammer or a rolling pin. The nougatine may be stored as is, chopped with a heavy knife, or ground into finer pieces in a food processor. Transfer to an airtight container. (*Nougatine will keep for 1 month at room temperature.*) If the nougatine pieces have stuck together, break them apart with a rolling pin or regrind in a food processor.

> **I prefer to use chopped almonds here because they mix into the sugar more evenly. That way each little piece becomes coated with caramel.**

Caramelized Hazelnut Paste *Praliné aux noisettes*

The French use the word *croquant* to refer to anything crunchy, such as *pralin* and *nougatine*. Don't let the word *praliné* fool you—this has nothing to do with the New Orleans specialty, delicious as it is. French *pralin* is a brittle made with hazelnuts (nougatine is made with almonds) and it gives a wonderfully intense flavor to butter creams and ice creams, as well as mousses and chocolate bonbons. Make a large quantity at a time, grind it into a paste, and keep it for up to six months in your refrigerator. If the paste separates and the oil comes to the top, simply blend it back into the paste with your electric mixer or food processor.

This recipe is a classic formula that can be multiplied or divided as you wish, as long as the proportions—six parts sugar, caramelized, to four parts hazelnuts—are respected. This is one of those recipes where a scale is essential; cup measurements do not have the precision needed to maintain the balance of the formula.

As always when working with caramel, be sure to use a heavy pot holder and not to splash the caramel on your skin. Sugar begins to caramelize at 340°F; sugar that is deep amber in color, almost burnt, may be as hot as 410°F. And, caramelized sugar will cling to your skin.   **Makes about 1 cup**

Vegetable oil

About 1 cup (4 ounces) whole hazelnuts, blanched or unblanched

¾ cup (6 ounces) plus 1 tablespoon sugar

2 teaspoons light corn syrup

1. Preheat the oven to 350°F. Line a baking sheet with aluminum foil and grease the foil lightly but evenly with vegetable oil. Set aside.

2. Spread the nuts on an ungreased baking sheet and toast them for 15 minutes, or until lightly browned. If unblanched, the skins should begin to split. Remove the nuts from the oven and while they are still warm, rub them between 2 terry-cloth towels to remove as much of the skin as possible. Keep the nuts warm in a turned-off oven while preparing the sugar.

3. Put the sugar and corn syrup in a medium heavy-bottomed saucepan. If you have an unlined copper caramelizing pot with a pour spout, clean it first with salt and white vinegar, then use it here; this is the ideal pot for caramelizing, as it conducts heat so quickly and evenly. Add 3 tablespoons water to wet all the sugar without dissolving it, or even making it pourable.

Begin heating the sugar over low to medium heat. The heat should remain on the bottom of the pot; flames should not come up the side of the pot at any time. As soon as you begin heating the sugar, wash any crystals clinging to the inside of the pot into the rest of the sugar, using a pastry brush dipped in water. Do this before the pot gets too hot, so that the water from the brush does not simply evaporate against the pot and the brush does not burn. However, if you notice sugar crystals still clinging to the pot once it heats, try to wash them down with a more generous dose of water on the brush. Heat the sugar without disturbing the pot until the sugar begins to boil clear. Once the sugar boils clear, swirl it from time to time to distribute the heat within the syrup. When the sugar just begins to take on a light amber color, watch it carefully and swirl the pot often. It will go to deep caramel within just a few minutes. When caramel reaches 360 to 365°F turn off the heat and immediately stir in the warm nuts, mixing evenly. Pour the mixture onto the foil-lined baking sheet and spread it with the wooden spoon. Scrape as much out of the pot as possible, but do not touch it with your fingers, as it is still extremely hot. Allow the mixture to cool completely. It will become very brittle.

4. Lift the nut brittle off the aluminum foil and break it up coarsely, then chop it with a heavy chef's knife for *pralin* or *croquant*. Place the pralin in a food processor and blend until smooth. Place in an airtight container. (*The paste may be refrigerated for up to 6 months. Stir or process in any oil that rises to the top before using.*)

> **I like to use an unlined copper or stainless steel pot to caramelize sugar: the former because it conducts the heat quickly and is especially made for just this purpose, the latter because I can see the color changes in the sugar more easily. A black pot would obscure these color changes.**

Chocolate-Hazelnut Paste *Gianduja*

Gianduja **is a spread made from hazelnuts and chocolate. It adds a delightful flavor to creams and mousses and is ideal for sandwiching Hazelnut Macaroons (page 161) or filling puff pastry Straws (page 152). In France, children love their morning baguette spread with a thin layer of gianduja, sold everywhere under the brand name Nutella. This recipe makes a stiffer version that can be used at room temperature as a bonbon center or warmed slightly for a spread.** **Makes about 2 cups**

   1 cup Caramelized Hazelnut Paste (page 320), at room temperature

   8 ounces milk chocolate, melted and cooled but still fluid

1.   Put hazelnut paste in the bowl of an electric mixer or in a food processor and stir to an even consistency.

2.   Add the chocolate, all at once, and blend quickly until smooth. The mixture will become extremely thick. Wrap in plastic or store in an airtight container at room temperature. (*The spread will keep for 2 months at room temperature. Knead to soften.*)

Pistachio Paste *Pâte de pistaches*

Pistachios are plentiful in Europe, and they are becoming more and more a part of the modern French pastry chef's repertoire, often replacing the more classic almonds or hazelnuts. Fine Pistachio Paste can be used to flavor Crème Anglaise (page 328) as well as ice creams, butter cream, and mousse. A coarser paste is used to fill Chocolate-Pistachio Rolls (page 139), a variation on *pains au chocolat.* **Makes about 1 cup**

   ½ cup plus 1 tablespoon (4 ounces) sugar

   2 teaspoons light corn syrup

   Seeds from ½ vanilla bean

   1½ cups (6 ounces) lightly toasted shelled pistachios, skins removed (see page 10)

1.   Place the sugar and corn syrup in a small heavy saucepan. Add just enough water to wet the sugar, 2 to 3 tablespoons. Wash down any sugar crystals clinging to the inside of the pot with a wet pastry brush. Place the pot over low heat and heat, without moving the pot.

2. When the sugar boils clear, add the vanilla seeds and the pistachios. Bring back to a boil and cook for 5 minutes. Let cool to tepid.

3. Pour the mixture into a food processor and process to a smooth paste. For a coarser paste, process using pulses to the desired consistency. Cool completely and store in an airtight container in the refrigerator. (*The paste will keep well several months in the refrigerator. Stir before using.*)

Chocolate Glaze I *Glaçage au chocolat I*

A perfect chocolate glaze pours smoothly and shines at any temperature. This particular glaze meets those criteria. It is ideal for chilled or frozen cakes. The glaze will keep well in the refrigerator, remaining soft so that you can easily spoon out whatever quantity you need for a cake and warm it.
Makes about 3 cups, enough for three 9-inch cakes

> 1 cup milk
>
> 1 pound bittersweet chocolate, finely chopped
>
> 1 tablespoon vegetable oil
>
> 1 tablespoon light corn syrup
>
> ¼ recipe (½ cup) Simple Syrup (page 334)

1. Bring the milk to a boil in a small saucepan. Pour this over the chocolate in a medium mixing bowl and let stand, without stirring, for 5 minutes. Whisk until smooth.

2. Whisk in the oil, corn syrup, and Simple Syrup, whisking until there are no streaks. Pour the glaze through a medium mesh strainer, into a bowl if using immediately or into a container with a tight-fitting lid if storing. Use immediately or cool to room temperature, cover, and refrigerate. (*The glaze will keep in an airtight container for several weeks in the refrigerator. Warm the glaze in a small bowl set in simmering water. It will melt very quickly.*)

> **For any chocolate glaze, avoid melting the chocolate at too high a temperature and avoid melting the glaze to more than 100°F. This will keep your glaze shiny when it sets up. Stir with a wooden spoon, not a whisk.**

Chocolate Glaze II *Glaçage au chocolat II*

This glaze also pours beautifully and remains shiny. It sets up at room temperature, and is suitable for cakes and pastries that do not require refrigeration. It is also suitable for refrigerated pastries, such as éclairs, when you want a hard, shiny glaze. Another use for this glaze is to mask cakes before glazing with warm Chocolate Glaze I. Doing this gives the cake a completely smooth surface.   Makes about 2½ cups

> 6 ounces (1½ sticks) unsalted butter
>
> 10 ounces bittersweet chocolate, finely chopped
>
> 2 tablespoons light corn syrup

1.   Clarify the butter by putting it in a small shallow saucepan and melting it over low heat. When the butter separates, using a shallow spoon, skim the foam that rises to the top. Keep the butter warm.

2.   Meanwhile, melt the chocolate in a heatproof bowl set in, not over, simmering water. Stir often and remove the bowl from the water bath before it is completely melted. The chocolate should not be hotter than tepid. Whisk until smooth.

3.   Pour the butter into the chocolate. Leave the water you see in the bottom of the pan.

4.   Add the corn syrup and whisk the mixture until smooth. There should be no streaks. Pour through a medium mesh strainer. Use immediately or cool to room temperature and store in a covered container. (*This glaze can be stored in an airtight container at room temperature for up to 1 week. Spoon as much as you need and warm the glaze in a heatproof bowl set in simmering water. Do not overheat when melting.*)

Glaze for Fruit Tarts and Desserts *Nappage*

A fresh fruit tart with a thick layer of apricot or red currant glaze has always seemed incongruous to me. However, glaze is sometimes needed to keep sliced fruit from drying out or to keep certain fruits from turning brown. It can also give shine to a dull-finished tart or cake.

This glaze uses pectin rather than gelatin as a gelling agent. Powdered pectin is sold under various brand names in 1¾- or 2-ounce packets, usually in the baking section of the supermarket. The glaze can be made in large batches, then frozen in smaller batches (½ cup at a time) in zipper-type freezer bags. The glaze will enhance, not detract from, the flavor of any fruit tart or dessert.

This recipe has vanilla seeds in it, and some may remain in the final glaze, if you do not have a very fine strainer. If you do not want to see the seeds, omit the vanilla bean altogether or replace it with a 2-inch whole cinnamon stick.   **Makes about 3 cups**

2 tablespoons powdered pectin

1 cup plus 2 tablespoons (8 ounces) sugar

1 vanilla bean, split lengthwise, or one 2-inch cinnamon stick

Zest of 1 lemon, cut into thin strips

Zest of 1 orange, cut into thin strips

8 leaves of fresh mint

1.   Place the pectin and the sugar in a small mixing bowl and stir with a whisk. Set aside.

2.   Pour 2½ cups water into a small saucepan and add the vanilla bean and the citrus zests. Heat the liquid without bringing it to a boil. It must be lukewarm (105 to 110°F) in order to dissolve the pectin.

3.   Add the sugar and pectin to the liquid and heat to a simmer, stirring constantly with a whisk or a wooden spoon. The mixture will foam quite a bit. Simmer for 3 minutes. Remove from the heat and add the mint leaves. Let the mixture infuse for 15 minutes.

4.   While still quite warm, pour the mixture through a fine mesh strainer. If you do not think your strainer is fine enough, line it with several layers of cheesecloth. Cool completely before covering and storing. (*The glaze will keep in an airtight container in the refrigerator for 1 week or up to 3 months in the freezer.*)

The glaze can be used to make a topping for mousse. For chilled or frozen raspberry mousse, for example, melt ½ cup of glaze in a double boiler until completely liquefied (100°F). Add ¼ cup strained raspberry puree. Paint the mousse with this topping. It will gel on contact with the cold mousse. The glaze works with any fruit juice or puree except pineapple and lemon, which are too acidic or enzymatic and would break apart the pectin.

Streusel

Streusel adds a delicate crunch to a baked fruit tart. The topping is common in German pastries, so, not surprisingly, it has found its way into a lot of Alsatian recipes as well. Sometimes it is flavored with cinnamon or vanilla; sometimes chopped nuts are added.

Streusel should be mixed only until it starts to come together. If the mixture begins to mass, stop mixing and refrigerate the dough until cold. Put the cold dough back in the mixer and use the paddle to break apart the big pieces. This Streusel may be less delicate, but it will still be quite usable.

This recipe is a formula with equal amounts by weight of flour, sugar, and butter. Multiply by any factor, as long as the quantities are not too large for your mixer. Streusel must be blended evenly for even baking and browning. Makes about 1½ cups, enough for one 10-inch tart

4 ounces (1 stick) very cold unsalted butter, in small pieces

½ cup plus 1 tablespoon (4 ounces) sugar

¾ cup (4 ounces) all-purpose flour, unsifted

½ teaspoon ground cinnamon (optional)

1 cup (4 ounces) chopped walnuts or pecans (optional)

Seeds from ½ vanilla bean (optional)

1. Place the butter, sugar, and flour in the bowl of an electric mixer or in a food processor. Mix with the paddle attachment or process using pulses until the butter is completely broken up.

2. Add the cinnamon, nuts, and/or the vanilla seeds, if using. Continue mixing until the Streusel begins to come together. Stop mixing when the pieces are the size of chickpeas.

3. Use immediately or refrigerate. (*Streusel will keep in an airtight container in the refrigerator for up to 1 week or for up to 1 month in the freezer. Store in zipper bags, then break clumps apart with your fingertips.*)

Sauces *Les Sauces*

Crème Anglaise
  Hazelnut Praline Sauce / *Sauce pralinée*
  Pistachio Sauce / *Sauce aux pistaches*

Caramel Sauce / *Sauce au caramel*
  Chocolate-Caramel Sauce / *Sauce au caramel chocolatée*

Fresh Berry Sauce / *Coulis de fruits rouges*

Caramel-Berry Sauce with Chocolate / *Coulis au caramel chocolaté*

Buttered Applesauce with Vanilla / *Compote de pommes vanillée*
  Chunky Applesauce / *Compote de pommes rustique*
  Spicy Applesauce / *Compote de pommes épicée*

Simple Syrup / *Sirop à 30° Baumé*

Crème Anglaise

This is one of the most basic and versatile recipes in the French pastry chef's repertoire. It is a simple yet rich and delicious sauce to serve with desserts. It is the basis for Bavarian cream, many mousses, and ice creams. In fact, if you have an ice cream machine, you can make the most perfect vanilla ice cream by simply churning chilled *Crème Anglaise*.

By changing the liquid in Crème Anglaise from milk and cream to something else (one part cream and 3 parts fruit juice or puree, for example) but using the same cooking techniques, you can create a wide variety of sauces, mousses, and custards.   **Makes about 3 cups**

I cup whole milk

I cup whipping cream

I vanilla bean, split lengthwise

½ cup (about 3½ ounces) sugar, divided in half

5 large egg yolks

1. Prepare an ice bath by placing a medium stainless steel or glass bowl inside a much larger one. Fill the larger bowl with ice cubes to surround the inner bowl completely. Place a medium sieve (preferably stainless steel, not plastic) over the inner bowl.

2. Bring the milk, cream, vanilla bean, and half the sugar to a boil in a 1½-quart stainless steel saucepan over medium heat. Keep a wire whisk in the pot, so that if the liquid starts boiling, you can stir down the foam and prevent it from boiling over.

3. In a medium stainless steel or glass bowl, whisk together the eggs and the remaining sugar until the mixture is thick and pale yellow. Pour the boiled milk into the eggs and whisk immediately. As soon as the mixture appears homogeneous, pour it back into the pot and place it over medium heat. Stir constantly with a wooden spoon, making sure to run the spoon over the entire bottom of the pot, so as to cook the custard evenly and keep the bottom from burning.

4. Once the custard begins to thicken, start checking the spoon. Lift it after every few stirs and run your finger over the back. If your finger leaves a streak, the sauce is done. Take care not to let this cream come to a boil, or it will curdle.

5. Immediately pour the Crème Anglaise through the strainer into the inner bowl. If there is any sauce left in the bottom of the pan, scrape it out with a rubber spatula and press it through the strainer. Use a pitcher to pour cold water over the ice. Pour the water only to the level of the custard, so that the inner bowl does not float and risk tipping its contents into the ice bath. If you accidentally pour water into the custard, whisk it in immediately.

6.   Remove the vanilla bean from the strainer and scrape the seeds into the sauce. Remove the strainer. Allow the sauce to cool completely, whisking it every few minutes to help dissipate the heat. Refrigerate the sauce in a container with a lid. (*Crème Anglaise will keep in an airtight container for up to 5 days in the refrigerator.*)

- **Crème Anglaise is not like Pastry Cream (page 308), which you can bring to a boil, since the starch in that preparation stabilizes the egg yolks and prevents them from curdling. If you are using a candy thermometer, it should read 176°F (plus or minus 2°). The eggs will begin to curdle at 180°F.**

- **Although you may feel uneasy about cooking the custard over high heat, it is actually better to cook it quickly, thereby giving any microbes less of an opportunity to multiply.**

Hazelnut Praline Sauce *Sauce pralinée*

Whisk several tablespoons to taste of Caramelized Hazelnut Paste (page 320) into chilled Crème Anglaise.

Pistachio Sauce *Sauce aux pistaches*

Whisk several tablespoons, to taste, of Pistachio Paste (page 322) into chilled Crème Anglaise. Since the sugar in this paste has not been caramelized, the sauce will taste very sweet.

Caramel Sauce *Sauce au caramel*

As delicious on a banana split as it is with Caramel Mousse (page 122), this sauce is gooey, simple, and very satisfying. You will find many uses for it, so keep a jar in the refrigerator.

As always when working with caramel, be sure to use a heavy pot holder and not to splash the caramel on your skin. Sugar begins to caramelize at 340°F; sugar that is deep amber in color, almost burnt, may be as hot as 410°F. And, caramelized sugar will cling to your skin. Be sure to prepare the sugar in a deep pot, so that none of the caramel splashes out.   Makes about 3 cups

1 ½ cups plus 3 tablespoons (12 ounces) sugar

1 tablespoon corn syrup

2 cups whipping cream, at room temperature

1 teaspoon vanilla extract

1 tablespoon dark rum (optional)

1.   Put the sugar in a large, deep, heavy-bottomed stainless steel saucepan. Add the corn syrup and ½ cup water, then stir with a wooden spoon to wet all the sugar without dissolving it, or even making it pourable.

2.   Begin heating the sugar over low to medium heat. The heat should remain on the bottom of the pot; flames should not come up the side of the pot at any time. As soon as you begin heating the sugar, wash any crystals clinging to the inside of the pot into the rest of the sugar, using a pastry brush dipped in water. Do this before the pot gets too hot, so that the water from the brush does not simply evaporate against the pot and the brush does not burn. However, if you notice sugar crystals still clinging to the pot once it heats, try to wash them down with a more generous dose of water on the brush. Heat the sugar without disturbing the pot until the sugar begins to boil clear. Once the sugar boils clear, swirl it from time to time to distribute the heat within the syrup. When the sugar just begins to take on a light amber color, watch it carefully and swirl the pot often. Once the caramel has reached 370°F, turn off the heat and quickly but carefully whisk in the cream. Use a long-handled whisk and wrap a towel around your hand to protect yourself from splattering caramel. Avoid standing directly over the pot until the eruption has subsided.

3.   Pour the hot sauce through a medium mesh strainer to remove any pieces of caramel. Whisk in the vanilla and the rum, if desired. Let cool. Use while warm or refrigerate in an airtight container. Stir before using, as the sugar portion may sink. (*Caramel Sauce will keep in an airtight container for up to 2 weeks in the refrigerator. Warm it in a hot water bath or directly over low heat in a stainless steel pot. Whisk constantly if heating directly.*)

- **Be careful when preparing this sauce. The caramelized sugar is close to 400°F, and when the cold cream hits it, kaboom! Use a fairly deep pot so that when the caramel starts to boil up, it does not boil over. Use a whisk with a long handle, so that your hand is not inside the pot. And wrap your whisking hand in a towel. Even if the sauce temperature drops down to 200°F, you would not want to feel it on your skin.**

- **Use a stainless steel pan for this recipe. For one reason, you will be whisking in cream and a pot made of another material could react with the metal whisk moving against it. For another, it is very difficult to see subtle changes in color in enameled pots or those made of a dark material.**

Chocolate-Caramel Sauce *Sauce au caramel chocolatée*

Omit the vanilla and rum. Instead, whisk in 3 ounces finely chopped bittersweet chocolate. This must be done while the sauce is still hot. Strain.   Makes about 3¼ cups.

Fresh Berry Sauce *Coulis de fruits rouges*

There is no real recipe for *coulis*, other than berries, sugar, and lemon juice. How much sugar and lemon juice depends entirely on how sweet and how flavorful the berries are. Just add sugar and lemon juice gradually until you attain the flavor you like.

If using frozen berries, be sure to thaw them in the refrigerator before pureeing. If thawed slowly in the refrigerator, these berries will separate less.

Fresh or frozen strawberries, raspberries, blackberries, or a combination

Granulated or powdered sugar

Freshly squeezed lemon juice

Finely chopped fresh mint (optional)

1.   If using strawberries, stem, hull, and cut them into pieces. Whatever berries you use, puree them in a food processor or blender until smooth. If you have a lot of berries, puree in batches.

2.   Press raspberries or blackberries through a medium mesh strainer. Whisk in granulated or powdered sugar, add lemon juice to taste, and fresh mint, if desired. (*Coulis will keep in an airtight container for up to 3 days in the refrigerator or for up to 1 month in the freezer. If freezing, freeze without the lid on to allow for expansion, then cover. Thaw in the refrigerator. Stir before using.*)

Caramel-Berry Sauce with Chocolate

Coulis au caramel chocolaté

Lisa Gardner, the pastry chef at Maple Drive Restaurant in Beverly Hills, is the creator of this subtle sauce. It is the perfect accompaniment to a chocolate or a fruit dessert. The recipe is only a guide-line, since the actual proportions will depend upon the sweetness of your berries.   **Makes 2 cups**

About ½ cup Chocolate-Caramel Sauce (page 331)

About 1½ cups Fresh Berry Sauce (page 331)

Sugar, to taste (optional)

Simple Syrup (page 334) (optional)

Lemon juice (optional)

Heat the caramel sauce in a small saucepan over very low heat. When it is of an even consistency, stir in the berry sauce. Taste and adjust the flavoring. You may add more caramel sauce, sugar, syrup, or lemon juice to attain the flavor you want. The berry flavor should be pronounced; the others should remain subtle. Use at room temperature. (*The sauce will keep in an airtight container for up to 3 days in the refrigerator. Stir to mix or heat slightly over very low heat.*)

Buttered Applesauce with Vanilla

Compote de pommes vanillée

Applesauce is widely used in French pastries, often covered with sliced apples. It adds moistness to such pastries as Rustic Apple Tartlets (page 28).

Golden Delicious is the perfect apple for applesauce. It is not particularly juicy, so small pieces cook down to a thick sauce that is not watery. If you want a chunkier applesauce, as for Normandy Apple Tart (page 90), add large chunks of apple. These will cook without losing their shape.

Adding a vanilla bean to the applesauce gives a lovely, subtle flavor. It also adds black dots, so if you don't want to see these in your pastry, leave out the vanilla bean. You can replace it with a stick of cinnamon, if you wish. Butter, added at the end, lends a richness to the compote, as well as helping thicken it. If you prefer a fat-free applesauce, leave out the butter.   **Makes about 3 cups**

1 pound ripe Golden Delicious apples, peeled, cored, and cut into small pieces

½ cup plus 1 tablespoon (4 ounces) sugar

Zest and juice of 1 lemon

1 vanilla bean, split lengthwise, or one 2-inch stick cinnamon (optional)

2 ounces (½ stick) unsalted butter, at room temperature

1. Place the apples, sugar, lemon zest and juice, and the vanilla bean or cinnamon stick, if using, in a large stainless steel saucepan. Mix well and cook over low heat, stirring often with a wooden spoon. Cook until the apples are completely cooked and can be mashed, 20 to 30 minutes. Let cool to tepid.

2. Remove the vanilla bean or cinnamon stick, scraping the seeds back into the mixture. Puree the applesauce in a blender, food processor, or food mill. When it is completely smooth, whisk in the butter in small pieces. If you are using a food processor or blender, add the butter while the motor is still running. Cool completely. (*Applesauce will keep in an airtight container for 2 weeks in the refrigerator. Cover the top surface of the applesauce with plastic wrap before sealing the container.*)

Chunky Applesauce *Compote de pommes rustique*

Set aside half the apples in large chunks or wedges. Cook the rest of the apples with the sugar, lemon juice and zest, and vanilla bean or cinnamon stick, if using. Halfway through the cooking process, stir in the apple chunks and cook until they are tender but not falling apart. Do not puree or add any butter. Stir in the vanilla seeds, if desired, then discard the pod. Cool the compote in a shallow, baking dish. This will help the juices evaporate and yield a thicker applesauce.

Spicy Applesauce *Compote de pommes épicée*

While this version is not particularly French, it is quite delicious. It can be prepared chunky or smooth. From the original recipe, omit the vanilla bean but use the cinnamon stick. Add a ½-inch piece of peeled ginger, a few gratings of nutmeg, and a pinch of ground cloves. Remove the whole spices before pureeing.

Simple Syrup *Sirop à 30° Baumé*

Mixed with an appropriate alcohol or fruit juice, simple syrup has traditionally been used to add flavor and moisture to an otherwise neutral and dry sponge. Over time, the uses for this syrup have
evolved to include the base for sorbets and glazes.

Since the syrup must be cool, even cold, when used, I keep a quart or so on hand in the refrigerator at all times. Thus I am not frustrated when I prepare all the components for, say, an Opera
Cake (page 66), only to discover that I have to boil and cool some syrup before I can assemble the
cake.

Degrees Baumé refer to the density of the syrup. No need to buy a density meter: If you follow the recipe, your syrup will be at the right level of density.   Makes about 4 cups

2½ cups water

4 cups (1¾ pounds) sugar

1.   Pour the water into a medium saucepan. Stir in the sugar.

2.   Bring the mixture to a boil, then reduce the heat and simmer for 15 minutes. Allow the
syrup to cool completely before using. (*Simple Syrup will keep well in an airtight container in the refrigerator almost indefinitely.*)

When making syrup, always place the liquid in the pan before the sugar. This ensures that
all the sugar crystals come in contact with the water as the sugar is poured in.

Preserves and Flavorings

Les Confitures et les parfums

Apricot Preserves / *Confiture d'abricots*

Raspberry Preserves / *Confiture de framboises*

Chestnut Cream with Vanilla / *Crème de marrons vanillée*

Candied Orange Peel / *Zestes d'oranges confits*

Coffee Flavoring / *Essence de café*

Apricot Preserves *Confiture d'abricots*

This delicious fruit makes a thick and savory spread. For the best results, use the following method, which yields preserves with lots of chunks:

- **Use a quantity of sugar that equals two-thirds the weight of the fruit.**
- **Boil the sugar first, then poach the fruit in the syrup.**

If you prefer a less chunky version, cut the fruit into small pieces to start. But retain the method to make preserves that cook less than by conventional methods and thus retain a brighter color. They are also less likely to stick to the bottom of the pan and burn.

I always keep at least a small amount of apricot preserves on hand for glazes. Making apricot glaze for tarts or cakes is simple. Heat some of these preserves in a small saucepan and strain them through a mesh sieve. The glaze may not be as clear or shiny as a bona fide apricot glaze, but it is more flavorful and less stiff.

This recipe works well with any stone fruit—peaches, plums, nectarines, even cherries. Be sure to determine the quantity of sugar needed by weighing the fruit *after* removing the pits.   **Makes about 8 half-pint jars**

3½ pounds ripe apricots (about 3 pounds, pitted)

4½ cups (about 2 pounds) sugar

Juice of 1 lemon

1.   Thoroughly wash and dry 8 half-pint jars and their lids. Keep them hot.

2.   Wash and quarter the apricots, discarding the pits. If you wish, cut the fruit into small pieces. Weigh the apricots, then weigh two-thirds that amount of sugar.

3.   If you have an unlined copper preserving pot, use that. Otherwise, use a wide, low-sided stainless steel pot. Put the sugar and lemon juice in the pot, then add just enough water to wet all the sugar. Stir the sugar with your hand, so you can feel for and break up any large clumps.

4.   Place the sugar over medium heat. Brush down any sugar crystals clinging to the inside of the pot, using a clean pastry brush dipped in water. Do not stir or move the pot before the sugar comes to a boil. Once the sugar begins to boil clear, observe it carefully. It will boil quickly at first, and there will be a lot of froth. As the syrup thickens, the bubbles will form and burst more slowly. Cook until the syrup measures 248 to 250°F on a candy thermometer (hard ball stage).

5.   At this point, carefully spoon in about one-third of the apricots. Allow the sugar to come back to a boil, then add another third. Repeat one more time. Continue cooking the preserves, stirring often and skimming away any froth that hardens on the surface. As the mixture begins to thicken—how long this takes depends on the water content of the fruit—start testing the preserves for doneness. Drop a spoonful onto a chilled plate. If the preserves set up immediately, becoming firm and not running on the plate when it is tilted, the mix has been cooked enough. If not, continue to cook. Stir frequently, for as the mixture thickens, it can scorch.

6.   When the preserves are ready, line up the jars next to the pot. Using a long-handled ladle or spoon that fits inside the rim of the jars, carefully fill the jars to about ½ inch from the top. Wipe the rims clean with a damp cloth. If you are using two-part lids, place the lids on top of the jars and screw on the bands, but do not tighten them immediately. Do the same with one-part lids. Once all the jars have been covered, tighten the bands. Cool at room temperature. As they cool, the preserves and the headroom air inside the jars will contract and suck the lids down. You will actually hear the lids pop.

7.   Once the jars are cool, wipe them if necessary and label them with the contents and date. Check for any lids that are still up. Those jars should be refrigerated and used first. (*Properly sealed jars can be stored in a cool, dry place for up to 1 year.*)

If you do not want to jar the preserves, cool them in a glass or stainless steel bowl, transfer them to a container with a tight-fitting lid, and store the preserves in the refrigerator. They will keep for several months.

Raspberry Preserves *Confiture de framboises*

These preserves are made in the same proportions of fruit to sugar as the Apricot Preserves and follow the same technique. This method virtually poaches the berries, forcing a lot of their juices into the syrup, because the heat causes some of the berries to burst, though a lot are left intact. The preserves are nice and chunky and retain the beautiful color of the fruit. Makes about 8 half-pint jars

3 pounds ripe raspberries, picked over

4½ cups (about 2 pounds) sugar

Juice of 1 lemon

1. Thoroughly wash and dry 8 half-pint jars and their lids. Keep them hot.

2. Weigh the raspberries, then weigh two-thirds that amount in sugar.

3. If you have an unlined copper preserving pot, use that. Otherwise, use a wide, low-sided stainless steel pot. Put the sugar and lemon juice in the pot, then add just enough water to wet all the sugar. Stir the sugar with your hand, so you can feel for and break up any large clumps.

4. Place the pot over medium heat. Brush down any sugar crystals clinging to the inside of the pot, using a clean pastry brush dipped in water. Do not stir or move the pot before the sugar comes to a boil. Once the sugar begins to boil clear, observe it carefully. It will boil quickly at first, and there will be a lot of froth. As the syrup thickens, the bubbles will form and burst more slowly. Cook until the syrup measures 248 to 250°F on a candy thermometer (hard ball stage).

5. At this point, carefully spoon in about one-third of the berries. Allow the sugar to come back to a boil, then add another third. Repeat one more time. Continue cooking the preserves, stirring often and skimming away any froth that hardens on the surface. As the mixture begins to thicken—how long this takes depends on the water content of the fruit—start testing the preserves for doneness. Drop a spoonful onto a chilled plate. If the preserves set up immediately, becoming firm and not running on the plate when it is tilted, the mix has been cooked enough. If not, continue to cook. Stir frequently, for as the mixture thickens, it can scorch.

6. When the preserves are ready, line up the jars next to the pot. Using a long-handled ladle or spoon that fits inside the rim of the jars, carefully fill the jars to about ½ inch from the top. Wipe the rims clean with a damp cloth. If you are using two-part lids, place the lids on top of the jars and screw on the bands, but do not tighten them immediately. Do the same with one-part lids. Once all the jars have been covered, tighten the bands. Allow the jars to cool at room temperature. As they cool, the preserves and the headroom air inside the jars will contract and suck the lids down. You will actually hear the lids pop.

7. Once the jars are cool, wipe them if necessary and label them with the contents and date. Check for any lids that are still up. Those jars should be refrigerated and used first. (*Properly sealed jars can be stored in a cool, dry place for up to 1 year.*)

Because it conducts heat so quickly and evenly, copper is ideal for cooking preserves. It will, however, react with the acid in the fruit, so the preserves must be removed immediately. Unlike aluminum, which gives off harmful ions when it comes into contact with acids, copper will, itself, tarnish. In other words, the fruit is harmful to the copper, not vice versa.

Chestnut Cream with Vanilla
Crème de marrons vanillée

Chestnut cream is a spread that takes full advantage of the starchy-sweet richness of chestnuts. Have it plain on bread or toast, mixed in with yogurt or, at its most decadent, on a spoon. I use this cream to make Chestnut Paris-Brest (page 35) and Mont Blanc (page 160), both of which can also be made with canned chestnut puree. I leave little chunks of chestnuts in the cream. They become saturated with sugar, not unlike *marrons glacés*, or glazed chestnuts.

The drawback to making chestnut cream is peeling the chestnuts. If you can find frozen or jarred peeled whole chestnuts (see page 104) and are sure they are good quality, use them. **Makes about six 12-ounce jars**

4 pounds fresh chestnuts, peeled (see page 340), or 3 pounds frozen or jarred peeled chestnuts

8 cups whole milk

2 vanilla beans, split lengthwise

6¾ cups (about 3 pounds) sugar

continued

1.   Thoroughly wash and dry 6 wide-mouth 12-ounce jars and their lids. Keep warm.

2.   Put the chestnuts in a large pot. Add the milk and the vanilla beans and bring to a boil over medium heat. Reduce the heat and simmer until the chestnuts are tender and the milk has been absorbed, about 20 minutes. Stir frequently to prevent the chestnuts from sticking. Let cool.

3.   Remove the vanilla beans and scrape the seeds back into the chestnuts. Carefully and working in batches, puree the chestnuts in a blender or food processor or with a handheld blender. The puree will be quite thick.

4.   While you are pureeing the chestnuts, bring the sugar to a boil with 2 cups of water in a very large heavy-bottomed pot or a clean copper preserving pot Brush down any sugar crystals clinging to the inside of the pot, using a clean pastry brush dipped in water. Cook the sugar to 248 to 250°F on a candy thermometer (hard ball stage).

5.   When the sugar is ready, add about one-third of the pureed chestnuts, stirring with a heavy wooden spoon. Return to a boil, then add another third of the puree. Repeat one more time. Cook the cream for 10 to 15 minutes, or until it is quite thick and no clumps of puree remain (although there will be chunks of chestnut). Stir frequently to prevent burning and to help break up the chestnut clumps.

6.   When the cream is ready, line up the jars next to the pot. Using a long-handled kitchen spoon, spoon the cream into the jars, leaving about a ½ inch of head space at the top. Tap the jars lightly on the table between additions to knock out any air bubbles. When all the jars have been filled, wipe the rims with a damp cloth, then place the lids on top of the jars. Loosely screw the bands onto the lids, then tighten them once all the jars have been covered. Cool the jars at room temperature, verifying that the lids are popping.

7.   Wipe the jars if necessary, then label them with the contents and date. Check for any lids that are still up. Those jars should be refrigerated and used first. *(Properly sealed jars can be stored in a cool place for up to 6 months.)*

How to Peel Chestnuts

Cut an X into the domed side of each chestnut with a paring knife. Place the chestnuts in a large pot and cover them with water. Bring to a boil over medium heat and let the chestnuts boil for 2 or 3 minutes. Reduce the heat to a slow simmer. Remove a few at a time with a skimmer and peel them, removing the inner skin as well as the shell. Do not worry about breaking the chestnuts.

Candied Orange Peel *Zestes d'oranges confits*

Candied citrus peel adds terrific flavor and texture to pastries and chocolates. You can make candied peel easily at home, and this particular recipe gives you peel with an unusual spicy flavor. You can easily vary the spices and the type of citrus peel. Make sure the peel is from organic fruit.

Leave the peels in large pieces; they will be easier to store and less likely to crystallize or fall apart. Cut strips or dice as needed. Makes about 8 ounces

8 brightly colored organic oranges, preferably navel

2¼ cups (1 pound) sugar

1 piece star anise

8 black peppercorns, crushed

1 vanilla bean, split lengthwise

3 tablespoons lemon juice

1. Wash the oranges, then cut off and discard the ends. Make a few vertical cuts down the sides of the oranges and peel away the skins. Use the oranges for another purpose. Flatten the peel and cut away the pith with a thin, sharp knife. You should have peels that are ⅛ inch thick.

2. Bring a large pot of water to a boil and add the peels. Boil for 2 minutes, remove with a skimmer, and rinse under cold water. Repeat this blanching process twice, using fresh water each time. The third time, rinse in cold water and drain.

3. Put ½ cup water and the remaining ingredients in a large saucepan and bring to a boil. Lower the heat and add the orange peels. Cook, covered, over low heat for 1½ hours. Uncover and leave the peels in the syrup for 8 hours, covered by a piece of parchment paper placed directly on the surface of the syrup.

4. Using tongs, remove the peels from the syrup and place the pieces on a wire rack. Set the rack over the pot and let the peels drain completely. Transfer the peels to a covered jar and keep refrigerated. (*Candied peel will keep for 3 months.*)

Coffee Flavoring *Essence de café*

Excellent coffee flavoring is available in France and in the United States in gourmet grocery stores. Many old-school pastry chefs still prefer to make their own, and you can do the same. It's a great way to use up leftover caramelized sugar. Save the leftover caramel in a metal container, pouring it while it is still molten. Once you have a significant amount, transform it into Coffee Flavoring. This recipe can be multiplied or divided according to the quantity of caramelized sugar you have on hand.

Makes about 2 cups

1½ cups (1 pound) caramelized sugar

¼ cup water

4 heaping tablespoons instant coffee dissolved in 2 tablespoons boiling water

1. Heat the caramelized sugar in a metal container directly over low heat until the caramel that is against the metal begins to melt. Quickly transfer the caramel to a large heavy saucepan. Continue heating until the caramel is completely melted and just begins to smoke. Turn off the heat.

2. Using a wire whisk, quickly stir in ¼ cup water. Be careful: This will sputter quite a bit. Stir in the dissolved coffee. Cool to room temperature. Strain the flavoring into a covered jar and refrigerate. (*This flavoring will keep in the refrigerator for up to 6 months.*)

Techniques

A FRENCH CHEF ONCE TOLD me, "La recette est dans la main," by which he meant the recipe is not what's written on a piece of paper but how you do it. You can have the greatest recipes and ingredients in the world, but without the techniques and tricks to execute the recipes, you may only have a recipe for disaster. That is not to say that the techniques employed constantly by home and professional bakers alike even approach difficulty. The techniques described here are simply tricks that must be practiced until they become second nature.

Piping

The first time I used a pastry bag—make that the first ten times—I doubt that I extruded two things, rosettes, ladyfingers, or whatever, that were even close to the same size and shape. It looks easy, but it is actually quite awkward to do at first. Here are a few tips:

Fit the tip onto the bag, then twist the bag and stuff it into the tip.

- Slide the pastry tip onto the narrow end of the pastry bag, then twist the bag into the top of the tip, plugging the bag.

- Fill the bag with a rubber spatula, a large spoon, or a pastry scraper, taking care not to form air pockets.

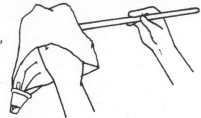

Use a large spoon or a spatula to fill the bag, cuffed over your hand.

- Never fill the bag to the top. Do not place more batter, dough, or cream in the bag than you can comfortably squeeze through the tip with one hand. It's easy to refill the bag.

- If piping out cookies onto a baking sheet, touch the bottom edge of the pastry tip to the pan. Squeeze the bag with your stronger hand and guide the bag with your other hand, holding the bag lightly from below. Pull the bag in a straight line, squeezing evenly and using the tip against the pan as a guide. When you have reached the desired length, stop squeezing and pulling the bag, and with the guiding hand, sharply pull the tip straight up. Then place the tip at the next position, leaving room for spreading if necessary, and start again.

- If piping out decorations or, say, round meringues, hold the bag vertically about one inch above your starting point, then evenly squeeze out the design, taking care to not drag the pastry tip through whatever you have just piped out.

Melting Chocolate

When melting chocolate, whatever the kind, chop it first and place it in a stainless steel or glass bowl. This bowl should sit just inside a pot with the lip of the bowl hanging over the edge of the pot so that no water or steam can come up around the bowl. If this happens, it could cause the chocolate to seize (stiffen), and if you are in the first stages of chocolate tempering, it could cause the chocolate to cloud later on. Pour enough water into the pot so that when the chocolate-filled bowl is placed inside, the level of the water is at the level of the chocolate line. The part of the bowl that contains the chocolate should be jacketed in water. Remember, steam is hotter than simmering water and can burn your chocolate.

Heat the water until it is just barely simmering. As the chocolate starts to melt, stir it with a wooden spoon. Then, depending on the chocolate's ultimate use, bring it to the desired temperature.

Cooking Sugar

The first time I made Italian meringue—the one that requires cooked sugar—I was working in a Paris pastry shop. I was nearly laughed out of the kitchen when I asked for the candy thermometer. It seemed that only an American wimp would ask for such a convenience.

In the age-old method, still in use today, the baker first plunges his or her fingers into cold water, quickly grabs some boiling sugar between these theoretically cooled fingertips, then plunges them and the sugar immediately back into the cold water. The baker then tests the doneness of the sugar by rolling it into a ball and pulling it between the fingers to see if strands form or even if the sugar cracks. It is certainly a very hands-on method.

Now that I can sense heat again in my right hand, I have come to realize that all those blisters were for nought. A good candy thermometer, one that measures in small (not more than two-degree) increments and has a wire cage around it, is a wonderful tool. (The cage keeps the thermometer from touching the pot, which is hotter than the sugar.) The thermometer is accurate, and once you have learned to "read" the bubbles in boiling sugar, you don't have to insert it until the sugar is just about ready.

The more folksy method of dropping a bit of boiling sugar into cold water from a spoon and then rolling the mass between your fingers is less accurate, but unless you need to have the sugar at a very precise temperature, as for pulled sugar or blown sugar pieces, I find it to be quite sufficient. What is more, this method will give you a real feel for the sugar. You may want to use this method in conjunction with an accurate thermometer the first couple of times you cook sugar. This will help develop your sense of when it is ready.

Caged candy thermometer

Keep Your Sugar Crystal Clear

Cooking sugar—regardless of the stage you ultimately want (soft ball, hard crack, caramel, or whatever)—is a simple chemical reaction: Take a solid, apply heat, and it goes to a different state, namely, liquid. In this case, the solid is crystal table sugar, which is sucrose. A sucrose molecule is composed of two rings of carbon that are bonded together. At room temperature, these molecules are very stable. As heat is applied, the bonds begin to break and the sugar liquefies. As the sugar cools down, however, it wants to go back to its most stable room-temperature state, crystalline.

A phenomenon called seeding takes place in saturated solutions, of which melted sugar (not diluted with water) is one. All it takes is the introduction of one sugar crystal into a pot of melting sugar, and all the sugar tries to go back to its more stable crystalline form. Even as you continue to apply heat and some of the sugar continues to melt, other previously melted sugar is seeded and becomes crystalline again. When this happens, you can pretty much give up the project and start over. Do one of the following to prevent seeding:

- As soon as you put the pan on the stove to melt the sugar, brush down any sugar crystals that cling to the inside of the pot with a pastry brush dipped in water. These crystals must be removed to prevent their falling into the pot while heating.

- Add some strained freshly squeezed lemon juice to the pot before heating (about 1 table-spoon juice per pound of sugar). The acidity of the juice will stabilize the sugar. The lemon flavor will remain, however, so if this is not desired, go to the next option.

- Add an invert sugar, which is very stable as a liquid at room temperature, to the pot before heating. The most commonly available invert sugar is glucose, and its most common form is corn syrup. Add about 2 tablespoons corn syrup per pound of sugar.

You may have encountered another phenomenon with caramelized sugar: it tends to become sticky at room temperature, and even melted under refrigeration. This is because during the caramelizing process water molecules are boiled off. This is not a natural state for sucrose. Sugar loves water. It pulls it out of the air, even refrigerator air, which is moist. When you remove that water by heating, the sugar will do what it can to absorb more water from its surroundings, still seeking stability at whatever temperature. The best way to avoid this problem is to caramelize just before serving, or at least to not expect the same crispness after several hours of refrigeration. For instance, if you are serving Crème Brûlée (page 50), you can prepare the custard up to three days ahead. Caramelize the top no more than one hour before serving. Napoleons (page 41) and some other pastries may be caramelized at the last minute with a blowtorch.

Working with Dough

You've probably read many recipes for tart and quiche doughs that warned you not to overknead the dough or to reroll dough scraps more than once. Here are a few simple tricks which will help you avoid overworking rolled doughs.

- Always work on cold dough, as cold as you can have it and still be able to roll it.

- Form the dough into a thin disk, about one inch thick, before chilling. Or form a large batch of dough into a log that you can cut into one-inch slices. Place the chilled disk on a lightly floured work surface. Lightly flour the top of the dough. Tap the dough evenly across the top with the side of a rolling pin, then rotate the disk a quarter-turn and tap it evenly again. This will spread the dough and actually begin to roll it out without the mechanical action of rolling. Tapping does not build up gluten anywhere near as fast as rolling.

- Once you have tapped the dough to a size where you can roll it easily, do so, making sure that the dough is of an even thickness all over. If the edges begin to split, patch them as you roll. When baked, this patching will show more in Flaky Pastry Dough (page 348) than in Sweet Short Dough (page 348) because of the proportion of butter, which helps the dough melt together. Roll the dough to about 3 inches beyond the diameter of the tart pan.

• Pick up the dough by rolling it around the rolling pin. Transfer the dough to the pan. Pick up the edge of the dough and lay the dough into the bottom of the tart pan so that the dough fits into the angle. Do not stretch the dough, or it will stretch back and shrink during baking. Take a scrap of dough, roll it into a ball, dip it in flour, and push it into this bottom angle. This action will fit the dough completely into the pan without your having to touch it too much and risk having the dough melt and stretch. Let any excess dough hang over the top edge of the pan, run the rolling pin over it to cut, and remove the scraps.

• Chill the tart shell for at least one hour (or wrap and freeze) before filling and/or baking.

• Partially bake the crust until lightly browned for 10 to 15 minutes at 375°F, if desired. Let cool completely before filling it with a butter-based cream, or the heat from the crust could cause the cream to melt and separate. This prebaking ensures that a tart crust—even a tart with a baked filling—will be thoroughly baked and will remain crisp.

On Tarts of All Sizes

All the world loves a tart, and there is a tart to fit everyone's taste: fruit tarts made with sweet dough or puff pastry, savory tarts and quiches, large tarts, individual tarts, mini-tarts. Most of the recipes in this book are for large tarts. Most of these can be reduced to individual tarts or mini tartlets, keeping a few things in mind:

1. It takes about approximately 8 ounces of dough to line a 10-inch fluted tart pan. Quiche pans are a bit deeper and may require slightly more dough.

2. Individual tarts, which are usually about 4 inches in diameter, require about 2 to 3 ounces of dough each and can be lined in the same way as large tarts. You will create more scraps when lining individual tarts, so be sure to have extra dough on hand. See page 348 for ways to reuse the scraps.

3. There is a real art to lining mini tartlet pans without losing your mind. These are not rolled individually. Instead, line up several 1- to 2-inch tartlet molds on a work surface so that they are as close together as possible. Stagger rows so that the edges of one row's molds fill the spaces of the previous row's molds. On a lightly floured surface, roll out a sheet of dough to the same dimensions as the space occupied by the pans. Starting at the edge farthest from you, roll the dough onto the rolling pin. Lift the pin, hold it over the pans, and starting with the row closest to you, lay the dough lightly over all the tins, unrolling it as you do so. If some are not covered, do not worry; you can do this with a second rolling. It is important to avoid stretching the dough.

Pull off a walnut-sized chunk of fresh or scrap dough and roll it into a ball. Dip it in flour, then use the ball of dough to push the sheet of dough into each pan. Dip the dough ball in more flour to keep it from sticking. Once all the molds have been lined, take two rolling pins (or use a straight-sided bottle if you do not have two pins), lay them together at one end of the array of pans, and roll them across the tops to cut away the excess dough. Using two pins will keep the pans from rocking back and forth as you run them across. Place the lined pans on a baking sheet and refrigerate for at least one hour or up to twenty-four hours. Or you can freeze them, with or without Almond Cream (see page 314). Prick each lined pan with the tines of a fork before filling with Almond Cream or before baking unfilled. This is not required for mini quiches, or other mini tartlets that are filled before baking. These will bake in about ten minutes at 375°F and do not require any pie weights.

4. If you adapt a large recipe to make individual or mini tarts, you will need more filling than for a large tart. Here are some general guidelines:

- A 4-inch individual tart requires 1½ tablespoons Almond Cream for baking, not including what you may be using for filling, as in the Italian Prune Plum Tart (page 26), and about 3 tablespoons Pastry Cream. Mini tartlets require about ½ teaspoon Almond Cream and 1 or 2 teaspoons Pastry Cream or whatever cream you are using.

- Individual quiches take about ¼ cup filling each. Mini quiches take just a few teaspoonfuls.

Leftover Dough

Previously rolled dough acts differently than fresh dough, but this does not mean that scraps should be discarded. This is especially true of puff pastry scraps, since so much goes into making the dough. There are ways to store and reuse these scraps without risk of changing the quality of the finished product. In fact, dough scraps can sometimes improve it. Just follow these tips and suggestions for scrap use.

Sweet Short Dough (page 294): These dough scraps can be rerolled twice with little problem. After the first rolling, gather the scraps and refrigerate them for at least one hour before rerolling. After the second rolling, distribute a small portion of scraps evenly over fresh dough or actually mix them into a batch of dough while it is being prepared. The scraps will break up sufficiently so as to not make the dough tough. When preparing Rolled Butter Cookies (page 172), use only freshly prepared dough or dough that has never been rolled, as these cookies tend to shrink and toughen. Reserve any scraps you create for another use. This is also the case for scraps used in tart shells, though here hardness is less of an issue.

Flaky Pastry Dough (page 293): This dough has a much higher proportion of gluten than *pâte sucrée*, which has a lot of sugar to separate the gluten strands. Do not use any scraps that have been rerolled more than once. Even first-run scraps should be mixed with fresh dough, using no more than 10 percent. Mix these scraps (which may be refrigerated or frozen) in with a fresh batch of dough while it is being mixed, or distribute them on top of a fresh disk of dough. You can even fold a few scraps into a batch of puff pastry.

Puff Pastry (page 296): Puff pastry scraps should not be rerolled more than once. This dough is subjected to so much rolling during preparation that the gluten really develops. It gives the dough necessary body. As you create scraps, lay them one on top of another, wrap in plastic, and refrigerate (if you are making another batch of puff pastry within a few days) or freeze for up to one month (even if the original dough was frozen). Do not form the scraps into a ball, or they will puff in all directions. Lay chilled or thawed scraps on rolled-out fresh puff pastry before completing the last turn. Do not use the scraps earlier in the process, or the gluten in the scraps will overdevelop. Use this dough for recipes that do not require full puff pastry or dough that needs maximum puff. It is ideal for Napoleons (page 41), Tarte Tatin (page 30), or any other pastry that requires pricking the dough all over to prevent rising.

Yeasted Dough: If you find yourself with leftover neutral bread dough, refrigerate it for up to five days. You may need to punch this dough down daily. When you make your next batch of bread—even if it is not the same neutral dough—mix the leftover dough in when you add the liquid to the flour. It will act like a starter and give the new dough a little extra boost. This may add a somewhat sour taste, from the fermentation of the old dough. It will also give the bread larger pores and a more rustic look. In fact, many country bread bakers use 10 percent leftover dough in their fresh bread doughs. This trick can even be used for Brioche Dough (page 268). Brioche scraps can be frozen, then thawed in the refrigerator and added to the fresh dough while still cold. Make sure to mix the scraps in completely.

Peeling and Preparing Whole Fruit

Here are a few little tricks for peeling fruit. These tricks could make the difference between a perfectly presentable fruit and something that should be made into a smoothie.

Cut a small slice off the stem end and off the blossom end, so that the fruit can rest on either end. If you are cutting pineapple, use a serrated knife, which will cut through the rind and fibers inside more easily than a chef's knife. For all other fruits, use a sharp knife with a thin blade, such as a fish-fillet knife. Starting from the top bare surface of the fruit and working downward, cut away the rind in the thinnest possible strips, always following the shape of the fruit. Keep the strips narrow to help keep you from cutting too far into the flesh of the fruit. After you've cut all the way around the fruit, turn it over so that it is sitting on the opposite bare side. Trim away any peel you may have missed. Cut the fruit according to the recipe instructions.

- For whole or sliced pineapple, cut straight down with a corer to remove the thick, fibrous core. Slice crosswise.

- For pineapple pieces, cut the pineapple in half from top to bottom. Cut a V down the middle of each half and remove the core. Cut the halves first into wedges and then into smaller pieces.

- For kiwi slices, turn the fruit on its side and cut crosswise into thin slices.

- For apples, either core with an apple corer and leave whole, or cut in half, cut away the core with a paring knife, and slice.

Preparing a Mango

Place the mango on a cutting board so that it sits naturally. Using a sharp fish-fillet knife, slice the mango horizontally, passing over its large, flat seed. Turn the mango over and repeat. If slicing or pureeing the mango, cut the halves into wedges then, holding the blade flat against the cutting board, cut the flesh away from the skin. Peel the skin from the seed portion and with the seed flat on the board, cut straight down around the seed to remove this more fibrous flesh.

Cut the mango horizontally, above and below the flat seed.

For decorative halves, which are lovely on a fruit platter, use a paring knife to cut crosshatches in the flesh of each half. Cut down to the skin with the tip of the knife, but do not cut through the skin. Make the cuts ½ inch apart. Hold the ends of the halves with your thumbs and forefinger, then flip the mango halves inside out by placing your fingers against the skin. Cubes of the mango will then pull easily from the skin.

Hold the knife flat against the cutting board to cut the fruit from the peel.

How to Puree Mango Peel and pit 3 mangoes. Process in a food processor or blender. Press the puree through a medium mesh strainer to remove the fibers. Measure the volume. Add 2 teaspoons lemon juice per mango to the puree to help preserve the color. Freeze the puree in ½-cup batches. Label the container with the amount and date. The puree may be frozen in an airtight container or zipper bag for up to six months. This will make about 1½ cups of puree.

Cut straight down around the seed to remove more fruit.

Equipment

WHILE IT MAY BE tempting to run out and buy all the latest and the greatest equipment and utensils for the kitchen, you can make phenomenal pastries with very little equipment. Here are some suggestions, most of which are probably familiar to you. You may have many of these items in your toolbox already.

Acetate: Available in art supply stores in sheets or rolls.

Baking sheets: Get the largest that will fit in the oven, two rimless, two with shallow rims. Choose pans that are flat and heavy-duty, so that they will retain their shape when heated.

Blender: A conventional blender is good for grinding nuts, pureeing fruits, and the like. If you have to choose between a heavy-duty blender and a food processor, choose the food processor. Its broad bottom makes it more efficient for most tasks and easier to clean. A handheld, or inversion, blender is like a wand with a motor on one end and a covered, spinning blade on the other. It is ideal for pureeing liquid in a bowl or pot, eliminating the need to pour it into a food processor or blender, then pureeing in batches.

Cake pans: 8-, 9-, and 10-inch straight-sided pans, two of each, should meet most of your baking needs.

Caramelizing pot: Made of unlined copper for fast, even heat conduction, with a pour spout, this is not necessary but handy to have if you do a lot of sugar work. Clean before each use with vinegar and coarse salt.

Citrus zester: A little gadget that creates strips of citrus zest.

Cookie cutters: Keep several sizes of both plain and fluted cookie cutters.

Cooling racks: You will need several wire racks in various shapes and sizes (round, rectangular). Be sure you have enough rack space to cool several cake layers, loaves of bread, or batches of cookies at once.

Dipping forks: You can use your fingertips to dip chocolate centers, but dipping forks will help retain the centers' shapes.

Dough scraper: A rigid or flexible piece of plastic that fits in your hand. It is excellent for filling pastry bags.

Entremets rings: These are of fairly low priority, unless you plan to make lots of charlottes or mousse cakes. Entremets rings made of stainless steel are far superior to springform pans for these specialties.

Food processor: Useful for grinding nuts or pureeing fruits. Do not use a food processor for making doughs; it tends to overmix and heat doughs.

Knives: Invest in heavy, stainless steel knives with bolted handles. You will need at least one 4-inch paring knife, a fish-filleting knife with a flexible blade, and at least one chef's knife (10-inch blade, if you're buying only one). A serrated knife for breads and for slicing cakes is a must. The longer, the better: I have a serrated knife with a very sharp 14-inch blade.

Madeleine pans: This is one pan for which there is no improvisation.

Measuring spoons and cups: Use glass cups for liquids and metal or plastic cups for dry ingredients.

Mixer: An electric mixer is crucial. If you can afford it, buy a heavy-duty stand-alone mixer. These mixers usually come with a dough hook.

Mixing bowls: It is helpful to have several in various sizes. They should be made of glass or stainless steel (other materials may be porous or may react with their contents).

Parchment paper: This is widely available in housewares stores as well as in many supermarkets.

Pastry bags: These should be made of supple material for squeezing and cleaning ease. Start with small (8-inch), medium (12-inch), and large (16-inch) bags and several plain and fluted (star) tips. Be sure to clean all thoroughly after each use.

Pastry brushes: Get brushes with natural bristles, which are usually softer than synthetic and easier to wash, in various sizes, including at least two 1-inch brushes, one of which can be for grease only.

Pots and pans: You will need pots and pans in various sizes, preferably heavy-duty. I use pans that have aluminum on the outside, for fast even heating, and stainless steel on the inside, so that they do not react with their contents. Whatever equipment you choose, be sure it's nonreactive (stainless steel or enamel-coated cast iron).

Rolling pin: For ease in picking up doughs and better control, a solid rolling pin (no handles) is preferable.

Scale: A scale is essential in a pastry kitchen. One with sliding weights, not a spring scale, is preferable. Spring scales are considerably less precise, and the mechanism tends to break down.

Slotted spoons or skimmers: Ideal for removing poached fruit from their liquids as well as skimming impurities from the surface of simmering liquids.

Spatulas, rubber: A flexible spatula, ideal for scraping bowls. "Spoonulas" are now widely available. These rubber spatulas have a slight indentation in the head, making them quite versatile.

Spatulas, stainless steel: An assortment of spatulas ranging in length from 4 to 16 inches with straight, not tapered, blades will come in very handy. You will also need one or two offset (bent) spatulas. I use a 4-inch offset spatula quite a bit.

Springform pans: You will need 9- and 10-inch pans for the recipes in this book.

Strainers: Strainers should be stainless steel, fine and medium mesh. Medium mesh is a good replacement for an old sifter; it loosens and lightens dry ingredients with no risk of adding metal shavings.

Tart rings: Bottomless tart ring and pans with removable bottoms in various sizes, including several 4-inch rings for individual tarts, are a must for tart baking.

Thermometers: You will need a candy thermometer until you can safely and comfortably eyeball sugar and custards. The best are calibrated in small increments (maximum 2°F) and have a wire cage around the glass. An oven thermometer is a must, as even the best oven can go out of calibration.

Whisks: Have at least two on hand, preferably with wooden handles and stainless steel wires. Use a small whisk for small bowls and a medium-sized whisk for medium to large bowls.

Terminology

THROUGHOUT THIS BOOK, I have defined French terms in the recipes where they are used, so that you do not need to thumb through the book for definitions. However, there are certain terms used repeatedly in English but not necessarily defined.

Nonreactive cookware

It is extremely important, especially when preparing creams or custards, whipping egg whites, or working with acidic fruits, to use nonreactive bowls and cookware. Try to use glass or stainless steel bowls, which do not react with their contents. Any type of porous bowl may absorb whatever you are mixing (and perhaps retain bacteria), so avoid ceramic bowls. Even glazed ceramic (which may have cracks in the glaze) is not great, as these bowls often are not heat resistant. For pots, stainless steel is best: It will not react with its contents. You can whisk milk in a stainless steel pot, for example, and it will not darken, as it would in an aluminum pot. I never use dark-colored pots and pans, either. Not only do some of them contain aluminum, but their color makes it difficult to see subtle changes in color. The best example of this is caramelizing sugar. You may not see it change from deep amber to burned sugar until it is too late.

Folding

This refers to a method of mixing, in which a rubber spatula is dipped down in the middle of a mixing bowl, taking other ingredients with it. The spatula is brought up along the side of the bowl, flipping whatever was on the bottom of the bowl over onto the top. All the while, the bowl is turned. Folding is especially important for fragile mixes, such as those made with egg whites or whipped cream, which could collapse or overmix with another blending method.

Whisking or whipping

These are interchangeable terms for a technique used to incorporate air into a mix. If you are working by hand, use a wire whisk and a rapid stirring motion. If you are using an electric mixer, use the whisk attachment, if available, or double beaters.

Spoons (teaspoons, tablespoons)

Unless otherwise stated, these are level spoonfuls. Scoop whatever you are measuring, then scrape across the top of the spoon with a metal spatula or the flat side of a knife. Do not shake or tap the spoon to level it; this will compact whatever is in the spoon. The same goes for cup measurements.

Weight

I cannot stress enough the importance of weighing ingredients, instead of measuring them in cups or spoons. A pound is a pound, but a cup of flour sometimes weighs 4 ounces, sometimes 5 ounces, depending upon how compacted it was in its container. Buy a scale if you don't have one. The recipes in this book have both weight and volume measurements. Get used to using weight. This is especially important, of course, for dry ingredients, but it can be significant for liquid ingredients as well.

Sifting

The French sift their flour through a flat sieve, or *tamis*. At home, I use a medium mesh bowl strainer. If your flour, or whatever you are sifting, is weighed first, then you know that you have the right amount. Sifting serves to take out any lumps and, in some cases, to combine the flour with other dry ingredients. The recipes in this book were prepared with flour that was sifted after measuring or weighing.

Beating egg whites until stiff but not dry

Egg whites that are overbeaten will not hold up any ingredients that are folded into them. Start beating egg whites on low speed, until they froth. Increase the speed to medium and continue to beat until soft peaks form, that is, when the whip is lifted, a peak that gently falls over is formed). Gradually add sugar to tighten the whites. This will bind them somewhat so that when they are stiff, they do not crack apart. In other words, they are not "dry."

Glossary

à l'anglaise. To cook something, usually a sauce or a base for ice cream or mousse, in the style of a crème anglaise; that is, until the mixture coats the back of a spoon.

bain-marie. *See* water bath.

biscuit. From the French, meaning twice cooked, this term originally referred to sponge bases that were first cooked on the stove, then baked in the oven, as is a génoise (originally called *biscuit à la génoise*). The term has now become a generic one for sponge-type bases.

brown butter. *Beurre noisette* is the French term for hazelnut butter, which is salted or unsalted butter that has been melted over medium-high heat until it froths, takes on a light brown color, and gives off a nutty aroma. Brown butter imparts a subtle flavor to cakes and tarts.

chausson. A turnover pastry, from the French word meaning slipper.

choux. From the French word for cabbages, this term refers to cream puffs of any size, before they are filled. *Pâte à choux* is cream puff dough, but the common term in the bakery kitchen, or *laboratoire*, is *la pâtache*.

clarified butter. Butter that has been melted then allowed to settle, so that the whey solids and water separate from the butterfat. The whey and water can be removed, leaving a pure fat that does not burn easily, and that leaves no solids when mixed into a glaze.

couverture. Coating chocolate, containing 60 percent or less cocoa paste (or liqueur).

croquant. Literally meaning crunching, this term refers to anything that adds crunch to a recipe, such as *nougatine, pralin*, or streusel.

détrempe. The flour, water, sugar, and salt (plus yeast) portion of croissant dough or puff pastry, before the folding-in of the butter block.

double boiler. *See* water bath.

entremets. Literally *entre les mets*, or between courses, this term has come to signify any finished cake, such as a Charlotte or an Opéra.

feuilletage. Puff pastry or paste, also called *pâte feuilletée.*

fond. Generally, any base, such as a meringue disk, a génoise, or a *fond de succès* (hazelnut or almond meringue). *Fond* can also refer to a base for a soup or a sauce, such as *fond de volaille* (poultry base or stock) or *fond de veau* (veal base or stock).

ganache. This generic term refers to a blend of chocolate and milk and/or cream, and may include butter (*ganache beurrée*) or flavorings (e.g., *ganache au café, ganache pralinée*). Ganaches are widely used as centers for bonbons, to fill cakes, and to sandwich cookies, such as macaroons.

glaçage. An opaque glaze, such as chocolate or fondant, for cakes or pastries, or the operation of glazing.

gluten. The protein component of wheat and many other grains, such as rice and rye. Strands of this protein can be increased in length by mechanical kneading; it is the building up of gluten that gives bread its body and suppleness.

mise en place. From the French, meaning put in place, this term refers to components prepared in advance.

motte. A lump of butter. French pastry chefs and bakers buy their butter in 15-kilo bulk cylinders. This is economical, and the butter is generally of better quality than that found in small blocks. In fact, many cheese shops also sell *beurre en motte*; customers ask for the quantity they want, and the shopkeeper cuts away that amount with a wire.

nappage. A clear or translucent glaze for cakes or tarts. This term also refers to glazing with *nappage.*

nougatine. Brittle made from caramelized sugar and chopped almonds. A generation ago, this product was widely used as decoration, or even as the base for large presentation cakes (see *pièce montée*). The brittle is prepared, then rolled out in front of the oven, to keep it pliable, with a heavy, solid metal rolling pin. The brittle must then be cut before it hardens. Today, nougatine is still used for decoration, but more so to add crunch to fillings for cakes and ice creams.

pâte. The French word for dough or paste (also noodles), as in *pâte à choux* (choux paste or cream puff dough) or *pâte feuilletée* (leafy or flaky dough, or puff paste). In generic terms, *la pâte* simply means the dough.

pièce montée. A large presentation cake, usually a *croquembouche* (cream puff tower), decorated with spun caramel and *dragées* (sugar-coated almonds). This can also refer to a tiered wedding cake.

pralin. Brittle made from caramelized sugar and toasted hazelnuts, this product is ground to make *praliné*, or *pâte pralinée* (caramelized hazelnut paste). It can also be finely chopped to add texture to a pastry cream or butter cream, or the top of a cake.

salé(e). Salty or savory.

seizing (chocolate). The reaction that occurs when water comes in contact with melted chocolate. The water reacts with the cocoa butter and causes the chocolate to stiffen, sometimes irreversibly.

sucré(e). Sweet.

tamis. French-style sifter, consisting of a deep, round wooden or metal frame around a screen. Dry ingredients are placed inside the tamis, then shaken back and forth. The blended and clump-free ingredients come out the bottom.

tour (le). The station in a French pastry shop where doughs, particularly puff pastry and croissant dough, are made. The term comes from *tourner*, or to turn, reflecting what happens to these doughs. The *tourier* is one who makes doughs.

vanilla. See page 12.

water bath. Called a *bain-marie* in French, it has uses both in the oven and on top of the stove. On the stovetop, it is a double boiler, composed of a pot of simmering water with a bowl set into it, so that no steam escapes and enters whatever is in the bowl. This is important for the melting of chocolate. In the oven, a water bath is a large pan half filled with hot water and holding custards. It prevents a leathery crust from forming on top of the custard and promotes even baking. The custard begins heating immediately from the heat transmitted by the hot water surrounding its base.

zest. The outermost, colored skin of a citrus fruit, without the bitter white pith underneath. This portion of the skin can be grated or stripped, from the fruit, using a fine grater or a zester, and added to a recipe to impart the flavor of the fruit without adding liquid.

Mail-Order Sources

FORTUNATELY, MOST OF THE recipes in this book can be prepared from ingredients available in supermarkets, with an occasional trip to a gourmet or specialty food shop. The equipment, too, is readily available at specialty shops or by mail order. Here is a list of sources for both ingredients and equipment.

The Baker's Catalogue
P.O. Box 876
Norwich, VT 05005-0876
(800) 827-6836
Extensive line of ingredients and equipment

Chef's Catalog
P.O. Box 620048
Dallas, TX 75262
(800) 338-3232
Extensive line of equipment

Entner-Stuart Premium Syrups
P.O. Box 1417
Corvallis, OR 97339
(800) 377-9787
All-natural flavored syrups, perfect for
soaking sponge layers or boosting the flavor
of juices and purees

Frontier Cooperative Herbs
3021 78th Street
P.O. Box 299
Norway, IA 52318
(800)669-3275
Natural and organic products; bulk herbs and
spices

Joie de Vivre
P.O. Box 875
Modesto, CA 95353
(209) 869-0788
Ingredients, including Clément Faugier
chestnut products and Valrhona chocolate

Sheila Linderman
6103 Pine Crest Drive
Los Angeles, CA 90042-4344
(323) 344-0044
Madagascar vanilla beans and extract

Melissa's/World Variety Produce
P.O. Box 21127
Los Angeles, CA 90021
(800) 468-7111
Exotic fruits and vegetables, packaged herbs
and spices, vanilla beans

Pacific Island Imports
333 Washington Boulevard, Suite 106
Marina Del Rey, CA 90292
(310) 544-3929
Tahitian vanilla beans and extract

Sur La Table (Catalog Division)
1765 Sixth Avenue South
Seattle, WA 98134-1608
(800) 243-0852
Extensive catalog of equipment; some
ingredients

Van Rex Gourmet Foods
2055 51st Street
Vernon, CA 90058
(323) 581-7999
Full line of imported pastry ingredients;
excellent chocolates

Index